W9-BWV-996

Criminal Justice Interactive

Companion Text

Robert Mutchnick

Indiana University of Pennsylvania

Prentice Hall

Boston Columbus Indianapolis New York San Francisco Upper Saddle River

Amsterdam Cape Town Dubai London Madrid Milan Munich Paris Montreal Toronto

Delhi Mezico City Sao Paolo Sydney Hong Kong Seoul Singapore Taipei Tokyo

Editor in Chief: Vernon Anthony
Acquisitions Editor: Tim Peyton
Editorial Assistant: Lynda Cramer
Director of Marketing: David Gesell
Senior Marketing Manager: Adam Kloza
Senior Marketing Coordinator: Alicia Wozniak
Senior Managing Editor: JoEllen Gohr
Project Manager: Jessica H. Sykes
Senior Operations Supervisor: Pat Tonneman
Operations Specialist: Laura Weaver
Senior Art Director: Diane Ernsberger
Text Designer/Composition/Full-Service Project Manager: Naomi Sysak
Cover Art: Jeff Vanik
Cover Designer: Diane Lorenzo
Lead Media Project Manager: Karen Bretz
Printer/Binder: Bind-Rite Graphics/Robbinsville
Cover Printer: Lehigh-Phoenix Color/Hagerstown
Text Font: Times Roman

Copyright © 2010 Pearson Education, Inc., publishing as Prentice Hall, 1 Lake Street, Upper Saddle River, New Jersey 07458. All rights reserved. Manufactured in the United States of America. This publication is protected by Copyright, and permission should be obtained from the publisher prior to any prohibited reproduction, storage in a retrieval system, or transmission in any form or by any means, electronic, mechanical, photocopying, recording, or likewise. To obtain permission(s) to use material from this work, please submit a written request to Pearson Education, Inc., Permissions Department, 1 Lake Street, Upper Saddle River, New Jersey 07458.

Many of the designations by manufacturers and seller to distinguish their products are claimed as trademarks. Where those designations appear in this book, and the publisher was aware of a trademark claim, the designations have been printed in initial caps or all caps.

10 9 8 7 6 5 4 3 2 1

Prentice Hall
is an imprint of

PEARSON

www.pearsonhighered.com

ISBN 10: 0-13-505722-1
ISBN 13: 978-0-13-505722-3

Brief Contents

Contents

Criminal Justice Interactive: A User's Guide

This companion text is designed to be used with *Criminal Justice Interactive* online. Together, the *Criminal Justice Interactive* online media (designed to encourage active learning) and this printed companion text (designed to make it easy to review key concepts) make up a "hybrid" learning system. Like hybrid cars that utilize both gas and electricity to deliver an efficient driving experience, *Criminal Justice Interactive* uses both interactive multimedia materials and a concise printed text to deliver an efficient (and engaging) learning experience.

HOW TO USE THE *CRIMINAL JUSTICE INTERACTIVE* TEXT

While *Criminal Justice Interactive* online is designed to deliver an active and engaging learning experience, this companion text is designed to be used for reviewing key ideas and concepts when you are not online. Using this text, you can quickly find and review just the information you need. Features of the companion text include:

- *A concise and straightforward presentation of all key concepts in an outline format*. Instead of overwhelming you with too much text, this book includes just the facts and ideas that you need to know in order to succeed in this course.
- *A logical and easy-to-use organization*. All topics are presented in numbered modules. In addition to the Contents, a Chapter Outline is included at the start of each chapter. These features make it easy to quickly find the material you are looking for.
- Learning Objectives *and* Key Terms *at the beginning of each chapter*. These lists quickly summarize the important ideas and vocabulary that you will need to know in order to understand the concepts presented in each chapter.
- *Definitions of key terms in the margin next to where the term first appears, as well as in a comprehensive glossary at the end of the book*. Having key terms defined both when you first read them and again in a glossary at the back of the book makes reviewing key term definitions efficient and easy.
- *Icons throughout the text, which let you know when related multimedia resources are available online*. After you've read about a topic, you can go online for more information on that topic. This will help reinforce your understanding of what you have read.
- *Comprehensive Chapter Summaries*. These will help you make sure that you have learned what you were supposed to in the chapter.

- *A list of application and review materials related to each chapter that are available online.* There are many resources available online to help you apply and review what you have read in the book. There is a handy list of these resources at the end of each chapter.

HOW TO USE *CRIMINAL JUSTICE INTERACTIVE* ONLINE (WWW.PEARSONHIGHERED.COM/CJI)

The online companion to this printed text is a complete multimedia introduction to criminal justice. To access *Criminal Justice Interactive* online you will need to register at www.pearsonhighered.com/cji with the access code that was included with this book.

If your copy of the book did not include an access code, you should be able to purchase one at your college bookstore. You may also purchase an access code at www.mypearsonstore.com.

At *Criminal Justice Interactive* online you will explore a three-dimensional city environment and enter virtual buildings to access overviews of the major processes and functions of the criminal justice system. You will be able to:

- Watch episodes of an original dramatic movie connected to the learning material in each section.
- Learn key concepts and important topics through interactive learning modules.
- Apply key concepts with simulation activities that put you in the role of people working in the criminal justice system.
- Check your understanding of and ability to think critically about key concepts through online assignments, review questions, and essay questions.

The purpose of the *Criminal Justice Interactive* online is to provide you with an engaging introduction to criminal justice that encourages active learning by:

- *Presenting* key concepts
- Letting you *apply* key concepts
- Allowing you to *review* key concepts

Chapter 1

The Criminal Justice System

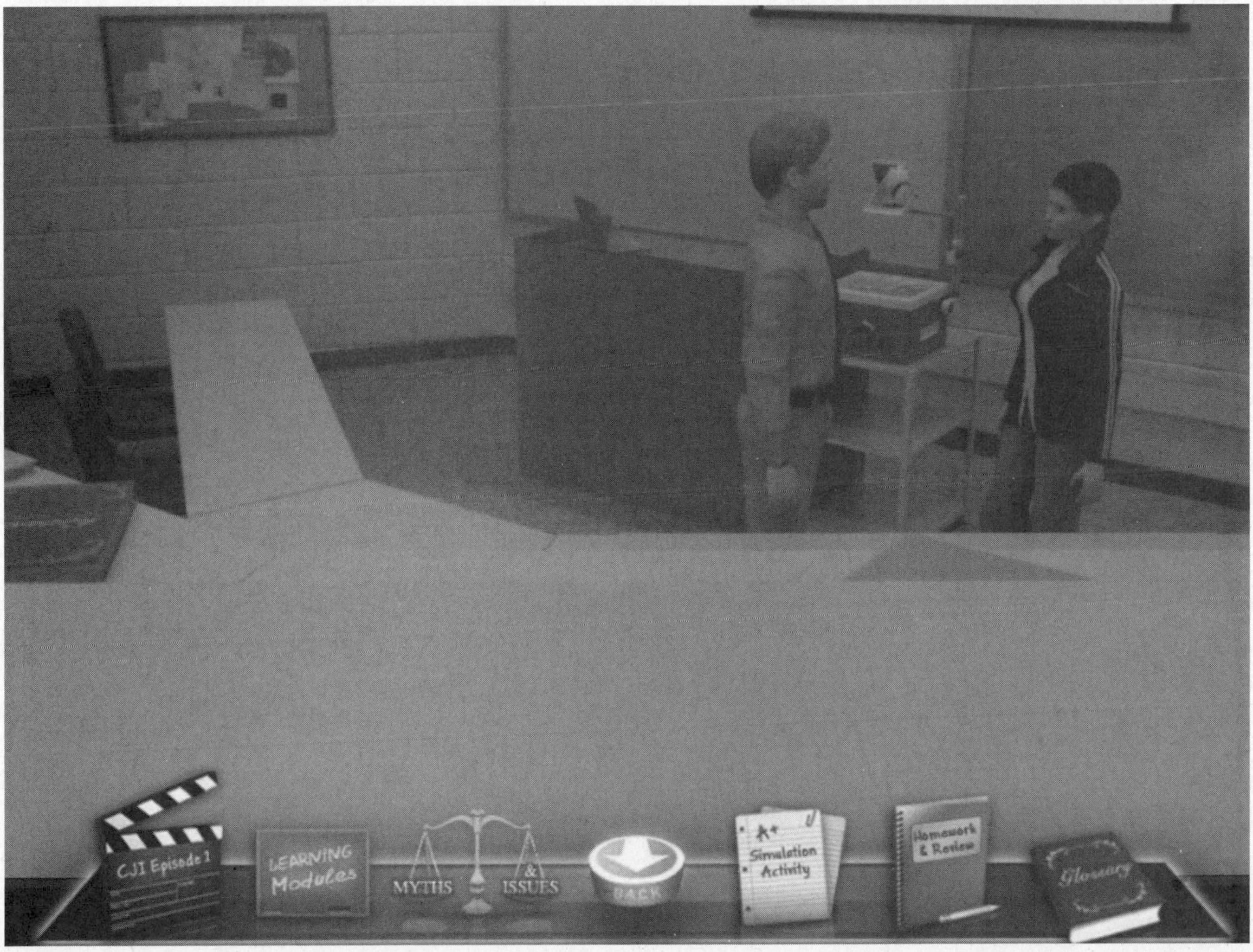

CHAPTER OUTLINE

- 1.0 The criminal justice system
- 1.1 The criminal justice system core components
  - 1.1.2 Crime
  - 1.1.3 Criminal justice
  - 1.1.4 Criminal justice system
- 1.2 Criminal justice goals
  - 1.2.1 The criminal justice system was established to meet certain goals.
  - 1.2.2 Five different goals of the criminal justice system
  - 1.2.3 Retribution
  - 1.2.4 Deterrence
  - 1.2.5 Incapacitation
  - 1.2.6 Rehabilitation
  - 1.2.7 Restoration
- 1.3 Steps in the criminal justice process
  - 1.3.1 The steps
  - 1.3.2 Investigation and arrest
  - 1.3.3 Booking
  - 1.3.4 First appearance
  - 1.3.5 Preliminary hearing
  - 1.3.6 Information and indictment
  - 1.3.7 Arraignment
  - 1.3.8 Trial
  - 1.3.9 Sentencing
  - 1.3.10 Corrections
- 1.4 Due process vs. crime control
  - 1.4.1 Packer identified two models in 1968.
  - 1.4.2 Selected amendments to the U.S. Constitution and Bill of Rights
- 1.5 The criminal justice funnel
  - 1.5.1 Most of the crime that occurs is *not* known to law enforcement.
  - 1.5.2 The *dark figure of crime*
  - 1.5.3 Police discretion
  - 1.5.4 Stages of the criminal justice funnel
  - 1.5.5 Depending on how one looks at the data, of the 500 cases known to the police, approximately 14 individuals are incarcerated, representing just about 3%.

LEARNING OBJECTIVES

After reviewing the online material and reading this chapter, you should be able to:

1. Explain the five major goals of the criminal justice system: deterrence, incapacitation, retribution, rehabilitation, and restoration.
2. Describe the structure of the criminal justice system and its three major components: the police, courts, and corrections.
3. Describe the steps in the criminal justice process: occurrence of a crime, investigation and arrest, pretrial activities, trial, sentencing, and corrections.
4. Understand the due process and crime control models of criminal justice and discuss the tension between them.
5. Define terms related to the criminal justice system.

KEY TERMS

arraignment
arrest
bail
booking
concurrent sentences
consecutive sentences
corrections
crime
crime control model
criminal justice
criminal justice funnel
criminal justice system
dark figure of crime
deterrence
due process model
exclusionary rule
felony
first appearance
general deterrence
grand jury
halfway houses
incapacitation
incarceration
indictment
individual rights
information
just desserts
law enforcement
lex talionis
misdemeanor
nolo contendere (no contest)
parole
plea bargaining
police discretion
preliminary hearing
probable cause
probation
rehabilitation
release on recognizance (ROR)
restoration
restorative justice
retribution
specific deterrence
trial
warrant

1.0 The criminal justice system

1.1 The criminal justice system core components

CRIME

Conduct in violation of the criminal laws of a state, the federal government, or a local jurisdiction, for which there is no legally acceptable justification or excuse.

CRIMINAL JUSTICE

In the strictest sense, the criminal (penal) law, the law of criminal procedure, and the array of procedures and activities having to do with the enforcement of this body of law. Criminal justice cannot be separated from social justice because the kind of justice enacted in our nation's criminal courts is a reflection of basic American understandings of right and wrong.

CRIMINAL JUSTICE SYSTEM

The aggregate of all operating and administrative or technical support agencies that perform criminal justice functions.

1.1.1 **Crime** is conduct in violation of the criminal laws of a state, a federal government, or local jurisdiction for which there is no legally acceptable justification or excuse.

1.1.2 **Criminal justice** is the criminal (penal) law, the law of criminal procedure, and the array of procedures and activities having to do with the enforcement of this body of law.

1.1.3 **Criminal justice system** is the aggregate of all operating and administrative or technical support agencies that perform criminal justice functions including the basic divisions of the operational aspects of criminal justice and law enforcement.

- The criminal justice system can be viewed as an umbrella under which its components and subcomponents (including the making of criminal law, the development of criminal procedure, probation and parole) are at different levels of government (local or municipal, county, state, and federal).

1.2 Criminal justice goals

1.2.1 The criminal justice system was originally established to meet certain goals. Over time, the goals have changed. The different components of the system may have different goals that suggest the perception that the system is really a process rather than a system.

ARREST

The act of taking an adult or juvenile into physical custody by authority of law for the purpose of charging the person with a criminal offense, a delinquent act, or a status offense, terminating with the recording of a specific offense. Technically, an arrest occurs whenever a law enforcement officer curtails a person's freedom to leave.

- Law enforcement works hard to remove offenders from the community by means of **arrest** and begins processing these offenders through the system.
- Law enforcement would like these offenders removed from free society for as long as possible.
- If an offender's case makes it through the courts and to the sentencing phase of the system, the offender, even if he or she has committed a serious crime, may be released back into the community without serving any time in incarceration.
- On the surface it may appear that law enforcement and the courts are often working at opposite purposes to meet conflicting goals.

For more on whether or not the criminal justice system is a system and process, visit Criminal Justice Interactive online > The Criminal Justice System > Myths and Issues Videos > Issue 1: Is the Criminal Justice System Really a System?

1.2.2 Five different goals of the criminal justice system:

- Retribution
- Incapacitation
- Deterrence
- Rehabilitation
- Restoration

For more on the goals of the criminal justice system, visit Criminal Justice Interactive online > The Criminal Justice System > Learning Modules > 1.1: Criminal Justice Goals.

1.2.3 **Retribution** is the act of taking revenge on a criminal perpetrator. It is also known as **just desserts**. This model of criminal sentencing holds that criminal offenders deserve the punishment they receive at the hands of the law, and that punishments should be appropriate to the type and severity of the crime committed. At one point in time, most societies punished all offenders and the punishment could, in some instances, inflict more harm or hurt than the offense itself

- The concept of ***lex talionis*** is known as the law of retaliation.
  - Taken from Hammurabi's Code, approximately 210 B.C.E., *lex talionis* delineated both crimes and punishments.
  - An "eye for an eye, a tooth for a tooth," taken from the Old Testament, is often used to define *lex talionis* and the goal of retribution.
- Those who believe in retribution believe that those who commit crimes get what they deserve.
- Retribution focuses on past behavior.

RETRIBUTION
The act of taking revenge on a criminal perpetrator.

JUST DESSERTS
A model of criminal sentencing that holds that criminal offenders deserve the punishment they receive at the hands of the law and that punishments should be appropriate to the type and severity of the crime committed.

LEX TALIONIS
Taken from Hammurabi's Code, approximately 210 B.C.E., that delineated both crimes and punishments. The law of retaliation, based on the concept of an eye for an eye, a tooth for a tooth.

1.2.4 **Deterrence** is a goal of the criminal justice system that seeks to inhibit criminal behavior through the fear of punishment; the overall goal is crime prevention.

- Two types of deterrence:
  - **Specific deterrence**
    - A goal of criminal sentencing that seeks to prevent a particular offender from engaging in repeat criminality
    - Individuals need to understand that there are consequences for actions and the only way to avoid such consequences in the future is to desist from such behavior. Examples:
      - Points on a person's license for speeding: Earning enough points can result in the offender's insurance being cancelled or their premiums being dramatically increased.

DETERRENCE
A goal of criminal sentencing that seeks to inhibit criminal behavior through the fear of punishment.

SPECIFIC DETERRENCE
A goal of criminal sentencing that seeks to prevent a particular offender from engaging in repeated criminality.

- ❐ Incarceration for conviction of a crime: The purpose is that the offender learns that there are consequences for committing a crime, and that while the person is incarcerated, he or she is not able to commit another crime against free society.
- ❐ The death penalty is the ultimate form of specific deterrence: Executing an offender ensures that the specific offender will never commit another crime.

GENERAL DETERRENCE

A goal of criminal sentencing that seeks to prevent others from committing crimes similar to the one for which a particular offender is being sentenced by making an example of the person sentenced.

- ❖ **General deterrence**
  - ◆ A goal of criminal sentencing that seeks to prevent others from committing crimes similar to the one for which a particular offender is being sentenced by making an example of the person sentenced. Examples:
    - ❐ In colonial times in the United States, colonists who were found guilty of offenses could be placed on display in stocks in the town square so that all the other townspeople could see and be reminded of the possible punishment for committing an offense.
    - ❐ Wearing the letter A attached to the clothing of women who were found guilty of adultery not only marked those women, but also served as a general deterrence to others.
    - ❐ Countries that have public punishments, such as public executions or chopping off limbs, are using general deterrence to prevent others from committing similar crimes.

- ■ Deterrence focuses on future behavior and preventing a recurrence of the unwanted behavior

INCAPACITATION

The use of imprisonment or other means to reduce the likelihood that the offender will commit future offenses.

1.2.5 **Incapacitation** is the use of imprisonment or other means to reduce the likelihood that an offender will commit future offenses.

- ■ Intends to protect the members of society by removing those who choose not to adhere to the laws.
- ■ During incapacitation, the offender is prevented from committing another crime against free society. Examples:
  - ❖ County jails
  - ❖ Minimum-, medium-, and maximum-security, and supermax prison facilities
    - ◆ Supermax facilities are reserved for the worst of the worst federal prisoners who are segregated from everyone. In supermax facilities, the inmate is locked in their single occupant cell 23 hours per day with one hour for exercise.

- ❖ Penal colonies
  - ◆ Australia began as a penal colony with serious offenders in England being transported to Australia, never to return to England.

- Incapacitation is a more limited goal than deterrence because it only focuses on the time period the offender is under the direct control of the criminal justice system.
- Incapacitation is only interested in restraint, not punishment.

1.2.6 **Rehabilitation** is the attempt to reform a criminal offender.

REHABILITATION
The attempt to reform a criminal offender. Also, the state in which a reformed offender is said to be.

- The goal seeks to change the behavior of the offender, typically through treatment or programs. Examples include: Alcoholics Anonymous, GED programs, group and individual counseling, career counseling, parenting classes, technical and skill programs
- In the late 1970, the public tended to accept the philosophy that nothing works and the move away from rehabilitation and back to incapacitation began.
  - ❖ The move back to incapacitation was helped by reports that upwards of 90% of offenders released from treatment programs recidivated (returned to a life of crime).
    - ◆ Involves correcting the behavior of the offender, usually through treatment or education, by providing him or her with the necessary skills and emotional strength to either return or stay in society and function without violating the law.

1.2.7 **Restoration's** goal is to make the victim whole again.

RESTORATION
A goal of criminal sentencing that attempts to make the victim "whole again."

- When an individual is victimized by a crime, either property or violent, they and their family experience trauma.
  - ❖ The trauma can be physical, psychological, emotional, and/or financial for all involved.
  - ❖ The trauma can be short term or permanent.
- In the past, the victim tended to be ignored by the justice system.
  - ❖ In a criminal action, the *victim*, for purposes of prosecution, is the state.
  - ❖ The *real* victim (the citizen) would, if possible, be called as a witness on behalf of the state to testify at the trial and this will most likely victimize the victim yet again.
- Attempts at restoration can include activities such as cleaning up litter or washing cars have been vandalized; painting buildings that have been spray painted with graffiti; transportation to medical appointments; making payments to the victim or a general fund to reimburse victims for suffering, lost wages, and medical expenses.

- Federal Comprehensive Crime Control Act, 1994
  - ❖ If sentenced to probation, the defendant must also be ordered to pay a fine, make restitution, and/or work in community service.

RESTORATIVE JUSTICE

A sentencing model that builds on restitution and community participation in an attempt to make the victim "whole again."

- **Restorative justice (RJ)** is a sentencing model that builds on restitution and community participation in an attempt to make the victim whole again.
  - ❖ Also referred to as balanced and restorative justice.
    - ◆ Both the safety of the community and the offender's accountability are considered in repairing the harm; hence the term balanced.
    - ◆ The justice system has a responsibility to protect the community. However, the community can participate in its own safety; the community is the facilitator in the restorative process.

1.3 Steps in the criminal justice process

1.3.1 The steps:

- Investigation and arrest
- Booking
- First appearance
- Preliminary hearing
- Information and indictment
- Arraignment
- Trial
- Sentencing
- Corrections

1.3.2 Investigation and arrest

PROBABLE CAUSE

A set of facts and circumstances that would induce a reasonably intelligent and prudent person to believe that a specified person has committed a specified crime. Also, reasonable grounds to make or believe an accusation. Probable cause refers to the necessary level of belief that would allow for police seizures (arrests) of individuals and full searches of dwellings, vehicles, and possessions.

WARRANT

In criminal proceedings, a writ issued by a judicial officer directing a law enforcement officer to perform a specified act and affording the officer protection from damages if he or she performs it.

- **Probable cause** is a set of facts and circumstances that would induce a reasonably intelligent and prudent person to believe that a specified person has committed a specified crime.
- Also refers to the necessary level of belief that would allow police to arrest individuals and search dwellings, vehicles, and possessions.
- **Warrant** is a writ issued in criminal proceedings by a judicial officer directing a law enforcement officer to perform a specified act, and protects the officer from any damages related to the act.
  - ❖ In criminal proceedings, a writ issued by a judicial officer directing a law enforcement officer to perform a specified

act and affords the officer protection from damages if he or she performs it.

- ❖ Police acting under the authority of a warrant are afforded protection from lawsuits for actions related to the enforcement of the warrant.

- Arrest is the act of taking an adult or juvenile into physical custody by authority of law for the purpose of charging the person with a criminal offense, a delinquent act, or a status offense, terminating with the recording of a specific offense.
    - ❖ Technically, an arrest occurs whenever a **law enforcement** officer curtails a person's freedom to leave. The officer does *not* have to tell the citizen that they are under arrest; only that they cannot leave the current location.
    - ❖ After arrest and prior to questioning, defendants are required to be advised of their constitutional rights (a result of the Supreme Court decision of *Miranda* v. *Arizona* [1966]):
        - ◆ "You have the right to remain silent."
        - ◆ "Anything you say can and will be used against you in a court of law."
        - ◆ "You have the right to talk to a lawyer for advice before we ask you any questions, and you have the right to have him with you during questioning."
        - ◆ "If you cannot afford a lawyer, one will be appointed for you before any questioning if you wish."
        - ◆ "If you decide to answer questions now without a lawyer present, you will still have the right to stop at any time and may talk with a lawyer before starting to speak again."
        - ◆ "Do you wish to talk or not?"
        - ◆ "Do you want a lawyer?"
    - ❖ Although it is typical that the *Miranda* warnings are given at the time of arrest, it is not necessary or required.
    - ❖ The *Miranda* warnings are required to be read prior to questioning.
        - ◆ If the police in the field are not going to question the suspect, they do not have to provide the suspect with his *Miranda* warnings.
        - ◆ *Miranda* warnings are read when a suspect is first arrested, usually to make sure that anything the suspect says from that point forward can be used against the suspect should the case go forward.

LAW ENFORCEMENT

The generic name for the activities of the agencies responsible for maintaining public order and enforcing the law, particularly the activities of preventing, detecting, and investigating crime and apprehending criminals.

BOOKING

A law enforcement or correctional administrative process officially recording an entry into detention after arrest and identifying the person, the place, the time, the reason for the arrest, and the arresting authority.

1.3.3 **Booking** is a law enforcement or correctional administrative process of officially recording an entry into detention after arrest and identifying the person, the place, the time, the reason for the arrest, and the arresting authority.

- The booking process often includes:
  - Identifying the place, time, and reason for arrest
  - Photographing and fingerprinting of the suspect
  - Obtaining the address of suspect
  - Recording the suspect's date of birth
  - Recording the suspect's weight and height
- Suspects are again advised of their rights and asked to sign a form acknowledging they have been read their rights and that they understand them.
  - The suspect may be asked to sign a form outlining each individual right.
  - In some instances, the reading of the rights and the acknowledgement that they have been read is videotaped.

FIRST APPEARANCE

An appearance before a magistrate during which the legality of the defendant's arrest is initially assessed and the defendant is informed of the charges on which he or she is being held. At this stage in the criminal justice process, bail may be set or pre-trial release arranged. Also called initial appearance.

BAIL

The money or property pledged to the court or actually deposited with the court to effect the release of a person from legal custody.

RELEASE ON RECOGNIZANCE (ROR)

The release of a defendant into their own care or care of another without posting bond.

PRELIMINARY HEARING

A proceeding before a judicial officer in which three matters must be decided: (1) whether a crime was committed, (2) whether the crime occurred within the territorial jurisdiction of the court, and (3) whether there are reasonable grounds to believe that the defendant committed the crime.

1.3.4 **First appearance**, usually occurs within 24 to 48 hours after arrest, and the defendant is brought before a judicial officer.

- Defendant is informed of the charges lodged against him or her and of his or her rights.
- Defendant may be provided with the opportunity for bail or release on recognizance.
  - **Bail** is the money or property pledged to the court or actually deposited with the court for the release of a person from legal custody.
  - **Release on recognizance (ROR)** is the release of a defendant into his or her own care, or the care of another without the posting of bond, cash, or property as collateral.
    - Defendant pays a percentage of the bail amount to the bonding company as a nonrefundable fee.
    - Bonding company agrees to be responsible to the court for the entire amount of the bail.
    - If the defendant does not show up for court, the judge can issue a warrant for his or her arrest and threaten to keep the bail money.
    - The bonding company will try to track down the defendant and bring him or her back, by force if necessary.
- An attorney is appointed for defendant if defendant is indigent.

1.3.5 **Preliminary hearing** occurs before a judicial officer and allows the defense counsel to assess the strength of the prosecution's case (discover function for defense). A preliminary hearing is designed to accomplish three issues:

- Whether a crime was committed
- Whether the crime was committed within the jurisdiction of the court
- Whether there are reasonable grounds to believe that the defendant committed the crime

1.3.6 Information and indictment

- **Indictment** is a formal written accusation submitted to the court by a grand jury, alleging that a specific person has committed a specified offense, usually a **felony**.
- **Grand jury**
  - ❖ A body of persons who have been selected according to law and sworn to hear evidence against accused persons and determine whether there is sufficient evidence to bring those persons to trial, to investigate criminal activity generally, and to investigate the conduct of public agencies and officials.
  - ❖ *True bill* is the decision of a grand jury that sufficient evidence exists to indict an accused person.
  - ❖ *No-bill*, sometimes called a *no true bill*, is the decision of a grand jury not to indict an accused person as a result of insufficient evidence.
  - ❖ Not all states use the grand jury system; some rely on the prosecutor's office to engage in these activities.
- **Information** is a formal written accusation submitted to a court by a prosecutor, alleging that (a) specified person(s) has committed (a) specified offense(s).

1.3.7 **Arraignment** is a hearing before the court having jurisdiction in a criminal case in which the:

- Identity of the defendant is established; defendant is informed of the charges against him or her; defendant is informed of his or her rights; and defendant is requested to enter a plea. Acceptable pleas can include:
  - ❖ Guilty
  - ❖ Not guilty
  - ❖ ***Nolo contendere*** is a plea of no contest and is used when the defendant does not wish to contest conviction.
    - ◆ Because the plea does *not* admit guilt, it cannot provide the basis for later civil suits that might follow a criminal conviction or the revocation of a license.
    - ◆ Spiro Agnew, who was vice president of the United States under Richard Nixon, was one of the first persons to use the *nolo contendere* plea to avoid losing his license to practice law in the state of Maryland.

INDICTMENT

A formal, written accusation submitted to the court by a grand jury, alleging that a specified person has committed a specified offense, usually a felony.

FELONY

A criminal offense punishable by death or by incarceration in a prison facility for at least one year.

GRAND JURY

A group of jurors who have been selected according to law and have been sworn to hear the evidence, and to determine whether there is sufficient evidence to bring the accused person to trial to investigate criminal activity generally, or to investigate the conduct of a public agency or official.

INFORMATION

A formal written accusation submitted to the court by a prosecutor, alleging that a specified person has committed a specific offense.

ARRAIGNMENT

Strictly, the hearing before a court having jurisdiction in a criminal case in which the identity of the defendant is established, the defendant is informed of the charge and of his or her rights, and the defendant is required to enter a plea. Also, in some usages, any appearance in criminal court prior to trial.

***NOLO CONTENDERE* (NO CONTEST)**

A plea of no contest. A no-contest plea is used when the defendant does not wish to contest conviction. Because the plea does not admit guilt, however, it cannot provide the basis for later civil suits that might follow a criminal conviction.

- If a defendant "stands mute" (refuses to enter a plea), the judge will enter a plea of "not guilty" on his or her behalf.
- Federal Rules of Criminal Procedure specify that arraignment shall be conducted in open court and shall consist of reading the indictment or information to the defendant or stating to him or her the substance of the charge and calling on him or her to plead thereto.
  - ❖ Defendant shall be given a copy of the indictment or information before he or she is called upon to plead.

PLEA BARGAINING

The process of negotiating an agreement among the defendant, the prosecutor, and the court as to an appropriate plea and associated sentence in a given case. Plea bargaining circumvents the trial process and dramatically reduces the time required for the resolution of a criminal case.

- **Plea bargaining** is the process of negotiating an agreement among the defendant, the prosecutor, and the court as to an appropriate plea and associated sentence in a given case.
  - ❖ Plea bargaining circumvents the trial process and dramatically reduces the time required for the resolution of a criminal case.
  - ❖ Any plea-bargain agreement requires a judge's approval.
  - ❖ Plea bargaining is one of the points in the criminal justice system that results mostly in cases of attrition.
  - ❖ Reasons prosecutor may be willing to plea bargain:
    - ◆ A prosecutor may decide the case is weak, and rather than risk dismissal, opt for a negotiated plea.
    - ◆ Defense attorney may see no hope of having his or her client acquitted of the offense, and therefore, is keenly interested in limiting the sentence imposed by the court.
    - ◆ The prosecutor may be able to get the defendant to testify against someone else in exchange for a negotiated plea.
    - ◆ Because of limited resources, the prosecutor may be willing to negotiate a plea to be able to use the limited resources for more important cases.
  - ❖ Reasons a defendant may be willing to plea bargain:
    - ◆ Defendant knows he or she is guilty and is likely to receive a harsher sentence if he or she goes through with a trial.
    - ◆ Defendant believes the charge will be reduced if he or she pleads guilty.
    - ◆ Defendant anticipates receiving a reduced sentence if he or she pleads guilty.
    - ◆ By pleading guilty to one charge, the prosecutor agrees to drop other charges.

TRIAL

In criminal proceedings, the examination in court of the issues of fact and relevant law in a case for the purpose of convicting or acquitting the defendant.

1.3.8 **Trial** is the examination in a court of the issues of fact and law for the purpose of reaching judgment of conviction or acquittal of the defendant(s).

- Prosecutor, representing the state, is required to present his or her side of the case first.

- Defense is entitled to cross-examine all of the state's witnesses.
- Once state has completed the presentation of its case, the defense has the opportunity to present its case.
- State has opportunity to cross-examine the witnesses presented by the defense.
- After summations by the prosecutor and the defense, the case is sent to the jury or judge for determination of guilt or innocence.
- For less serious offenses, some states allow bench trials to occur before a judge if defendants waive their right to a trial by jury.
- When a jury is unable to reach a decision, the jury is called deadlocked. The judge declares a mistrial and the defendant may be tried again with a new jury.

1.3.9 Sentencing occurs when a defendant is convicted.

- Eighty-two percent of all sentences are imposed in criminal cases because of guilty pleas rather than trials.
- Presentence investigation report is a report completed by a probation officer, and addresses issues about defendant that relate to the decision process of the sentencing phase.
- Judge sentences defendant to a combination of the following:
  - Fine
  - Probation
  - Electronic monitoring
  - Incarceration
  - Capital punishment (for selected offenses)
- Types of sentences
  - **Consecutive sentences** are two or more sentences imposed at the same time, which are served in sequence with the other sentence(s).
  - **Concurrent sentences** are two or more sentences imposed at the same time for more than one offense and to be served at the same time.

1.3.10 **Corrections**

- Community-based corrections
  - **Probation** is a sentence of imprisonment that is suspended and conditional freedom is granted to the defendant as long as the person meets certain conditions of behavior. Conditions can include maintaining employment, going to school, or refraining from drugs and alcohol.
  - **Parole** is the status of an offender conditionally released from prison by discretion of a paroling authority prior to the expiration of sentence.

CONSECUTIVE SENTENCES

Two or more sentences imposed at the same time after conviction for more than one offense, and served in sequence with the other sentence. Also, a new sentence for a new conviction, imposed upon a person already under sentence for a previous offense, which is added to the previous sentence, thus increasing the maximum time the offender may be confined or under supervision.

CONCURRENT SENTENCES

Two or more sentences imposed at the same time after conviction for more than one offense, and served in sequence with the other sentence. Also, a new sentence for a new conviction, imposed upon a person already under sentence for a previous offense, which is added to the previous sentence, thus increasing the maximum time the offender may be confined or under supervision.

CORRECTIONS

A generic term that includes all government agencies, facilities, programs, procedures, personnel, and techniques concerned with the intake, custody, confinement, supervision, treatment, and presentencing and predisposition investigation of alleged or adjudicated adult offenders, youthful offenders, delinquents, and status offenders.

PROBATION

A sentence of imprisonment that is suspended. Also, the conditional freedom granted by a judicial officer to a convicted offender, as long as the person meets certain conditions of behavior.

PAROLE

Status of an offender conditionally released from prison by discretion of a paroling authority prior to the expiration of sentence.

- ◆ Conditions of parole are established and offender is placed under direction of a parole officer.
- ◆ **Halfway houses** are community-based group homes designed to provide residential services to individuals who are released on parole, or for some of newly released offenders to ease into living in the outside world.

HALFWAY HOUSES

Temporary living situations that provide a way for newly released offender to ease in to living in the outside world. When in the halfway house, the offender is still under the control of the justice system.

- ■ **Incarceration** typically is the placement of an individual in a county jail, a state prison, or penitentiary.

INCARCERATION

An expensive sentencing option that removes dangerous persons from the general public so they are no longer able to continue their criminal activities and the community is better protected.

For more on the steps in the criminal justice process, visit Criminal Justice Interactive online > The Criminal Justice System > Learning Modules > 1.2 Criminal Justice Process.

1.4 Due process vs. crime control

1.4.1 Herbert Packer identified two models in 1968—the crime control and due process models.

- ■ **Crime-control model** is a criminal justice perspective that emphasizes the efficient arrest and conviction of criminal offenders; often referred to as assembly line justice. In a crime-control model, the interests of the community are favored over **individual rights**.
- ■ **Due process model** is a criminal justice perspective that emphasizes individual rights at all stages of justice system processing; Packer refers to this model as obstacle course justice.
  - ❖ Based on the notion that society would rather a guilty person goes free than to convict an innocent person.
  - ❖ Due process of law involves the course of legal proceedings according to the rules established for prosecution guaranteed by the Fourteenth Amendment and addressed in the Fourth, Fifth, Sixth, and Eighth Amendments.

CRIME-CONTROL MODEL

A criminal justice perspective that emphasizes the efficient arrest and conviction of criminal offenders.

INDIVIDUAL RIGHTS

The rights guaranteed to all members of American society by the U.S. Constitution (especially those found in the first ten amendments to the Constitution, known as the Bill of Rights). These rights are particularly important to criminal defendants facing formal processing by the criminal justice system.

DUE PROCESS MODEL

A criminal justice perspective that emphasizes individual rights at all stages of justice system processing.

1.4.2 Selected amendments to the U.S. Constitution and Bill of Rights:

- ■ Fourth Amendment
  - ❖ Prohibition against unreasonable searches and seizures
  - ❖ **Exclusionary rule**
    - ◆ Prohibits use of items obtained as a result of unreasonable search and seizure as evidence against a criminal defendant.
- ■ Fifth Amendment
  - ❖ Prohibition against double jeopardy
  - ❖ Privilege against forced self-incrimination

EXCLUSIONARY RULE

The understanding based on U.S. Supreme Court precedent that incriminating information must be seized according to constitutional specifications of due process or it will not be allowed as evidence in a criminal trial.

- Sixth Amendment
  - ❖ The right to a jury trial
  - ❖ The right to a public trial
  - ❖ The right to a speedy trial
  - ❖ The right to confront witnesses
  - ❖ The right to compulsory process to obtain witnesses
  - ❖ The right to assistance of an attorney in all felony cases
  - ❖ The right to assistance of an attorney in **misdemeanor** cases in which a term of incarceration in a jail or prison can be imposed.

MISDEMEANOR

An offense punishable by incarceration, usually in a local confinement facility, for a period whose upper limit is prescribed by statute in a given jurisdiction, typically one year or less.

- Eighth Amendment
  - ❖ The prohibition against cruel and unusual punishment
- Fourteenth Amendment
  - ❖ "No State shall make or enforce any law which shall abridge the privileges or immunities of citizens of the United States, nor shall any State deprive any person of life, liberty, or property, without due process of law; nor deny any person within its jurisdiction the equal protection of the law . . .."

For more on due process vs. crime control, visit Criminal Justice Interactive online > The Criminal Justice System > Learning Modules > 1.3 Due Process vs. Crime Control.

For more on the way due process and crime control work, visit Criminal Justice Interactive online > The Criminal Justice System > Myths and Issues Videos > Issue 2: Crime Control vs. Due Process.

1.5 The criminal justice funnel

The criminal justice funnel is a way to visually represent the number of crimes and offenders who proceed through the criminal justice system.

CRIMINAL JUSTICE FUNNEL

A visual representation of the number of crimes and offenders who proceed through the criminal justice system.

1.5.1 Most of the crime that occurs is *not* known to law enforcement. Our knowledge of the actual amount of crime that occurs is at best an estimate.

1.5.2 The ***dark figure of crime*** is crime that is not reported to the police and that remains unknown to officials.

DARK FIGURE OF CRIME

A crime that is not reported and is therefore unknown to officials.

- The dark figure of crime is dark because we do not know what percentage of crime it represents.
- Examples of reasons crimes are not known to the police:
  - ❖ Victim does not even know a crime was committed.
  - ❖ Victim was involved in a crime at the time he or she was victimized, such as when a prostitute is robbed by a client.

- Victim does not report crime because he or she does not have insurance, such as when a person had uninsured jewelry stolen and believes the police won't be able to recover it.
- Victim is embarrassed to report the crime, such as when an off-duty law enforcement officer is assaulted and wants to keep it from his fellow officers.
- It is a white-collar crime that has gone undiscovered, such as when a stockbroker sells insider information about a stock.

POLICE DISCRETION
The opportunity of law enforcement officers to exercise choice in their daily activities.

1.5.3 Police discretion

- The opportunity of law enforcement officers to exercise choice in their daily activities
- Law enforcement officers make decisions regarding the laws they enforce, which in turn influences which offenders enter the *criminal justice funnel.*
- At each stage of the criminal justice funnel, criminal justice personnel make decisions as to which cases to continue in the system and which cases are to be kicked out.

1.5.4 Stages of the criminal justice funnel

- The funnel is widest at the top and continues to narrow as people proceed through the system to its narrowest point at the end of the system.
- Of approximately every 1,000 crimes that occur, approximately 500 are known to law enforcement.
- Crimes known to law enforcement
  - This is the first stage, and represents the widest part of the funnel.
  - Of the crimes known to law enforcement, not all crimes result in arrest.
    - For a number of reasons, law enforcement may not be able to make an arrest.
      - The suspect may have died.
      - The suspect may have left the jurisdiction and not able to be extradited, even though law enforcement knows where the suspect is.
    - Law enforcement may also use their discretion to choose not to make an arrest.
      - The suspect may be willing to exchange information for not being arrested, for that will enable law enforcement officers to arrest a larger fish.

- The suspect may be a police informant that the police need to protect because of the information the informant may provide.

- Of the approximately 500 crimes known to law enforcement, 400 (80%) remain unsolved.

- Prosecution stage of the funnel
  - Of the approximately 100 individuals arrested, approximately 35 are juveniles and 65 are adults.
    - The 35 juveniles, once identified as juveniles, are immediately removed from the criminal justice system and placed in the juvenile justice system, except for those waived to the adult court.
  - Of the 35 juveniles passed to the juvenile justice system, approximately 30 are put on probation or have their cases dismissed, while approximately five are retained in the system.
  - Of the 65 adults, the prosecutor retains jurisdiction, approximately 40 cases are retained for prosecution, and the other 25 are kicked out of the system.
  - For numerous reasons, the prosecutor may choose not to prosecute a case.
    - There may be, from the prosecutor's perspective, insufficient evidence to obtain a conviction; therefore, it does not make sense to continue the case in the system.
    - There may be a technical problem with the case. For instance, the rights of the suspect may have been violated, thereby making it difficult or impossible for the prosecutor to obtain a conviction.
    - The prosecutor may have limited resources and can only prosecute a limited number of cases each fiscal year.
    - The prosecutor may be concerned about his or her record of wins and losses and how it will influence his or her re-election chances, and may only take a case forward if he or she is confident it can be won.
- Pretrial stage of the funnel
  - Of the 40 cases that are accepted for prosecution, approximately 30 of them will go to trial. In approximately 10 of the cases, the offender will jump bail or flee.
- Trial stage of the funnel
  - Of the approximately 30 cases that go to trial, approximately 11 of the offenders will be acquitted, 2 will be found guilty, and 17 will be plead guilty.

- Sentencing stage of the funnel
    - This is the last stage of the criminal justice funnel and represents the narrowest part of the funnel. Of the 19 offenders sentenced, approximately 4 will be placed on probation, 1 will receive another type of sentence, and 14 will likely be incarcerated.

1.5.5 Of every 500 cases known to the police, approximately 14 individuals are incarcerated, representing just about 3%. If one just considers the 100 crimes cleared by arrest, then the approximately 14 who are incarcerated represent 14% of the cases.

For more on the criminal justice funnel, visit Criminal Justice Interactive online > The Criminal Justice System > Simulation Activity: The Criminal Justice Funnel.

CHAPTER SUMMARY

- There are five major goals of the criminal justice system. Deterrence seeks to inhibit criminal behavior through the fear of punishment. The use of imprisonment or other means to reduce the likelihood that an offender will commit future offenses is known as incapacitation. Retribution is the act of taking revenge on a criminal perpetrator. Rehabilitation is the attempt to reform a criminal offender. The goal of criminal sentencing that attempts to make the victim whole again is called restoration.
- The steps in the criminal justice process include investigation and arrest, booking, first appearance, preliminary hearing, information and indictment, arraignment, trial, sentencing, and corrections.
- There are two models of criminal justice: the crime-control model and the due process model. The crime-control model emphasizes the interest of the community over the individual, while the due process model focuses on individual rights at all stages of the criminal justice system.
- The criminal justice funnel is a visual representation of the number of crimes and offenders who proceed through the criminal justice system. Most individuals who go through the funnel never reach the narrowest part of the funnel—the sentencing phase.

ONLINE@CRIMINAL JUSTICE INTERACTIVE

Learning Modules

1.1 Criminal Justice Goals
1.2 Criminal Justice Process
1.3 Due Process vs. Crime Control

Myths and Issues Videos

Myth vs. Reality: Crime Has Been Steadily Increasing
Issue 1: Is the Criminal Justice System Really a System?
Issue 2: Crime Control vs. Due Process

Simulation Activity: The Criminal Justice Funnel

Homework and Review

In the News
Web Activity
Review Questions
Essay Questions
Flashcards

Chapter 2

Defining and Measuring Crime

CHAPTER OUTLINE

- 2.0 Defining and measuring crime
- 2.1 Defining crime
  - 2.1.1 Ways to categorize crime
- 2.2 How crimes are measured
  - 2.2.1 Uniform Crime Report (UCR)
  - 2.2.2 NIBRS: The new UCR
  - 2.2.3 The National Crime Victimization Survey (NCVS)
  - 2.2.4 Comparisons of the UCR and the NCVS
- 2.3 Violent crime
  - 2.3.1 Murder
  - 2.3.2 Forcible rape
  - 2.3.3 Robbery
  - 2.3.4 Aggravated assault
- 2.4 Property crime
  - 2.4.1 Burglary
  - 2.4.2 Larceny-theft
  - 2.4.3 Motor vehicle theft
  - 2.4.4 Arson
- 2.5 White-collar and organized crime
  - 2.5.1 White-collar crime
  - 2.5.2 The extent of white-collar crime
  - 2.5.3 Similarities between white-collar crimes and other crimes
  - 2.5.4 Occupational crime
  - 2.5.5 Consumer fraud
  - 2.5.6 Insurance fraud
  - 2.5.7 Tax fraud
  - 2.5.8 Bribery, corruption, and political fraud
  - 2.5.9 Corporate crime
  - 2.5.10 Organized crime
- 2.6 Examination of Part II offenses
  - 2.6.1 Offenses that are generally less serious are categorized as Part II offenses.
  - 2.6.2 Includes offenses for recorded arrests, not for crimes reported to the police
  - 2.6.3 A Part II arrest is counted each time a person is taken into custody.
  - 2.6.4 List of Part II offenses (arrest figures for 2006)
- 2.7 Women and crime
  - 2.7.1 Women as victims
  - 2.7.2 Women as offenders

LEARNING OBJECTIVES

After reviewing the online material and reading this chapter, you should be able to:

1. Discuss the definition of crime from various perspectives: legalistic, political, sociological, and psychological.
2. Describe, compare, and contrast two primary sources of crime statistics (Uniform Crime Report and National Crime Victimization Survey).
3. Describe the following major types of crime as defined by the FBI's Uniform Crime Report: violent crimes, property crimes, white-collar crime, and organized crime.
4. Define terms related to identifying and measuring crime.

KEY TERMS

aggravated assault
arson
assault
Bureau of Justice Statistics
burglary
carnal knowledge
clearance
clearance rate
corporate crime
crime
Crime Index
crime rate
felony
forcible rape
incident-based reporting
larceny-theft
law
mala en se crimes
mala prohibita crimes
misdemeanor
motor vehicle theft
murder
National Crime Victimization Survey (NCVS)
occupational crime
organized crime
Part I offenses
Part II offenses
property crime
robbery
serial murder
sexual battery
Uniform Crime Report (UCR)
violent crime
white-collar crime

2.0 Defining and measuring crime

2.1 Defining crime

2.1.1 Ways to categorize crime

- **Crime** is defined as conduct in violation of the criminal laws of the federal government, a state, or a local jurisdiction, for which there is no legally acceptable justification or excuse.
- Misdemeanor vs. felony
  - **Misdemeanor** is an offense punishable by incarceration, usually in a local confinement facility, for a period whose upper limit is prescribed by status in a given jurisdiction.
  - **Felony** is an offense punishable by death or by incarceration in a prison facility for at least one year.
  - The distinction between misdemeanor and felony is actually made when the law enforcement officer decides what **law** was violated by the offender's behavior, or the prosecutor decides with which crime to actually charge the offender.
- *Mala en se* crimes vs. *mala prohibita* crimes
  - ***Mala en se* crimes** are acts that are regarded, by tradition and convention, as wrong in themselves such as murder, rape, etc.
  - ***Mala prohibita* crimes** are acts that are considered wrong only because there is a law against them.
    - These acts may not be necessarily wrong in themselves. In fact, the laws relating to these acts may change over time depending on the attitudes and values of society, and include such crimes as marijuana possession and underage drinking.
- Crimes against person vs. crimes against property
  - The Uniform Crime Reports (UCR), Part I index crimes separates the eight crimes in the index into categories of crimes against the person (violent crime) vs. crimes against property.
    - The Part I index crimes are the crimes used to determine the crime rates that are regularly reported for public consumption in the news.
  - Crimes against persons (violent crime): murder, forcible rape, robbery, aggravated assault
  - Crimes against property: burglary, larceny-theft, arson
  - The above crimes are all felonies. The list could be extended beyond Part I index crimes to include other

CRIME
Conduct in violation of the criminal laws of a state, the federal government, or a local jurisdiction, for which there is no legally acceptable justification or excuse.

MISDEMEANOR
An offense punishable by incarceration, usually in a local confinement facility, for a period whose upper limit is prescribed by statute in a given jurisdiction, typically one year or less.

FELONY
A criminal offense punishable by death or by incarceration in a prison facility for at least one year.

LAW
A rule of conduct, generally found enacted in the form of a statute, that proscribes or mandates certain forms of behavior. Statutory law is often the result of moral enterprise by interest groups that, through the exercise of political power, are successful in seeing their valued perspectives enacted into law.

***MALA EN SE* CRIMES**
Acts that are regarded, by tradition and convention, as wrong in themselves.

***MALA PROHIBITA* CRIMES**
Acts that are considered wrong only because there is a law against them.

felonies or misdemeanors to both the crimes against person and crimes against property.

- There are many additional ways to categorize crimes and the above are just a few examples.

For more on the defining crime, visit Criminal Justice Interactive online > Defining and Measuring Crime > Learning Modules > 2.1 Defining Crime.

2.2 How crimes are measured

2.2.1 **Uniform Crime Report** (UCR) is a statistical reporting program run by the FBI's Criminal Justice Information Services (CJIS) division.

UNIFORM CRIME REPORT
A statistical reporting program run by the FBI's Criminal Justice Information Services (CJIS) division. The UCR Program publishes *Crime in the United States,* which provides an annual summation of the incidence and rate of reported crimes throughout the United States.

- The UCR Program publishes *Crime in the United States*, which provides an annual summation of the incidence and rate of reported crimes throughout the United States.
- History and development
    - In the 1920s, the International Association of Chiefs of Police (IACP) worked to develop a program of national crime statistics.
    - In 1927, the IACP created the Committee on Uniform Crime Reporting. The committee identified seven crimes that would be used for comparing crime:
        - Murder
        - Forcible rape
        - Robbery
        - Aggravated assault
        - Burglary
        - Larceny
        - Motor vehicle theft
    - IACP released its first report in 1930. Four hundred cities were surveyed, 43 states were represented, and approximately 20% of the total U.S. population was included.
        - IACP lobbied the U.S. Congress to pass legislation authorizing the Uniform Crime Report.
        - Congress authorized the U.S. attorney general to survey crime in America by passing Title 28, Section 534 on June 11, 1930.
            - "The Attorney General shall—(1) acquire, collect, classify, and preserve criminal identification, crime, and other records . . .."
        - The attorney general authorized the Bureau of Investigation to be the agency responsible for meeting the requirements of Title 28, Section 534.

- ❖ In 1935, the Bureau of Investigation was renamed the Federal Bureau of Investigation (FBI).

■ Today

- ❖ Approximately 17,000 law enforcement agencies contribute data monthly on a voluntary basis to the FBI to assist with publication of the UCR.
- ❖ Total number of the seven original crimes known to the police for 2007: 11,251,818.
- ❖ The seven original crimes by number and percent of total for 2007, by change in percent for 2007/2008:

Crime	Number	%	% change
	2007	2007	2007/2008
Murder	16,929	0.15	−4.4
Forcible rape	90,427	0.80	−2.2
Robbery	445,125	3.96	−1.1
Aggravated assault	855,856	7.61	−3.2
Burglary	2,179,140	19.37	+1.3
Larceny-theft	6,568,572	58.38	−0.6
Motor vehicle theft	1,095,769	9.74	+13.1

- ❖ **Crime Index** is now defunct, but was once an inclusive measure of the violent and property crime categories of the UCR, also known as the "Part I offenses."
  - ◆ There were originally seven crimes included in the Part I offenses.
  - ◆ Arson was added as a Part I offense to the property category in 1979.
  - ◆ The Crime Index is useful for geographic and historical purposes because it uses the concept of a crime rate.
    - ❒ **Crime rate** refers to the number of offenses reported for each unit of population. For standardization purposes, crime rates are typically reported per 100,000.
- ❖ **Clearance rate** is a traditional measure of investigative effectiveness that compares the number of reported or discovered crimes to the number of crimes solved through arrest or by other means, such as the death of the suspect.
  - ◆ Once an arrest has been made, a crime is regarded as "cleared" for reporting purposes.
  - ◆ **Clearance** by exceptional means can result when law enforcement authorities believe they know whom the perpetrator of a crime is, but cannot make an arrest.

CRIME INDEX

An inclusive measure of the violent and property crime categories, or Part I offenses of the Uniform Crime Reports. The Crime Index has been a useful tool for geographic (state-to-state) and historical (year-to-year) comparisons because it employs the concept of a crime rate (the number of crimes per unit of population). However, the addition of arson as an eighth index offense and the new requirements with regard to the gathering of hate-crime statistics could result in new Crime Index measurements that provide less-than-ideal comparisons.

CRIME RATE

The number of offenses reported for each unit of population. Typically reported as the number of crimes per 100,000 residents.

CLEARANCE RATE

A traditional measure of investigative effectiveness that compares the number of crimes reported or discovered to the number of crimes solved through arrest or other means (such as the death of the suspect).

CLEARANCE

The event in which a known occurrence of a Part I offense is followed by an arrest or another decision that indicates that the crime has been solved.

- Historical trends
  - Since the beginning of the UCR there have been four major shifts in the crime rates:
    - The first shift occurred in the early 1940s.
      - Young males made up the most "crime-prone" segment of society.
      - Crime decreased sharply due to the large number of young men entering the military.
      - From 1933 to 1941 the Crime Index declined from 770 to 508 offenses per every 100,000 members of the population.
    - Second shift occurred between the 1960s and 1990s.
      - Dramatic increase in most forms of crime
      - Baby boom
        - With World War II ending in 1945 and many young men returning to civilian life, birthrates skyrocketed.
        - By 1960, baby boomers were entering their teenage years, which is the most crime-prone time of life.
      - The disproportionate number of young people produced a dramatic increase in most major crimes.
      - From 1960 to 1980, crime rates rose from 1,887 to 5,950 offenses per U.S. resident.
    - Third shift occurred between 1991 and 2000.
      - Significant declines in the rate of most major crimes being reported.
      - Crime Index dropped from 5,897 to 4,124 offenses per 100,000 U.S. population, sending it to levels not seen since 1975. Suggested reasons for decline:
        - Well-funded national effort to combat crime beginning with Safe Streets Act of 1968
        - Growth in popularity of innovative police programs such as community policing
        - Aggressive approach to gun control, including Brady Handgun Violence Prevention Act
        - Strong victims' movement and enactment of the 1984 federal Victims of Crime Act and the 1994 Violence Against Women Act
        - Sentencing reform

        - "War on drugs" begun during the 1970s has resulted in stiff penalties for drug dealers and repeat drug offenders.
        - Increased use of death penalty
        - Substantial growth in use of incarceration
        - Advances in forensic science and the advent of DNA evidence
    - Fourth shift occurred in 2001.
        - Shift may be taking place now, but too early to tell.
        - As size of teenage population continues to increase, the "crime-prone" segment increases.
        - Some researchers are predicting that crime rates will peak around 2010.

- UCR Technology
    - Crime clock is the yearly calculation of crime in the United States.
        - Clock is not rate based and does not allow for easy comparisons over time.
        - Distinguishes between two categories of Part I offenses:
            - Violent crime—one every 22.4 seconds
                - Murder—one every 31 minutes
                - Forcible rape—one every 5.8 minutes
                - Robbery—one every 1.2 minutes
                - Aggravated assault—one every 36.8 seconds
            - Property crime—one every 3.2 seconds
                - Burglary—one every 14.15 seconds
                - Larceny-theft—one every 4.8 seconds
                - Motor vehicle theft—one every 28.8 seconds

2.2.2 National Incident-Based Reporting System (NIBRS): The new UCR

INCIDENT-BASED REPORTING

Compared with summary reporting, a less restrictive and more expansive method of collecting crime data in which all of the analytical elements associated with an offense or arrest are compiled by a central collection agency on an incident-by-incident basis.

- **Incident-based** rather than "summary-based" like the UCR
- City, county, state, and federal law enforcement agencies furnish detailed data on crime and arrest activities at the incident level.
- Goals of NIBRS:
    - Enhance the quality, quantity, and timeliness of crime data collection by law enforcement.
    - Improve the methodology used for computing, analyzing, auditing, and publishing the collected data.
- Advantages of NIBRS:
    - The ability to break down and combine crime offense data into specific information
    - Distinguishes between attempted and completed crimes

- ❖ Records each offense occurring in an incident
- ❖ Records rape of males and females
- ❖ Restructures definition of assault
- ❖ Collects weapon information for all violent offenses
- ❖ Provides details on arrests for the eight index crimes and 49 other offenses

- NIBRS replaces old Part I and Part II offenses with 22 general offenses:
  - ❖ Arson
  - ❖ Assault
  - ❖ Bribery
  - ❖ Burglary
  - ❖ Counterfeiting
  - ❖ Embezzlement
  - ❖ Extortion
  - ❖ Forcible sex offenses
  - ❖ Fraud
  - ❖ Gambling
  - ❖ Homicide
  - ❖ Kidnapping
  - ❖ Larceny
  - ❖ Motor vehicle theft
  - ❖ Narcotics offenses
  - ❖ Nonforcible sex offenses
  - ❖ Pornography
  - ❖ Prostitution
  - ❖ Receiving stolen property
  - ❖ Robbery
  - ❖ Vandalism
  - ❖ Weapons violation
- In addition, the NIBRS collects data on the following crimes:
  - ❖ Bad checks
  - ❖ Vagrancy
  - ❖ Disorderly conduct
  - ❖ Driving under the influence
  - ❖ Drunkenness
  - ❖ Nonviolent family offenses
  - ❖ Liquor law violations
  - ❖ "Peeping Tom" activity
  - ❖ Runaways
  - ❖ Trespass

- NIBRS collects the following information on each incident:
  - Administrative segment
    - Originating agency identifier (OAI)
    - Incident number
    - Incident date/hour
    - Exceptional clearance indicator
    - Exceptional clearance date
  - Victim segment
    - Victim number
    - Victim UCR offense code
    - Type of victim
    - Age of victim
    - Sex of victim
    - Race of victim
    - Ethnicity of victim
    - Resident status of victim
    - Homicide/assault circumstances
    - Justifiable homicide circumstances
    - Type of injury
    - Related offender number
    - Relationship of victim to offender
  - Offense segment
    - UCR offense code
    - Attempted/completed code
    - Alcohol/drug use by offender
    - Type of location
    - Number of premises entered
    - Method of entry
    - Type of criminal activity
    - Type of weapon/force used
    - Bias crime code
  - Property segment
    - Type of property loss
    - Property description
    - Property value
    - Recovery date
    - Number of stolen motor vehicles
    - Number of recovered motor vehicles
    - Suspected drug type

    - Estimated drug quantity
    - Drug measurement unit
- Offender segment
    - Offender number
    - Age of offender
    - Sex of offender
    - Race of offender
- Arrestee segment
    - Arrestee number
    - Transaction number
    - Arrest date
    - Type of arrest
    - Multiple clearance indicator
    - UCR arrest offense code
    - Arrestee armed indicator
    - Age of arrestee
    - Sex of arrestee
    - Race of arrestee
    - Ethnicity of arrestee
    - Resident status of arrestee
    - Disposition of arrestee under 18

- The FBI began collecting crime data in NIBRS format in 1989. The intended date of full implementation was 1999. By 2001, only 21 state crime reporting programs had been certified for NIBRS participation and 15 more were nearing completion of the certification process.

2.2.3 The **National Crime Victimization Survey** (NCVS) started in 1972 partially as a response to problems with UCR.

- Based on victim self-reports rather than police reports.
- Designed to estimate the occurrence of all crimes, whether reported or not.
- **Bureau of Justice Statistics** collects/publishes data.
- Data collected through a cooperative arrangement with the U.S. Census Bureau.
- Interested in the "dark figure of crime" (crimes not reported to the police and remain unknown to officials).
- Surveys 56,000 households about victimization (about 120,000 individuals).
- Surveys individuals over 12 years of age.
- Sample interviewed twice per year.

NATIONAL CRIME VICTIMIZATION SURVEY (NCVS)

A now defunct but once inclusive measure of the UCR Program's violent and property crime categories, or what are called Part I offenses. The Crime Index, long featured in the FBI's publication *Crime in the United States*, was discontinued in 2004. The index had been intended as a tool for geographic (state-to-state) and historical (year-to-year) comparisons via the use of crime rates (the number of crimes per unit of population). However, criticism that the index was misleading arose after researchers found that the largest of the index's crime categories, larceny-theft, carried undue weight and led to an underappreciation of changes in the rates of more violent and serious crimes

BUREAU OF JUSTICE STATISTICS

A U.S. Department of Justice agency responsible for the collection of criminal justice data, including the annual National Crime Victimization Survey.

FORCIBLE RAPE

The carnal knowledge of a female forcibly and against her will. For statistical reporting purposes, the FBI defines forcible rape as "unlawful sexual intercourse with a female, by force and against her will, or without legal or factual consent." Statutory rape differs from forcible rape in that it generally involves nonforcible sexual intercourse with a minor. *See also* carnal knowledge and rape.

CARNAL KNOWLEDGE

Sexual intercourse, coitus, sexual copulation. Carnal knowledge is accomplished "if there is the slightest penetration of the sexual organ of the female by the sexual organ of the male."

ROBBERY

The unlawful taking or attempted taking of property that is in the immediate possession of another by force or violence and/or by putting the victim in fear. Armed robbery differs from unarmed, or strong-arm robbery in that it involves a weapon. Contrary to popular conceptions, highway robbery does not necessarily occur on a street, and rarely in a vehicle. The term highway robbery applies to any form of robbery that occurs outdoors in a public place.

ASSAULT

An unlawful attack by one person upon another. Historically, assault meant only the attempt to inflict injury on another person; a completed act constituted the separate offense of battery. Under modern statistical usage, however, attempted and completed acts are grouped together under the generic term assault.

BURGLARY

By the narrowest and oldest definition, breaking and entering of a dwelling house of another during the nighttime with the intent to commit a felony.

- List of households surveyed revised every three years.
- Includes data on seven crimes (definitions are those used by the National Crime Victimization Survey):
  - **Forcible rape** is defined as the **carnal knowledge** through the use of force or threat of force, including attempts. Rapes include victimization of both males and females.
  - Sexual assault includes a wide range of victimizations, separate from rape or attempted rapes.
    - These crimes include attacks or attempted attacks generally involving unwanted sexual contact between victim and offender.
    - Sexual assaults may or may not involve force and include such things as grabbing or fondling.
    - Sexual assault also includes verbal threats.
  - **Robbery** is defined by NCVS as a completed or attempted theft, directly from a person, of property or cash by force or threat of force, with or without a weapon.
  - **Assault** is defined by NCVS as an unlawful physical attack on a person, whether aggravated or simple, and includes attempted assaults with or without a weapon, but still excludes rape and attacks involving theft or attempted theft (which are classified as robbery).
  - **Burglary** is defined by NCVS as unlawful or forcible entry or attempted entry of a residence, garage, shed, or other structure on the premises, usually but not always involving theft.
  - **Personal and household larceny** (NCVS) is the attempted or completed theft of property or cash without personal contact.
  - **Motor vehicle theft** (NCVS) is stealing or the unauthorized taking of a motor vehicle, including attempted theft.
- NCVS employs a hierarchical counting system.
  - It counts only the most "serious" incident in any series of criminal events perpetrated against the same individual.
- Includes both attempted and completed offenses.
- Highlights of NCVS statistics for the recent years:
  - Approximately 15% of American households are touched by crime every year.
  - Nearly 16 million victimizations are reported to the NCVS per year.
  - City residents are about twice as likely as rural residents to be victims of crime.
  - About half of all violent crimes and slightly more than one-third of all property crimes are reported to the police.

- Victims of crime are more often men than women.
- Younger people are more likely than the elderly to be the victims of crime.
- Blacks are more likely than whites or members of other racial groups to be victims of violent crimes.
- Violent victimization rates are highest among people in lower income families.
- Young males have the highest violent victimization rates; elderly females the lowest.
- The chance of violent criminal victimization is much higher for young black males than for any other segment of the population.
- Number of victimizations for 2006:
  - Forcible rape: 272,350
  - Robbery: 711,570
  - Aggravated assault: 1,354,750
  - Burglary: 3,539,760
  - Larceny: 14,275,150
  - Motor vehicle theft: 993,910
- According to NCVS data, household crime rates are highest when:
  - Headed by blacks
  - Headed by younger people
  - There are six or more members in the household.
  - Headed by renters
  - Located in central cities
- Problems with NCVS data
  - Overreporting due to victims' misinterpretation of events
  - Underreporting due to embarrassment of reporting crime to interviewers
  - Underreporting due to fear of getting in trouble
  - Underreporting due to forgetting about victimization
  - Inability to record the personal criminal activity of those interviewed, such as drug use or gambling
  - Inadequate question format, which invalidates responses
  - Does not include data on individuals under 12.

PERSONAL AND HOUSEHOLD LARCENY

The unlawful taking or attempted taking, carrying, leading, or riding away of property, from the possession or constructive possession of another. Motor vehicles are excluded. Larceny is the most common of the eight major offenses, although probably only a small percentage of all larcenies are actually reported to the police because of the small dollar amounts involved.

MOTOR VEHICLE THEFT

The theft or attempted theft of a motor vehicle. Motor vehicle is defined as a self-propelled road vehicle that runs on land surface and not on rails. The stealing of trains, planes, boats, construction equipment, and most farm machinery is classified as larceny under the UCR/NIBRS Program, not as motor vehicle theft.

2.2.4 Comparisons of the UCR and the NCVS

- Both provide crime estimates.
- The type(s) of crime they choose to measure creates limitations.

- UCR
    - Homicide
    - Rape
    - Robbery (personal and commercial)
    - Assault (aggravated)
    - Burglary (commercial and household)
    - Larceny (commercial and household)
    - Motor vehicle theft
    - Arson
- NCVS
    - Rape
    - Robbery (personal)
    - Assault (aggravated and simple)
    - Burglary (household)
    - Larceny (personal and household)
    - Motor vehicle theft

- The type(s) of crime they exclude from measurement creates limitations:
    - UCR: assault (simple)
    - NCVS: homicide, commercial crimes
- Both are limited by the methods they use to gather crime data.
    - UCR uses data based only on crimes reported to the police.
    - NCVS uses data based on self-report of selected households.
- NCVS collects more detailed information than the UCR.
    - UCR provides information on:
        - Crime clearances
        - Persons arrested
        - Persons charged
        - Law enforcement officers killed and assaulted
        - Characteristics of homicide victims
    - NCVS provides information on victims':
        - Age
        - Race
        - Sex
        - Education
        - Income
        - Relationship (if any) to offender
        - Crime:
            - Time
            - Place of occurrence

  - ❐ Whether or not it was reported to police
  - ❐ Use of weapons
  - ❐ Occurrence of injury
  - ❐ Economic consequences

- UCR is sponsored by the FBI, whereas the NCVS is sponsored by the Bureau of Justice Statistics.

For more on how crime is measured, visit Criminal Justice Interactive online > Defining and Measuring Crime > Learning Modules > 2.2 How Crimes are Measured.

For practice comparing UCR and NCVS data, visit Criminal Justice Interactive online > Defining and Measuring Crime > Simulation Activity: The Extent of Crime.

2.3 Violent crime

VIOLENT CRIME

A UCR/NIBRS summary offense category that includes murder, rape, robbery, and aggravated assault.

MURDER

The unlawful killing of a human being. Murder is a generic term that in common usage may include first- and second-degree murder, manslaughter, involuntary manslaughter, and other similar offenses.

2.3.1 **Murder** (UCR) is the willful (nonnegligent) killing of one human being by another.

- Does not include suicides, justifiable homicides, deaths caused by negligence or accidents, or murder attempts.
- In 2007, 16,929 murders were reported.
- Murder rate—5.6 for every 100,000 persons in the United States.
- Weapon of choice—firearms (68% of murders)
  - Firearms (68% of murders)
    - Handguns (49.63%)
    - Rifles (3%)
    - Shotguns (3.1%)
    - Other guns (1%)
    - Firearms, types not stated (11.5%)
  - Knives were used 12.1% of the time.
  - Blunt objects (clubs, hammers, etc.) were used 4.4% of the time.
  - Personal weapons (hands, fists, feet, etc.) were used 5.8% of the time.
- It is the index crime least likely to occur, but most likely to be cleared.
- Murder rates tend to peak annually in the warmest months (typically July and August).
- Murder is most common in the southern states.

- Murder and victims' age:
  - Infant (under age of one) victims: 210
  - Victims aged 75 and over: 261
  - Young adults between 20 and 24 were most likely to be victims.
- Murder and relation to victim:
  - Of all murders, 12.97% were classified by offenders as "strangers."
  - Relationship between victim and perpetrator had not been determined in 46.17% of murders.
  - Largest category of known relationship was officially listed as "acquaintances."
- Arguments are listed as the largest circumstance involved in murders.
- Types of murderers
  - Thrill killing involves impulsive violence motivated by the killer's decision to kill a stranger as an act of daring or recklessness.
  - Gang killings involve members of teenage gangs who make violence part of their group activity; FBI records about 1,000 gang killings each year.
  - Cult killings occur when members of religious cults are ordered to kill by their leaders.
  - **Serial murder** is the killing of several people in three or more separate events.

SERIAL MURDER
The killing of several people in three or more separate events.

    - Types of serial murderers (typology developed by Ronald Homes and James DeBurger):
      - Visionary killers commit murders in response to some inner voice or vision that demands that some person or category of persons be killed.
      - Mission-oriented killers are motivated to rid the world of a particular type of undesirable person such as prostitutes.
      - Hedonistic killers are thrill-seeking murderers who get excitement and sometimes sexual satisfaction from killing.
      - Power-/control-oriented killers enjoy having complete control over their victims. If they rape or mutilate their victims, the violence is motivated not by sex, but by the pleasure of having power over another human being.
      - Mass murderers kill four or more victims at one location within one event.

2.3.2 Forcible rape (UCR) is defined as carnal knowledge of a female forcibly and against her will.

- For the UCR reports, reported rapes, by definition, must be of females.
  - The FBI states, "Sex attacks on males are excluded [from the crime of forcible rape] and should be classified as assaults or other sex offenses, depending on the nature of the crime and the extent of injury."
  - **Sexual battery**
    - Some jurisdictions refer to same-sex rape as sexual battery although they are not included in the FBI's UCR data.

SEXUAL BATTERY

Intentional and wrongful physical contact with a person, without his or her consent, that entails a sexual component or purpose.

- Statutory rape differs from forcible rape in that it involves sexual intercourse with a female who is under the age of consent, regardless of whether or not she is a willing partner.
- Rape is one of the least reported of all offenses.
  - Estimates are that only one out of every four forcible rapes that actually occur are reported to the police.
- Reasons women have not reported forcible rape in the past:
  - Victim's fear of embarrassment
  - Insensitive handling by law enforcement officials
  - Trauma of physical examination
  - Many states permitted women's past sexual history to be revealed in detail in courtroom if trial ensued.
- In 2007, 90,427 forcible rapes were reported.
- From 2007 to 2008, there was a 2.2% decrease in the number of offenses reported.
- Greatest number of forcible rapes reported during the hot summer months. November through February recorded the lowest number of reports.
- Frequently committed by a man known to the victim
- Contemporary wisdom holds that forcible rape is often a planned violent crime that serves the offender's need for power rather than sexual gratification ("power thesis").
- Most rapes are committed by acquaintances of the victim and often betray a trust or friendship.
  - Date rape
    - Appears to be far more common than previously believed.
    - Date rape drug Rohypnol is often used to render female victim unconscious.

    - ❖ Rape within marriage
        - ◆ A growing concern in American criminal justice

2.3.3 Robbery (UCR) is the taking or attempting to take anything of value from the care, custody, or control of a person or persons by force or threat of force or violence and/or by putting the victim in fear.

- Armed robbery differs from unarmed or strong-armed robbery because of the use of a weapon.
- A personal crime that involves a face-to-face confrontation
- Robbery is a personal crime. Individual citizens are typical targets of robbers.
- Guns are discharged in 20% of all robberies.
- Purse snatching and pocket picking are *not* classified as robbery. They are considered to be larceny-thefts under UCR reporting.
- In 2007, most robberies occurred on the street/highway.
- In 2007, banks, gas stations, convenience stores, and other businesses were the second most common targets.
- Residential robberies accounted for only 15.2% of total robberies in 2007.
- In 2007, 445,125 robberies were reported.
    - ❖ Forty-five percent of reported robberies occurred outdoors (highway robberies).
    - ❖ Strong-armed robberies (no weapon used) accounted for 33% of total robberies reported.
    - ❖ While guns were used in 35% of all robberies, they were discharged in only 20% of all robberies.
    - ❖ Knives were used in 7% of all robberies.
    - ❖ Three percent of robbery victims were also raped.
- Robbery is primarily an urban offense.
    - ❖ Robbery rate in large cities in 2006 was 207.5 per every 100,000 inhabitants.
    - ❖ Robbery rate in rural areas in 2006 was 15.9 per every 100,000 inhabitants.
- Eighty-eight percent of those arrested for robbery in 2006 were male.
- Sixty-five percent of those arrested for robbery in 2006 were under the age of 25.
- Fifty-nine percent of those arrested for robbery in 2006 were minorities.

2.3.4 **Aggravated assault** (UCR) is an unlawful attack by one person upon another for the purpose of inflicting severe or aggravated bodily injury. This type of assault is usually accompanied by a weapon or by other means likely to produce death or great bodily harm.

AGGRAVATED ASSAULT

The unlawful, intentional inflicting, or attempted or threatened inflicting, of serious injury upon the person of another. While aggravated assault and simple assault are standard terms for reporting purposes, most state penal codes use labels like first-degree and second-degree to make such distinctions.

- Assault
  - ❖ Historically, assault meant only the attempt to inflict injury on another person and required no actual touching.
- Battery
  - ❖ Means offensive touching such as slapping, hitting, or punching a victim.
  - ❖ Today most states just use the term *assault* to represent the attempt and the completed act.
- An assault can also involve "offensive touching," such as when a man kisses a woman against her will or puts his hands on her body.
- Two types of assault
  - ❖ Simple assault may involve pushing and shoving or even fistfights.
  - ❖ Aggravated assault can involve use of weapon, and the victim requires medical assistance.
- In 2007, the FBI reported 855,856 cases of aggravated assault.
  - ❖ Because those who committed assaults were often known to their victims, 54% of all aggravated assaults in 2006 were cleared by arrest.
- Summer months have the greatest frequency of reported assaults. The least frequent are January, February, November, and December.
- Those arrested for assault tend to be young, male, and white.
- Assault victims tend to be male.
- Highest rates of assault occur in urban areas, and in southern and western regions of country.
- Most common weapons used:
  - ❖ Blunt instruments (34%)
  - ❖ Hands, feet, and fists (25%)
  - ❖ Firearms (22%)
  - ❖ Knives (19%)

For more on violent crime, visit Criminal Justice Interactive online > Defining and Measuring Crime > Learning Modules > 2.3 Violent Crime.

PROPERTY CRIME

A UCR/NIBRS summary offense category that includes burglary, larceny-theft, motor vehicle theft, and arson.

2.4 Property crime

2.4.1 Burglary (UCR) is the unlawful entry of a structure to commit a felony or theft. The use of force to gain entry need not have occurred.

- Three sub-classifications for burglary: forcible entry; unlawful entry where no force is used; attempted forcible entry
- Structures include: apartment, house, barn, house trailer or houseboat when used as a permanent dwelling, railroad car (but not an automobile), stable, or vessel (ship).
- In 2007, 2,179,140 burglaries were reported with a clearance rate of 12.6%.
- Total dollar loss as a result of burglaries is estimated to be around $4.3 billion for 2007, with an average loss per offense of $1,991.
- Daytime burglaries are more common than nighttime burglaries.
- Of all burglaries, 67.9% were of residential properties.
- Of all burglaries, 32.4% were unlawful entries.
- Of all burglaries, 6.5% were attempted forcible entries.
- Ten percent of all burglaries were those in which a household member was home.
  - Residents who were home during a burglary suffered a greater than 30% chance of becoming the victim of a violent crime.

LARCENY-THEFT

The unlawful taking or attempted taking, carrying, leading, riding away of property, from the possession or constructive possession of another. Motor vehicles are excluded. Larceny is the most common of the eight major offenses, although probably only a small percentage of all larcenies are actually reported to the police because of the small dollar amounts involved.

PART I OFFENSES

A UCR/NIBRS offense group used to report murder, rape, robbery, aggravated assault, burglary, larceny-theft, motor vehicle theft, and arson, as defined under the FBI's UCR/NIBRS Program. Also called major crimes.

2.4.2 **Larceny-theft** (UCR) is the unlawful taking, carrying, leading, or riding away of property from the possession or constructive possession of another.

- The most common of the eight major offenses of the Part I index crimes
- One of the least likely of the **Part I offenses** to be cleared by an arrest
- Larceny is oftentimes not reported to the police because:
  - Victim does not have insurance.
  - Victim believes police can do nothing.
  - Victim does not realize he or she is a victim; they think they may have lost the item.
- Some states distinguish between simple and grand larceny.
  - Grand larceny is usually defined as theft of valuables in excess of a certain set dollar amount, such as $200.
- UCR lists the following offenses as types of larceny:
  - Theft from motor vehicles
  - Shoplifting
  - Thefts of motor vehicle parts and accessories

- ❖ Thefts from buildings
- ❖ Bicycle thefts
- ❖ Pocket picking
- ❖ Purse snatching
- ❖ Thefts from coin-operated machines
- ❖ Theft of farm animals and farm machinery

- Not included in list of larcenies:
  - ❖ Embezzlement
  - ❖ Con games
  - ❖ Forgery
  - ❖ Worthless checks
  - ❖ Computer software/information thefts
- In 2007, there were 6,568,572 reported larceny-thefts.
- Total dollar amount of property stolen was placed at $5.8 billion, with an average value of property of $886 per offense.
- Most common form of larceny is the theft of motor vehicle parts, accessories, and contents:
  - ❖ Tires
  - ❖ Wheels
  - ❖ Hubcaps
  - ❖ Radar detectors
  - ❖ Stereos
  - ❖ CD players
  - ❖ Cassette tapes
  - ❖ Compact discs
  - ❖ Cellular phones

2.4.3 Motor vehicle theft (UCR) is defined as the theft or attempted theft of a motor vehicle.

- Motor vehicle is defined by UCR as self-propelled vehicles that run on the ground and not on rails, and includes automobiles, motorcycles, motor scooters, trucks, buses, and snowmobiles. Excluded are trains, airplanes, bulldozers, most farm machinery, ships, boats, and spacecraft.
- Motor vehicle theft has one of the highest rates of reporting to the police because insurance companies require a police report to pay a claim of a stolen auto.
- In 2007, 1,095,769 motor vehicles were reported stolen with a rate of 363.3 per 100,000 residents.
- The estimated value of motor vehicles stolen in 2007 was $7.4 billion, with the average value of each vehicle reported stolen being $6,755.

- The clearance rate for reported stolen vehicles is 12.6%.
  - Clearance rate for city agencies is 9.4%.
  - Clearance rate for rural county agencies is 26%.
- Motor vehicle theft has very low clearance rate because:
  - Autos are stolen and shipped overseas for sale.
  - Autos are stolen and "chopped" for parts.
- Automobiles accounted for 73.4% of the motor vehicle thefts reported stolen in 2007.
- Typical offender is a young male under the age of 25.
- In 2007, 93.1% of the nation's motor vehicle thefts occurred in metropolitan statistical areas.
- Carjacking is the taking of an auto directly from the control of an individual (*not* considered a motor vehicle theft).
  - The FBI estimates that carjackings account for slightly more than 1% of all motor vehicle thefts.

ARSON

The burning or attempted burning of property, with or without the intent to defraud. Some instances of arson result from malicious mischief, some involve attempts to claim insurance monies, and some are committed in an effort to disguise other crimes, such as murder, burglary, or larceny.

2.4.4 **Arson** (UCR) is any willful or malicious burning or attempting to burn, with or without intent to defraud, a dwelling house, public building, motor vehicle or aircraft, personal property of another, etc.

- Some instances of arson are the result of malicious mischief, attempts to claim insurance money, or to disguise other crimes such as murder, burglary, and larceny.
- In 2007, 64,332 arsons were reported.
  - Arson of structures such as houses, storage buildings, and manufacturing facilities reported was 27,598 (42.9%).
  - Arson of vehicles reported was 17,948 (27.9%).
  - Arson of property such as crops, timber, fences, etc., was 18,784 (29.2%).
- The average dollar loss per reported arson in 2007 was $17,289; arsons of industrial/manufacturing structures resulted in the highest average dollar losses of $114,699 per arson.
- In 2007, arson offenses decreased 6.7% when compared to 2006.
- Nationwide, the rate of arson was 24.7 offenses for every 100,000 residents.

For more on property crime, visit Criminal Justice Interactive online > Defining and Measuring Crime > Learning Modules > 2.4 Property Crime.

WHITE-COLLAR CRIME

Crime committed, usually by a person of high social status, in the course of an occupation.

2.5 White-collar and organized crime

2.5.1 **White-collar crime** is crime usually committed by a person of high social status or in a position of power in the course of an occupation.

- Many criminologists do not recognize that violations of public and corporate trust by those in authority are as harmful as predatory acts committed by people in a lower social class.

2.5.2 The extent of white-collar crime

- The dollar loss from white-collar crime is likely significant, far exceeding all other crimes combined, because it is so difficult to detect.
  - NIBRS (2007)
    - Fraud (1999): 157,749
    - Counterfeiting/forgery (1999): 91,697
    - Embezzlement (1999): 20,694
- Some do not see white-collar crime as harmful and financially impactful as street crime:
  - The economic losses from white-collar crime are spread over millions of victims.
  - Trauma to the victims is less than that in street crime.
- Types of white-collar crime
  - Individual crimes committed by individuals for direct personal gain in the course of their occupational duties.
  - **Corporate crime** committed to further corporate goals rather than personal gain.

CORPORATE CRIME

A violation of a criminal statute either by a corporate entity or by its executives, employees, or agents acting on behalf of and for the benefit of the corporation, partnership, or other form of business entity.

2.5.3 Similarities between white-collar crimes and other crimes

- Similarities:
  - Like other crimes, they involve violence and theft.
  - They result in loss of property and in injury and death.
- Two important differences:
  - White-collar crimes involve far more victimization and harm.
  - Victimization from white-collar crimes is much less apparent.

2.5.4 **Occupational crime** is any act punishable by law that is committed through opportunity created in the course of an occupation that is legal.

OCCUPATIONAL CRIME

Any act punishable by law that is committed through opportunity created in the course of an occupation that is legal.

- Occupational crimes include job-related law violations of both white- and blue-collar workers where the motive is direct personal gain.
- Two major types
  - Employee theft is stealing job-related items or merchandise from one's place of employment; one of the most widespread of all crimes with costs of $2 trillion per year.
  - Workplace theft occurs at all employee levels, including senior staff and management; embezzlement involves taking of money (as opposed to merchandise) for personal use; ranges from stealing from the cashbox to adjusting financial records.

- Occupational fraud
    - Securities-related crimes
        - Crimes committed by those who work in the stocks and bonds field, and who misuse their position for personal gain.
            - Fraud against the government
                - Affects all levels of government.
                - Wide range of activities make up this type of fraud, such as bid rigging, payoffs and kickbacks for contracts, filing false claims against a budget, or a company/business hiring a former government employee or family/friends of government officials to gain influence.
                - The costs of such fraud are impossible to accurately measure, but they likely total in the hundreds of billions annually.

2.5.5 Consumer fraud

- A consumer is deceived into surrendering money; businesses use deceptive advertising to entice consumers to purchase a product that may be fraudulent.

2.5.6 Insurance fraud

- Policyholders/third parties filing false claims
- A member of a company is an accomplice to a policyholder filing a false claim.
- Insurance companies that sell policies with no intent to ever pay claims
- High-ranking managers embezzle and debit the money as claims.
- Businesses like auto repair defraud insurance companies for services through intentional overcharging and/or charging for work not actually done.

2.5.7 Tax fraud

- This type of fraud occurs when a business attempts to reduce the amount of taxes that are owed through deception, misinformation, etc.
- The IRS estimates that the net tax gap (the difference between taxes that were paid and those that should have been paid) for 2001 was $290 billion.

2.5.8 Bribery, corruption, and political fraud

- Political officials accept payment, favors, etc., in return for favorable decisions or preferential treatment.
- This includes a wide range of behaviors: judges who accept bribes, mayors who award contracts for kickbacks, members of Congress voting in certain ways in return for payment.

2.5.9 Corporate crimes, including corporate thefts, are crimes committed either by a corporation or by individuals that may be identified with a corporation.

- There are three major forms of corporate theft.
  - Deceptive advertising refers to advertising that is misleading, false, or deceptive.
  - Financial fraud is when corporate executives engage in fraud that serves/benefits the company, such as money laundering.
  - Price-fixing is conspiracy between business competitors to sell the same product or service at the same price, driving the price artificially higher.

2.5.10 **Organized crime** is defined by the FBI as "crime committed by any group, having formalized structure whose primary objective is to obtain money through illegal activities."

ORGANIZED CRIME

The unlawful activities of the members of a highly organized, disciplined association engaged in supplying illegal goods and services, including but not limited to gambling, prostitution, loan sharking, narcotics, labor racketeering, and other unlawful activities.

- The FBI (1999) categorizes organized crime as "traditional" or "nontraditional."
  - Traditional organized crime is what is generally referred to as the "Mafia," the "Mob," "La Cosa Nostra," or the "Syndicate."
  - Nontraditional organized crime refers to more recent groups, such as Asian, Russian/Eastern European, or Nigerian/West African.
- Historical overview of organized crime
  - The roots of the Mafia are in Sicily, Italy, and pre-date organized crime in the United States.
  - La Cosa Nostra refers to a large number of organized criminal groups that flourished in U.S. cities before the Italians arrived, and included individuals in Jewish and Irish communities.
- Prohibition and official corruption
  - Prohibition provided organized crime with a new business and income stream.
  - Prior to Prohibition, the Mafia focused on gambling, protection rackets, and loan sharking.
  - The selling of liquor and related activities gave Mafia families the opportunity to accumulate great wealth during the depression.
- Types of organized crime
  - The FBI (1999) lists a wide variety of activities that organized crime groups engage in:
    - Historically, these have been gambling, prostitution, drug trafficking, loan sharking, labor racketeering, and murder for hire.

        - More recently, these include financial institution fraud, health care fraud, fraud against the government, money laundering, and securities fraud.
    - Other organized crime groups in the United States
        - Black Mafia
        - Cuban Mafia
        - Haitian Mafia
        - Columbian Cartels
        - Russian Mafiya
        - Asian criminals: Chinese Tongs, Japanese Yakuza, Vietnamese gangs, Taiwan's Triads
        - Inner-city gangs: Los Angeles Crips, Los Angeles Bloods, Chicago Vice Lords
        - International drug rings
        - Outlaw motorcycle gangs: Hell's Angels, Pagans
    - Transnational organized crime
        - Unlawful activity undertaken and supported by criminal groups operating across national boundaries
        - Transnational crime is now a major force in world finance, able to affect countries at critical stages of their economic development.
            - Examples of world's major crime clans: South American cocaine cartels, Italian Mafia, Russian Mafiya, West African crime groups
            - Russian organized crime has grown quickly since the collapse of the Soviet Union and has taken root in the United States and other countries.

For more on white-collar crime, visit Criminal Justice Interactive online > Defining and Measuring Crime > Learning Modules > 2.5 White-Collar and Organized Crime.

For more on the costs of white-collar crime, visit Criminal Justice Interactive online > Defining and Measuring Crime > Myths and Issues Videos > Myth vs. Reality: Street Crime Is More Costly to Society than White-Collar Crime.

2.6 Examination of Part II offenses

2.6.1 Offenses that are generally less serious are categorized as Part II offenses.

2.6.2 Includes offenses for recorded arrests, *not* for crimes reported to the police

2.6.3 A Part II arrest is counted each time a person is taken into custody.

2.6.4 List of **Part II offenses** (arrest figures for 2006):

PART II OFFENSES

A UCR/NIBRS offense group used to report less serious offenses. Agencies are limited to reporting only arrest information for Part II offenses, with the exception of simple assault.

- Simple assault (1,305,757)
- Curfew offenses and loitering (159,907)
- Embezzlement (20,012)
- Forgery and counterfeiting (108,823)
- Disorderly conduct (703,504)
- Driving under the influence (1,460,498)
- Drug offenses (1,889,810)
- Fraud (280,693)
- Gambling (12.307)
- Liquor offenses (645,734)
- Offenses against the family (e.g., nonsupport) (131,491)
- Prostitution and related offenses (79,673)
- Public drunkenness (553,188)
- Runaways (114,179)
- Sex offenses (e.g., statutory rape) (87,252)
- Stolen property (e.g., receiving) (122,722)
- Vandalism (300,679)
- Vagrancy (36,471)
- Weapons offenses (e.g., carrying) (200,782)

2.7 Women and crime

2.7.1 Women as victims

- Women, as a group, are victimized far less frequently than men in all of crime except for rape.
    - Males age 12 and older are victims of crimes at a rate of approximately 2,500 per 100,000 residents.
    - Females age 12 and older are victims of crimes at a rate of approximately 1,800 per 100,000 residents.
- Injuries
    - When it is a violent crime, women are more likely to be injured than men (29% vs. 22%).
    - Women are also more likely to adjust how they live in an attempt to reduce the likelihood of their victimization; these can include: where they travel, when they travel, always

traveling in pairs, types of residences (security systems, deadbolt locks, etc.).

- A Bureau of Justice analysis found:
  - Women who are victims of violent crime are twice as likely to be victimized by strangers as by people whom they know.
  - Separated or divorced women are:
    - Six times more likely to be victims of violent crime than widows
    - Four-and-a-half times more likely to be victims of violent crime than married women
    - Three times more likely to be victims of violent crime than widowers and married men
  - Women living in central city areas are considerably more likely to be victimized than women in the suburbs.
  - Suburban women are more likely to be victimized than women living in rural areas.
  - Women from low-income families experience the highest amount of violent crime; victimization of women falls as family income rises.
  - Unemployed women, female students, and those in the armed forces are the most likely victims of violent crime.
  - Black women are victims of violent crime more frequently than are women of any other race; Hispanic women are more frequently victimized than white women.
  - Women 20 to 24 are the most at risk for violent victimization.

- National Violence Against Women Survey (NVAWS), 2000:
  - Physical assault is widespread among American women.
    - Fifty-two percent of surveyed women said they had been physically assaulted as a child or as an adult.
  - Approximately 1.9 million women are physically assaulted in the United States each year.
  - Eighteen percent of women experienced a completed or attempted rape at some time in their life.
  - Of those reporting rape:
    - Twenty-two percent were under 12 years of age.
    - Thirty-two percent were between 12 and 17 when first raped.
  - Native American and Alaska Native women were most likely to report rape and physical assault, while Asian/Pacific Islander women were least likely to report such victimization.

- ❖ Women report significantly more partner violence than do men. Twenty-five percent of surveyed women said they had been raped or physically assaulted by a current or former spouse, cohabitating partner, or date.
- ❖ Violence against women is primarily partner violence. Seventy-six percent of the women who had been raped or physically abused since age 18 were assaulted by a current or former husband, cohabitating partner, or date, compared with 18% of the men.

2.7.2 Women as offenders. The following statistics are taken from the *Sourcebook of Criminal Justice Statistics*, 2007.

- Although women make up 52% of the population, they account for proportionately less of all arrests:
  - ❖ All crimes: 24.5% (1.6% increase over 2006)
  - ❖ Violent crimes: 18.4% (1.2% increase over 2006)
  - ❖ Property crimes: 33.8% (12.7% increase over 2006)
- Violent offenses:
  - ❖ Murder and non-negligent manslaughter: 10.5% (6% decrease from 2006)
  - ❖ Forcible rape: 1.1% (19.5% decrease from 2006)
  - ❖ Robbery: 13.1% (2.9% increase over 2006)
  - ❖ Aggravated assault: 21.4% (1.1% increase over 2006)
- Property offenses (percentage of all arrests for category):
  - ❖ Burglary: 15% (2% increase over 2006)
  - ❖ Larceny-theft: 40.2% (15.2% increase over 2006)
  - ❖ Motor vehicle theft: 18.2% (10.9% decrease from 2006)
  - ❖ Arson: 15.2% (14% decrease from 2006)
- Part II offenses in 2007, women represented the following percent of all arrests:
  - ❖ Other assaults: 25.5% (1.8% increase over 2006)
  - ❖ Forgery and counterfeiting: 39% (9.3% decrease from 2006)
  - ❖ Fraud: 45% (10.6% decrease from 2006)
  - ❖ Embezzlement: 51.8% (10.6% increase over 2006)
  - ❖ Stolen property: buying, receiving, possessing: 19.4% (3.4% decrease from 2006)
  - ❖ Vandalism: 17.2% (0.2% increase over 2006)
  - ❖ Weapons: carrying, possessing, etc.: 8% (7.7% decrease from 2006)
  - ❖ Prostitution and commercialized vice: 68.2% (2% increase over 2006)
  - ❖ Sex offenses (except forcible rape and prostitution): 7% (3.6% decrease over 2006)

- Drug abuse violations: 19.5% (1.7% decrease from 2006)
- Gambling: 17.2% (19.5% increase over 2006)
- Offenses against the family: 25% (0.9% increase over 2006)
- Driving under the influence: 20.9% (4% increase over 2006)
- Liquor law violations: 27.9% (1.8% increase over 2006)
- Public drunkenness violations: 16.1% (10.2% increase over 2006)
- Disorderly conduct violations: 27% (0.9% decrease from 2006)
- Vagrancy offenses: 23.8% (11.3% decrease from 2006)
- All other offenses (except traffic): 23.4% (0.7% decrease from 2006)
- Suspicion offenses: 20.6% (11.2% decrease from 2006)
- Curfew and loitering law violations: 30.3% (4.6% decrease from 2006)
- Runaways: 55.9% (4.2% decrease from 2006)

CHAPTER SUMMARY

- There are many ways to categories crime. Misdemeanor is an offense punishable by incarceration, usually in local confinement, while a felony is far more serious and is punishable by death or incarceration for at least one year. *Mala en se* crimes are crimes that are wrong because they are inherently evil. *Mala prohibita* crimes are acts that are considered wrong only because there are laws against them. Crimes against persons include murder, forcible rape, robbery, and aggravated assault. Crimes against property are burglary, larceny-theft, and arson.
- There are several sources of crime statistics. The Uniform Crime Rate (UCR) is a statistical reporting program run by the FBI's Criminal Justice Information Services division. UCR Program publishes an annual summary of the incidence and rate of reported crimes throughout the United States. The National Incident-Based Reporting System (NIBRS) is incident-based rather than summary-based. Among the NIBRS's several advantages is the fact that it breaks down crime offense data into specific information, distinguishes between attempted and completed crimes, and collects weapons information for all violent offenses. The National Crime Victimization Survey (NCVS) is based on victim self-reports rather than police reports and is collected by the Bureau of Justice Statistics. It includes more detailed information than the UCR.
- The various crimes defined as violent crimes include murder, forcible rape, robbery, and aggravated assault. Murder is the willful (non-negligent) killing of one human being by another. Forcible rape is carnal knowledge through the use of force or threat of force, including attempts. The NIBRS reports on rapes of both males and females. Robbery is defined by NCVS as a completed or attempted theft, directly from a person, of property or cash by force or threat of force, with or without a weapon. Aggravated assault is an unlawful attack by one person upon another for the purpose of inflicting severe or aggravated bodily injury.

- Property crimes include burglary/theft, larceny, motor vehicle theft, and arson. Burglary/theft is defined by NCVS as unlawful or forcible entry or attempted entry of a residence, garage, shed, or other structure on the premises, usually but not always involving theft. Larceny is the completed or attempted theft of property or cash without personal contact. Motor vehicle theft (NCVS) is stealing or unauthorized taking of a motor vehicle including attempted theft. Arson is any willful or malicious burning or attempting to burn, with or without intent to defraud, a dwelling house, public building, motor vehicle or aircraft, personal property of another, etc.
- White-collar crime is crime committed, usually by a person of high social status or in a position of power, in the course of an occupation. Although many do not see white-collar crime as being harmful or financially impactful as other crimes, the dollar loss from white-collar crime is likely significant, far exceeding all other crimes combined. White-collar crimes include crimes such as occupational theft (employee and workplace theft and fraud), consumer fraud, insurance fraud, tax fraud, bribery, corruption, political fraud, and corporate crime.
- The FBI defines organized crime as "crime committed by any group, having formalized structure whose primary objective is to obtain money through illegal activities." Organized crime in the United States pre-dates the arrival of the Italians and included individuals in the Jewish and Irish communities. Once the Italian Mafia arrived, the organized crime group participated in gambling, protection rackets, and loan sharking. The Mafia found a new business and income stream during Prohibition—they participated in the illegal selling of liquor—and accumulated great wealth. More recent activities of organized crime include fraud as well as gambling, prostitution, and drug trafficking. Today, organized crime also operates across national boundaries and involves worldwide crime clans.
- Part II offenses are generally less serious and include such acts as simple assault, running away, and disorderly conduct.
- Women in general are victimized far less frequently than men in all crimes except rape. As participants in crime, although women represent 52% of the population, they account for a much lower percentage of criminal arrests.

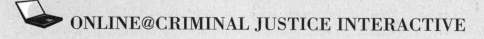

ONLINE@CRIMINAL JUSTICE INTERACTIVE

Learning Modules

2.1 Defining Crime
2.2 How Crimes are Measured
2.3 Violent Crime
2.4 Property Crime
2.5 White-Collar and Organized Crime

Myths and Issues Videos

Myth vs. Reality: Street Crime Is More Costly to Society than White-Collar Crime
Issue 1: Crime vs. Deviance
Issue 2: Full Law Enforcement: Actuality or Imagination

Simulation Activity: The Extent of Crime

Homework and Review

In the News
Web Activity
Review Questions
Essay Questions
Flashcards

Chapter 3

Explaining Criminal Behavior

CHAPTER OUTLINE

3.0 Explaining criminal behavior

3.1 Introduction

- 3.1.1 Crime vs. deviance
- 3.1.2 Theory is a set of interrelated propositions.

3.2 Classical School

- 3.2.1 Classical theory

3.3 Biological School

- 3.3.1 Basic assumptions
- 3.3.2 Phrenology
- 3.3.3 Atavism
- 3.3.4 Criminal families
- 3.3.5 Somatotyping

3.4 Psychological School

- 3.4.1 Basic assumptions
- 3.4.2 Behavioral conditioning
- 3.4.3 Psychoanalytic theory
- 3.4.4 Behaviorism

3.5 Sociological theories

- 3.5.1 Basic assumptions
- 3.5.2 Origins
- 3.5.3 Social ecology school
- 3.5.4 Anomie theory
- 3.5.5 Subcultural theory
- 3.5.6 Focal concerns
- 3.5.7 Subculture of violence
- 3.5.8 Life course perspective

LEARNING OBJECTIVES

After reviewing the online material and reading this chapter, you should be able to:

1. Explain the major theoretical perspectives on criminal behavior (classical, biological, psychological, sociological) and apply these theories to actual crimes and criminal behavior.
2. Discuss how crime theories influence the criminal justice system.
3. Discuss factors that make it difficult for criminologists to definitively explain crime.
4. Define terms related to theories of criminal behavior.

KEY TERMS

anomie
atavism
behavioral conditioning
Biological School
body types
born criminal
Chicago School
Classical School
concentric zone theory
conformity
criminal subculture
focal concerns
free will
hedonism
life course perspective
middle-class measuring rod
Mobilization for Youth
modes of adaptation
phrenology
Positive School
psychoanalysis
Psychological School
psychopath
reaction formation
social disorganization
social ecology
sociopath
status frustration
strain theory
subculture of violence

3.0 Explaining criminal behavior

3.1 Introduction

3.1.1 Crime vs. deviance

- Crime is conduct in violation of the criminal laws of a state, the federal government, or a local jurisdiction, for which there is no legally acceptable justification or excuse. These crimes include murder or shoplifting.
- Deviance is a violation of social norms defining appropriate behavior under a particular set of circumstances.
- Criminal behavior is also deviant behavior, while all deviant behavior is not necessarily criminal behavior.
    - For deviant behavior to be elevated to the level of criminal behavior it must be converted into law, approved by a legislative body, written down, and codified.

3.1.2 Theory is a set of interrelated propositions that attempt to describe, explain, predict, and ultimately control a group of events.

- Even though some theorists have posited grand theories intended to explain all crime, there is probably no single cause of crime.
- Theory can be classified in a variety of ways according to various criteria.
    - For the purposes of this book, theory will be organized into five categories (each theoretical approach will be discussed in its own section below).
        - Classical
        - Biological
        - Psychological
        - Sociological
        - Conflict

For more on whether criminologists can reasonably determine the causes of crime, visit Criminal Justice Interactive online > Explaining Criminal Behavior > Myths and Issues Videos > Myth vs. Reality: Criminologists Know What Causes Crime.

For more on whether crime theory ultimately matters and to whom, visit Criminal Justice Interactive online > Explaining Criminal Behavior > Myths and Issues Videos > Issue 1: Does Crime Theory Matter, and If So, to Whom?

3.2 Classical School

3.2.1 Classical theory is an approach to crime causation and criminal responsibility that grew out of the Enlightenment and that emphasized the role of free will and reasonable punishments.

- Basic assumptions of classical theory:
  - Individuals have **free will**; individuals choose to engage in crime after considering various courses of action and then selecting the one he or she believes is the most desirable.
  - Focus is on the crime, not the criminal.
  - Punishments of offenders need to be certain, swift, and severe enough to prevent crime.
- Classical approach evolved in the eighteenth century, in part, as an extension of the application and works of the Enlightenment theorists: Montesquieu, Voltaire, Hume, Locke, Rousseau, Hobbes.
- Cesare Beccaria (1738–1794) is considered by many to be the father of the **Classical School**.
  - Published *Essays on Crime and Punishment* (1764), considered to be a radical departure from the general operating philosophy of the day. The book was written after Beccaria had visited a prison in Milan and saw the conditions under which the prisoners lived and functioned.
  - Beccaria presented nine guiding principles about crime and how society should respond to lawbreakers:
    - Social action should be based on the utilitarian principle of "the greatest happiness for the greatest number."
    - The sovereign's right to punish is founded on the importance of defending public liberty, and the punishments are to be just in proportion; liberty is to be preserved by the sovereign and considered sacred and valuable.
    - Punishments are set by the legislator by the making of penal laws; the magistrate cannot increase the punishment already determined by law.
    - Obscurity in the law is evil.
      - Crimes will be less frequent if the code of laws is more universally read and understood.
      - A scale of crimes should be formed where the most serious consist of those that immediately tend to the dissolution of society, and the last of the smallest possible injustice done to a private member of that society.

FREE WILL
Individuals choose to engage in crime after considering various courses of action and then selecting the one he or she believes is the most desirable.

CLASSICAL SCHOOL
An eighteenth-century approach to crime causation and criminal responsibility that grew out of the Enlightenment; emphasized the role of free will and reasonable punishments. Classical thinkers believed that punishment, if it is to be an effective deterrent, has to outweigh the potential pleasure derived from criminal behavior.

- The intent of punishment is to prevent the criminal from doing future injury to society and to prevent others from committing similar offenses.
  - Punishments and the mode of inflicting them ought to make the strongest and most long-lasting impressions on the minds of others while inflicting the least torment to the body of the criminal.
- Secret accusations are an abuse.
- Torture during the criminal trial is a cruelty and should be abolished.
  - No man is judged a criminal until he has been found guilty and is entitled to the public protection.
  - Torture is a flawed tool of investigation where the strong go free and the feeble are convicted.
- There are advantages to immediate punishment.
  - The smaller the interval of time between the punishment and the crime, the stronger and more lasting will be the association.
- Crimes are prevented more effectively by certainty of punishment than by severity.

- Many of Beccaria's ideas have been incorporated into our criminal justice system:
  - The punishment should only be just enough to deter crime.
  - Abolition of physical punishment and the death penalty
  - Presumption of innocence
  - Right to confront accusers
  - Right to a speedy trial
  - Right against self-incrimination

- Jeremy Bentham (1784–1832) was influenced by the work of Beccaria.
  - Developed **hedonism** as the major explanation for human behavior during the eighteenth century; hedonism is the concept that people would automatically attempt to maximize pleasure and minimize pain.
    - In the hedonistic calculus, individuals seek pleasure while at the same time trying to avoid pain.
    - Individuals make "free-will" decisions to commit crime based on weighing the advantages and the disadvantages of the action.

HEDONISM

The major explanation for human behavior during the eighteenth century; the concept that people would automatically attempt to maximize pleasure and minimize pain.

        - ◆ In considering pleasure or pain, the following are considered: intensity, duration, certainty or uncertainty, proximity or remoteness.
        - ◆ Crime can be prevented by structuring criminal justice.
    - ❖ To deter individuals from committing crime, the punishment/disadvantages must outweigh the gains/advantages of committing the crime.
- ■ Theorists of the Classical School such as Beccaria and Bentham were concerned with why individuals committed crime, rather than whether or not the crime was committed.

For more on classical theory, visit Criminal Justice Interactive online > Explaining Criminal Behavior > Learning Modules > 3.1 Theories of Crime.

3.3 Biological School

BIOLOGICAL SCHOOL
A perspective on criminological thought that holds that criminal behavior has a physiological basis.

3.3.1 Basic assumptions

- ■ Behavior is predetermined and is constitutionally or genetically based.
- ■ The brain is the controlling factor in human behavior.
- ■ Treatment is the appropriate response to criminal behavior.
- ■ Focus is on the individual rather than on the crime.

3.3.2 **Phrenology** is the belief that the characteristics of personality can be seen in the brain and are mirrored in bumps in the skull.

PHRENOLOGY
The chief practitioners of this believed that the characteristics of the brain are mirrored in bumps in the skull.

- ■ Franz Joseph Gall (1758–1828) is considered to be the *father* of phrenology.
    - ❖ One of the first to present the idea that the organs of the body determined one's mental state and behavior
    - ❖ *Crainioscopy* name given by Gall to the study of the head and the brain that later became known as phrenology.
    - ❖ Basic propositions of crainioscopy:
        - ◆ The brain is the organ of the mind.
        - ◆ The brain consists of localized faculties or functions.
        - ◆ The shape of the skull reveals underlying development (or lack of development) of areas within the brain.
        - ◆ Personality can be revealed by a study of the skull.
    - ❖ Gall never systematically tested his theory in a way that would meet today's scientific standards.
- ■ Johann Gaspar Spurzheim (1776–1853), a student of Gall, introduced the study of phrenology to the United States.
- ■ Phrenology remained a viable approach in the United States until the turn of the twentieth century.

ATAVISM

A condition characterized by the existence of features thought to be common in earlier stages of human evolution.

3.3.3 **Atavism** is a condition characterized by the existence of features thought to be common in earlier stages of human evolution.

- Cesare Lombroso (1835–1909), Italian physician, while employed to do autopsies on prisoners, identified abnormalities of the brain as well as other physical abnormalities and compared individuals' heads and bodies.
    - Borrowed term *atavism* from Charles Darwin (1809–1882) who had first used the term in his work *On the Origin of Species* (1859).
        - Lombroso used the term atavism to represent those individuals who had not fully evolved and therefore were not as civilized; they were considered throwbacks to an earlier era.
    - *Criminal Man* (1876) was published by Lombroso outlining his theory.
        - Stigmata were physical characteristics that identified a criminal.
            - The more stigmata the individual possessed, the more likely he was atavistic and therefore a criminal.
        - Examples of stigmata:
            - Elongated ears that stick out
            - Extra-long arms
            - Large lips
            - Crooked nose
            - Excessive body hair
            - Prominent cheekbones
            - Two different color eyes
            - A retreating forehead
        - Lombroso also identified behavioral atavisms:
            - Dullness to a sense of touch
            - Greater sensitivity to pain
            - Laziness
            - Absence of remorse
            - Impulsiveness
            - Greater agility
    - For Lombroso, atavism implied a **born criminal**.
        - Lombroso believed at varying times during his career that between 70% to 90% of criminals were born criminal.
    - Lombroso also identified career criminals and criminaloids. These individuals committed crimes because of greed, passion, or circumstance in their behavior.

BORN CRIMINAL

Lombroso considered them as displaying atavistic traits; characterized a biological throwback.

- ❖ Lombroso has become known as the father of the **Positive School**.
  - ◆ Positive School was in direct contrast to the Classical School.
    - ❒ Assumptions of the Positive School
      - Behavior is determined (no free will).
      - Crimes should be defined socially.
      - Focus should be on criminal, not on crime.

POSITIVE SCHOOL

An approach to criminal justice theory that stresses the application of scientific techniques to the study of crime and criminals. Includes a philosophy with several varieties, the first being a product of eighteenth century Enlightenment philosophy, with its emphasis on the importance of reason and experience.

- ■ Sir Charles Buckman Goring (1870–1919) studied 3,000 prisoners and compared them along physiological criteria to noncriminals.
  - ❖ Found no significant differences between the criminal group and the noncriminal group, thereby dealing a major setback to the work and theories of Lombroso.
- ■ Earnest A. Hooton (1887–1954) trained as a physical anthropologist and studied the relationship between physiology and crime.
  - ❖ Constructed profiles of 13,873 male prisoners in 10 different states and measured them on 107 different characteristics.
  - ❖ Compared prisoners to a control group of 3,203 civilian volunteers.
  - ❖ Used many of Lombroso's concepts in his study.
  - ❖ Found differences between criminals and noncriminals across a wide range of physical features.
  - ❖ Concluded that prisoners demonstrated a decided physical inferiority.

3.3.4 Criminal families. The study of criminal families considers crime genetic.

- ■ Richard Dugdale (1841–1883) did the first study of mental degeneration as an inherited contributor to crime.
  - ❖ Studied the Juke family using the family tree method.
    - ◆ Family lineage began in America with "Max," a descendant of Dutch immigrants to New Amsterdam in the early eighteenth century.
      - ❒ Two of Max's sons married into the notorious "Juke family of girls," six sisters who were illegitimate.
      - ❒ The male Jukes were reputed to have been vicious while one of the sisters named Ada, had an especially bad reputation and eventually came to be known as "the mother of criminals."
  - ❖ Findings
    - ◆ Over a 75-year time period, the heirs of Ada included 1,200 people, most of whom were social degenerates; only a handful of socially productive progeny could be identified.

- Arthur H. Estabrook continued the work of Richard Dugdale. He extended the study to include 2,094 descendants and found just a few who were normal.
- Henry Goddard (1866–1957) studied the heredity of "feeble-mindedness," or those who today we would call "intellectually-challenged," using the Kallikak family that had two clear lines of descent.
    - One line was an outgrowth of an affair that Martin Kallikak had with a feeble-minded barmaid who had a son by Martin, which produced a total of 480 identifiable descendants.
        - Over half the descendants were determined to be feeble-minded.
    - The second line of 496 descendants was the result of Martin Kallikak's marriage to a virtuous Quaker girl; only three of the descendants in this line were determined to be abnormal.
    - Goddard's research techniques were called into question and within 10 years of publishing his 1912 book, Goddard acknowledged the flaws in his research and no longer promoted the findings.

3.3.5 Somatotyping was developed by William Sheldon (1893–1977).

- Somatotyping is the classification of human beings into types according to body build and other physical characteristics relating them to specific personalities.
    - Studied 200 juvenile delinquents between 15 and 21 at Hayden Goodwill Institute, Boston, Massachusetts.
    - Determined that young males had one of three **body types**: endomorph, mesomorph, or ectomorph.
        - Endomorph
            - Physical characteristics
                - Soft roundness throughout the various regions of the body
                - Short tapering limbs
                - Small bones
                - Soft, velvety skin
            - Personality characteristics
                - Viscerotonic: having sociable, comfort-loving temperament. Loves:
                    - Physical comfort
                    - Food
                    - Affection
                    - Approval
                    - Company of others

BODY TYPES

These theories suggest that certain physical features may result in a propensity to crime.

- Mesomorph
  - Physical characteristics
    - Predominance of muscle, bone, and connective tissue
    - Muscular, strong
  - Personality characteristics
    - Somatic: pertaining to body or trunk
    - Active
    - Assertive
    - Aggressive
    - Noisy
    - Loves power and to dominate others
- Ectomorph
  - Physical characteristics
    - Thinness
    - Fragility
    - Delicacy of body
  - Personality characteristics
    - Cerebrotonic: having a shy, inhibited temperament
    - Private
    - Restrained
    - Inhibited
    - Hyper-attentive

❖ Measuring system

- Each of the three body types is identified by a rating scale of 0 to 7.
  - If an individual does not have any evidence of the body type, the individual is rated as a "0" for that body type.
  - If the person has an extreme amount of the body type the individual is rated as a "7."
- Normal American males are rated as 4.0–4.0–3.5 (endomorphy, mesomorphy, ectomorphy).
- Normal American females are rated as 5.0–3.0–3.5 (endomorphy, mesomorphy, ectomorphy).
  - Everyone's body type has the three components to some degree.

For more on biological theories, visit Criminal Justice Interactive online > Explaining Criminal Behavior > Learning Modules > 3.1 Theories of Crime.

PSYCHOLOGICAL SCHOOL

A perspective on criminological thought that views offensive and deviant behavior as the product of dysfunctional personality. Psychological thinkers identify the conscious, and especially the subconscious, contents of the human psyche as major determinants of behavior.

BEHAVIORAL CONDITIONING

A psychological principle that holds that the frequency of any behavior can be increased or decreased through reward, punishment, and association with other stimuli.

PSYCHOANALYSIS

A theory of human behavior, based on the writings of Sigmund Freud, that sees personality as a complex composite of interacting mental entities.

3.4 Psychological School

3.4.1 Basic assumptions

- The individual is the main unit of analysis.
- Personality is the major motivational element within individuals.
- Crime results from inappropriately conditioned behavior or from dysfunctional mental processes.
- Defective or abnormal mental processes may have a number of causes, including diseased minds or inappropriate or improper conditioning.

3.4.2 **Behavioral conditioning** is a psychological principle that holds that the frequency of any behavior can be increased or decreased through reward, punishment, and/or association with other stimuli.

- Ivan Pavlov (1849–1936), Russian physiologist, worked with dogs that salivated whenever food was presented to them.
  - Pavlov gave the dogs food only when a bell was rung, causing them to associate the food with the ringing of the bell.
  - After the dogs were conditioned to associate the food with the bell, Pavlov had the bell rung, but no food was provided.
  - The dogs continued to salivate each time the bell was rung, even though no food was forthcoming.
  - Pavlov won the Nobel Prize for Medicine in 1904 as a result of his work in the area of behavioral conditioning.

3.4.3 Psychoanalytic theory

- Sigmund Freud (1856–1939), trained as a physician and neurologist.
  - Freud is most closely associated with psychology and **psychoanalysis** (a term he coined).
    - Theory of human behavior based on the writings of Freud that sees personality as a complex composite of interacting mental elements.
  - Major contribution was to take study of mind from the medical paradigm and to develop a psychological paradigm. A psychological paradigm focuses on unconscious forces and drives.
  - Freud identified three elements of the personality:
    - Id
      - Source of drives, which are seen as primarily sexual
      - Id is like a small child.

- ❒ Comprises our instincts and unsocialized biological drives.
- ❒ Has to be controlled, or we cannot operate in society.
- ❒ At an early age, the ego and the superego start controlling the id.

◆ Ego

- ❒ A rational mental entity that outlines paths through which the desires of the id can be fulfilled
- ❒ Often referred to as the *reality principle* because of the belief that it relates desires to practical behavioral alternatives.
- ❒ Part of the personality that learns to solve problems
- ❒ Acts as a control or brake for the id
- ❒ Analyzes situations so that the id does not cause trouble

◆ Superego

- ❒ A guiding principle, often compared to the conscience that judges the quality of the alternatives presented by the ego according to the standards of right and wrong.
- ❒ Can be compared to the "little voice" that tells us what is right and what is wrong.

❖ Freud did not concern himself with crime; however, from a psychoanalytical perspective, crime is the result of at least three conditions:

◆ Weak superego

- ❒ Cannot responsibly control the drives that emanate from the id.
- ❒ An inadequate superego may result in the following types of crimes:
  - Sex crimes
  - Crimes of passion
  - Murder
  - Other violent crimes
- ❒ Individuals without a fully developed superego are often categorized as:
  - **Psychopaths** and **sociopaths** (now used interchangeably)

◆ Sublimation

- ❒ A process by which one thing is symbolically substituted for another
- ❒ Deemed necessary when the direct pursuit of one's desires is not possible.

PSYCHOPATH

A person with a personality disorder, especially one manifested in aggressively antisocial behavior, which is often said to be the result of a poorly developed superego. Also called sociopath.

SOCIOPATH

A person with a personality disorder, especially one manifested in aggressively antisocial behavior, which is often said to be the result of a poorly developed superego. Also called psychopath.

- Death wish (Thanatos)
  - The often unrecognized desire of animate matter to return to the inanimate
  - Individuals engage in potentially self-destructive activities, including smoking, speeding, skydiving, bad diets, and fighting.
  - The self-destructive wish may also motivate offenders to commit crimes that are themselves dangerous or self-destructive, such as burglary, assault, murder, prostitution, or drug use.
  - Criminals who leave evidence behind, sometimes even items of personal identification like a driver's license, may be responding to some basic need for apprehension and punishment.

3.4.4 Behaviorism is the assessment of human psychology through the examination of objectively observable and quantifiable actions, as opposed to subjective mental states.

- B.F. Skinner (1904–1990) developed the theory called behaviorism, which claimed that behavior is determined by rewards and punishments.
  - Based on psychological principle of operant conditioning, which is the altering of behavior by giving a subject rewards or punishments for a specified action until the subject associates the action with pleasure or pain
  - Concerned with observable behavior rather than psychological behavior, which is not observable
  - Undesirable behavior can be eliminated, modified, or replaced by taking away the reward value or by rewarding a more appropriate behavior.
  - Behaviorism is used extensively in therapeutic communities in which residents are placed on token systems that reward appropriate behavior.

For more on psychological theories, visit Criminal Justice Interactive online > Explaining Criminal Behavior > Learning Modules > 3.1 Theories of Crime.

3.5 Sociological school

3.5.1 Basic assumptions of the Sociological School

- Social groups, social institutions, the arrangements of society, and social roles all provide the proper focus for study.
- Group dynamics, group organization, and subgroup relationships form the basis from which criminal activity develops.

- The structure of society and the relative degree of social organization or social disorganization are important factors contributing to the prevalence of criminal behavior.

3.5.2 Origins

- Sociology is largely an American contribution.
- Often traced to the work of the **Chicago School** of the 1920s and 1930s.
  - ❖ A sociological approach that emphasizes demographics (the characteristics of population groups) and geographics (the location of such groups relative to one another). This approach sees the **social disorganization** that characterizes delinquency areas as a major cause of criminality and victimization.
  - ❖ Explained criminality as a product of society's impact upon the individual.
    - ◆ The structure of prevailing social arrangements, the interaction between individuals and groups and the social environment were all seen as major determinants of criminal behavior.

3.5.3 **Social Ecology** School is an outgrowth of the research activities of the Department of Sociology at the University of Chicago.

- Main theorists/researchers: Robert Park, Ernest Burgess, Clifford Shaw, and Henry McKay
- Robert E. Park (1864–1944) and Ernest W. Burgess (1886–1966) developed **concentric zone theory**.
  - ❖ Began mapping the city of Chicago based on the social characteristics of the city.
    - ◆ Model consisted of five zones:
      - ❒ Central business district
      - ❒ Transitional zone
        - Many recent immigrant groups reside in this zone.
        - Housing has deteriorated.
        - Factories abound.
        - Numerous abandoned buildings
      - ❒ Working-class zone
        - Consists of small, single-family homes.
        - Typically well-kept homes and manicured yards
        - Single-car garages for those homes that have garages

CHICAGO SCHOOL

A sociological approach that emphasizes demographics (the characteristics of population groups) and geographics (the mapped location of such groups relative to one another). Sees the social disorganization that characterizes delinquency areas as a major cause of criminality and victimization.

SOCIAL DISORGANIZATION

A condition said to exist when a group is faced with social change, uneven development of culture, maladaptiveness, disharmony, conflict, and lack of consensus.

SOCIAL ECOLOGY

A criminological approach that focuses on the misbehavior of lower-class youths and sees delinquency primarily as the result of social disorganization.

CONCENTRIC ZONE THEORY

A conception of the city (Chicago) as a series of distinctive circles radiating from the central business district used to describe differences in crime rates.

- ❒ Residential zone
  - Single-family homes
  - Typically larger than in the working-class zone
  - Two- and three-car garages attached to homes
- ❒ Commuter zone
  - Considered the suburbs
  - Large homes on sizable tracks of land
- ❖ One way to visualize concentric zone theory is to picture a bull's-eye target with the center of the target being the central business district and the outer circle being the commuter zone.

- ■ Clifford Shaw and Henry D. McKay (1899–1980) studied social disorganization of neighborhoods of delinquent youths and concluded that there were some elements in bad neighborhoods that caused crime.
  - ❖ Shaw and McKay adapted the work of Park and Burgess' concentric zone theory and related it to the study of crime.
  - ❖ Discovered that the amount of crime increased as one moved towards the center of the city.
  - ❖ Zone 2, the zone of transition, consistently demonstrated the highest crime rates.
    - ◆ This zone is called the zone of transition because it is the zone to which immigrants move before they become integrated into other parts of the city.
    - ◆ Crime in this zone is dependent upon structural elements such as:
      - ❒ Poverty
      - ❒ Illiteracy
      - ❒ Lack of schooling
      - ❒ Unemployment
      - ❒ Illegitimacy
    - ◆ The aforementioned elements lead to social disorganization, which leads to crime.
  - ❖ Shaw and McKay concluded that delinquents were no different from nondelinquents in terms of such characteristics as personality, intelligence, and physical condition.
  - ❖ Neighborhoods with the worst delinquency problems also had the highest rates of other social problems including deteriorated housing, infant mortality, and tuberculosis.

ANOMIE

A socially pervasive condition of normlessness. Also, a disjunction between approved goals and means.

3.5.4 **Anomie** theory is a socially pervasive condition of normlessness.

- ■ Anomie, as used by Robert King Merton, means a disjunction between approved goals and available means.

- Émile Durkheim (1858–1917), a French sociologist, refined use of the term anomie to mean a specific form of suicide that resulted when there was a sudden and unexpected upheaval in the norms of society creating a situation of normlessness.
- Robert King Merton (1910–2003) applied the term anomie, but defined it very differently than Durkheim.
  - According to Merton, anomie was a disjunction between approved goals and means to achieve these goals.
    - The goals are the general societal goals.
    - The means are those that are generally accepted by society to pursue the goals.
  - Merton believed that while the same goals and means are held out by society as desirable for everyone, they are *not* equally available to all.
    - Opportunities are *not* equally distributed throughout society and some people turn to illegitimate means to achieve the goals they are pressured to reach.
  - Merton developed five **modes of adaptation**:
    - Conformist
      - Accepts society's goals and the socially accepted means to obtain the goals
      - The conformist typically engages in law-abiding behavior.
      - Example: college students. By attending college, they are deferring their gratification until they begin their careers.
    - Innovator
      - Accepts the societal goals while rejecting the approved means of obtaining the goals
      - This type of adaptation often results in the commission of property crime and white-collar crime.
      - Examples: an embezzler, a stripper
    - Ritualist
      - Rejects the societal goals while still adhering to the approved means that are available
      - This individual does not typically violate the law, but has given up on success as defined by society and just does the best he or she can with what he or she has.
      - Examples: individuals trapped in minimum-wage jobs (typically unskilled jobs that do not require any education) and have difficulty making ends meet.

MODES OF ADAPTATION

Merton's five ways of adapting to strain caused by restricted access to the socially approved goals and means.

- Retreatist
  - Rejects both the goals provided by society and the means to obtain the goals
  - This type of adaptation often results in drug use and addiction, some victimless crimes, or a retreat from society as hermits.
  - Examples: dropouts, drug addict, hermit
- Rebel
  - Rejects the goals and means as established by society and substitutes with their own goals and means
  - This type of adaptation results in political crimes such as environmental protests.
  - Examples: hippies who continue to live the hippie lifestyle, survivalists

STRAIN THEORY
These theories require that people be motivated to commit criminal and delinquent acts.

- Merton hypothesized that individuals succumb to the strain of society in a theory called **strain theory**.
  - The causes of crime can be connected to the pressure on culturally or materially disadvantaged groups or individuals to achieve the goals held by society, even if the means to those goals require the breaking of laws.
- Merton believed that the adaptation categories are not intentionally selected by the individuals who occupied them, but are imposed on people by structural aspects of society.
- Those who share the goals promoted by society, but find their means to attain the goals systematically blocked, experience anomie.

3.5.5 Subcultural theory

CRIMINAL SUBCULTURE
The primary focus would be on profit-making activities and violence would be minimal; criminal "trades" would be practiced under the loose supervision of organized crime.

REACTION FORMATION
The process whereby a person openly rejects that which he or she wants or aspires to but cannot obtain or achieve.

- A theoretical perspective based on the idea that a subculture is composed of a group of people who participate in a shared system of values and norms different from those of the larger culture, which may become a **criminal subculture**.
  - Subcultural explanations of crime suggest that group values support criminal behavior.
- Albert K. Cohen (b. 1918)
  - **Reaction formation**
    - The process whereby a person openly rejects what he or she wants or aspires to but cannot obtain or achieve.
    - It is the reaction that causes the development of gangs and continues the subculture.

- **Middle-class measuring rod**
  - Cohen suggested that a measuring rod holds young people accountable to middle-class ideals such as school performance, neatness, nonviolent behavior, and language proficiency.
- Nonutilitarian delinquency
  - Youths who choose delinquent behavior are alienated from middle-class lifestyles and achieve status identity from subcultural peers through destructive behavior.
- **Status frustration**
  - Children, especially those from deprived backgrounds, experience status frustration because they are aware they can't achieve middle-class goals.

MIDDLE-CLASS MEASURING ROD
A set of standards that are difficult for the lower-class child to attain that include sharing, delaying gratification, and respecting others' property.

STATUS FRUSTRATION
Lower-class children lose ground in the search for status and suffer from this.

- Richard Cloward (1926–2001) and Lloyd Ohlin (1918–2008)
  - Cloward and Ohlin combined the work of Merton and Sutherland.
    - From Merton, they used the access to the legitimate opportunity structure.
    - From Sutherland, they used access to the illegitimate opportunity structure.
  - Cloward and Ohlin believed that the access to the illegitimate opportunity structure had to be reduced while increasing access to the legitimate structure.
  - If a person has access to both structures, they can choose whether or not to be delinquent; if they have access to only one structure, they do not have a choice.
  - Closing down the illegitimate structure and opening up the legitimate one will have the desired effect of reducing delinquency and increasing **conformity**.
  - **Mobilization for Youth** (1962)
    - A subculture project in New York City designed to increase educational and job opportunities for youths in deprived communities.
    - A federally-funded program designed to open access to the legitimate opportunity structure. Examples of programs: midnight basketball, schools open late to provide tutoring, and sports programs.

CONFORMITY
Striving for socially approved goals and following normal means of achieving them. Most people adapt this way; if not, according to Merton, the very existence of society would be threatened.

MOBILIZATION FOR YOUTH
A subculture project in New York City designed to increase educational and job opportunities for youths in deprived communities.

3.5.6 **Focal concerns** theory is a theory developed by Walter B. Miller in which the emphasis on specific values contributes to the involvement in delinquency by members of the lower class.

- Lower-class culture is characterized by:
  - A system of values that establish and maintain a way of life
  - Attitudes that go against norms of the middle class and may be considered as purposely nonconforming

FOCAL CONCERNS
A theory developed by Walter B. Miller in which the emphasis on specific values contributes to the involvement in delinquency by members of the lower class. The six focal concerns identified by Miller include: trouble, toughness, smartness, excitement, fate, and autonomy.

- Focal concerns
  - Trouble
    - A dominant feature of lower-class culture
    - Is a situation or behavior that results in unwelcome or complicated involvement with official authorities or agencies of middle-class society. Examples: fighting, sexual adventures while drinking
  - Toughness
    - Lower-class individuals develop the characteristic of toughness, either spiritually or physically, or they run the risk of being seen as weak.
    - Toughness can be represented by: physical strength, athletic ability, tattooing, absence of sentimentality, view of women as conquest objects.
  - Smartness
    - The capacity to outsmart, outfox, and outwit others, as well as the capacity to avoid being outsmarted oneself
  - Excitement
    - The search for thrills
    - An attempt to overcome boredom
    - Includes activities such as drinking, fighting, gambling, and sexual adventures
  - Fate
    - The concept of luck forms behavior
    - Many lower-class individuals feel their lives are influenced by factors over which they have little control.
  - Autonomy
    - Lower-class individuals want to take charge of their own lives.
    - Manifests itself in statements like "I can take care of myself," and "No one's going to push me around."

SUBCULTURE OF VIOLENCE

Those in this subculture learn a willingness to resort to violence and share a favorable attitude toward the use of violence. A cultural setting in which violence is a traditional and often accepted method of dispute resolution.

3.5.7 **Subculture of violence** coined by Wolfgang and Ferracuti

- Those in this subculture learn a tendency toward violence and share a favorable attitude toward the use of violence; violence becomes the traditional and accepted method of resolving disputes.
- Wolfgang and Ferracuti examined homicide rates in Philadelphia during the 1950s and concluded that murder was viewed as a way of life among certain groups.
- They also determined that subcultures do not conflict with the larger society of which they are a part.
- The subculture of violence does not require that all individuals share the basic value of violence or that they express violence in all situations.

- A propensity for violence in a subculture depends on learned behavior.
- Subcultures generally don't see violence as criminal or immoral, so deviant individuals do not have to struggle with feelings of guilt about their crimes.

For more on sociological theories, visit Criminal Justice Interactive online > Explaining Criminal Behavior > Learning Modules > 3.1 Theories of Crime.

3.5.8 Life course perspective

LIFE COURSE PERSPECTIVE
Developmental theory concept that individuals and their influencing factors change over time, usually in patterned ways

- Life course researchers examine trajectories and transitions through the life span.
  - ❖ A path of development that is marked by a sequence of transitions such as changes in career, marriage, parenthood, and criminal behavior
  - ❖ Turning points that identify significant events in a person's life and represent the opportunity for people to turn either away from, or toward deviance and crime
- Robert Sampson and John Laub identified the perspective of life course.
  - ❖ Life course perspective believes that criminal behavior tends to follow an identifiable pattern throughout a person's life cycle.
  - ❖ In the lives of those who eventually become criminal, crime-like or deviant behavior:
    - ◆ Is relatively rare during early childhood
    - ◆ Tends to begin as sporadic instances during early adolescence
    - ◆ Becomes more common during late teens and early adult years
    - ◆ Gradually diminishes as the person gets older
  - ❖ Linked lives
    - ◆ Highlights the fact that no one lives in isolation.
    - ◆ Events in the life course are constantly being influenced by families, friends, acquaintances, employers, and teachers.

CHAPTER SUMMARY

➢ There are a number of theories that have been developed to explain criminal behavior. The Classical School, which developed in the eighteenth century, holds that individuals commit crimes as a result of free will and that punishment can deter crime if the punishment outweighs the pleasure derived from the crime. The Biological School claims that criminal behavior has a physiological basis.

The Psychological School rests on the perspective of criminological thought that views offensive and deviant behavior as the product of dysfunctional personality. Sociological theories contend that social groups, social institutions, the arrangements of society, and social roles all affect criminal behavior.

➢ Each of these theories uniquely impacts the criminal justice system and, in part because there is no single theory, can complicate the ways that criminologists explain crime.

ONLINE@CRIMINAL JUSTICE INTERACTIVE

Learning Modules

3.1 Theories of Crime

Myths and Issues Videos

Myth vs. Reality: Criminologist Know What Causes Crime
Issue 1: Does Crime Theory Matter, and If So, to Whom?
Issue 2: What Influence Do Crime Theories Have on the Criminal Justice System?

Simulation Activity: Explaining Criminal Behavior

Homework and Review

In the News
Web Activity
Review Questions
Essay Questions
Flashcards

Chapter 4

Criminal Law

CHAPTER OUTLINE

LEARNING OBJECTIVES

After reviewing the online material and reading this chapter, you should be able to:

1. Discuss four sources of laws in the United States: Constitutions (state and federal), statutes and codes (state and federal), judicial decision, and administrative agencies.
2. Define and contrast criminal law and civil law.
3. Define, describe, and present the three elements that must be present for a crime to have been committed (*actus reus*, *mens rea*, concurrence) and be able to identify these elements in actual criminal cases.
4. Define and describe four broad legal defense categories: alibi, justification, excuse, and procedural.
5. Define terms related to criminal law.

KEY TERMS

actus reus
administrative law
alibi
Bill of Rights
case law
civil law
codification
common law
concurrence
corpus delicti
criminal law
criminal negligence
criminal procedure
double jeopardy
due process
duress
entrapment
felony
guilty but mentally ill (GBMI)
inchoate offense
insanity defense
justification
law
McNaughten rule
mens rea
misdemeanor
necessity
precedent
procedural law
rule of law
self-defense
stare decisis
statutory law
strict liability
summary offense
treason
U.S. Constitution

4.0 Criminal law

4.1 Sources and types of law

4.1.1 Definitions of law

- **Law** is a rule of conduct, generally found enacted in the form of a statute, that proscribes or mandates certain forms of behavior.
- **Statutory law** is written or codified law; the law on the "books," as enacted by a government body or agency having the power to make laws.
  - ❖ Statutory law is often the result of moral enterprise by interest groups that, through the exercise of political power, are successful in seeing their perspectives enacted into law.
- **Case law** is the body of judicial **precedent**, historically built upon legal reasoning and past interpretations of statutory law that serves as a guide to decision making, especially in the courts.
- **Codification** is defined as the act or process of rendering laws in written form.

4.1.2 Brief history of **criminal law**

- Code of Hammurabi, one of the earliest known codification of laws, is an ancient code of 250 laws instituted by Hammurabi, King of Babylon, around 1750 B.C.E. dealing with criminal and civil matters.
- Mosaic code was the code of the Israelites, approximately 1200 B.C.E., which is the foundation of Judeo-Christian moral teachings and is the partial basis for the U.S. legal system. Mosaic code is based on belief that God entered into a covenant with the tribes of Israel in which they agreed to obey His law, as presented by Moses, in return for God's special care and protection.
- Twelve Tables were a set of Roman law created around 451 B.C.E. formulated by a special commission of 10 men in response to pressures from lower class. The original code was written on 12 bronze tablets and represented a collection of rules related to family, religious, and economic life. The Twelve Tables are based on common and fair practices generally accepted among early tribes, which existed prior to the establishment of the Roman Empire.
- Justinian Code was an effort to preserve Roman values and traditions by Emperor Justinian who ruled Roman Empire from 527–565 C.E. (Common Era). The Justinian Code consisted of three legal documents:
  - ❖ The Institutes
  - ❖ The Digest
  - ❖ The Code

LAW
A rule of conduct, generally found enacted in the form of a statute, that proscribes or mandates certain forms of behavior. Statutory law is often the result of moral enterprise by interest groups that, through the exercise of political power, are successful in seeing their valued perspectives enacted into law.

STATUTORY LAW
Written or codified law; the "law on the books," as enacted by a government body or agency having the power to make laws.

CASE LAW
The body of judicial precedent, historically built on legal reasoning and past interpretations of statutory laws, that serves as a guide to decision making, especially in the courts.

PRECEDENT
A legal principle that ensures that previous judicial decisions are authoritatively considered and incorporated into future cases.

CODIFICATION
The act or process of rendering laws in written form.

CRIMINAL LAW
The branch of modern law that concerns itself with offenses committed against society, its members, their property, and the social order. Also called penal law.

- Private laws concerned with contracts, personal possessions, injuries to citizens, and the legal status of various people (including slaves, guardians, husbands and wives).
- Public laws concerned with organization of the Roman state, Senate, government office.

- Magna Carta or "Great Charter," was a guarantee of liberties consisting of 63 clauses signed by King John of England in 1215 that influenced many modern legal and constitutional principles.
  - Law had two functions:
    - Limited capricious decision-making powers of the King.
    - Gave people certain protections from the government.
  - The two functions of law became extremely important in the modern criminal justice system.
  - In 1613, the Magna Carta was interpreted during a judicial revolt to support individual rights and jury trials.
  - One specific provision of the Magna Carta, designed originally to prohibit the King from prosecuting the barons without just cause, focused on individual rights and was expanded into the concept of **due process** of law.

4.1.3. Sources of law

- Natural law refers to rules of conduct inherent in human nature and in the natural order that are thought to be knowable through intuition, inspiration, and the exercise of reason, without the need for reference to created laws. Examples: Ten Commandments, inborn tendencies, and the idea of sin
  - Used by early Christian church as a powerful argument in support of its interests
    - Thomas Aquinas (1225–1274): Any man-made law that contradicts natural law is corrupt in the eyes of God.
    - Religious practice, which strongly reflected natural law conceptions, was central to the life of early British society.
    - The U.S. Declaration of Independence is built around natural law; when Thomas Jefferson wrote of inalienable rights to "Life, Liberty, and the pursuit of Happiness," he referred to the natural law due of all men and women.
- English **common law** is law originating from usage and custom rather than from written statutes.
  - Refers to an unwritten body of judicial opinion, originally developed by English courts, that is based on non-statutory customs, traditions, and precedents that help guide judicial decision making

DUE PROCESS

A right guaranteed by the Fifth, Sixth, and Fourteenth Amendments of the U.S. Constitution and generally understood, in legal contexts, to mean the due course of legal proceedings according to the rules and forms established for the protection of individual rights. In criminal proceedings, due process of law is generally understood to include the following basic elements: a law creating and defining the offense, an impartial tribunal having jurisdictional authority over the case, accusation in proper form, notice and opportunity to defend, trial according to established procedure, and discharge from all restraints or obligations unless convicted.

COMMON LAW

Law originating from usage and custom rather than from written statutes. The term refers to an unwritten body of judicial opinion originally developed by English courts that is based on nonstatutory customs, traditions, and precedents that help guide judicial decision making.

- Common law has often been called the major source of modern criminal law in the United States.
- English common law is judge-made law that is refined and changed by the actual decisions that judges make when ruling on cases before them. These decisions are then handed down from generation to generation; the general idea is that similar cases should be treated the same way.

STARE DECISIS

A legal principle that requires that, in subsequent cases on similar issues of law and fact, courts be bound by their own earlier decisions and by those of higher courts having jurisdiction over them. The term literally means "standing by decided matters."

- ***Stare decisis***, a term literally meaning "standing by decided matter," is a legal principle that requires that, in subsequent cases on similar issues of law and fact, courts be bound by their own earlier decisions and by those of higher courts having jurisdiction over them.
  - The rule requires judges to follow precedent in judicial interpretations; however, prior decisions can be overruled or modified by higher courts of appeal.

U.S. CONSTITUTION

Produced by the Constitutional Convention and ratified in 1789, the U.S. Constitution is the oldest written constitution continuously in effect.

BILL OF RIGHTS

The first ten amendments to the U.S. Constitution. Drafted by James Madison as a response to concerns that the U.S. Constitution did not include a declaration of individual rights. The U.S. Constitution identified what a government could do, but said nothing about what it could not do. The Bill of Rights was ratified in 1791.

- **U.S. Constitution** is the final authority in all questions pertaining to the rights of individuals, the power of the federal government and the states to create laws and to prosecute offenders, and the limits of punishments that can be imposed; created by federal Constitutional Convention, which met in Philadelphia, Pennsylvania, in 1787.
  - **Bill of Rights**:
    - Amendment I: Congress shall make no law respecting an establishment of religion, or prohibiting the free exercise thereof; or abridging the freedom of speech, or of the press; or the right of the people peaceably to assemble, and to petition the Government for a redress of grievances.
    - Amendment II: A well regulated Militia, being necessary to the security of a free State, the right of the people to keep and bear Arms, shall not be infringed.
    - Amendment III: No Soldier shall, in time of peace be quartered in any house, without the consent of the Owner, nor in time of war, but in a manner to be prescribed by law.
    - Amendment IV: The right of the people to be secure in their persons, houses, papers, and effects, against unreasonable searches and seizures, shall not be violated, and no Warrants shall be issue, but upon probable cause, supported by Oath or affirmation, and particularly describing the place to be searched, and the persons or things to be seized.
    - Amendment V: No person shall be held to answer for a capital, or otherwise infamous crime, unless on a presentment or indictment of a Grand Jury, except in cases arising in the land or naval forces, or in the Militia, when in actual service in time of War or

public danger; nor shall any person be subject for the same offense to be twice put in jeopardy of life or limb; nor shall be compelled in any criminal case to be a witness against himself, not be deprived of life, liberty, or property, without due process of law, not shall private property be taken for public use, without just compensation.

- Amendment VI: In all criminal prosecutions, the accused shall enjoy the right to a speedy and public trial, by an impartial jury of the State and district wherein the crime shall have been committed, which district shall have been previously ascertained by law, and to be informed of the nature and cause of the accusation; to be confronted with the witnesses against him; to have compulsory process for obtaining witnesses in his favor; and to have the Assistance of Counsel for his defence.
- Amendment VII: In Suits at common law, where the value in controversy shall exceed twenty dollars, the right of trial by jury shall be preserved, and no fact tried by a jury, shall be otherwise re-examined in any Court of the United States, than according to the rules of the common law.
- Amendment VIII: Excessive bail shall not be required, nor excessive fines imposed, nor cruel and unusual punishments inflicted.
- Amendment IX: The enumeration in the Constitution, of certain rights, shall not be construed to deny or disparage others retained by the people.
- Amendment X: The powers not delegated to the United States by the Constitution, nor prohibited by it to the States, are reserved to the States respectively, or to the people.

4.1.4. Types of law

- Criminal law is the branch of modern law that concerns itself with offenses committed against society, members thereof, their property, and the social order; also called penal law.
  - Violations of criminal law result in punishment upon conviction in a court of law.
  - Criminal acts injure not just the individual, but society as a whole.
    - Historically, in England, when an act occurred, even if was directly against another citizen, it was considered to have violated the "King's peace;" hence the idea today that a crime is against society.
    - When a crime is prosecuted today, it is done so by the state with the victim being a witness for state.

- Criminal law is composed of both statutory and case law.
  - Statutory law is written or codified law; the "law on the books," as enacted by a government body or agency having the power to make laws.
  - Case law, also called the "law of precedent," is built on legal reasoning and past interpretations of statutory laws that serves as a guide to decision making, especially in the courts.

CIVIL LAW

The branch of modern law that governs relationships between parties.

- **Civil law** is the branch of modern law that governs relationships between parties.
  - Also referred to as tort law, civil law determines private rights and liabilities and provides a formal means of regulating noncriminal relationships between and among people, businesses and other organizations, and agencies of the government. Civil law includes:
    - Breach of contracts
    - Divorce
    - Contested wills
    - Child support and custody
    - Workmen's compensation
    - Negligence
    - Product liability
    - Libel
    - Slander
    - Transfer of property
  - Because civil suits are private wrongs, the individual/ company/government entity must set the wheels of justice in motion by filing a suit in civil court
    - Parties in a civil suit are referred to as:
      - Plaintiff—the person/company/government entity that files the lawsuit
      - Defendant—the person/company/government entity being sued
    - Since the outcome is to assess liability, the final disposition usually involves the awarding of money to the aggrieved party in the form of compensatory damages.
      - Compensatory damages are payments for an actual injury or economic loss.
      - Punitive damages are monetary damages awarded when a defendant's acts are found to be malicious, violent, oppressive, fraudulent, wanton, or grossly reckless.

For more on the distinctions and sources of civil and criminal law, visit Criminal Justice Interactive online > Criminal Law > Learning Modules > 4.1 Sources of Law and Types of Law.

- **Administrative law** is law made and enforced by administrative/regulatory agencies either at the federal or state levels.
  - ❖ Rules and regulations created to control the activities of industry, business, and individuals. Examples:
    - ◆ Tax laws
    - ◆ Health codes
    - ◆ Pollution laws
    - ◆ Vehicle registration/inspection
    - ◆ Building codes
    - ◆ Agriculture
    - ◆ Product safety
    - ◆ Immigration

ADMINISTRATIVE LAW
Law made and enforced by administrative/regulatory agencies either at the federal or state levels.

- Case law is the body of judicial precedent, historically built on legal reasoning and past interpretations of statutory laws that serves as a guide to decision-making, especially in the courts. Also called the "law of precedent."
  - ❖ When a court renders a decision it is written down, including the rationale for the decision.
  - ❖ The reasoning provided for the decision is to be taken into account by other courts when they have similar cases.
  - ❖ *Stare decisis* is a legal principle that requires that, in subsequent cases on similar issues of law and fact, courts be bound by their own earlier decisions and by those of higher courts having jurisdiction over them.
- **Procedural law** is the part of the law that specifies the methods to be used in enforcing substantive law.
  - ❖ **Criminal procedures** are rules and laws intended to guard against discrimination in the application of justice for those accused of a crime.
    - ◆ The U.S. Constitution through the Fourth, Fifth, Sixth, and Eighth Amendments provide the foundations for basic criminal procedure. Examples: general rules of evidence, search and seizure requirements, and procedures following an arrest.

PROCEDURAL LAW
The part of the law that specifies the methods to be used in enforcing substantive law. See also criminal procedure.

CRIMINAL PROCEDURE
Rules and laws intended to guard against discrimination in the application of justice for those accused of a crime. The U.S. Constitution through the Fourth, Fifth, Sixth, and Eighth Amendments provide the foundations for basic criminal procedure. The part of the law that specifies the methods to be used in enforcing substantive law.

4.2 Crime elements

4.2.1 ***Actus reus*** is an act in violation of the law, also referred to as a guilty act, and includes both an action taken by an individual or a failure of an individual to act.

- Crimes of commission are crimes that involve an act that the law prohibits, such as murder, rape, and shoplifting.
- Crimes of omission are crimes that involve the failure to act when the law requires an individual to take action, such as child neglect or failure to file taxes.

ACTUS REUS
An act in violation of the law. Also, a guilty act.

- One can "think" about committing a crime, but without engaging in the illegal act, thinking alone is *not* enough to make it a crime.
- Crimes can also be committed by:
  - Speaking. Example: yelling "fire" in a crowded theater
  - Making threats. Example: threatening the life of the president of the United States
  - Attempted criminal act. Examples: Attempting to break into a house with the intent to burgle constitutes attempted burglary; attempting to murder someone but failing (as when a gun misfires) constitutes attempted murder.
  - Stalking
    - Antistalking laws exist to prevent harassment and intimidation even when no physical harm occurs.

MENS REA

The state of mind that accompanies a criminal act. Also, a guilty mind.

4.2.2 ***Mens rea*** is the state of mind that accompanies a criminal act; also referred to as *guilty mind.*

- The concept of the "guilty mind" is based on the assumption that individuals have the ability to make reasonable decisions about right and wrong and to choose between alternatives of conduct.
- Types of *mens rea*:
  - Purposeful (intentional), also known as "direct intent." Example: An individual intentionally fires a gun at an individual, hitting and killing him.
  - Knowing. The person is aware that the act could result in illegal behavior and/or harm. Example: A bartender serves alcohol to a drunk woman with the intent of obtaining sexual favors from the woman; however, when leaving the bar, the woman falls down a flight of stairs hitting her head and dies. The bartender was aware that serving the drinks to an already intoxicated person could possibly result in physical harm, although the bartender had no intention of harming the individual.
  - Reckless. Activity that increases the probability of harm. Example: Store owner decides to set fire to his store to collect insurance money for his failing business, and as a result two of his employees die in the fire. Store owner can be charged with the homicides since he should have known there was the probability that individuals in the store might not be able to escape and may die.
  - **Criminal negligence** is behavior in which a person fails to reasonably perceive substantial and unjustifiable risks of dangerous consequences; assumes person should have known better. Example: Father leaves a small baby strapped in a car seat locked in a hot car in the parking lot while he shops, and child dies as a result. Father can be charged with negligent homicide since he should have known better.

CRIMINAL NEGLIGENCE

Behavior in which a person fails to reasonably perceive substantial and unjustifiable risks of dangerous consequences.

- *Mens rea* must be inferred from a person's action and from all circumstances that surround those actions.
- "Purposeful" and "knowing" constitute the most clear cases of *mens rea.*
- "Reckless" and "negligent" *mens rea* constitute sufficient grounds for criminal prosecution.
- *Mens rea* vs. motive. *Mens rea* and motive are *not* the same. A motive is a person's reason for committing a crime.
- **Strict liability** is liability without fault or intention.
    - ❖ Strict liability offenses do not require *mens rea*. Example: An individual who owns a chimpanzee that escapes from his cage and attacks an individual has strict liability for the actions of the chimpanzee, even though the owner took all reasonable measures to prevent the escape. Because the owner knows the chimpanzee is a wild animal that has the potential to cause serious harm if given the opportunity, he is still responsible even though he took reasonable precautions.

STRICT LIABILITY

Liability without fault or intention. Strict liability offenses do not require *mens rea*.

4.2.3 **Concurrence** (of *actus reus* and *mens rea*) is the coexistence of (1) an act in violation of the law (*actus reus*) and (2) a culpable mental state (*mens rea*).

- The "guilty act" and the "guilty mind" *must* concur in time to be able to convict an individual of a crime.
- If there is too much time between the guilty mind and the actual guilty act, the guilty mind could *not* have informed the guilty act and the two required elements are not present. Example: A young man gets into a fight with an individual and threatens to kill the individual. Three years later when driving down a street near his house, he swerves to avoid hitting a child who has run between two parked cars. His car jumps the curb, hitting and killing the individual he had threatened to kill three years earlier. In this case, there is no concurrence of the guilty act and the guilty mind.

CONCURRENCE

The coexistence of (1) an act in violation of the law (*actus reus*) and (2) a culpable mental state (*mens rea*).

For more about *actus rea, mens rea,* and concurrence, visit Criminal Justice Interactive online > Criminal Law > Learning Modules > 4.2 Crime Elements.

For practice in learning to recognize these elements, visit Criminal Justice Interactive online > Criminal Law > Simulation Activity: Explaining Criminal Behavior.

4.2.4 ***Corpus delicti***, a term that literally means "the body of crime," refers to the facts that show a crime has occurred.

- *Not* a statutory element of a crime
- For a person to be tried for a crime, it must first be shown that the offense has, in fact, occurred.

CORPUS DELICTI

The facts that show that a crime has occurred. The term literally means "the body of the crime."

4.3 Categories of crime

FELONY

A criminal offense punishable by death or by incarceration in a prison facility for at least one year.

4.3.1 **Felony** is a criminal offense punishable by death or by incarceration in a prison facility for at least one year.

- Examples of felonies:
  - Homicide
  - Forcible rape
  - Aggravated assault
  - Robbery
  - Burglary
  - Motor vehicle theft
  - Arson
  - Larceny
- Range of penalties include:
  - Fine
  - Confiscation of property
  - Probation
  - Incarceration
  - Death sentence
- The incarceration of a felon is grounds for uncontested divorce.
- Convicted felons typically lose certain privileges upon release from prison:
  - Right to hold public office
  - Right to vote
  - Ability to enter certain professions
  - Right to carry or possess a firearm
  - Right to serve on a federal grand or petit jury
  - Right to federal jury service
  - Right to enlistment in any of the armed forces
- Capital felony is a case in which most states seek the death sentence; some states also include a life sentence without parole as sentence in a capital felony case. Typically, these are restricted to murder cases.
- There is variation in what states define as felonies. Examples: prostitution, gambling, illegal drug possession

MISDEMEANOR

An offense punishable by incarceration, usually in a local confinement facility, for a period whose upper limit is prescribed by statute in a given jurisdiction, typically one year or less.

4.3.2 **Misdemeanor** is an offense punishable by incarceration, usually in a local confinement facility, for a period whose upper limit is prescribed by statute in a given jurisdiction, typically one year or less. For a crime to be a misdemeanor, it must take place in front of the officer or a civilian witness who must sign a complaint in order for the arrest to occur.

- Considered a minor offense in comparison to a felony. Examples:
  - ❖ Petty theft
  - ❖ Simple assault
  - ❖ Disorderly conduct
  - ❖ Public intoxication
  - ❖ Disturbing the peace

4.3.3 **Summary offenses or violations**, in some jurisdictions, are minor crimes that are sometimes described as ticketable or punishable by a fine. Examples: jaywalking, spitting on sidewalk, littering, certain traffic violations such as failure to wear a seat belt

SUMMARY OFFENSE

A violation of the criminal law. Also, in some jurisdictions, a minor crime such as jaywalking, that is sometimes described as ticketable. See also offense.

For more on these three categories of crime (felony, misdemeanor, and summary offense), visit Criminal Justice Interactive online > Criminal Law > Learning Modules > 4.3 Categories of Crime.

4.3.4 **Treason** and espionage

TREASON

A U.S. citizen's actions to help a foreign government overthrow, make war against, or seriously injure the United States. Also, the attempt to overthrow the government of the society of which one is a member. The only crime specifically mentioned in the U.S. Constitution. (Daniel Oran, Oran's Dictionary of the Law [St. Paul, MN: West, 1983], p. 306.)

- Treason is a U.S. citizen's actions to help a foreign government overthrow, make war against, or seriously injure the United States (Dan Oran, *Oran's Dictionary of the Law*, 1983, p. 306). Treason is the only crime specifically mentioned in the Constitution, and is also a crime under the laws of most states.
- Espionage is the gathering, transmitting, or losing of information related to the national defense in such a manner that the information becomes available to enemies of the United States.

4.3.5 **Inchoate offense** is an offense not yet completed; an offense that consists of conduct that is a step toward the intended commission of another crime. *Inchoate* means "incomplete or partial."

INCHOATE OFFENSE

An offense not yet completed. Also, an offense that consists of an action or conduct that is a step toward the intended commission of another offense.

- Conspiracy
  - ❖ When a person conspires to commit a crime; any action undertaken in the furtherance of the conspiracy is generally regarded as a sufficient basis for arrest and prosecution. Example: A man decides that he wants to end the life of his wife and asks around if anyone knows of a "hitman." An undercover police officer contacts the husband and says that he is available to do the work. The husband asks the undercover officer how much he would charge to get rid of his wife, and when and how it can be done. The discussion with the undercover officer is sufficient to demonstrate intent and can result in the husband being charged with conspiracy to commit murder.

- Attempt
    - An individual dressed in black from head to toe, including a ski mask, found in the back of a house carrying a screwdriver may be arrested for attempted burglary, especially if the back door shows pry marks that match the marks left by the screwdriver.

4.3.6 Felony/misdemeanor distinctions

- The classification of a crime as a felony or a misdemeanor affects the following:
    - Conditions under which law enforcement can make an arrest and the degree of force that is authorized
    - The charges the prosecutor will be able to press against the defendant
    - The care the judge exercises in accepting a guilty plea and the admission of evidence into the record
    - The availability of procedural and constitutional safeguards
    - Availability of counsel to represent the defendant
    - Determination of which court will have trial jurisdiction
    - The type of sentence that can be imposed
    - Conditions of release from incarceration
    - Size of the jury

4.4 Legal defenses

4.4.1 There are four types of recognized defenses: alibi, justification, excuse, and procedural.

ALIBI

A statement or contention by an individual charged with a crime that he or she was so distant when the crime was committed, or so engaged in other provable activities, that his or her participation in the commission of that crime is impossible.

4.4.2 **Alibi** is a statement or contention by an individual charged with a crime that he or she was so distant when the crime was committed or so engaged in other provable activities, that his or her participation in the commission of the crime is impossible.

- Based on the premise that an individual is actually innocent.
- The use of an alibi is best supported by witnesses and documentation. Example:
    - The defendant was on a plane flying across the country when the crime occurred. He has a plane ticket stub in his name and the individual who sat next to him is available to testify that the defendant was on the plane at the time of the crime.

JUSTIFICATION

A legal defense in which the defendant admits to committing the act in question but claims it was necessary in order to avoid some greater evil.

4.4.3 **Justification** is a legal defense in which the defendant admits to committing the act in question but claims it was necessary in order to avoid some greater evil.

- Types of justifications: self-defense, defense of home and property, necessity, consent, and resisting unlawful arrest

- **Self-defense** is the protection of oneself or of one's property from unlawful injury or from the immediate risk of unlawful injury. Also, the justification that the person who committed an act that would otherwise constitute an offense reasonably believed that the act was necessary to protect self or property from immediate danger.
    - A defendant who hurts an attacker can generally use self-defense as their defense at trial.
    - Retreat rule mandates that a defendant is required to use an avenue of escape if it is available rather than defending himself or herself from the attacker. If there is no avenue of retreat, the defendant can use defensive force to protect himself or herself.
    - Defensive force must be proportionate to the amount of force or perceived degree of threat that an individual is defending against.
    - Reasonable force is the degree of force that is appropriate in a given situation and is not excessive; the minimum degree of force necessary to protect oneself, one's property, a third party, or the property of another in the face of substantial threat.
- Defense of others is the use of reasonable force to defend others who are, or appear to be, in imminent danger.
    - Self-defense cannot be claimed by an individual who joins an illegal fight merely in order to assist a friend or family member.
    - The defense of a third party requires that the third party be free from fault.
    - Alter ego rule in some jurisdictions is a **rule of law** that holds that a person can only defend a third party under certain circumstances and only to the degree that the third party could act on his or her own. A person who aids a third party whom he sees being attacked may become criminally liable if that third party initiated the attack.
- Defense of home and property
    - Most jurisdictions allow the owner of property to justifiably use reasonable, nondeadly force to prevent others from unlawfully taking or damaging one's property.
        - Use of deadly force is *not* justified unless the perpetrator of the illegal act intends to commit, or is in the act of committing a violent act against another human being. This includes setting booby traps such as spring-loaded shotguns, electrified gates, or explosive devices.

SELF-DEFENSE

The protection of oneself or of one's property from unlawful injury or from the immediate risk of unlawful injury. Also the justification that the person who committed an act that would otherwise constitute an offense reasonably believed that the act was necessary to protect self or property from immediate danger.

RULE OF LAW

The maxim that an orderly society must be governed by established principles and known codes that are applied uniformly and fairly to all of its members.

NECESSITY

A legal defense based on the claim that the committing of the crime was more beneficial than adhering to the law. There is no intent to violate the law.

- **Necessity** is the claim that some illegal action was needed to prevent an even greater harm.
  - *Crown* v. *Dully and Stephens* (late 1800s)
    - Famous English case involving a shipwreck that left 33 sailors and a cabin boy adrift in a lifeboat
    - After days at sea without rations, two of the sailors decided to kill and eat the cabin boy. The sailors were then rescued and put on trial for killing the cabin boy. The sailors' defense was necessity, since killing the cabin boy was necessary for their survival, without which they all would have died. English court rejected the defense. The court reasoned that the cabin boy was not a direct threat to the survival of the men. The sailors were convicted of murder and sentenced to death, although they were spared the gallows by royal intervention.
    - The defense of eating another human was upheld for when the human is already dead and eating was necessary for survival. Example: South American soccer team's plane crashed in the Andes mountains and some of the soccer players, who survived the crash, ate thc flcsh of those who died.
- Consent claims that whatever harm was done occurred only after the injured person gave his or her permission for the behavior in question. Examples:
  - Preppy murder case, which involved the strangulation of a young woman during rough sex in Central Park. The young woman supposedly gave consent to participate in rough sex that resulted in her death. The defendant pleaded guilty to first-degree manslaughter.
  - Performance art case, which involved a performance artist in front of a paying audience, who had an assistant shoot him in the upper arm while he stood in front of a canvas on which the blood spattered. The defense of consent was provided by the artist's assistant.
  - Condom rape case, which involved Joel Valdez who was found guilty of rape in 1993 after the jury rejected his claim that the act became consensual once he complied with the victim's request he use a condom. A determining factor was that Valdez was drunk and armed with a knife at the time of the rape.
- Resisting unlawful arrest
  - An individual has the right to resist arrest if the arrest is unlawful.
  - Some states have statutory provisions allowing individuals to resist unlawful arrests.

- Such states usually allow that a person may use a reasonable amount of force other than deadly force, to resist an unlawful arrest or unlawful search by a law enforcement officer if the officer uses or attempts to use greater force than necessary to make the arrest or search.
- Such laws are inapplicable in cases where the defendant is the first to resort to using force.

4.4.4 Excuse claims that the individual who engaged in the unlawful behavior was at the time not legally responsible for his or her actions and should not be held accountable under the law.

- Some particular condition was occurring at the time that would cause the defendant not be held responsible. Examples: age, duress, mistake, involuntary intoxication, unconsciousness, provocation, insanity
- The defense of age rests in the ancient belief that children cannot reason logically until around age 7; also called the "defense of infancy."
  - In most jurisdictions, children below the age of 7 cannot be charged with even a juvenile offense.
  - All states have an age that an individual is a considered a juvenile and above which the individual is considered to be an adult.
  - If individuals are categorized as juveniles, they cannot be found guilty of a criminal violation; instead they are adjudicated.
- **Duress** is any unlawful threat or coercion used by a person to induce another to act (or to refrain from acting) in a manner he or she otherwise would not (or would).
  - Often referred to as "coercion"
  - Usually *not* a useful defense when the crime committed involves serious physical harm since the harm committed may outweigh the coercive influence

DURESS

A legal defense in which the defendant claims he or she was compelled to take part in a crime by others.

- Mistake: two types
  - Mistake by law
    - Rarely acceptable; "ignorance of the law is no excuse."
  - Mistake of fact
- Involuntary intoxication as a result of drugs and/or alcohol
  - Involuntary intoxication is rarely a successful defense to criminal charges because it is self-induced.
  - When people are "tricked" into consuming intoxicating substances it can be used as defense to exonerate.
    - Secretly "spiked" punch, popular aphrodisiacs, LSD-laced desserts—all might be ingested by individuals unknowingly.

- Unconsciousness, rarely used as a defense, relies on the premise that individuals cannot be held responsible for anything he or she did while unconscious. Examples: sleepwalking, epileptic seizures, neurological dysfunction
- Provocation recognizes that a person can be emotionally enraged by another who intended to elicit just such a reaction.
    - Commonly used as a defense in barroom brawls
    - Has been used in cases where wives kill husbands and children kill fathers, claiming years of abuse
    - This defense is generally more acceptable in minor offenses than in serious violations of law.

INSANITY DEFENSE
A legal defense based on claims of mental illness or mental incapacity.

- **Insanity** is a legal defense based on claims of mental illness or mental incapacity.
    - The insanity defense is *not* frequently used; one study showed it has been used in less than 1% of felony cases.
    - The definition of insanity is a legal one, *not* a psychiatric one.
    - Prior to the 1800s, the insanity defense did not exist.

MCNAUGHTEN RULE
A rule determining insanity, which asks whether the defendant knew what he or she was doing or whether the defendant knew that what he or she was doing was wrong.

- Insanity defenses
    - **McNaughten rule** is based on the case of Daniel McNaughten who attempted to kill Sir Robert Peel, the British Home Secretary, but instead killed his secretary Edward Drummon. Lawyers for McNaughten argued he suffered from vague delusions centered on the idea that the Tories, a British political party, were persecuting him. Medical testimony indicated that McNaughten did not know what he was doing at the time of the shooting. The jury accepted the medical claim and the case established what has become known as the McNaughten rule.
        - Under the McNaughten rule, a person is not guilty of a crime if at the time of the crime the person did not know what he or she was doing or did not know that what he or she was doing was wrong; the inability to distinguish right from wrong must be the result of some mental defect or disability.
        - In most states, the burden of proving insanity falls on the defendant.

For more on the McNaughten rule and the insanity defense, visit Criminal Justice Interactive online > Criminal Law > Myths and Issues Videos > Myth vs. Reality: The Insanity Defense Is Often Used Successfully.

    - Irresistible impulse rule
        - Defendant knew what he or she was doing was wrong; however, he or she couldn't help himself or herself. Eighteen states use some form of irresistible impulse rule.

- Lorena Bobbitt successfully employed the irresistible impulse defense against charges of malicious wounding. Bobbitt's attorney argued that, in her mind, it was her husband's penis from which she could not escape and the impulse to sever the organ became irresistible.
- Criticism: All of us have compulsions, but we do not act on them; we control them.

❖ Durham rule was created in 1871 by a New Hampshire court; 19 states now use this test.

- A person is not criminally responsible for his or her behavior if his or her illegal actions were the result of some mental disease or defect.
- Jurors must be able to see the criminal activity in question as a "product" of mental deficiencies harbored by the defendant.

❖ Substantial capacity test claims that the subject's insanity should be defined as the lack of substantial capacity to control one's behavior and represents a blending of the McNaughten and the irresistible impluse rules.

- The test requires judgment to the effect that the defendant either has, or lacked the mental capacity, to understand the wrongfulness of his or her act or to conform his or her behavior to the requirements of the law.
- This test does *not* require total mental incompetence, nor does the rule require the behavior in question to live up to the criterion of total irresistibility.
- The problem of establishing just what constitutes "substantial mental capacity" has plagued this rule from its conception.

❖ Brawner rule places responsibility for deciding insanity squarely on the shoulders of the jury.

- Created in 1972 by the same judge who adopted the Durham rule
- The jury decides if the defendant can be justly held responsible for the criminal act in the face of any claims of insanity.

❖ Temporary insanity, widely used in the 1940s and 1950s, claims that the defendant was insane during the criminal event but is no longer.

- Proof of temporary insanity is the responsibility of the defendant.
- This type of plea has become less popular as state legislatures have regulated the circumstances under which it can be made.

❖ Diminished capacity is based on the claim that mental condition, which may be insufficient to exonerate a defendant of guilt, may be relevant to specific mental elements of certain crimes or degrees of crime.

- Similar to the insanity defense
- Many jurisdictions have done away with this type of defense.

GUILTY BUT MENTALLY ILL (GBMI)

A verdict, equivalent to a finding of "guilty," that establishes that the defendant, although mentally ill, was in sufficient possession of his or her faculties to be morally blameworthy for his or her acts.

- **Guilty but mentally ill (GBMI)** is a verdict equivalent to a finding of "guilty" that establishes that the defendant, although mentally ill, was in sufficient possession of his or her faculties to be morally blameworthy for his or her acts.
  - A person can be held responsible for a specific criminal act even though a degree of mental incompetence may be present in his or her personality.
  - A jury must return a finding of guilty but mentally ill if every element necessary for a conviction has been proved beyond a reasonable doubt.
    - The defendant is found to have been mentally ill at the time the crime was committed.
    - The defendant was not found to have been legally insane at the time the crime was committed.

- Insanity defense under federal law, requires severe mental disease or defect, and as a result the defendant was unable to appreciate the nature and quality or the wrongfulness of the act.
  - The act places the burden of proof of insanity on the defendant.
  - In *Jones* v. *U.S.* (1983), the Court ruled that defendants can be required to prove their insanity when it becomes an issue in their defense.
  - In *Ake* v. *Oklahoma* (1985), the Court held that the government must ensure access to a competent psychiatrist whenever a defendant indicates that insanity will be an issue at trial.

4.4.5 Procedural defense is when a defendant was discriminated against in the justice process in some manner, or some important aspect of official procedure was not properly followed. As a result, the defendant should be released from criminal liability.

- Types of procedural defenses:
  - Entrapment
  - Double jeopardy
  - *Collateral estoppel*
  - Selective prosecution
  - Denial of speedy trial
  - Prosecutorial misconduct
  - Police fraud

- **Entrapment** is an improper or illegal inducement to crime by agents of enforcement; also a defense that may be raised when such inducements occur.
    - Entrapment defenses argue that enforcement agents effectively created a crime where there would otherwise have been none.
    - Idea for criminal activity probably originated with official agents of the criminal justice system. Example: Automaker John DeLorean was arrested in 1982 by federal agents at Los Angeles airport. FBI videotape that was secretly made showed DeLorean allegedly dealing with undercover agents and holding packets of cocaine. DeLorean was charged with narcotics smuggling violations, but claimed entrapment, saying he was set up by the police to commit a crime that he would not have been involved in were it not for their urging. DeLorean was found not guilty because he was able to demonstrate that the police had initiated the idea and that a police informant repeatedly threatened him not to pull out of the deal.

ENTRAPMENT

An improper or illegal inducement to crime by agents of law enforcement. Also, a defense that may be raised when such inducements have occurred.

- Double jeopardy is a common law and prohibits a second trial for the same offense.
    - Fifth Amendment of the U.S. Constitution makes it clear that no person may be tried twice for the same offense.
        - Double jeopardy clause protects against three distinct abuses:
            - A second prosecution for the same offense after acquittal
            - A second prosecution for the same offense after conviction
            - Multiple punishments for the same offense
        - **Double jeopardy** does not apply in cases of trial error; convictions that are set aside because of some error in proceedings at a lower court level will permit a retrial on the same charges.
        - When a defendant's motion for a mistrial is successful, or when members of the jury cannot agree upon a verdict, a second trial may be held.
    - Defendants may be tried in both federal and state courts without necessarily violating the principle of double jeopardy.
    - Because criminal and civil laws differ as to purpose, it is possible to try someone in civil court to collect damages for a possible violation of civil law even if he or she was found not guilty in criminal court. Example: O. J. Simpson civil trial in 1997 is an example of damages being collected in civil court even though Simpson was found not guilty in the criminal trial.

DOUBLE JEOPARDY

A common law and constitutional prohibition against a second trial for the same offense.

- *Collateral estoppel* applies to facts that have been determined by a valid and final judgment. Such facts cannot become the object of new litigation. Example: If defendant has been acquitted of a murder charge by virtue of an alibi, it would not be permissible to try that person again for the murder of a second person killed along with the first.
- Selective prosecution occurs when defense may be available where two or more individuals are suspected of criminal involvement, but not all are actively prosecuted.
  - ❖ Based on the Fourteenth Amendment's guarantee of "equal protection of the laws," when prosecution proceeds unfairly on the basis of some arbitrary and discriminatory attribute such as race, sex, friendship, age, or religious preference, the defense of selective prosecution offers some protection.
- Denial of a speedy trial is a defense that can be used when a defendant has been languishing.
  - ❖ Sixth Amendment to U.S. Constitution guarantees a right to a speedy trial.
  - ❖ Most speedy trial laws set a reasonable period, such as 90 or 120 days following arrest, for a person to be brought to trial.
  - ❖ If limit set by law is exceeded, the defendant must be set free and no trial can occur.
- Prosecutorial misconduct is an action undertaken by prosecutors that gives the government an unfair advantage or that prejudices the rights of a defendant or a witness. Examples:
  - ❖ When prosecutors hide information that would help the defense
  - ❖ When prosecutors knowingly permit false testimony
  - ❖ When prosecutors make biased statements to the jury in closing arguments
- Police fraud is caused when evidence against a defendant is concocted and planted by police officers.

For more on legal defenses, visit Criminal Justice Interactive online > Criminal Law > Learning Modules > 4.4 Legal Defenses.

CHAPTER SUMMARY

➢ The law in the United States comes from a number of sources. The U.S. Constitution is based on natural law, rules of conduct that are inherent in human nature. Modern criminal law is based on common law, judge-made law that is refined and changed by the actual decisions of the courts. The U.S. Constitution is the final authority in all questions regarding the rights of individuals.

- There are a number of different types of law. Criminal law is the branch of modern law that concerns itself with offenses committed against society. Civil law is the branch of modern law that governs the relationships between parties and regulates noncriminal relationships. Administrative law is law made and enforced by administrative or regulatory agencies. Case law is judicial precedent, built on past interpretations of statutory laws. Procedural law specifies the methods to be used in enforcing substantive law.
- For a crime to occur, three elements have to be present. *Actus reus* is the guilty act, an act in violation of law. *Mens rea* is the guilty mind, the state of mind that accompanies a criminal act. Concurrence is the coming together of the *actus reus* and *mens rea*. *Corpus delicti*, a term that means body of crime, refers to the facts that show a crime has occurred.
- There are several categories of crime. A felony is a criminal offense punishable by incarceration in a prison for at least one year. A misdemeanor is an offense punishable by incarceration usually in a local facility and usually for less than a year. A summary offense is a minor crime that is punished by a ticket or a fine. Other categories of crime include treason/espionage and inchoate offenses.
- In defense of a crime, there are four broad legal categories. An alibi is a contention that the individual charged with the crime was so distant when the crime occurred that it would have been impossible for him or her to commit it. Justification, which includes the category of self-defense, is a defense in which the defendant admits committing an act but claims it was necessary to avoid some greater evil. Necessity is the claim that some illegal action was needed to prevent an even greater harm and includes issues regarding insanity defenses. A procedural defense occurs when the defendant claims that some important aspect of official procedure was not followed or that the defendant was in some way discriminated against.

ONLINE@CRIMINAL JUSTICE INTERACTIVE

Learning Modules

4.1 Sources of Law and Types of Law
4.2 Crime Elements
4.3 Categories of Crime
4.4 Legal Defenses

Myths and Issues Videos

Myth vs. Reality: The Insanity Defense Is Often Used Successfully
Issue 1: Does Society Legislate Morality by Punishing Immoral Behavior?
Issue 2: Is There "Equal Justice Under the Law"?

Simulation Activity: Recognizing the Elements of Crime

Simulation Activity: Explaining Criminal Behavior

Homework and Review
In the News
Web Activity
Review Questions
Essay questions
Flashcards

Chapter 5

The Police: History, Structure, and Functions

CHAPTER OUTLINE

- 5.0 The police: History, structure, and functions
- 5.1 History and professionalism of police
  - 5.1.1 History of police in England
  - 5.1.2 History of police in America
- 5.2 Modern American policing eras
  - 5.2.1 Policing eras: Political, reform, and community
- 5.3 Levels of law enforcement: Federal, state, local, and private
  - 5.3.1 Federal law enforcement agencies
  - 5.3.2 State and local agencies
  - 5.3.3 Women in law enforcement
  - 5.3.4 Private protective services
- 5.4 Police roles and functions
  - 5.4.1 Mission of police
  - 5.4.2 Operational strategies
- 5.5 Police organization
  - 5.5.1 Two basic organizational types
  - 5.5.2 Line operations in police organizations
  - 5.5.3 Staff operations
  - 5.5.4 Chain of command
- 5.6 Policing styles
  - 5.6.1 James Q. Wilson
  - 5.6.2 Three styles of policing

LEARNING OBJECTIVES

After reviewing the online material and reading this chapter, you should be able to:

1. Discuss the history of the police in the United States and the three major eras of American policing: political era, reform era, and community era.
2. Describe and compare the roles and the responsibilities of the following levels of law enforcement: federal, state, local, and private.
3. Describe the general roles of police in American society: enforcing the law, apprehending offenders, preventing crime, and keeping the peace.
4. Describe the primary operational strategies utilized by the police: patrol, emergency response, investigation, problem solving, and support services.
5. Describe the typical organizational structure of a police agency/department.
6. Define, describe, and apply three policing styles: legalistic, watchman, and service.
7. Discuss the history and current state of women and minorities in law enforcement.
8. Define terms related to the history, structure, and functions of the police.

KEY TERMS

bailiffs
bobbies
chain of command
comes stabuli
constable
corruption
crime prevention
Drug Enforcement Administration (DEA)
highway patrol
hue and cry
hundred
legalistic style
police–community relations
private protective services
service style
sheriff
shire reeve
state police
tithing
vigilantism
watch and ward
watchman style

HUE AND CRY

During medieval times, the method used to alert townspeople of the occurrence of a crime. Anyone within hearing distance was required to give pursuit to apprehend the offender. If the offender was not apprehended, the townspeople were fined by the King.

TITHING

From the Old English tithe, paying one tenth, it came to represent ten families grouped together for peace-keeping purposes.

HUNDRED

In England during medieval times, the hundred represented the grouping of ten tithings (ten families to each tithing) for purposes of maintaining order in a community.

COMES STABULI

A non-uniformed mounted law enforcement officer of medieval England. Early police forces were small and relatively unorganized but made effective use of local resources in the formation of posses, the pursuit of offenders, and the like.

CONSTABLE

First appeared in England after the Norman conquest of 1066. Meaning "count of the stable," those who held the position were responsible for maintaining the weapons of the townsfolk. Eventually became responsible for maintaining the "King's peace."

5.0 The police: History, structure, and functions

5.1 History and professionalism of police

5.1.1 History of police in England

- King Arthur's Court, fifth century
  - Knights of King Arthur roamed the land enforcing rights, safeguarding travelers, and suppressing wrongdoing.
  - Their shields, which they would die to protect, may be the origin of the shield worn by modern law enforcement officers.
- Alfred the Great, ninth to tenth century, developed the Pledge System, based on a program of mutual responsibility.
  - The king (known as the Crown) placed the responsibility squarely on citizenry of each district.
  - It was each man's duty to raise the "**hue and cry**" when a crime was committed. (Neighbors were required to pursue the criminal; if neighbors failed to catch the criminal they were fined by the Crown.)
    - **Tithing**
      - Crown divided families in a town into groups of 10 families.
      - Basic foundation of Mutual Pledge System
      - Only needed to enforce two laws: murder and theft
    - **Hundred**
      - As the size of the tithings increased and reached the size of 10 times 10, or 100 families, they were called hundreds (ten tithings).
      - If the village was near the coast, log walls or fortresses were built and the area became known as a borough.
    - ***Comes stabuli*** is a nonuniformed mounted law enforcement officer of medieval England; considered first real police officer.
      - Early police forces were small and relatively disorganized, but made effective use of local resources in the formation of posses, the pursuit of offenders, etc.
      - Our modern-day term "**constable**" comes from this term.
      - Appointed by local nobleman and placed in charge of weapons and equipment of each shire (shire is administrative equivalent of a county)

- **Shire reeve** was responsible to the local nobleman for ensuring that citizens enforced the law effectively.
  - The origin of today's **sheriffs**
  - Crown appointed a shire reeve to supervise each county.
  - Gradually branched out from supervisory post to pursue and apprehend lawbreakers

SHIRE REEVE

Chief law enforcement officer of a shire, the equivalent of a county in the United States. We derived the term sheriff from shire reeve.

SHERIFF

The elected chief officer of a county law enforcement agency. The sheriff is usually responsible for law enforcement in unincorporated areas and for the operation of the county jail.

- Invasion of England by France; 1066 Duke of Normandy crowned King of all England, King William I
  - ❖ Installed strong central government based on King's law
  - ❖ Substituted mutilation for death penalty and instituted the wager of battle to decide right and wrong.
    - ◆ In a wager of battle, the accused could challenge accuser to battle; the winner won his case.
  - ❖ Circuit judges were created by descendants of William I. Circuit judges relieved shire reeves and constables of their judicial powers so they could focus on enforcement of law.
- In 1166, Henry the Law-Giver created Leges Henrici (Laws of Henry).
  - ❖ Trial by jury, called *Assizes*, jury of one's peers
    - ◆ Designed to settle disputes over ownership or possession of land
    - ◆ Decision final, no appeal
  - ❖ Felonies
    - ◆ Offenses against King's peace included arson, robbery, murder, false coinage, and crimes of violence.
- King John developed the Magna Carta in 1215.
  - ❖ Provided that all cities and villages would have their own liberties and customs
  - ❖ Every man entitled to trial by jury.
  - ❖ Separation of state and local governments
  - ❖ Gave due process of law
- Edward I (1272–1307) set up a curfew and night watch program.
  - ❖ Statute of Winchester (1285) was a law that created a **watch and ward** system in English cities and towns that codified early police practices, protecting property against fire, guarding gates of town/city, and arresting those who committed offenses.
  - ❖ Night watch program allowed for gates of Westminster to be locked at night (Westminster was then the capital of England).

WATCH AND WARD

System in England in the 1400s and 1500s, in which individuals would patrol at night and call out the time as he patrolled. Intent was to scare off individuals who were engaged in illegal activity by announcing the presence of the watchman.

BAILIFFS
An armed law enforcement officer responsible for maintaining order in the court and ensuring that the rules of court are followed.

- Mandated the draft of eligible males to serve as night watch people
- Institutionalized the use of the "hue and cry"
- Required that citizens maintain weapons in their home for answering the call to arms
- **Bailiffs** hired as night watchmen to enforce curfew and guard gates.

- Edward II (1326) established justice of the peace.
  - Designed to supplement shire reeve and the Mutual Pledge System
  - Originally, justices of the peace were noblemen appointed by the Crown to help shire reeve police the county.
  - Soon they took on judicial functions in addition to law enforcement duties.
    - Settled matters of wages, prices, conditions of labor, and pretrial preliminary hearings to determine if there was enough evidence to hold a person for trial
  - Constable became an assistant to the justice of the peace and duties were expanded to include:
    - Supervising night watchmen
    - Investigating offenses
    - Serving summonses
    - Executing warrants
    - Taking charge of prisoners
    - Separation of justice and constable into judge and police officer roles developed.
  - During remainder of fourteenth century, law enforcement became increasingly responsible to central government of King.
    - Justice of the peace, as appointee of King, exercised great control over the locally appointed constable.
    - Constable no longer an independent official of the Mutual Pledge System; now served the justice of the peace.
  - Relationship remained this way for justice of the peace and the constable for the next 500 years.
  - Mutual Pledge System began to decline as people began to pay others to assume their law enforcement responsibilities.
  - Constable often paid their deputies or other substitutes to do their work year after year.
- Eighteenth- and nineteenth-century England
  - Cities began to grow rapidly as a result of the industrial revolution and crime increased.

- Paid night watch force was developed; responsible for guarding city against thieves and vandals; ultimately proved ineffective.
  - Night watchmen merely roamed streets of city calling out weather, time, and "all is well;" "all is well" cry warned thieves and vandals and prevented encounters with criminals.
- Civilian associations responded first to the increase in crime by establishing their own private law enforcement associations.
  - The Boy Street Horse and Foot Patrol (1750) patrolled streets and highways leading to London; represented the first real detective unit.

■ Nineteenth century

- Sir Robert Peel, Home Secretary, father of police administration, proposed London have a group of civilians paid by the community to serve as police officers.
  - In 1829, Parliament passed the "Act for Improving the Police In and Near the Metropolis," which developed into the London Metropolitan Police.
  - London Metropolitan Police was uniformed for easy identification: top hats, three-quarter-length coats of royal blue, white pants, armed with a club.
    - Called "**bobbies**" after Sir Robert Peel
    - Original force of 1,000
    - Structured along military lines
    - Commanded by two magistrates (later commissioners)
- In 1835, Parliament passed legislation allowing (not requiring) every borough over 20,000 people to form a police force.
  - Town council, a body of elected representatives, allowed to appoint from its members a watch committee, which in turn appointed chief of police and officers of force.
- In 1839, County Police Act passed by Parliament that gave magistrates responsibility to fix strength of force and to appoint and dismiss chief constable in counties. Fifteen of the 52 counties adopted police forces by 1840.
- In 1883, women entered law enforcement.
  - London Metropolitan Police appointed two women to supervise women convicts.

BOBBIES
The popular British name given to members of Sir Robert (Bob) Peel's Metropolitan Police Force.

5.1.2 History of police in America

■ Seventeenth and eighteenth centuries

- American colonists brought structures from their European homelands.

- Shire reeve was responsible for law enforcement in the counties.
- Constable was responsible for law enforcement in the towns.
- Before American Revolution, the Crown appointed the sheriffs and constable; after the Revolution, popular election determined sheriffs and constables.

❖ Night watch system known as rattle watch, since they carried rattles on their rounds to scare criminals and remind citizens of their presence.
- Adopted by large cities, Boston and New York, in 1636
- In 1658, paid watchmen were hired in New York.
- In 1693, the first uniformed officer was employed by New York City.
- In 1731, the first neighborhood, or precinct station, was constructed.

VIGILANTISM

Individuals who without legal authorization conduct a trial of an accused. More typical in the Old West.

❖ **Vigilantism** is the act of taking the law into one's hands.
- Charles Lynch, Virginia farmer in late 1700s
  - ❒ With associates, Lynch tracked and punished offenders.
  - ❒ The punishment was usually "lynching," which refers to punishing a person, usually by hanging, without due process, and is named after Charles Lynch.

■ In the nineteenth century, rising crime prompted cities to develop their own police forces.

❖ Daytime/nighttime forces had problems of competition because they each had different administrations; this resulted in inefficiencies.

❖ In 1844, New York legislature pass bill to authorize first unified day/night police force. Boston followed suit in 1855, establishing a unified force.

❖ Citizen involvement in law enforcement
- In 1800s, people often took the law into their own hands, especially in western United States.

❖ In 1902, International Association of Chiefs of Police (IACP) was formed, immediately creating a clearinghouse for criminal identification.

❖ In 1910, Alice Stebbins Wells became the first sworn female police officer in the world serving with the Los Angeles Police Department.
- By 1915, the U.S. Census Bureau reported that 25 cities employed female police officers.

        - In 1915, International Association of Policewomen, now the International Association of Women Police was formed in Baltimore.
        - In 1918, Ellen O'Grady became the Deputy Police Commissioner for the City of New York, the first woman to hold a high administrative post in a major police department.

For more on women in police enforcement, visit Criminal Justice Interactive online > The Police: History, Structure, and Functions > Myths and Issues Videos > Issue 1: Women and Minorities in Law Enforcement.

    - In 1915, Fraternal Order of Police (FOP) initiated operations patterning itself after labor unions but prohibiting strikes.

- State law enforcement agencies
    - In 1835, Texas provisional government established the Texas Rangers.
        - Actually a military unit established in three companies; were responsible for border patrol
        - Their primary task was apprehension of Mexican cattle rustlers.
    - In 1865, Massachusetts became the next state to create a **state police** force to control vice within the state.
    - In 1905, Pennsylvania created what is considered to be the first contemporary state police force under Governor Pennypacker. Originally called the Pennsylvania Constabulary. Today it is known as the Pennsylvania State Police.
        - Created as a response to riots in coal regions since local law enforcement was not up to the task.
        - Newly hired state police were transferred to opposite sides of the state to ensure that they would not have local ties to the miners who were rioting, enabling them to enforce the laws without conflict.
        - Also provided law enforcement in rural areas

STATE POLICE

A state law enforcement agency whose principal functions usually include maintaining statewide police communications, aiding local police in criminal investigations, training police, and guarding state property. The state police may include the highway patrol.

For more on history and professionalism of the police in England and the United States, visit Criminal Justice Interactive online > The Police: History, Structure, and Functions > Learning Modules > 5.1 History and Professionalism of the Police.

5.2 Modern American policing eras

5.2.1 Policing eras: political era (1840–1930), reform era (1930–1970), community era (1970–today)

- Political era represented close ties between law enforcement and public officials.
  - Often during the early part of this era, officers "purchased" lucrative beats by paying ward officials.
  - Law enforcement was part of the political machine.
- Reform era occurred when citizens called for reform and the removal of politics from law enforcement.
  - During this era, law enforcement took pride in their professional approach to fighting crime.
  - Emphasis was placed on solving crime and arresting offenders.
  - Serious crackdown on organized crime, especially from federal agents
  - Individuals like August Vollmer and O. W. Wilson were instrumental in leading the professionalism approach.
- During the community era, community policing developed. The focus was on integrating the police with the community in the form of a partnership.
  - In some instances, law enforcement officers were encouraged to live within the communities in which they worked.
  - Officers walking beats interacting with members of the community in a positive way was emphasized.
  - Law enforcement paid attention to "quality of life" offenses to help both keep the peace and reduce crime.
  - **Police–community relations (PCR)** is an area of police activity that stresses the need for the community and the police to work together effectively, and emphasizes the notion that the police derive their legitimacy from the community they serve.
    - For most departments, interest in police–community relations began in the 1960s.
      - The social unrest of the 1960s helped to re-focus law enforcement toward a community relations approach.

POLICE–COMMUNITY RELATIONS (PCR)

An area of police activity that recognizes the need for the community and the police to work together effectively. PCR is based on the notion that the police derive their legitimacy from the community they serve. Many police agencies began to explore PCR in the 1960s and 1970s.

For more on modern American policing eras, visit Criminal Justice Interactive online > The Police: History, Structure, and Functions > Learning Modules > 5.2: Modern American Policing Eras.

5.3 Levels of law enforcement: federal, state, local, and private

5.3.1 Federal law enforcement agencies

- First federal agency
  - In 1789, Revenue Cutter Service was created to patrol shores of United States to prevent smuggling and to ensure collection of revenue on imported goods.
- U.S. Marshal Office is the oldest continuous operating agency created in 1789.
  - Thirteen U.S marshals assigned to President George Washington's attorney general.
  - As the United States moved west, U.S. marshals were needed to serve as main law enforcement in the new territories.
  - "Wild" Bill Hickok and Wyatt Earp were U.S marshals.
  - After Civil War when most territories became states, U.S. marshals became bailiffs of U.S. District Courts.
- Other early federal agencies
  - Immigration and Naturalization Service created in 1891; the Border Patrol is part of this agency.
  - Secret Service (1865), under the U.S. Department of Treasury, created to control flood of counterfeit currency as a result of the Civil War; after assignation of William McKinley, the Secret Service was given the responsibility of protecting the President.
  - Internal Revenue Service (1862)
- Federal law enforcement in the twentieth century
  - Federal Bureau of Investigation (FBI), originally Bureau of Investigation, created in 1908 and designed to serve as the investigative arm of the U.S. Department of Justice.
    - Six attorneys were originally hired because other agencies could not stem the rising tide of American political and business **corruption**.
    - White Slave Traffic Act (1910) necessitated a coordinated interstate law enforcement effort to fight organized prostitution.
    - Incidents of sabotage and espionage on American soil during World War I also contributed to the rapid growth of the Bureau of Investigation.
    - Espionage Act of 1917 provided a legal basis for the bureau's investigation into subversive activities.
    - J. Edgar Hoover appointed Director of FBI in 1924.
      - Bureau opened its Identification Division.
        - Served as a national clearinghouse for information on criminals

CORRUPTION
The abuse of police authority for personal or organizational gain. See police corruption.

- Began operation with 810,188 fingerprint cards received from the Federal Penitentiary at Leavenworth, Kansas, and from the International Association of Chiefs of Police.
- In 1930, the agency reorganized and was renamed the Federal Bureau of Investigation (FBI).
- In 1932, the Crime Laboratory opened with a borrowed microscope.
- Collects data for Uniform Crime Report (1930)
- Mission: "To protect and defend the United States against terrorist and foreign intelligence threats, to uphold and enforce the criminal laws of the United States, and to provide leadership and criminal justice services to federal, state, municipal, and international agencies and partners. (FBI Web site: www.fbi.gov/).
- Current major administrative divisions within the FBI:
    - Administrative Services Division
    - Counterterrorism Division
        - The National Infrastructure Protection Center (NIPC) and the National Domestic Preparedness Office (NDPO) are assigned to this division.
        - The NIPC serves as the government's focal point for threat assessment, warning investigation, and response for threats or attacks against critical components of the U.S. infrastructure.
        - The NDPO coordinates all federal efforts to assist state and local first responders with planning, training, and equipment needs necessary to respond to incidents involving conventional or unconventional weapons of mass destruction.

❖ Criminal Investigative Division

- ◆ Coordinates investigations into organized crime including drugs, racketeering, and money laundering
- ◆ Investigates violent crime, including:
    - ❒ Wanted fugitives, escaped federal prisoners
    - ❒ Unlawful flight to avoid prosecution
    - ❒ Violent gangs

        - Serial murders
        - Kidnappings
        - Bank robberies
        - Crime on Indian reservations
        - Crimes against U.S. citizens overseas
        - Theft of government property
        - White-collar crimes, including:
            - Fraud against the government
            - Corruption of public officials
            - Health-care fraud
            - Election law violations
            - Business and economic frauds
            - Corruption crimes
        - Investigations into civil rights violations
    - This division contains, for example, the following sections:
        - Asset Forfeiture Program
        - Financial Crimes Section
        - Internet Fraud Complaint Center
- Criminal Justice Information Services Division
    - Headquartered in Clarksburg, West Virginia
    - Serves as the central repository for criminal justice information services in the FBI.
    - Provides state-of-the-art identification and information services to local, state, federal, and international criminal justice communities.
    - This division includes:
        - Fingerprint Identification Program
        - National Crime Information Center (NCIC) Program
        - Uniform Crime Reporting Program
        - Integrated Automated Fingerprint Identification System
    - Finance Division
    - Information Resources Division
    - Inspection Division
    - Investigative Services Division
    - Laboratory Division
        - Operates one of the largest and most comprehensive crime laboratories in the world
        - The only full-service federal forensic laboratory in the United States

- Offers laboratory services free of charge to all law enforcement agencies in the United States
- Laboratory activities include:
  - Crime scene searches
  - Special surveillance photography
  - Latent fingerprint examinations of evidence (including DNA testing)
  - Court testimony by laboratory personnel

- Other federal law enforcement agencies
  - Department of Justice
    - Bureau of Prisons
    - **Drug Enforcement Administration (DEA)**
      - First created as the Bureau of Narcotics and Dangerous Drugs in 1914 as part of Harrison Act
      - Various agencies combined in 1973 to create the Drug Enforcement Administration.
    - Federal Bureau of Investigation
    - U.S. Marshal Service
    - Immigration and Naturalization Service
  - Department of Homeland Security
    - U.S. Customs and Border Protection
    - Federal Emergency Management Agency
    - Immigration and Customs Enforcement
    - Transportation Security Administration
    - U.S. Citizenship and Immigration Services
    - U.S. Coast Guard
    - U.S. Secret Service
    - Office of Inspector General
  - Department of the Treasury
    - Bureau of Alcohol, Tobacco, and Firearms
    - Internal Revenue Service
    - Federal Law Enforcement Training Center
  - Department of Interior
    - Fish and Wildlife Service
    - National Park Service
    - U.S. Park Police
  - Department of Defense
    - Criminal Investigation Division
    - Office of Special Investigations

DRUG ENFORCEMENT ADMINISTRATION (DEA)

Drug Enforcement Administration was created by President Nixon in 1973 to establish a single unified command to combat an all-out global war on drugs.

- ❒ Naval Investigation Service
- ❒ Defense Criminal Investigator Service

◆ Department of Transportation

- ❒ Federal Aviation Administration
- ❒ Federal Highway Administration
- ❒ Federal Railroad Associations

◆ General Services Administration

- ❒ Federal Protective Services

◆ U.S. Postal Service

- ❒ Postal Inspections Service

◆ Washington, D.C.

- ❒ Metropolitan Police Department

5.3.2 State and local agencies

■ State police (2000)

- ❖ Forty-nine state police agencies
  - ◆ Hawaii does *not* have a state police force.
- ❖ Approximately 87,064 full-time officers, of which approximately 56,384 are sworn
- ❖ Approximately 26,000 civilian employees
- ❖ Two types of state police agencies: centralized and decentralized
- ❖ Centralized model
  - ◆ Tasks of centralized agencies:
    - ❒ Assist local law enforcement in criminal investigations when asked.
    - ❒ Operate identification bureaus.
    - ❒ Maintain a centralized criminal records repository.
    - ❒ Patrol the state's highways.
    - ❒ Provide select training for municipal and county officers.
  - ◆ Examples of centralized state police agencies:
    - ❒ Pennsylvania
    - ❒ Michigan
    - ❒ New Jersey
    - ❒ New York
    - ❒ Vermont
    - ❒ Delaware

HIGHWAY PATROL

A state law enforcement agency whose principal functions are preventing, detecting, and investigating motor vehicle offenses and apprehending traffic offenders.

- Decentralized model
  - Tasks of decentralized agencies:
    - Draws clear distinction between traffic enforcement on state highways and other state-level law enforcement functions.
    - Typically creates two agencies to handle the two different tasks (sometimes called by other names): **highway patrol**, state bureau of investigation
  - Examples of decentralized agencies:
    - North Carolina
    - South Carolina
    - Georgia
  - Decentralized models often have other state law enforcement agencies designed to address specific areas:
    - State Wildlife Commission
    - Board of Alcohol Beverage Control
    - Enforcement and Theft Bureau
    - State University Police
    - Weigh Station Operations
    - Port Authorities

- County Law Enforcement (2000)
  - Approximately 3,000 sheriff departments
  - Approximately 293,823 full-time officers, of which approximately 164,711 are sworn
  - Approximately 22,737 part-time officers, of which approximately 10,300 are sworn
  - Approximately 89,000 civilian employees
  - Largest—Los Angeles Sheriff's Department with approximately 5,000 officers
  - Nearly two-thirds of all sheriff's departments employ fewer than 25 sworn officers.
  - Only 12 departments employ more than 1,000 officers.
- Metropolitan Police (2000)
  - Approximately 12,666 different police departments
  - Approximately 566,000 full-time police officers, of which approximately 440,920 are sworn
  - Approximately 62,000 part-time police officers, of which approximately 27,323 are sworn
  - Approximately 100,000 civilian employees
  - Largest municipal police department—New York City, with approximately 53,000 full-time employees, including about 40,000 full-time sworn officers

- ❖ Smallest municipal police departments
  - ◆ Approximately 2,245 departments have only one officer.
  - ◆ Departments that have only part-time officers: 1,164
- ❖ A few communities contract with private security firms for police services.

5.3.3 Women in law enforcement

- *Equality Denied: The Status of Women in Policing*, 2000, National Center for Women and Policing (2001)
  - ❖ Of all law enforcement personnel at the state, county, and local levels, women represent only 13% of sworn officers in departments with 100 or more officers.
  - ❖ Women of color fill only 4.8% of all sworn officers.
  - ❖ In 1990, women as sworn officers represented 9% of all officers, while in 2001 they represented 13%.
  - ❖ Of top command positions, women hold 7.3% of all positions, while women of color hold 1.7% of the positions.
  - ❖ In terms of state law enforcement agencies, women hold 6.8% of the sworn officer positions, while at the municipal level they hold 14.5% of sworn officer positions, and at the county level it is 13.5%.

5.3.4 **Private protective services** are self-employed individuals and privately funded business entities and organizations providing security-related services to specific clientele for a fee, for the individual entity that retains or employs them, or for themselves in order to protect their persons, private property, or interests from various hazards.

PRIVATE PROTECTIVE SERVICES

Independent or proprietary commercial organizations that provide protective services to employers on a contractual basis.

- Private security personnel work for corporate employers and secure private interests.
- *Hallcrest Report II* (1990)
  - ❖ Nearly 2 million people are employed in private security.
  - ❖ Experts estimate that private security services cost American industries about $64.5 billion in 2000.
- Major reasons for quick growth of private security
  - ❖ Increase in crimes in the workplace
  - ❖ An increase in fear (real or perceived)
  - ❖ Fiscal crises of the states
  - ❖ Increased public and business awareness and use of more cost effective private security
- Development of private policing:
  - ❖ Specialized in railroad security and would protect shipments as well as hunt down thieves who had made a getaway.
  - ❖ Hired by railroads that were laying tracks to support westward expansion.

- ❖ An open eye was the symbol that represented constant vigilance; the term "private eye" may have been derived this.
- ❖ Pinkerton developed a code of ethics for his agents.
    - ◆ Code prohibited his men and women from accepting rewards, agents from working for one political party against another, and agents from handling divorce cases.

- ■ Henry Wells and William Fargo founded Wells Fargo agency in 1852 and supplied detective and protective services to areas west of Missouri.
- ■ Brink's Company began as a general package delivery service in 1859 and grew to a fleet of 85 armored wagons by 1900.
- ■ Burns International Detective Agency founded in 1909 by William J. Burns, former direction of the Bureau of Investigation.
- ■ Wackenhut Security Corporation founded in 1954 by George R. Wackenhut, a former FBI special agent.
- ■ Largest private security agencies in the United States
    - ❖ Security Bureau, Inc.
    - ❖ Wackenhut Corp.
    - ❖ Guardsmark, Inc.
    - ❖ American Protective Services
    - ❖ Globe Security
    - ❖ Wells Fargo Guard Services
    - ❖ Advance Security, Inc.
    - ❖ Pinkerton's, Inc.
    - ❖ Allied Security, Inc.
    - ❖ Burns International Security Services
- ■ Types of private security personnel
    - ❖ Bank guards
    - ❖ Company guards
    - ❖ Loss-prevention specialists
    - ❖ Railroad detectives
    - ❖ Airport security
    - ❖ Automated teller machine services
    - ❖ Computer/information security
    - ❖ Executive protection
    - ❖ Hospital security
    - ❖ Nuclear facility security
    - ❖ School security
    - ❖ Store/mall
    - ❖ Bodyguards

- Private system of justice
  - Security executives order their managerial priorities as follows:
    - The protection of lives and property
    - Crime prevention
    - Loss prevention
    - Fire prevention
    - Success control
  - Conflict resolution, economic sanctions, or retraining sometimes supplant criminal prosecution as the most effective method of dealing with offenders.
  - Most frequently investigated crime is employee theft.

For more on how levels of law enforcement, visit Criminal Justice Interactive online > The Police: History, Structure, and Functions > Learning Modules > 5.3: Levels of Law Enforcement.

5.4 Police roles and functions

5.4.1 Mission of the police

- The basic purposes of policing include:
  - Enforcing the law
    - The police are required to enforce the laws of society.
    - Depending on their jurisdiction, the police are responsible for federal, state, and local statutes.
    - In reality, the police spend only a small amount of their time actually enforcing laws.
    - Ten percent to 20% of all calls to the police involve enforcing the law.
    - Policc also use their discretion in enforcing the law in part because in some jurisdictions, they are responsible for enforcing tens of thousands of laws making it impossible to enforce them all.
  - Apprehending offenders
    - Law enforcement officers make a determination of whether or not there are sufficient grounds to make a formal arrest of an individual or individuals.
    - If the crime committed is a felony, the law enforcement officer does not have to have observed the crime taking place to make an arrest.
    - If the crime is a misdemeanor, the law enforcement officer either has to have observed the offender committing the crime, or have a witness who is willing to file a complaint in order to effect an arrest.

- Response time, the time it takes an officer to respond to the scene of a crime, has been deemed crucial to "solving" a crime and making an arrest.
- The quicker the response time, the more likely the law enforcement officer is able to clear the crime by an arrest.
- In the case of Timothy McVeigh, the Oklahoma City bomber, law enforcement officers were able to arrest him within 90 minutes of the bombing of the federal building because of their quick response and investigation of the crime scene.

❖ Preventing crime

CRIME PREVENTION
The anticipation, recognition, and appraisal of a crime risk and the initiation of action to eliminate or reduce it.

- **Crime prevention** is the anticipation, recognition, and appraisal of a crime risk and the initiation of action to eliminate or reduce it.
- This represents a proactive approach to law enforcement.
- Modern crime prevention also includes reducing the public's fear of crime.
- Effective crime prevention means effective crime prediction.

❖ Preserving the peace

- Maintaining the peace cuts across many of the responsibilities and activities of law enforcement officers.
- Peacekeeping activities can include:
    - ❒ Leading funerals
    - ❒ Crowd control at concerts and sporting events
    - ❒ Assisting with crowd and vehicle control at parades
    - ❒ Protecting rights of unpopular groups to march/demonstrate
    - ❒ Maintaining peace between picketing strikers and those who choose to cross a picket line
- Many law enforcement agencies focus on quality-of-life issues or a minor violation of the law (sometimes called a petty crime) that demoralizes community residents and businesspeople.
- Examples of quality-of-life offenses that contribute to the deterioration of a neighborhood:
    - ❒ Panhandling
    - ❒ Graffiti
    - ❒ Vandalism
    - ❒ Prostitution
    - ❒ Corner drug dealing
    - ❒ Public urination

- Providing service
  - Law enforcement officers can be mobilized by any citizen who makes a phone call to the law enforcement agency or flags down a patrolling squad car.
  - The majority of calls/contacts law enforcement receives are for services that are non-emergency in nature.
  - Examples of service calls to which law enforcement officers respond:
    - Fires
    - Calls requiring an ambulance
    - Lost/missing children
    - Blocked driveways
    - Locked out of a car

5.4.2 Operational strategies

- Preventive patrol
  - The primary operational strategy
  - Routine patrol activities use the majority of personnel and budgetary resources of law enforcement agencies at the state and local levels.
  - Purpose of patrol
    - To provide for quick response to calls for assistance
    - To create a visible presence with the intent of deterring crime
    - To interrupt crimes in progress
    - To enhance the public's sense of safety and security
  - Computer-assisted dispatch (CAD)
    - Used by most law enforcement agencies
    - System assists with the following:
      - Prioritizing incoming calls for service.
      - Recording dispatches.
      - Recording the amount of time devoted to each call.
      - Recording who was dispatched or responded to the call.
  - The majority of law enforcement personnel regularly engage in preventive patrol:
    - Foot patrol
    - Squad car
    - Motorcycle
    - Segway personal transporter
    - Mounted (horse)

        - Bicycle
        - Watercraft (boat, jet ski)
        - Canine (K-9) assisted
        - Aircraft (plane, helicopter)
    - The majority of law enforcement activities are interactive in nature; law enforcement officers interface with members of the public as they perform their duties.
        - Law enforcement officers interact with two types of individuals:
            - Individuals who are victims or need assistance and welcome the presence of law enforcement
            - Individuals who are either suspects or perpetrators who do not want to interact with law enforcement officers
- Routine incident response
    - Routine incident responses are the second most common activity of law enforcement officers who are regularly involved in patrol.
    - Examples of routine incidents:
        - Traffic accidents
        - Double-parked cars
        - Vandalism/graffiti
    - Response time
        - Citizen satisfaction with law enforcement service is often linked to response time.
            - Response time is a measure of the time that it takes for law enforcement officers to respond to calls for service.
            - Response time is measured from the time a call is received by the law enforcement agency for service until the time an officer arrives on the scene to handle the call.
- Emergency response is probably the most important aspect of what police agencies do.
    - Often referred to as "critical incidents."
    - Examples of when emergency responses are used:
        - A crime in progress
        - A traffic accident with injuries
        - A natural disaster: hurricanes, tornadoes, floods, earthquakes
        - Incidents of terrorism
        - Officer needs assistance
        - Shots fired

- Criminal Investigation is the process of discovering, collecting, preparing, identifying, and presenting evidence to determine what happened and who is responsible when a crime has occurred.
  - Regardless of their rank or job responsibilities, any law enforcement officer can be involved in the initial stages of an investigation.
    - Typically, the first officer to arrive at the location of the call is responsible for two very specific activities:
      - Preserving evidence such as footprints, fingerprints, tire tracks, and other evidence related to the crime.
      - Conducting a preliminary investigation. A preliminary investigation refers to all of the activities undertaken by a police officer who responds to the scene of a crime, including determining whether a crime has occurred, securing the crime scene, and preserving evidence.
        - The preliminary investigation includes the following activities:
          - Meeting the needs of any injured individuals
          - Recording
            - Position of victims or injured individuals
            - Spontaneous statements given by victims, perpetrators, or witnesses
            - Unusual actions or activities of any of the victims, perpetrators, or witnesses
      - Providing superiors with an assessment of the crime scene and current status of the situation
      - Determining if a crime has been committed
      - Arresting or pursuing the suspected perpetrator or providing the information to headquarters so they can dispatch others to apprehend the offender
      - Determining the need for investigative specialists and arranging for their notification
      - Providing a report of all relevant activities
- Problem solving
  - Also referred to as "problem-oriented policing."
  - Designed to reduce chronic offending in the community.
  - SARA (scanning, analysis, response, assess) represents the methodology of problem-oriented policing.

- CAPRA (clients, acquired/analyzed, partnerships, respond, assess) is the problem-oriented policing methodology developed by the Royal Canadian Mounted Police.
    - CAPRA process
        - Law enforcement officials interact with community members who are most affected by crime issues.
        - Law enforcement officials collect and analyze data with the intent of understanding the causes of community problems.
        - By creating partnerships with the community, solutions are jointly developed.
        - Law enforcement officials create a workable plan to meet the jointly created solution.
        - Once implemented, the plan is periodically assessed to ensure success.

- Support services
    - Although the main focus of law enforcement is addressing the needs of the community, there are many support services operating in the background that are needed for law enforcement to operate.
    - Examples of support services:
        - Dispatch
        - Training
        - Human resources management
        - Property and evidence control
        - Record keeping
        - Equipment
        - Public relations
        - Recruitment
        - Research and development

For more on police roles and functions, visit Criminal Justice Interactive online > The Police: History, Structure, and Functions > Learning Modules > 5.4: Police Roles and Functions.

5.5 Police organization

5.5.1 Two basic organizational types associated with law enforcement agencies: line operations and staff operations.

5.5.2 Line operations in police organizations, field activities, or supervisory activities directly related to day-to-day police work.

- Authority flows from the top down.
- For those agencies that have line operations only, there are no support services such as media relations, training, or fiscal management divisions.

- All aspects of line operation law enforcement agencies are directly focused on providing field services.
- The majority of municipal police departments would qualify as small departments and therefore have line operations only.

5.5.3 Staff operations include police organizations and activities (like administration and training) that provide support for line operations.

- Line and staff agencies
  - ❖ Exist in law enforcement agencies that are of sufficient size to have internal support capabilities
  - ❖ In these agencies, line managers are largely unencumbered with duties such as:
    - ◆ Budgeting
    - ◆ Training
    - ◆ Scientific analysis of evidence
    - ◆ Legal advice
    - ◆ Shift assignments
    - ◆ Duty rosters
    - ◆ Personnel management
    - ◆ Research and development
  - ❖ Divisions are likely to exist between areas such as:
    - ◆ Enforcement
    - ◆ Investigation (field services)
    - ◆ Administrative services
      - ❒ Human resources management
      - ❒ Training and education
      - ❒ Materials supply
      - ❒ Finance management
      - ❒ Facilities management
  - ❖ Auxiliary and support services
    - ◆ Records
    - ◆ Property maintenance and control
    - ◆ Vehicle maintenance
    - ◆ Communication
    - ◆ Crime laboratory
    - ◆ Detention and jail services

5.5.4 **Chain of command** is the unbroken line of authority that extends through all levels of an organization, from the highest to the lowest.

CHAIN OF COMMAND
The unbroken line of authority that extends through all levels of an organization, from the highest to the lowest.

- The chain of command delineates who reports to whom.
- Law enforcement agencies typically utilize a quasi-military chain of command; most of the titles of ranks are similar to those used in the military: sergeant, lieutenant, captain, major.

- With unity of command, every individual has only one supervisor to whom he or she answers and from whom he or takes orders under normal circumstances.
- Span of control is the number of police personnel or the number of units supervised by a particular commander.

For more on police organization, visit Criminal Justice Interactive online > The Police: History, Structure, and Functions > Learning Modules > 5.5: Police Organization.

5.6 Policing styles

5.6.1 James Q. Wilson wrote *Varieties of Police Behavior: The Management of Law and Order in Eight Communities* (1968), and identified three styles of policing: watchman, legalistic, and service.

5.6.2 Three styles of policing

WATCHMAN STYLE
A style of policing marked by a concern for order maintenance. Watchman policing is characteristic of lower-class communities where police intervene informally into the lives of residents to keep the peace.

- **Watchman style**
  - This style of policing is characteristic of the political era of policing.
  - The focus of this style is "order maintenance."
  - Job is viewed as controlling illegal and disruptive behavior.
  - Informal intervention by law enforcement includes behaviors such as persuasion, threats, and "roughing up" a few folks periodically.
  - Style is used more frequently in lower-class neighborhoods as a method of keeping the peace.

LEGALISTIC STYLE
A style of policing marked by a strict concern with enforcing the precise letter of the law. Legalistic departments may take a hands-off approach to disruptive or problematic behavior that does not violate the criminal law.

- **Legalistic style**
  - This style of policing is characteristic of the reform era of police administration.
  - Committed to enforcing the "letter of the law" by making numerous arrests for all types of criminal behavior.
  - In terms of noncriminal behavior, law enforcement under this style takes a "hands-off" approach, also referred to as "laissez-faire policing."

SERVICE STYLE
A style of policing marked by a concern with helping rather than strict enforcement. Service-oriented police agencies are more likely to use community resources such as drug treatment programs to supplement traditional law enforcement activities than are other types of agencies.

- **Service style**
  - This style of policing is characteristic of the community era where problem solving is emphasized.
  - The goal of service reflects the need of the community.
  - Law enforcement is there to help members of the community.
  - Law enforcement works closely with other social service agencies to assist members of the community with their problems.

- Diversion from the formal justice system is used when possible.
  - Prosecutors will often agree not to prosecute if the defendant agrees to get help for their problem by participating in programs like family counseling or Alcoholics Anonymous.
  - Community citizens embrace such approaches because it tends to spare them the embarrassment of public airing of their problems.
- This style of policing tends to be found more frequently in wealthy neighborhoods.
- Law enforcement officers who work for departments that serve wealthy communities are well paid and highly educated.

For more on policing styles, visit Criminal Justice Interactive online > The Police: History, Structure, and Functions > Learning Modules > 5.6: Policing Styles.

CHAPTER SUMMARY

- Today's police structure has its origins as early as fifth-century England when the knights of King Arthur's courts enforced rights and suppressed wrongdoing. The development of the Magna Carta by King John resulted in separation of state and local government as well as provided for due process and trial by jury. The colonies in what is now the United States brought the police structures from their European homelands. The Crown appointed the officials (including constable and sheriff) who enforced the law; after the American Revolution, these positions were elected by popular vote. In the 1800s, many took the law into their own hands, especially in western United States. The 1900s saw the establishment of more organized police forces, primarily at the state and local levels.
- The modern policing eras include three distinct periods: political era (1840–1930), reform era (1930–1970), and community era (1970–present). The political era was characterized by close ties between law enforcement and public officials, with officers purchasing desirable beats. The reform era represented a move toward professionalism and an emphasis on solving crime and arresting offenders. During the community era, community policing developed with a focus on creating a partnership between police and the community.
- Today's law enforcement has four levels: federal, state, local, and private. Federal law enforcement agencies include the Department of Justice, the Department of Homeland Security, Department of Treasury, and Department of Interior. State police agencies exist in every state except Hawaii. There are two models of state agencies: centralized (whose duties include monitoring state highways and maintaining centralized records) and decentralized (states that maintain two agencies, typically highway patrol and state bureau of investigation). County and metropolitan agencies control local jurisdictions, and may include sheriffs and

city police forces. Private protective services are hired by businesses and organizations that need security-related services. They include such agencies as Wells Fargo, Burns International, and Allied Security.

- The mission of police includes enforcing the law, apprehending and arresting offenders, preventing crime, preserving peace, and providing service. These functions each require separate operational strategies. The police force also requires a wide range of support services, including dispatch, training, public relations, recruitment, and research and development.
- Police are organized by two organizational types: line operations and staff operations. Line operations involve field or supervisory activities related to day-to-day-work. Staff operations include police organizations and activities that provide support for line operations.
- Three types of policing styles have been identified. Watchman style policing, characteristic of the political era of policing, focuses on order maintenance and the control of illegal and disturbing behavior. The legalistic style, which reflects the reform era, is a style that is committed to enforcing the "letter of the law" and taking a hands-off approach to noncriminal behavior. Service style, which is characteristic of the community era, focuses on problem solving, helping members of the community, and diversion from formal justice system when possible.

ONLINE@CRIMINAL JUSTICE INTERACTIVE

Learning Modules

5.1 History and Professionalism of the Police
5.2 Modern American Policing Eras
5.3 Levels of Law Enforcement
5.4 Police Roles and Functions
5.5 Police Organization
5.6 Policing Styles

Myths and Issues Videos

Myth vs. Reality: CSI Solves Another Crime
Issue 1: Women and Minorities in Law Enforcement
Issue 2: Who Do the Police Represent?

Simulation Activity: Policing Styles

Homework and Review

In the News
Web Activity
Review Questions
Essay Questions
Flashcards

Chapter 6

The Police and the Constitution

CHAPTER OUTLINE

- 6.0 The police and the constitution
- 6.1 Introduction
  - 6.1.1 The legal environment for law enforcement
  - 6.1.2 Bill of Rights
  - 6.1.3 Constitutional amendments and the criminal justice process
  - 6.1.4 1960s
- 6.2 Individual rights
  - 6.2.1 Due process requirements
- 6.3 The Fourth Amendment
  - 6.3.1 The Fourth Amendment text
- 6.4 Search and arrest warrants
  - 6.4.1 Search and arrest warrants are derived from the Fourth Amendment.
- 6.5 Warrantless searches
  - 6.5.1 Laws and procedures
  - 6.5.2 Warrantless searches
  - 6.5.3 The exclusionary rule
  - 6.5.4 Fruit of the poisoned tree
  - 6.5.5 Plain-view doctrine
  - 6.5.6 Justification for warrantless searches
- 6.6 Arrest
  - 6.6.1 Definition of arrest
- 6.7 Interrogations and confessions
  - 6.7.1 Interrogations and confessions, and the Fifth Amendment
  - 6.7.2 Definition of interrogation
  - 6.7.3 Confessions
  - 6.7.4 Psychological manipulation
  - 6.7.5 Right to lawyer at interrogation
  - 6.7.6 Suspect rights: The *Miranda* decision
  - 6.7.7 Electronic eavesdropping
  - 6.7.8 USA PATRIOT Act of 2001
  - 6.7.9 Gathering electronic evidence
- 6.8 Remedies for violations of rights
  - 6.8.1 Violations of constitutional rights do occur.
  - 6.8.2 Four potential remedies: civil, criminal, nonjudicial, and exclusionary rule

LEARNING OBJECTIVES

After reviewing the online material and completing this chapter, you should be able to:

1. Discuss how the Fourth Amendment provides legal rights in regard to search and seizure.
2. Define the following requirements for a search or arrest warrant: neutral magistrate, probable cause, and particularity.
3. Explain under what circumstances warrantless searches may be justified.
4. Discuss how the legal protections of the Fourth Amendment may be applied to interrogations and confessions.
5. Discuss the civil, criminal, and nonjudicial remedies available to individuals whose Constitutional rights have been violated.
6. Define terms related to criminal procedure.

KEY TERMS

anticipatory warrant
arrest
Bill of Rights
Electronic Communication Privacy Act
electronic evidence
emergency search
exclusionary rule
Fifth Amendment
fleeting-targets exception
Fourth Amendment
fruit of the poisoned tree
good-faith exception
illegal search and seizure
illegally seized evidence
interrogation
landmark case
latent evidence
magistrate
Miranda rights
Miranda warnings
plain view
probable cause
psychological manipulation
reasonable suspicion
search incident to arrest
search warrant
stop and frisk
suspicionless searches
warrant
warrantless searches
writ of *certiorari*

BILL OF RIGHTS

The first ten amendments to the U.S. Constitution. Drafted by James Madison as a response to concerns that U.S. Constitution did not include a declaration of individual rights. U.S. Constitution identified what a government could do, but said nothing about what it could *not* do. Bill of Rights was ratified in 1791.

FOURTH AMENDMENT

Provides right for people to be secure in their persons, houses, papers, and effects against unreasonable searches and seizures.

PROBABLE CAUSE

A set of facts and circumstances that would induce a reasonably intelligent and prudent person to believe that a specified person has committed a specified crime. Also, reasonable grounds to make or believe an accusation. Probable cause refers to the necessary level of belief that would allow for police seizures (arrests) of individuals and full searches of dwellings, vehicles, and possessions.

FIFTH AMENDMENT

Provides for protections against double jeopardy and against a defendant being compelled in any criminal case to be a witness against himself, or for a defendant being deprived of life, liberty, or property, without due process of law.

***MIRANDA* WARNINGS**

The advisement of rights due criminal suspects by the police before questioning begins. *Miranda* warnings were first set forth by the U.S. Supreme Court in the 1966 case of *Miranda* v. *Arizona*.

EXCLUSIONARY RULE

The understanding, based on U.S. Supreme Court precedent, that incriminating information must be seized according to constitutional specifications of due process or it will not be allowed as evidence in a criminal trial.

6.0 The police and the constitution

6.1 Introduction

6.1.1 The legal environment for law enforcement has become far more complex since the court decisions of the 1960s.

6.1.2 Prior to 1960, the **Bill of Rights** was acknowledged, but was not taken as seriously as it is today.

6.1.3 Constitutional amendments and the criminal justice process

- **Fourth Amendment**
  - Right against unreasonable search and seizure
  - Right against arrest without **probable cause**
- **Fifth Amendment**
  - Right against self-incrimination
  - Right to trial by jury
  - Right to know the charges
  - Right to cross-examine witnesses
  - Right to a lawyer
  - Right to compel witnesses on one's behalf
  - Right to a speedy trial
- Eighth Amendment
  - Right to reasonable bail
  - Right against cruel and unusual punishments
- Fourteenth Amendment
  - Right to due process
  - Applicability of constitutional rights to all citizens, regardless of state law or procedure

6.1.4 1960s

- Warren Court
  - Earl Warren was chief justice of the U.S. Supreme Court from 1953 to 1969.
  - Court became known as the Warren Court.
  - Chief Justice Warren led the court to address individual rights, the U.S. Constitution, and law enforcement activity.
- Under the Warren Court, the case involving Ernesto Miranda (*Miranda* v. *Arizona*, 1966) provided us with the infamous ***Miranda* warnings**; *Mapp* v. *Ohio* (p. 135) addressed issues related to the **exclusionary rule**.
- Burger Court
  - Warren E. Burger was chief justice of the U.S. Supreme Court from 1969 to 1986.

- ❖ Court became known as the Burger Court.
- ❖ Under the leadership of Burger, the U.S. Supreme Court began a shift to a conservative approach, reflecting the changes in attitudes and thinking in the United States.
  - ◆ The decisions of the Burger court:
    - ❐ Limited the exclusionary rule
    - ❐ Expanded police powers
    - ❐ Reduced opportunities for state prisoners to bring appeals to federal courts
    - ❐ Supported use of:
      - Preventive detention
      - "No knock" police searches
      - The death penalty
      - Three-strikes laws

- ■ Roberts Court
  - ❖ John G. Roberts (b. 1955)
  - ❖ Named to the Court as chief justice by President George W. Bush in 2005, upon the death of Chief Justice William Rehnquist
  - ❖ Roberts had previously been a judge on the U.S. Court of Appeals for the District of Columbia Circuit.
  - ❖ It is expected that Roberts will follow in the conservative footsteps of Rehnquist in the way he leads the court.

6.2 Individual rights

6.2.1 Due process requirements

- ■ Most due process issues that are of concern to law enforcement pertain to three major areas that have been decided by landmark cases:
  - ❖ Evidence and investigation, often called search and seizure
  - ❖ Arrest
  - ❖ Interrogation
- ■ **Landmark cases** are cases in which there is a precedent-setting court decision that produces substantial change in both the understanding of the requirements of due process and in the practical day-to-day operations of the justice system. Landmark cases have caused dramatic changes in both the way law enforcement carries out its responsibilities and how citizens' rights are handled.
- ■ **Writ of *certiorari*** is a writ issued from an appellate court for the purpose of obtaining from a lower court the record of its proceedings in a particular case.

LANDMARK CASE

A precedent-setting court decision that produces substantial changes in both the understanding of the requirements of due process and in the practical day-to-day operations of the justice system.

WRIT OF *CERTIORARI*

A writ issued from an appellate court for the purpose of obtaining from a lower court the record of its proceedings in a particular case. In some states, this writ is the mechanism for discretionary review. A request for review is made by petitioning for a writ of *certiorari*, and the granting of review is indicated by the issuance of the writ.

- ❖ In some states, this writ is the mechanism for discretionary reviews.
- ❖ A request for review is made by petitioning for a writ of *certiorari*, and the granting of review is indicated by the issuance of the writ.

6.3 The Fourth Amendment

WARRANT

In criminal proceedings, a writ issued by a judicial officer directing a law enforcement officer to perform a specified act and affording the officer protection from damages if he or she performs it.

ILLEGALLY SEIZED EVIDENCE

Evidence seized without regard to the principles of due process as described by the Bill of Rights. Most illegally seized evidence is the result of police searches conducted without a proper warrant or of improperly conducted interrogations.

INTERROGATION

The information-gathering activity of questioning suspects.

6.3.1 "The right of the people to be secure in their persons, houses, papers, and effects, against unreasonable searches and seizures, shall not be violated, and no **Warrants** shall issue, but upon probable cause, supported by Oath or affirmation, and particularly describing the place to be searched, and the persons or things to be seized."

- ■ The Fourth Amendment addressed, in part, illegally seized evidence.
  - ❖ **illegally seized evidence** is evidence seized without regard to the principles of due process as described by the Bill of Rights.
    - ◆ Most illegally seized evidence is the result of police searches conducted without a proper warrant or of improperly conducted **interrogations**.
      - ❒ Warrant is a writ issued in criminal proceedings by a judicial officer directing a law enforcement officer to perform a specified act and affording the officer protection from damages if he or she performs it.

For more on The Fourth Amendment, visit Criminal Justice Interactive online > The Police and the Constitution > Learning Modules > 6.1 The Fourth Amendment.

6.4 Search and arrest warrants

6.4.1 Search and arrest warrants are derived from the Fourth Amendment.

- ■ Have very specific requirements
- ■ Provide an additional protective layer between the goals of officers and the privacy of the public
- ■ A warrant requires three elements:
  - ❖ Neutral **magistrate** is a judge who has no connection to the case.
    - ◆ Judge reviews the officer's affidavit and makes an evaluation of the circumstances to ensure that the invasion of a citizen's privacy is warranted.
    - ◆ Is designed to remove the emotion from the decision-making process.

MAGISTRATE

A judge for a low-level court that has very limited jurisdiction. Magistrate often is not required to have a law degree and handles minor criminal and civil matters.

- ❖ Probable cause
  - ◆ Search warrant requires that the officer completes a warrant application that describes how the indicated items are believed to be connected to the crime under investigation, why whose expectations exist, and where the items are expected to be found.
  - ◆ An arrest warrant requires that the officer completes the warrant application that provides sufficient evidence and logic to believe the identified individual is involved in the particular crime in question.
- ❖ Particularity refers to the fact that search and arrest warrants must provide very specific information about the arrest's or search's target.
  - ◆ In a search warrant, the specific site must be named by address and the specific rooms or spaces need to be indicated. Objects, papers, and other items related to the search must be named and itemized, along with their connection to the crime.
  - ◆ In an arrest warrant, the individual to be arrested must be identified clearly and completely, and the connection to the individual crime must be made.

For more on search and arrest warrants, visit Criminal Justice Interactive online > The Police and the Constitution > Learning Modules > 6.2 Search and Arrest Warrants.

6.5 **Warrantless searches**

WARRANTLESS SEARCHES

Search of a structure is permitted under certain circumstances with a warrant—when the suspect may escape, there is inherent danger, or when the possibility exists that evidence may be destroyed; *U.S.* v. *Reed*.

6.5.1 Laws and procedures guide any kind of formal search.

6.5.2 Warrantless searches are common and are contestable in court.

6.5.3 The exclusionary rule

- ■ *Weeks* v. *U.S.* (1914)
  - ❖ Freemont Weeks suspected of using mail to sell lottery tickets, a federal crime.
  - ❖ Weeks was arrested and federal agents searched Weeks' home.
  - ❖ Agents had no warrant for the search, but confiscated much incriminating evidence, including personal items such as clothes, papers, books, and even candy.
  - ❖ Prior to trial, Weeks' attorney asked for the return of Weeks' personal property, saying it had been illegally seized in violation of the Fourth Amendment.
  - ❖ Federal judge agreed and Weeks' personal property was returned.
  - ❖ Weeks was then convicted on remaining evidence.

- ❖ Weeks appealed and the case reached the Supreme Court.
- ❖ U.S. Supreme Court ruled.
  - ◆ If some of Weeks' personal property had been illegally seized, then the remainder of Weeks' property seized was also taken improperly; overturned the lower court's conviction.
  - ◆ Established what has become known as the exclusionary rule.
- ❖ The decision in *Weeks* was binding at the time only upon federal officers because it was federal agents who were involved in the illegal seizure.

FRUIT OF THE POISONED TREE

Doctrine based on the case *Silverthorne Lumber Co.* v. *U.S.* (1920), which posits that if the source of evidence is illegal then any evidence that results from the illegal search cannot be used since it is tainted.

SEARCH WARRANT

A document issued by a judicial officer that directs a law enforcement officer to conduct a search at a specific location for specified property or person relating to a crime, to seize the property or person if found, and to account for the results of the search to the issuing judicial officer.

ILLEGAL SEARCH AND SEIZURE

An act in violation of the Fourth Amendment of the U.S. Constitution, which reads, "The right of the people to be secure in their persons, houses, papers, and effects, against unreasonable searches and seizures, shall not be violated, and no warrants shall issue, but upon probably cause, supported by Oath or affirmation, and particularly described the place to be searched, and the person or things to be seized."

6.5.4 Fruit of the poisoned tree

- ■ *Silverthorne Lumber Co.* v. *U.S.* (1920)
  - ❖ In 1918, Frederick Silverthorne and his sons operated a lumber company and were accused of avoiding payment of federal taxes.
  - ❖ Federal agents asked them to turn over the company's books; they refused.
  - ❖ Shortly thereafter, without a warrant, federal agents seized the company's books.
  - ❖ Silverthorne's lawyers asked in court that the books be returned because no proper warrant had existed.
  - ❖ Prosecutor agreed and returned books, but not before making copies of some of the documents.
  - ❖ Silverthorne was convicted in federal court, and appealed to the U.S. Supreme Court.
  - ❖ U.S. Supreme court overturned conviction.
    - ◆ Evidence illegally seized cannot be used in a trial; therefore, neither can evidence that derives from an illegal seizure.
    - ◆ Principle today is called fruit of the poisoned tree doctrine.
      - ❒ Prohibits the admission of evidence obtained as a result of an illegal or initially tainted admission, confession, or search.
- ■ *U.S.* v. *Rabinowitz* (1950)
  - ❖ Federal agents arrested Rabinowitz on an arrest warrant for selling altered postage stamps in order to defraud other collectors.
  - ❖ Officers did not have a **search warrant**, but searched Rabinowitz's office, including his desk, file cabinet, and safe, and found 563 altered stamps.
  - ❖ U.S. Supreme Court denied Rabinowitz's appeal of **illegal search and seizure**.

    - Court ruled the Fourth Amendment provided against unreasonable searches, but that the search of Rabinowitz's one-room office was followed by a legal arrest.
    - Fourth Amendment protects people, not places.

- *Mapp* v. *Ohio* (1961)
  - Dolree Mapp was suspected of harboring a fugitive in her home who was wanted for a bombing.
  - Police went to her house on May 23, 1957, and were refused admission by Dolree Mapp.
  - Police forced their way in claiming to have a search warrant.
  - Dolree grabbed the supposed "warrant" and shoved it in her blouse.
  - Police retrieved the "warrant" from her blouse and searched the house.
  - Police found pornographic material, including photographs, in a trunk in the basement.
  - Bombing suspect was not found, but Mapp was arrested and convicted of possession of pornographic material.
  - At trial, no search warrant was produced. The Supreme Court of Ohio upheld conviction.
  - Mapp's conviction was overturned by U.S. Supreme Court because the evidence against Mapp was illegally obtained.
    - Fourteenth Amendment due process guarantee mandates that local police be held to same standard as federal agents.
    - Court specifically stated ". . . all evidence obtained by searches and seizures in violation of the Constitution is, by that same authority, inadmissible in a state court. Since the Fourth Amendment's right of privacy has been declared enforceable against the States through the Due Process clause of the Fourteenth Amendment, it is enforceable against them by the same sanction of exclusion as is used against the Federal Government . . .."

- *Chimel* v. *California* (1969)
  - Ted Chimel was convicted of the burglary of a coin shop based on evidence gathered at his home, which was the scene of arrest.
  - Officers had an arrest warrant, but not a search warrant.
  - Police searched the entire three-bedroom house, including the attic, small workshop, and garage.
  - Police realized search might be contested, but felt it was justified by claiming it was part of the arrest process, not to obtain evidence.

- Coins from the burglary were found in various places in Chimel's residence, including the garage.
- Chimel appealed the conviction.
- U.S. Supreme Court invalidated search of residence.
  - Search became invalid when it:
    - Went beyond the arrested person's area in "immediate control"
    - Was conducted for other than a valid reason
  - Officers may search:
    - Arrested person
    - Immediate control of arrested person
  - Officers can search to:
    - Protect the arresting officers.
    - Prevent evidence from being destroyed.
    - Keep defendant from escaping.

- *U.S.* v. *Leon* (1984)
  - Alberto Leon was placed under surveillance for drug trafficking based on a tip from a confidential informant.
  - Burbank police applied for a search warrant based on surveillance information that they observed.
  - Police searched Leon's three homes and found drugs. Leon was convicted of drug trafficking.
  - Federal court overruled state court's decision based on lack of original probable cause for issuing of warrant.
    - Upon a demonstration of probable cause, magistrates will issue warrants authorizing law enforcement officers to make arrests and conduct searches.
  - State appealed to U.S. Supreme Court.
  - U.S. Supreme Court reversed lower federal court ruling.
    - When law enforcement officers have acted in objective good faith or their transgressions have been minor, the evidence they have collected should not be inadmissible if later it is found the warrant is invalid.
    - Called "good-faith exception to the exclusionary rule."
      - **Good-faith exception** is an exception to the exclusionary rule and states that law enforcement officers who conduct a search, or who seize evidence, on the basis of good faith (when they believe they are operating according to the dictates of the law) and who later discover that a mistake was made (perhaps in the format of the application of the search warrant) may still use the seized evidence in court.

GOOD-FAITH EXCEPTION

An exception to the exclusionary rule. Law officers who conduct a search or who seize evidence on the basis of good faith (that is, when they believe they are operating according to the dictates of the law) and who later discover that a mistake was made (perhaps in the format of the application of the search warrant) may still provide evidence to be used in court.

- *Massachusetts* v. *Sheppard* (1984)
  - Officers executed a search warrant that failed to describe accurately the property to be seized.
  - The police were aware of the error but had been assured by the magistrate that the warrant was valid.
  - Sheppard was convicted, and then he appealed.
  - Massachusetts Supreme Court overturned lower-court ruling.
  - State appealed to U.S. Supreme Court, which reinstated the ruling of the court of original jurisdiction.
  - U.S. Supreme Court reiterated the good-faith exception.
- *Illinois* v. *Krull* (1987)
  - U.S. Supreme Court held that the good-faith exception applied to a warrantless search supported by state law even where the state statute was later found to violate Fourth Amendment rights.
- *Maryland* v. *Garrison* (1987)
  - Officers obtained a warrant to search an apartment believing it was the only apartment on the third floor.
  - When searching, they discovered there was another apartment on the floor and searched it, although it was not part of the original warrant.
  - Evidence the officers found was admitted into court.
  - U.S. Supreme Court upheld admissibility of evidence.
    - Supported the use of evidence obtained with a search warrant that was inaccurate in its specifics.
    - Evidence acquired in search is admissible based on the reasonable mistake of the officers.
- *Illinois* v. *Rodriguez* (1990)
  - Gail Fischer complained to police that she had been assaulted in a specific Chicago apartment.
  - Fischer led police to the apartment that she indicated she shared with the defendant; Fischer produced a key that she used to open the door.
  - Police, upon being admitted by Fischer, found Rodriguez asleep on the couch with drug paraphernalia and cocaine spread around him.
  - Police arrested Rodriquez for assault and possession of the controlled substance, and Rodriguez was convicted.
  - Rodriquez appealed based on fact that Fischer had not lived in the apartment for over a month and therefore did not have legal control over apartment.
  - U.S. Supreme Court rejected Rodriquez's appeal.

- No Fourth Amendment violation if police reasonably believed at the time of their entry that Fischer possessed authority to consent.

PLAIN VIEW

A legal term describing the ready visibility of objects that might be seized as evidence during a search by police in the absence of a search warrant specifying the seizure of those objects. To lawfully seize evidence in plain view, officers must have a legal right to be in the viewing area and must have cause to believe that the evidence is somehow associated with criminal activity.

6.5.5 **Plain-view** doctrine is a legal term describing the ready visibility of objects that might be seized as evidence during a search by police in the absence of a search warrant specifying the seizure of those objects.

- *Harris* v. *U.S.* (1968)
  - Police officer, inventorying an impounded vehicle, finds evidence of a robbery and Harris is convicted.
  - Harris appealed conviction based on illegal search.
  - U.S. Supreme Court rejected appeal.
    - Objects falling in plain view of an officer who has a right to be in the position to have that view are subject to seizure and may be introduced as evidence.
- Common plain-view situations:
  - Emergencies, such as crimes in progress
  - Fires
  - Accidents
- Plain-view doctrine applies only to sightings by the police under legal circumstances; that is, places where the police have a legitimate right to be, and typically, only if the sighting was coincidental.
- *U.S.* v. *Irizarry* (1982)
  - Agents arrested men in a hotel room in Isla Verde, Puerto Rico, on a valid arrest warrant.
  - Some drugs, which were in plain view, were seized in the room.
  - An agent, looking through the window of the room before the arrest, had seen a gun in the room.
  - When arrest was made, police searched the suspects and their immediate surroundings, seizing some drugs that were in plain view, but no gun was found.
  - Upon further search, the police noticed a ceiling tile in the bathroom had been moved.
  - Searching the ceiling of the bathroom, the police found guns and a substantial amount of cocaine.
  - U.S. Supreme Court overturned the admissibility of the guns and additional drugs.
    - The items of evidence found above the ceiling were not plainly visible to the agents standing in the room.
- *Arizona* v. *Hicks* (1987)
  - Officers responded to a shooting in an apartment.
  - A bullet fired in a second-floor apartment went through the floor, injuring a man in the apartment below.

- ❖ Police entered the apartment of James Hicks; the apartment was in considerable disarray.
- ❖ As police looked for who may have fired the shot, they discovered and confiscated a number of guns and a stocking mask that might be used in a robbery.
- ❖ In one corner the police noticed two stereo systems; one officer suspected they may have be stolen.
- ❖ The serial number of one component of the stereo system was visible from where it rested.
- ❖ The officer moved the other pieces of the stereo equipment to write down the other serial numbers.
- ❖ The serial number matched reportedly stolen equipment.
- ❖ Hicks was arrested and charged with armed robbery based on seized stereo equipment and was convicted.
- ❖ Hicks appealed, and U.S. Supreme Court upheld Hicks's appeal.
  - ◆ The officer's behavior became illegal when he moved the stereo equipment to record a serial number.
  - ◆ Persons have a "reasonable expectation to privacy," which means that officers lacking a search warrant, even when invited into a residence, must act more like guests than inquisitors.

■ *Horton* v. *California* (1990)

- ❖ A warrant was issued authorizing search of the home of Terry Brice Horton for stolen jewelry.
- ❖ The affidavit completed by the officer who requested the warrant alluded to an Uzi submachine gun and stun gun, weapons supposedly used in the jewelry robbery.
- ❖ The two guns were not listed in the warrant.
- ❖ When searching the home, the jewelry was not found, but a number of weapons were seized.
- ❖ Horton was convicted of robbery in part because of the introduction of the seized weapons as evidence.
- ❖ Horton appealed based on the fact that the police suspected Horton had the guns, and therefore should have listed them in the warrant.
- ❖ U.S. Supreme Court rejected Horton's appeal.
  - ◆ "Even though inadvertence is a characteristic of most legitimate plain-view seizures, it is not a necessary condition."
  - ◆ "Inadvertence" is no longer considered a condition necessary to ensure the legitimacy of a seizure, which results when evidence other than that listed in a search warrant is discovered.

EMERGENCY SEARCH

A search conducted by the police without a warrant, which is justified on the basis of some immediate and overriding need, such as public safety, the likely escape of a dangerous suspect, or the removal or destruction of evidence.

REASONABLE SUSPICION

The level of suspicion that would justify an officer in making further inquiry or in conducting further investigation. Reasonable suspicion may permit stopping a person for questioning or for a simple pat-down search. Also, a belief, based on a consideration of the facts at hand and on reasonable inferences drawn from those facts, that would induce an ordinarily prudent and cautious person under the same circumstances to conclude that criminal activity is taking place or that criminal activity has recently occurred. Reasonable suspicion is a general and reasonable belief that a crime is in progress or has occurred, whereas probable cause is a reasonable belief that a particular person has committed a specific crime. See also probable cause.

6.5.6 Justification for warrantless searches

- **Emergency searches** are property area searches conducted by the police without a warrant, which is justified on the basis of some immediate and overriding need such as public safety, the likely escape of a dangerous suspect, or the removal or destruction of evidence.
- Three threats that provide justification for emergency warrantless searches:
  - Clear dangers to life
  - Clear dangers of escape
  - Clear dangers of the removal or destruction of evidence
- *Warden* v. *Hayden* (1967)
  - Report that a robber had fled into building
  - Police searched residence without warrant.
  - Supreme Court approved of the search without a warrant.
    - "The Fourth Amendment does not require police officers to delay in the course of an investigation if to do so would gravely endanger their lives of the lives of others."
- *Maryland* v. *Buie* (1990)
  - U.S. Supreme Court extended the authority of police to search locations in a house where a potentially dangerous person could hide while an arrest warrant is being served.
  - Intention was to protect investigators from potential danger, and can even apply when officers lack a warrant, probable cause, or even **reasonable suspicion**.
- *Wilson* v. *Arkansas* (1995)
  - Court ruled that police officers generally must knock and announce their identity before entering a dwelling or other premises, even when armed with a search warrant.
  - Court added that the Fourth Amendment requires that searches be reasonable and "should not be read to mandate a rigid rule of announcement that ignores countervailing law enforcement interests."
    - Officers need *not* announce themselves when:
      - Suspects may be in the process of destroying evidence.
      - Officers are pursuing a recently escaped arrestee.
      - Officers' lives may be endangered by such an announcement.
  - This case has been called the "drug-law exception" to the knock and announce requirement.

- Wilson was a drug dealer who was apprehended by police who entered her unlocked house while she was flushing marijuana down a toilet.

- *Richards* v. *Wisconsin* (1997)
  - Supreme Court clarified its position on "no knock" exceptions.
  - Individual courts have a duty in each case to "determine whether the facts and circumstances of the particular entry justified dispensing with the requirement."
  - "A 'no-knock' entry is justified when the police have a reasonable suspicion that knocking and announcing their presence, under the particular circumstances would be dangerous or futile, or it would inhibit the effective investigation of the crime."
  - "This standard strikes the appropriate balance between the legitimate law enforcement concerns at issue in the execution of search warrants and the individual privacy interests affected by no-knock entries."
- *Illinois* v. *McArthur* (2001)
  - Tera McArthur called police officers to her trailer to keep the peace while she removed her belongings from the residence.
  - After emerging with her possessions, Tera McArthur spoke to a police officer who was on the scene, suggesting that officers should check the trailer because her husband had hidden marijuana in the trailer.
  - The officer requested permission from her husband to search the trailer, and he refused.
  - Another officer was sent to get the search warrant and the suspect, who had exited the trailer, was informed that he would have to remain on the porch and could not reenter the trailer unless a police officer accompanied him.
  - When the warrant arrived, the police searched the trailer and uncovered a small amount of marijuana and a marijuana pipe.
  - The suspect was convicted of drug charges, and appealed.
  - U.S. Supreme Court ruled that police officers with probable cause to believe that a home contains contraband or evidence of criminal activity may reasonably prevent a suspect found outside the home from reentering it while they apply for a search warrant.
- **Anticipatory warrants** are search warrants issued on the basis of probable cause to believe that evidence of a crime, while not presently at the place described, will likely be there when the warrant is executed.

ANTICIPATORY WARRANT

Search warrants issued on the basis of probable cause to believe that evidence of a crime, while not presently at the place described, will likely be there when the warrant is executed.

- *U.S.* v. *Grubbs* (2006)
  - An anticipatory search warrant had been issued for Grubbs's house based on a federal officer's affidavit stating the warrant could not be executed until a parcel containing a videotape of child pornography was received at the residence.
  - After the package was delivered, police executed the anticipatory search warrant and seized the tape and arrested Grubbs.
  - U.S. Supreme Court upheld the search and arrest.

For more on *Miranda* warnings, visit Criminal Justice Interactive online > The Police and the Constitution > Myths and Issues Videos > Myth vs. Reality: The *Miranda* Warnings Have to be Read Immediately Upon Arrest.

ARREST

The act of taking an adult or juvenile into physical custody by authority of law for the purpose of charging the person with a criminal offense, a delinquent act, or a status offense, terminating with the recording of a specific offense. Technically, an arrest occurs whenever a law enforcement officer curtails a person's freedom to leave.

6.6 Arrest

6.6.1 Arrest is the act of taking an adult or juvenile into physical custody by authority of law for the purpose of charging the person with a criminal offense, a delinquent act, or a status offense, terminating with the recording of a specific offense.

- Technically, an arrest occurs whenever a law enforcement officer curtails a person's freedom to leave.
- *U.S.* v. *Mendenhall* (1980)
  - Justice Potter Stewart of the U.S. Supreme Court set forth the "free to leave" test:
    - "A person has been 'seized' within the meaning of the Fourth Amendment only if in view of all the circumstances surrounding the incident, a reasonable person would have believed that he was not free to leave."
- *Payton* v. *New York* (1980)
  - U.S. Supreme Court ruled that unless the suspect gives consent or an emergency exists, an arrest warrant is necessary if an arrest requires entry into a suspect's private residence.

SEARCH INCIDENT TO ARREST

A warrantless search of an arrested individual conducted to ensure the safety of the arresting officer. Because individuals placed under arrest may be in possession of weapons, courts have recognized the need of arresting officers to protect themselves by conducting an immediate search of arrestees without obtaining a warrant.

- **Search incident to arrest**
  - *Terry* v. *Ohio* (1968)
    - Seasoned officer conducted a pat-down search of two men whom he suspected were casing a store, about to commit a robbery.
    - Arresting officer was a 39-year veteran of police work who testified the men "did not look right."
    - When the officer approached the two men, he suspected they might be armed.
    - Fearing for his life, the officer quickly spun the men around, put them up against a wall, patted down their clothing, and found a gun on Terry.

- Terry was convicted of carrying a concealed weapon.
- Terry appealed, arguing that the suspicious officer had no probable cause to arrest him, and therefore, no cause to search him.
- U.S. Supreme Court rejected appeal.
  - "We cannot blind ourselves to the need for law enforcement officers to protect themselves and other prospective victims of violence in situations where they may lack probable cause for an arrest."
  - Balanced interests of law enforcement and citizens' rights
  - Brought **stop and frisk** within the formal law of search and seizure, but relaxed the probable cause standard.
  - Upheld officers' right to stop and frisk individuals acting in a suspicious manner.
  - Stop and frisks require reasonable suspicion; facts lead officers to suspect that crimes may be occurring and that the suspects may be armed.

STOP AND FRISK

The detaining of a person by a law enforcement officer for the purpose of investigation, accompanied by a superficial examination by the officer of the person's body surface or clothing to discover weapons, contraband, or other objects relating to criminal activity.

- *Terry* case set standard for brief stop and frisk based upon reasonable suspicion.
  - Reasonable suspicion is the level of suspicion that would justify an officer in making further inquiry or in conducting further investigation.
  - Reasonable suspicion may permit stopping a person for questioning or for a simple pat-down search.
  - Reasonable suspicion is a general and reasonable belief that a crime is in progress or has occurred, whereas probable cause is a reasonable belief that a particular person has committed a specific crime.

- *U.S.* v. *Robinson* (1973)
  - Robinson was stopped for a traffic violation and arrested for driving with an invalid driver's license.
  - Upon search of Robinson after arrest, heroin was found.
  - Court held that the police may automatically search person subjected to a custodial arrest, regardless of the nature or severity of the crime (arrested for driving with invalid driver's license).
- *U.S.* v. *Sokolow* (1989)
  - Andrew Sokolow appeared suspicious to police because while traveling under an alias from Honolulu, Hawaii, he had paid $2,100 in $20 bills for two airplane tickets after spending a surprisingly small amount of time in Honolulu.

- Sokolow appeared nervous and checked no luggage.
- A warrantless airport investigation by DEA agents uncovered more than a kilogram of cocaine in the defendant's belongings.
- Sokolow was arrested and convicted of drug violations.
- Sokolow appealed conviction based on lack of probable cause.
- U.S. Supreme Court ruled that the legitimacy of such a stop must be evaluated according to a "totality of circumstances" criterion in which all aspects of the defendant's behavior, taken in concert, may provide the basis for a legitimate stop based upon reasonable suspicion, and therefore rejected Sokolow's appeal.

❖ *Minnesota* v. *Dickerson* (1993)

- Timothy Dickerson, who was observed leaving a building known for cocaine trafficking, was stopped by Minneapolis police officers after they noticed him acting suspiciously.
- Officers decided to investigate further and ordered Dickerson to submit to a pat-down search.
- The search revealed no weapons, but the officer conducting the search testified that he felt a small lump in Dickerson's jacket pocket that he believed to be a lump of crack cocaine.
- The officer reached into Dickerson's pocket and retrieved a small bag of cocaine.
- Dickerson was arrested, tried, and convicted of possession of a controlled substance.
- Dickerson appealed, claiming the pat-down search had been illegal.
- U.S. Supreme Court overturned the conviction.
  - "If an officer lawfully pats down a suspect's outer clothing and feels an object whose contour or mass makes it immediately apparent, there has been no invasion of the suspect's privacy beyond that already authorized by the officer's search for weapons."
  - However, "the officer never thought that the lump was a weapon, but did not immediately recognize it as cocaine."
    - The lump was determined to be cocaine only after the officer squeezed, slid, and otherwise manipulated the pocket's contents.
    - The Court took position that it went far beyond *Terry*.

- "While Terry entitled the officer to place his hands on the respondent's jacket and to feel the lump in the pocket, his continued exploration of the pocket after he concluded that it contained no weapon was unrelated to the sole justification for search under *Terry*," and was therefore was illegal.

- *Illinois* v. *Wardlow* (2000)
  - William Wardlow fled upon seeing a caravan of police cars converge in a Chicago neighborhood.
  - The police chased and caught Wardlow and conducted a pat-down search of his clothing for weapons.
  - The police discovered a handgun during the pat down and arrested Wardlow on weapons charges.
  - Wardlow was convicted and appealed, arguing that the police acted illegally in stopping him since they did not have reasonable suspicion that he had committed an offense.
  - The State Supreme Court of Illinois agreed with Wardlow and overturned the conviction.
  - The State of Illinois appealed to the U.S. Supreme Court.
  - The U.S. Supreme Court overturned the State Supreme Court saying that the officers' actions did not violate the Fourth Amendment.
  - This case involved a brief encounter between a citizen and a police officer on a public street and is governed by *Terry* under which an officer who has a reasonable suspicion that criminal activity is afoot may conduct a brief, investigatory stop.
  - An individual's presence in a high-crime area, by itself, is not enough to support a reasonable, particularized suspicion of criminal activity, but a location's characteristics are relevant in determining whether the circumstances are sufficiently suspicious to warrant further investigation.
  - In Wardlow's case, it was Wardlow's unprovoked flight that aroused the officers suspicions, and headlong flight is the consummate act of evasion.

- Use of force to arrest
  - Fleeing felon doctrine; historically, the fleeing felon doctrine dictated the use of force.
    - Deadly force can be used to apprehend any fleeing felony suspect; this was law in most states until the 1960s.
    - Reevaluation of doctrine in the 1960s; most states modified doctrine to only apply to "forcible felonies."
    - In the 1970s, most states limited doctrine to violent felonies.

        - *Tennessee* v. *Garner* (1985)
            - U.S. Supreme Court ruled the fleeing felon doctrine unconstitutional.
            - Other means of force
                - Some forms of force have generated considerable debate, including choke holds, mace, and high-speed chases.
- Vehicle searches
    - *Carroll* v. *U.S.* (1925)
        - First significant U.S. Supreme Court case involving an automobile
        - U.S. Supreme Court ruled a warrantless search of an automobile or other vehicle is valid if based on a reasonable belief that contraband is present.
    - *Preston* v. *U.S.* (1964)
        - Preston was arrested for vagrancy and his car was impounded, towed, and later searched.
        - Two guns were found in the glove compartment and additional incriminating evidence was found in the trunk during a search of the vehicle.
        - Preston was convicted on weapons possession and other charges.
        - Appealed based on illegal search
        - U.S. Supreme Court held for Preston.
            - The warrantless search of Preston's vehicle occurred while auto was in secure custody and therefore was illegal.
            - Court believed police could have obtained a warrant to conduct search of car.
    - *South Dakota* v. *Opperman* (1976)
        - U.S. Supreme Court held that a warrantless search of an impounded vehicle was legitimate for purposes of inventorying and safekeeping personal possessions of the car's owner.
        - The fact that marijuana turned up during inventorying is useable evidence because inventorying was legal.
    - *U.S.* v. *Ross* (1982)
        - Supreme Court found that officers had not exceeded their authority in opening a bag in the defendant's trunk, which was found to contain heroin.
        - Search was held to be justifiable on the basis of information developed from a search of the passenger compartment.
        - Court said "if probable cause justifies the search of a lawfully stopped vehicle, it justifies the search of

every part of the vehicle and its contents that may conceal the object of the search."

- *Colorado* v. *Bertine* (1987)
  - U.S. Supreme Court reinforced the idea that officers may open closed containers found in a vehicle while conducting a routine search for inventorying purposes.
- *Florida* v. *Wells* (1990)
  - U.S. Supreme Court agreed with lower court's suppression of marijuana discovered in a locked suitcase in the trunk of a defendant's impounded vehicle.
  - Court held that standardized criteria for authorizing the search of a vehicle for inventorying purposes were necessary before such a discovery could be legitimate.
  - Standardized criteria might take the form of department policies, written general orders, or established routines.
- *Ornelas* v. *U. S.* (1996)
  - Two experienced police officers stopped a car driven by two men who were known or suspected drug traffickers.
  - One of the officers noticed a loose panel above an armrest in the vehicle's back seat and then searched the car.
  - A package of cocaine was found beneath the panel, leading to the conviction of the defendants for drug charges.
  - Defendants appealed, arguing that there was no probable cause to search the car at the time of the stop.
  - The U.S. Supreme Court said "the model, age, and source of the car, and the fact that two men traveling together checked into a motel at 4 o'clock in the morning without reservations, formed a drug courier profile and . . . this profile together with the reports gave rise to a reasonable suspicion of drug trafficking activity."
  - In the court's view, reasonable suspicion became probable cause when the officer found the loose panel.
  - Probable cause permits a warrantless search of a vehicle under what has been called the **fleeting-targets** exception to the exclusionary rule.
    - Fleeting-targets exception is an exception to the exclusionary rule that permits law enforcement officers to search a motor vehicle based upon probable cause but without a warrant.
    - The fleeting-targets exception is predicated upon the fact that vehicles can quickly leave the jurisdiction of a law enforcement agency.

FLEETING-TARGETS EXCEPTION

An exception to the exclusionary rule that permits law enforcement officers to search a motor vehicle based on probable cause and without a warrant. The fleeting targets exception is predicated on the fact that vehicles can quickly leave the jurisdiction of a law enforcement agency.

- *Florida* v. *Jimeno* (1991)
    - Arresting officers stopped a motorist who gave them permission to search his car and a bag of cocaine was found on the floor of the car.
    - The defendant was convicted of possession. Jimeno appealed, saying that while he gave permission to search the car, it did not include permission to search the bag and other items in the car.
    - U.S. Supreme Court held that "a criminal suspect's Fourth Amendment right to be free from unreasonable searches is not violated when, after he gives police permission to search his car they open a closed container found within the car that might reasonably hold the object of the search."
- *Whren* v. *U.S.* (1996)
    - Officers may stop a vehicle being driven suspiciously and then search it once probable cause has developed, even if their primary assignment centers on duties other than traffic enforcement, or if a reasonable officer would not have stopped the motorist absent some additional law enforcement objective.
- *Knowles* v. *Iowa* (1998)
    - An Iowa police officer stopped Patrick Knowles for speeding and issued a citation, but did not make a custodial arrest; officer then conducted a full search of Knowles's car without consent and without probable cause.
    - Marijuana was found and Knowles was arrested and convicted.
    - Supreme Court overturned the conviction finding that while concern for officer safety during a routine traffic stop may justify the minimal intrusion of ordering a driver and passengers out of the car, it does not justify what it called the considerably greater intrusion attending a full field-type search.

- Roadblocks and motor vehicle checkpoints
    - *Michigan Department of State Police* v. *Sitz* (1990)
        - Case involved the legality of highway sobriety checkpoints including those at which nonsuspicious drivers are subjected to scrutiny.
        - U.S. Supreme Court ruled that such stops are reasonable insofar as they are essential to the welfare of the community as a whole.
    - *U.S.* v. *Martinea-Fuerte* (1976)
        - U.S. Supreme Court upheld brief, suspicionless seizures at a fixed international checkpoint designed to intercept illegal aliens.

- The Court noted that "to require that such stops always be based on reasonable suspicion would be impractical because the flow of traffic tends to be too heavy to allow the particularized study of a given car necessary to identify it as a possible carrier of illegal aliens."
  - Such a requirement also would largely eliminate any deterrent to the conduct of well-disguised smuggling operations even though smugglers are known to use these highways regularly.

- *Indianapolis* v. *Edmond* (2000)
  - In 1998, the Indianapolis Police Department established a narcotics checkpoint program.
  - Under the program, stopped drivers were told that they were at a drug checkpoint and officers examined each driver's license and registration while visually assessing the driver for signs of impairment.
  - Drug-sniffing dogs were then walked around the vehicle's exterior.
  - On average, motorists were stopped for three minutes.
  - In ruling the program illegal, the U.S. Supreme Court held that the Fourth Amendment prohibits even a brief seizure of a motorist under a program whose primary purpose is ultimately indistinguishable from the general interests of crime control.
  - The Court said that those programs whose purpose was to verify driver's licenses and vehicle registrations would continue to be permissible.

- Watercraft and motor homes
  - *U.S.* v. *Villamonte-Marquez* (1983)
    - A sailboat, occupied by Villamonte-Marquez that was anchored, was searched by a U.S. Customs officer after one of the crew members appeared unresponsive to being hailed.
    - The U.S. Customs officer thought he smelled marijuana after boarding the sailboat.
    - The officer saw burlap bales through an open hatch, which he suspected might be contraband; a search of the sailboat proved the officer correct.
    - Villamonte-Marquez was convicted on drug charges.
    - The conviction was appealed and the State Supreme Court overturned the conviction.
    - Upon appeal, the U.S. Supreme Court upheld the original conviction reasoning that a vehicle on the water can easily leave the jurisdiction of enforcement officials, just as a car or truck can; therefore, the warrantless search is legal.

- *California* v. *Carney* (1985)
  - U.S. Supreme Court extended police authority to conduct warrantless searches of vehicles to include motor homes.
  - Court reasoned that a vehicle's appointments and size do not alter its basic function of providing transportation.
- *U.S.* v. *Hill* (1988)
  - DEA agents developed evidence that led them to believe that methamphetamine was being manufactured aboard a houseboat traversing Lake Texoma in Oklahoma.
  - Because storm warnings had been issued for the area, agents decided to board and search the boat prior to obtaining a warrant.
  - During the search an operating amphetamine lab was discovered, and the boat was seized.
  - In appeal, the defendants argued that the houseboat search had been illegal because agents lacked a warrant to search their home.
  - The appellate court, however, in rejecting the claims of the defendants, ruled that a houseboat, because it is readily mobile, may be searched without a warrant when probable cause exists to believe that a crime has been or is being committed.

SUSPICIONLESS SEARCHES

A search conducted by law enforcement personnel without a warrant and without suspicion. Suspicionless searches are permissible only if based on an overriding concern for public safety.

- **Suspicionless searches**
  - *National Treasury Employees Union* v. *Von Raab* (1989)
    - U.S. Supreme Court in a 5–4 vote upheld a program by the U.S. Custom Service that required mandatory drug testing for all workers seeking promotions or job transfers involving drug interdiction and the carrying of firearms.
    - Court said "we think the government's need to conduct the suspicionless searches required by the Custom's program outweighs the privacy interest of the employees engaged directly in drug interdiction and of those who otherwise are required to carry firearms."
    - Compelling interest is a legal concept that provides a basis for suspicionless searches when public safety is at issue (urinalysis tests of train engineers are an example).
    - Suspicionless searches are searches conducted by law enforcement personnel without a warrant and without suspicion; they are permissible only if based upon an overriding concern for public safety.

- *Skinner* v. *Railway Labor Executives' Association* (1989)
  - This case was decided on the same day as the *National Treasury Employees Union* v. *Von Raab*.
  - Case involved evidence of drugs in a 1987 train wreck outside of Baltimore, Maryland, in which 16 people were killed and hundreds were injured.
  - U.S. Supreme Court voted 7–2 to permit the mandatory testing of railway crews for the presence of drugs or alcohol following serious train accidents.
- *Florida* v. *Bostick* (1991)
  - Broward County Sheriff's Department had routine practice of boarding buses at scheduled stops and asking passengers permission to search their belongings.
  - Terrance Bostick gave his permission to have his luggage searched.
  - Police found cocaine and Bostick eventually pleaded guilty to charges of drug trafficking.
  - Bostick was convicted of drug trafficking.
  - Florida Appeals Court overturned lower-court conviction.
  - State appealed to U.S. Supreme Court on basis that Bostick was constrained by the fact that the bus he wanted to ride was getting ready to leave, and not by the police that had boarded the bus.
  - U.S. Supreme Court upheld appeal of police.
    - Warrantless, suspicionless "sweeps" of buses, trains, planes, and city streets were permissible so long as officers:
      - Ask individual passengers for permission before searching their possessions
      - Do not coerce passengers to consent to a search
      - Do not convey the message that citizen compliance with the search request is mandatory
- *Bond* v. *U.S.* (2000)
  - A border patrol officer boarded a bus in Texas to check the immigration status of its passengers.
  - As the officer walked off the bus, he squeezed the soft luggage that passengers had placed in the overhead storage space.
  - As he squeezed the luggage, he noticed one that contained a "brick-like" object.
  - After a passenger admitted to owning the bag and consented to its search, the officer opened the bag and found a "brick" of amphetamine.

- The owner of the bag was indicted on federal drug charges and convicted.
- On appeal to the U.S. Supreme Court, the Court held that the border patrol officer's physical manipulation of the suspect's carry-on bag went beyond mere viewing and violated the Fourth Amendment's protection against unreasonable searches.

❖ *U.S.* v. *Drayton* (2002)

- Drayton, the driver of a bus, allowed three police officers to board the bus as part of a routine drug and weapons interdiction.
- One officer knelt on the driver's seat, facing the rear of the bus, while another officer stayed in the rear facing the front.
- The third officer, named Lang, worked his way from back to front.
- Lang approached passengers Christopher Drayton and Clifton Brown, Jr., who were seated together.
- Lang identified himself as a police officer and declared he was looking for drugs and weapons and asked if Drayton and Brown had any bags, to which they pointed overhead.
- Lang asked if he could search the bag, and Brown agreed, and the search revealed no contraband in the bag.
- Lang then asked Brown if he could pat him down, to which he agreed.
- The pat down of Brown revealed drug-like packets on both his thighs that resulted in his arrest.
- Lang asked Drayton if he could pat him down, to which he agreed, and the result was the same, resulting in his arrest.
- A further search of the two men revealed taped cocaine between their legs.
- Both were charged with federal drug crimes and convicted, although their attorney moved to suppress the evidence, arguing their consent to pat-down searches was invalid.
- On appeal, the Eleventh Circuit Court reversed the lower-court decision based on the belief that bus passengers do not feel free to disregard officers' requests to search in the absence of positive indication that consent may be refused.

❖ *U.S.* v. *Flores-Montano* (2004)

- Customs officials disassembled the gas tank of a car belonging to a man entering the country from Mexico and found it contained 37 kilograms of marijuana.

    - Officers admitted that their actions were not motivated by any particular belief that the search would reveal contraband. The Court held that Congress has always granted plenty of authority to conduct routine searches and seizures at the border without probable cause or a warrant.

- High-technology searches
  - *People* v. *Deutsch* (1996), California Appellate Court decision
    - A police officer drove by a house at 1:30 in the morning and did a thermal scan of the defendant's home.
    - A thermal imaging device identifies and can record differential temperatures associated with various parts of a dwelling without requiring officers to enter the structure.
    - The heat search of Dorian Deutsch's house revealed unusually warm areas of rooms that might be associated with the cultivation of drug-bearing plants such as marijuana.
    - Because no entry of the house was anticipated during the search, the officer acted without a search warrant.
    - Two hundred marijuana plants, which were being grown hydroponically under high-wattage lights in two walled-off portions of the home were seized.
    - Dorian Deutsch was convicted on drug charges.
    - On appeal, the California Appellate Court ruled that the scan was an illegal search because "society accepts a reasonable expectation of privacy" surrounding "nondisclosed activities within the home."
  - *Kyllo* v. *U.S.*(2001)
    - Officers conducted a warrantless search using thermal imaging.
    - As a result of the thermal scan, the officers applied for a search warrant of Kyllo's home.
    - More than one hundred marijuana plants were uncovered growing under bright lights.
    - Kyllo was convicted of drug manufacturing.
    - U.S. Supreme Court, on appeal, ruled that "where, as here, the Government uses a device that is not in general public use, to explore details of a private home, that would previously have been unknowable without physical intrusion, the surveillance is a Fourth Amendment search and is presumptively unreasonable without a warrant."

6.7 Interrogations and confessions

6.7.1 Interrogation and confessions, and the Fifth Amendment

- The Fifth Amendment protects against self-incrimination. There are four primary factors that affect self-incrimination.
  - Compulsion: If a person is forced to or intimidated into answering questions, information received may not be admissible.
  - Noncriminal application: Fifth Amendment protects only in criminal situations, including trials, grand jury, and future legal actions. If a compelled statement is not later used in a criminal proceeding, the defendant cannot litigate for violations of rights.
  - Witness: The protections of the Fifth Amendment apply only to those things a person may communicate; that is, testimony. It does not cover the production of physical evidence.
  - Witness against self: The Fifth Amendment protects only the person who makes the incriminating comments. It cannot be used to protect privacy or to protect another who has committed a crime.

6.7.2 Interrogation is the information-gathering activity of police officers that involves the direct questioning of suspects.

- U.S. Supreme Court has defined interrogation as any behaviors by the police "that the police should know are reasonably likely to elicit an incriminating response from the suspect." (*South Dakota* v. *Neville*, 1983)
  - Examples of behaviors that are considered to be interrogation:
    - Staged lineups
    - Reverse lineups
    - Positing guilt
    - Minimizing the moral seriousness of crime
    - Casting blame on the victim or society
  - Supreme Court has held that police words or actions normally attendant to arrest and custody do not constitute interrogation unless they involve pointed or directed questions.
  - Once police officers make inquiries intended to elicit information about the crime in question, interrogation has begun.

6.7.3 Confessions

- Physical abuse: *Brown* v. *Mississippi* (1936)
  - Robbery of a white store owner in Mississippi in 1934
  - During robbery, victim was killed.
  - Posse was formed and a local black man was taken into custody.

- ❖ Suspect was dragged from home, a rope put around his neck, and hoisted into a tree.
- ❖ Posse was hoping to get a confession out of man, but failed.
- ❖ Posse then arrested three other suspects and took them to local jail where they were whipped with belts and buckles until they confessed, perhaps falsely.
- ❖ Confessions were used at their trial, and all three defendants were convicted of murder.
- ❖ Mississippi Supreme Court upheld the convictions.
- ❖ U.S. Supreme Court reviewed convictions of the three men and overturned them.
- ❖ Court said it was difficult to imagine techniques more "revolting" to the sense of justice than those used in this case.

- Inherent coercion are the tactics used by police interviewers that fall short of physical abuse, but that nonetheless pressure suspects to divulge information.
- *Ashcraft* v. *Tennessee* (1944)
  - ❖ Ashcraft had been charged with murder of his wife Zelma.
  - ❖ Arrested Saturday night and interrogated by a team of skilled interrogators until Monday morning when he confessed.
  - ❖ During interrogation, he had bright light shined in his face, but was not physically mistreated.
  - ❖ Ashcraft was convicted of murder.
  - ❖ Supreme Court reversed the conviction.
  - ❖ Supreme Court made it plain that the Fifth Amendment guarantee against self-incrimination excludes any form of official coercion or pressure during interrogation.
- *Chambers* v. *Florida* (1940)
  - ❖ Four black men were arrested without warrants as suspects in a robbery and murder of an aged white man.
  - ❖ After several days of questioning in a hostile atmosphere, the men confessed to the murder.
  - ❖ The confessions were used as the primary evidence against the men at their trial and all three men were convicted.
  - ❖ Upon appeal, the U.S. Supreme Court overturned the convictions.
  - ❖ Court held that "the very circumstances surrounding their confinement and their questioning without any formal charges having been brought, were such as to fill petitioners with terror and frightful misgivings."

6.7.4 Psychological manipulation

- Psychological manipulation is manipulative action by police interviewers designed to pressure suspects to divulge information that are based upon subtle forms of intimidation and control.

PSYCHOLOGICAL MANIPULATION

Manipulation actions by police interviewers that are designed to pressure suspects to divulge information and that are based on subtle forms of intimidation and control.

- *Leyra* v. *Denno* (1954)
  - ❖ Detectives used a psychiatrist to question Leyra, who was charged with using a hammer to kill his parents.
  - ❖ Leyra had been led to believe that the psychiatrist was a medical doctor who had been sent to help him with his sinus problem.
  - ❖ The psychiatrist used subtle suggestions, telling Leyra that he would feel better if he confessed.
  - ❖ Leyra confessed and was found guilty.
  - ❖ Leyra appealed.
  - ❖ U.S. Supreme Court ruled that Leyra had been effectively and improperly duped by the police.
    - ◆ "Instead of giving petitioner the medical advice and treatment he expected, the psychiatrist by subtle and suggestive questions simply continued the police effort of the past days and nights to induce petitioner to admit his guilt."
- *Arizona* v. *Fulminante* (1991)
  - ❖ Oreste Fulminante was an inmate in a federal prison when he was approached secretly by a fellow inmate, who was an FBI informant.
  - ❖ The informant told Fulminante that other inmates were plotting to kill him because of a rumor that he killed a child.
  - ❖ Informant offered to protect Fulminante if he was told the details of the crime.
  - ❖ Fulminante described his role in the murder of his 11-year-old stepdaughter.
  - ❖ Fulminante was arrested, tried, and convicted for the murder.
  - ❖ Fulminante appealed his conviction based on the fact that his confession had been coerced because of the threat of violence.
  - ❖ U.S. Supreme Court agreed the confession had been coerced and ordered a new trial at which the confession could not be admitted into evidence.
  - ❖ At the same time the Court found that the admission of a coerced confession should be considered a harmless "trial error," which need not necessarily result in reversal of a conviction if other evidence still proves guilt.

6.7.5 Right to lawyer at interrogation

- *Escobedo* v. *Illinois* (1964)
  - ❖ Escobedo was arrested without a warrant for the murder of his brother-in-law. Escobedo made no statement during interrogation and was released.
  - ❖ A few weeks later, someone identified Escobedo as the murderer.

- Escobedo was again interrogated, and told they "had him cold."
- Escobedo asked to see his lawyer and was told he could not since an interrogation was underway.
- Escobedo's lawyer arrived at the jail and was told he can see his client after the questioning is complete.
- Meanwhile, Escobedo was told his lawyer did not want to see him.
- Escobedo confessed and was convicted, and his conviction was overturned.
- U.S. Supreme Court ruled Escobedo is entitled to counsel at police interrogations to protect the rights of the defendant and should be provided when the defendant desires.

- *Edwards* v. *Arizona* (1981)
    - Established a "bright-line rule" (that is, specified a criterion that cannot be violated) for investigators to use in interpreting a suspect's right to counsel.
    - Supreme Court reiterated its *Miranda* concern that once a suspect who is in custody and is being questioned has requested the assistance of counsel, all questioning must cease until an attorney is present.
- *Arizona* v. *Roberson* (1988)
    - U.S. Supreme Court ruled that the police may not avoid the suspect's request for a lawyer by beginning a new line of questioning, even if it is about an unrelated offense.
- *Minnick* v. *Mississippi* (1990)
    - U.S. Supreme Court held that interrogation may not resume after the suspect has had an opportunity to consult his or her lawyer if the lawyer is no longer present.
- *Davis* v. *U.S.* (1994)
    - A man being interrogated in the death of a sailor waives his ***Miranda* rights**; later, the man indicates that maybe he should talk to a lawyer.
    - Investigators asked the suspect clarifying questions, and he responded "No, I don't want a lawyer."
    - Upon conviction, he appealed, claiming that interrogation should have ceased when he mentioned a lawyer.
    - U.S. Supreme Court upheld conviction saying that "it will often be good police practice for the interviewing officers to clarify whether or not [the suspect] actually wants a lawyer."

***MIRANDA* RIGHTS**

The set of rights that a person accused or suspected of having committed a specific offense has during interrogation and of which he or she must by informed prior to questioning, as stated by the U.S. Supreme Court in deciding *Miranda* v. Arizona and other related cases.

6.7.6 Suspect rights: The *Miranda* decision

- *Miranda* v. *Arizona* (1966)
    - Ernesto Miranda was arrested in Phoenix, Arizona, and accused of kidnapping and rape.

- At police station Miranda was identified by the victim.
- After two hours of interrogation, Miranda signed a confession.
- Miranda was convicted of charges, and appealed to the U.S. Supreme Court.
- Court ruled that "the entire aura and atmosphere of police interrogation without the notification of rights and an offer of assistance of counsel tends to subjugate the individual to the will of his examiner."
- Court went on to say defendant "must be warned prior to any questioning that he has the right to remain silent, that anything he says can be used against him in a court of law, that he has the right to the presence of an attorney, and that if he cannot afford an attorney, one will be appointed for him prior to any questioning if he so desires."
- Unless and until such warnings and waiver are demonstrated by prosecution at trial, no evidence obtained as a result of interrogation can be used against him.

- *U.S.* v. *Dickerson* (2000)
  - Fourth Circuit U.S. Court of Appeals upheld an almost-forgotten law Congress had passed in 1968 with the intention of overturning *Miranda*.
  - Law says that "a confession . . . shall be admissible in evidence if it is voluntarily given." (Section 3501 of Chapter 223, Part II of Title 18 of the U.S. Code)
  - To determine voluntariness, the trial judge is to:
    - Take into consideration all the circumstances of the giving of the confession, including:
      - Time elapsing between arrest and arraignment
      - Whether the defendant knew the nature of the offense with which he was charged, or of which he was suspected of at the time of making the confession
      - Whether or not defendant was advised or knew that he was not required to make any statement and that any such statement could be used against him
      - Whether or not defendant had been advised prior to questioning of his right to assistance of counsel
      - Whether or not defendant was without the assistance of counsel when questioned and when giving his confession
  - *Miranda* was upheld by Court by a vote of 7–2.
  - U.S. Supreme Court held that *Miranda* is a constitutional rule (that is, a fundamental right inherent in the U.S. Constitution) that cannot be dismissed by an act of Congress.

- Waiver of *Miranda* rights by suspects
  - Knowing waiver can only be made if a suspect has been advised of his or her rights and was in a condition to understand the advisement
    - Example: suspect only speaks Spanish, buts right are read in English
  - Intelligent waiver
    - Requires defendant be able to understand the consequences of not invoking *Miranda* rights.
  - *Moran* v. *Burbine* (1986)
    - Supreme Court defined intelligent and knowing waiver as one "made with a full awareness both of the nature of the right being abandoned and the consequences of the decision to abandon it."
  - *Colorado* v. *Spring* (1987)
    - Supreme Court held that an intelligent and knowing waiver can be made even though a suspect has not been informed of all the alleged offenses about which he or she is about to be questioned.
  - U.S. District Court Judge William Byrne, Jr. approved the settlement of a class-action lawsuit against the Immigration and Naturalization Service in 1992.
    - *Miranda* rights were effectively extended to illegal immigrants living in the United States.
    - The printing of 1.5 million notices in several languages to be given to arrestees
    - Arrested illegal aliens must be told they may:
      - Talk to a lawyer.
      - Make a phone call.
      - Request a list of available legal services.
      - Seek a hearing before an immigration judge.
      - Possibly obtain release on bond.
      - Contact a diplomatic officer representing their country.
- Inevitable-discovery exception to *Miranda*
  - *Brewer* v. *Williams* (1977)
    - Robert Anthony Williams was convicted in 1969 of murdering a 10-year-old girl, Pamela Powers, around Christmas.
    - Williams had been advised of his rights.
    - Williams and detectives were riding in a car while the detectives were searching for the body of Pamela Powers.

- One detective made what has become to be known as the "Christian burial speech." Detective told Williams that with it being almost Christmas, it would be the "Christian thing to do" to see to it that Pamela has a decent burial rather than to have to lie in some field.
- Williams led detectives to Pamela's body and was convicted of murder.
- Supreme Court overturned conviction saying that the detective's remarks were "a deliberate eliciting of incriminating evidence from an accused in the absence of his lawyer."

- Public-safety exceptions to *Miranda*
  - *New York* v. *Quarles* (1984)
    - Victim reports to police her rape and that the suspect fled with a gun into a nearby A&P Supermarket.
    - Two police officers entered the store and apprehended the suspect.
    - One officer noticed that Quarles was wearing an empty shoulder holster.
    - Fearing that a child might find the discarded gun the officer quickly asked "Where is the gun?"
    - Quarles told the officer where the gun was.
    - Quarles was convicted of rape.
    - Quarles appealed, claiming the gun should have been suppressed as evidence since the officer had not read him his *Miranda* rights.
    - U.S. Supreme Court disagreed, stating that considerations of public safety were overriding and negated the need for advisement prior to limited questioning, which focused on the need to prevent further harm.
  - *Colorado* v. *Connelly* (1986)
    - Man approaches Denver police officer and says he wants to confess to the murder of a young girl.
    - Officer informs man of his *Miranda* rights, which the man waives, and continues talking; detective arrives and again man is informed of rights, which he again waives.
    - Man is taken to jail where he begins to hear "voices."
    - Later, man claims it was the voices that made him confess.
    - At trial, defense attorney moves to have confession suppressed because it was involuntary due to the defendant's mental condition.

- Man convicted and then appealed.
- Supreme Court rejects appeal, indicating the confession was not coerced by government officials and that "self coercion," be it through the agency or a guilty conscience or faulty thought process, does not bar prosecution based on information revealed willingly by the defendant.

❖ *Illinois* v. *Perkins* (1990)

- U.S. Supreme Court expanded its position to say that under appropriate circumstances, even the active questioning of a suspect by an undercover officer posing as a fellow inmate does not require *Miranda* warnings.
- Court found that, lacking other forms of coercion, the fact that the suspect was not aware of the questioner's identity as a law enforcement officer ensured that his statements were freely given.

■ *Miranda* and the meaning of interrogation

❖ *Rock* v. *Zimmerman* (1982)

- Suspect burned his own house and shot and killed a neighbor.
- When fire department arrives to put out fire, suspect shoots and kills fire chief.
- Police corner suspect in a field; suspect shouts at the police "How many people did I kill? How many people are dead?"
- Suspect convicted of the murders.
- Appeals conviction based on inadmissibility of statements because his rights had not been read to him.
- Supreme Court rejects appeal. *Miranda* warnings need only be given to individuals in custody.

❖ *South Dakota* v. *Neville* (1983)

- A man was suspected of driving while intoxicated, and was not read his rights.
- He was told he would stand to lose his driver's license if he did not submit to a Breathalyzer test.
- Man responded "I'm too drunk, I won't pass the test." His answer became evidence of his condition and was introduced at his trial.
- U.S. Supreme Court upheld conviction saying that the officers were found to have acted properly.

❖ *Arizona* v. *Mauro* (1987)

- A man willingly conversed with his wife in the presence of a police tape recorder, even after invoking his rights to keep silent.

- U.S. Supreme Court said the man had effectively abandoned his right to keep silent when he allowed his conversation to be taped.

- *Chavez* v. *Martinez* (2003)
  - Oliverio Martinez was blinded and paralyzed in a police shooting after he grabbed an officer's weapon during an altercation.
  - Chavez, a police officer, persisted in questioning Martinez while he was awaiting treatment despite his pleas to stop and the fact that he was obviously in great pain.
  - Court held that police questioning in the absence of *Miranda* warnings, even questioning that is overbearing to the point of coercion does not violate constitutional protections against self-incrimination, as long as no incriminating statements are introduced at trial.

- Nontestimonial evidence
  - Right to privacy
    - *Winston* v. *Lee* (1985)
      - Rudolph Lee, Jr., was found a few blocks from a store robbery with a gunshot wound in the chest.
      - Owner of store had reported that the robber had been hit when gunfire had been exchanged.
      - At hospital, store owner identifies Lee as the robber.
      - Prosecution sought to have Lee submit to surgery to remove bullet so it would have physical evidence linking Lee to the crime; Lee refused surgery.
      - Supreme Court upheld Lee's decision because such a magnitude of intrusion into Lee's body was unacceptable under right to privacy guaranteed by the Fourth Amendment.
  - Body cavity searches
    - *U.S.* v. *Montoya de Hernandez* (1985)
      - A woman known to be a "balloon swallower" arrived in the United States from Columbia, South America.
      - She was detained by customs officials and given a "pat-down" search by a female agent; agent reported that the woman's abdomen was firm and suggested an X-ray be taken.
      - Suspect refused the X-ray.
      - Suspect was given choice of submitting to further tests or being put on the next plane back to Columbia; the next plane was in 16 hours.

- ❒ Suspect was placed in room where she refused all food and drink.
- ❒ Court order was obtained to perform X-ray; X-ray revealed numerous balloons.
- ❒ Suspect was detained for four more days during which time she passed numerous balloons of cocaine-filled plastic condoms.
- ❒ Court upheld confinement as reasonably based as it was upon the supportable suspicion that she was "body-packing" cocaine; any discomfort she experienced resulted solely from the method she chose to smuggle illicit drugs.

6.7.7 Electronic eavesdropping

- *Olmstead* v. *U.S.* (1928)
  - ❖ Bootleggers used their personal telephones to discuss and transact business.
  - ❖ Federal agents tapped the lines and based their investigation and arrests upon conversations they overheard.
  - ❖ Defendants were convicted, and then they appealed.
  - ❖ Supreme Court ruled that telephone lines were not an extension of defendant's homes and therefore were not protected by the constitutional guarantee of security under the Fourth Amendment.
  - ❖ Subsequent federal statutes have modified the significance of *Olmstead*.
- *On Lee* v. *U.S.* (1952)
  - ❖ Recording devices carried on the body of an undercover agent or an informant were ruled to produce admissible evidence.
- *Berger* v. *New York* (1967)
  - ❖ Permitted wiretaps and bugs in instances where state law provided for use of such devices, and where officers obtained a warrant based upon probable cause.
- *Katz* v. *U.S.* (1967)
  - ❖ Federal agents had monitored a number of Katz's phone calls from a public phone using a device separate from the phone lines attached to the glass of the phone booth.
  - ❖ Supreme Court ruled that what a person makes effort to keep private, even in public places, requires a judicial decision in the form of a warrant issued upon probable cause, to unveil.
- *Lee* v. *Florida* (1968)
  - ❖ The Court applied the Federal Communications Act to record telephone conversations that may be the subject of police investigation, and held that evidence obtained without a warrant could not be used in state proceedings if it resulted from a wiretap.

    - ❖ The only person who has the authority to permit eavesdropping is the sender of the message.
- *U.S.* v. *Karo* (1984)
    - ❖ DEA agents had arrested James Karo for cocaine importation.
    - ❖ Officers had placed a radio transmitter inside a 50-gallon drum of ether purchased by Karo for use in processing cocaine.
    - ❖ The transmitter was placed inside the drum with the permission of the seller of the ether, but without a search warrant.
    - ❖ The shipment was followed to Karo's house, and Karo was arrested and charged with trafficking cocaine.
    - ❖ Karo was convicted, and appealed.
    - ❖ Supreme Court ruled that Karo's right of privacy had been violated inside his premises and that the evidence was tainted.
- Minimization requirements
    - ❖ *U.S.* v. *Scott* (1978)
        - ◆ Case established minimization requirement.
        - ◆ Minimization
            - ❐ Officers must make every reasonable effort to monitor only those conversations, through the use of phone taps, body bugs, and the like, which are specifically related to criminal activity under investigation.
        - ◆ As soon as it becomes obvious that a conversation is innocent, the monitoring personnel are required to cease their invasion of privacy.

ELECTRONIC COMMUNICATION PRIVACY ACT

A law passed by Congress in 1986 establishing due process requirements that law enforcement officers must meet in order to legally intercept wire communications.

- **Electronic Communications Privacy Act of 1986**
    - ❖ Act dealt with three specific areas of communications:
        - ◆ Wiretaps and bugs
        - ◆ Pen registers that record the numbers dialed from a phone
        - ◆ Tracing devices that determine the number from which a call emanates
    - ❖ Act also addressed procedures to be followed by officers in obtaining records relating to communications services, and it established requirements for gaining access to stored electronic communications and records of those communications.
- Telecommunications Act of 1996
    - ❖ This act makes it a federal offense for anyone engaged in interstate or international communications to knowingly use a telecommunications device to "create, solicit, or initiate the transmission of any comment, request, suggestion, proposal,

image, or other communication which is obscene, lewd, lascivious, filthy, or indecent with intent to annoy, abuse, threaten, or harass another person."

- ❖ A section of the law, known as the Communications Decency Act, criminalized the transmission to minors of "patently offensive" obscene materials over the Internet or other telecommunications services via computer.

6.7.8 USA PATRIOT Act of 2001

- Made it easier for police investigators to intercept many forms of electronic communication
- USA PATRIOT Act added felony violations of the Computer Fraud and Abuse Act to Section 2516(1) of Title 18 of the U.S. Code.
  - ❖ This is the portion of the federal law that lists specific types of crimes for which investigators may obtain a wiretap order for wire communications.
- The USA PATRIOT Act, which was renewed in 2005, made permanent 14 of the original 16 sections from the 2001 Act.
- Prior to passage of the USA PATRIOT Act, federal law allowed investigators to use an administrative subpoena to compel Internet service providers to provide a limited class of information such as a customer's name, address, length of service, and means of payment.
  - ❖ Administrative subpoena is a subpoena authorized by federal or state statute or by a federal or state grand jury or trial court.
  - ❖ USA PATRIOT Act amended portions of the federal code to update and expand the types of records that law enforcement authorities may obtain with a subpoena.
    - ◆ Records of session times and durations, as well as any temporarily assigned network address, may now be obtained.

6.7.9 Gathering **electronic evidence** is information and data of investigative value that are stored in or transmitted by an electronic device.

ELECTRONIC EVIDENCE
Information and data of investigative value that are stored or transmitted by an electronic device.

- Types of electronic devices:
  - ❖ Computers
  - ❖ Removable disks
  - ❖ CDs
  - ❖ DVDs
  - ❖ Magnetic tape
  - ❖ Flash memory chips
  - ❖ Cellular telephones
  - ❖ Personal digital assistants

- Electronic evidence has special characteristics:
  - It is latent.
  - It can transcend national and state borders quickly and easily.
  - It is fragile and can easily be altered, damaged, compromised, or destroyed by improper examination.
  - It may be time sensitive.
- Electronic evidence is "**latent evidence**" because it is not readily visible to the human eye under normal conditions.

LATENT EVIDENCE

Evidence of relevance to a criminal investigation that is not readily seen by the unaided eye.

For more on interrogations and confessions, visit Criminal Justice Interactive online > The Police and the Constitution > Learning Modules > 6.4 Interrogations and Confessions.

For more on the USA PATRIOT Act and how it affects freedom, visit Criminal Justice Interactive online > The Police and the Constitution > Myths and Issues Videos > Issue 1: The Loss of Some Personal Liberty as a Result of the USA PATRIOT Act May Actually Protect Liberty.

6.8 Remedies for violations of rights

6.8.1 In spite of the fact that there are laws that protect the constitutional rights of citizens, violations of those rights do occur.

6.8.2 There are four potential remedies to rights violations: civil, criminal, and nonjudicial remedies, as well as the exclusionary rule.

- Civil remedies
  - Legal liability
    - State officers can be liable if they violate constitutional rights while acting in their official capacity (also called under "color of law").
  - Immunity
    - Federal law enforcement officers can be sued for constitutional rights violations as well.
    - Some officials have absolute or limited immunity and are protected from most legal actions based on their behaviors even if they do violate constitutional rights.
  - Defenses to liability
    - Situations in which federal or state officers may not be sued. Immunity conditions protect officers.
- Criminal remedies
  - Several federal laws apply to criminal malfeasance by state and federal officers. Most require proof of a specific intent on the part of the officer and a noteworthy violation for conviction.

  - ❖ Penalties may include imprisonment or fines, according to the specific law, the offense, and the circumstances.
  - ❖ State criminal laws apply equally to officers of the law as well as to ordinary citizens.
  - ❖ Many states also have laws that specifically apply to misconduct by law enforcement officers. Limited immunity is applied to certain acts, such as deadly force committed in the line of duty to protect others.
- Nonjudicial remedies
  - ❖ Internal review: Internal affairs officers investigate complaints from citizens and colleagues about specific officers or situations; personnel or legal action may result from these probes.
  - ❖ Civilian review occurs when citizens investigate complaints from other citizens about specific officers or situations. These external review systems may have more public credibility but are less effective in identifying and disciplining officer excesses.
  - ❖ Mediation occurs when a neutral party or ombudsman investigates complaints and assists the involved parties in coming to a mutually acceptable resolution. The mediation process avoids litigation, but provides an avenue for the resolution of conflict and complaints.
- Exclusionary rule
  - ❖ Not initially part of the Bill of Rights. U.S. Courts began to recognize the importance of regulating how evidence was collected. Still controversial, many circumstances exist where thc exclusionary rule does not apply.
  - ❖ Evidence obtained in violate of the exclusionary rule may still be admissible if the link between the illegal search and the evidence is sufficiently weak, if the illegal evidence is supported by an independent source, or if the evidence would have been found regardless of violations. Examples: good faith, fleeting targets

For more on remedies for violations of rights, visit Criminal Justice Interactive online > The Police and the Constitution > Learning Modules > 6.5 Remedies for Violations of Rights.

For more on exceptions to the exclusionary rule, visit Criminal Justice Interactive online > The Police and the Constitution > Myths and Issues Videos > Issue 2: Exceptions to the Exclusionary Rule.

CHAPTER SUMMARY

- The Fourth Amendment addresses the issue of legal rights, especially in regard to search and seizure. The Fourth Amendment sets the standards by which evidence can be seized or buildings searched according to principles of due process set forth in the Bill of Rights. Most illegal searches are conducted without a proper warrant and illegal interrogations are conducted through the use of improper procedures.
- Search or arrest warrants have three requirements: a neutral magistrate, probable cause, and particularity. A neutral magistrate is a judge who has no connection to the case and is able to make a neutral evaluation. Probable cause requires that a search warrant or arrest warrant is completed properly by the officer. Particularity requires that search and arrest warrants provide very specific information about the arrest's or search's target.
- There is a body of case law that supports the validity of searches. Warrantless searches may be justified in certain cases. Emergency searches are property area searches conducted by the police without a warrant. Anticipatory warrants are search warrants issued on the basis of probable cause to believe that evidence of a crime, while not presently at the place described, will likely be there when the warrant is executed.
- The Fifth Amendment protects individuals against self-incrimination, as well as giving them other rights. This is especially relevant in terms of interrogations and confessions. There are four primary factors that affect self-incrimination. Compulsion refers to the fact that when a person is forced or intimidated into answering questions, the information gleaned from that conversation may not be admissible. Noncriminal application contends that the Fifth Amendment protects only in criminal situations. If a compelled statement is not later used in a criminal proceeding, the defendant cannot litigate for violations of rights. Witness posits that the protections of the Fifth Amendment apply to testimony. It does not cover the production of physical evidence. Witness against self indicates that the Fifth Amendment protects only the person who makes the incriminating comments; it does not protect privacy or protect others who have committed a crime.
- In spite of the fact that there are laws and judicial decisions that protect citizens' rights, violations do occur. When violations occur, there are several remedies. Civil remedies include legal liability (state officials can be liable if they violate constitutional rights), immunity (federal law enforcements can also be sued for constitutional rights violations, unless they have absolute or limited immunity), and defenses to liability (there are situations in which federal or state officers may not be sued). In addition, criminal remedies exist. Several federal laws apply to criminal malfeasance by state and federal officers. Penalties may include imprisonment or fines. State criminal laws apply equally to officers and ordinary citizens. Many states have specific laws that apply to misconduct by law enforcement officers. Nonjudicial remedies include internal reviews within internal affairs, civilian reviews, when citizens investigate, and mediation, when a neutral party investigates complaints. The exclusionary rule sets specific requirements regarding the links between illegal search and evidence.

ONLINE@CRIMINAL JUSTICE INTERACTIVE

Learning Modules

6.1 The Fourth Amendment
6.2 Search and Arrest Warrants
6.3 Warrantless Searches
6.4 Interrogations and Confessions
6.5 Remedies for Violations of Rights

Myths and Issues Videos

Myth vs. Reality: The *Miranda* Warnings Have to be Read Immediately upon Arrest
Issue 1: The Loss of Some Personal Liberty as a Result of the USA PATRIOT Act May Actually Protect Liberty
Issue 2: Exceptions to the Exclusionary Rule

Simulation Activity: Warrants and Searches

Homework and Review

In the News
Web Activity
Review Questions
Essay Questions
Flashcards

Chapter 7

The Police: Issues and Challenges

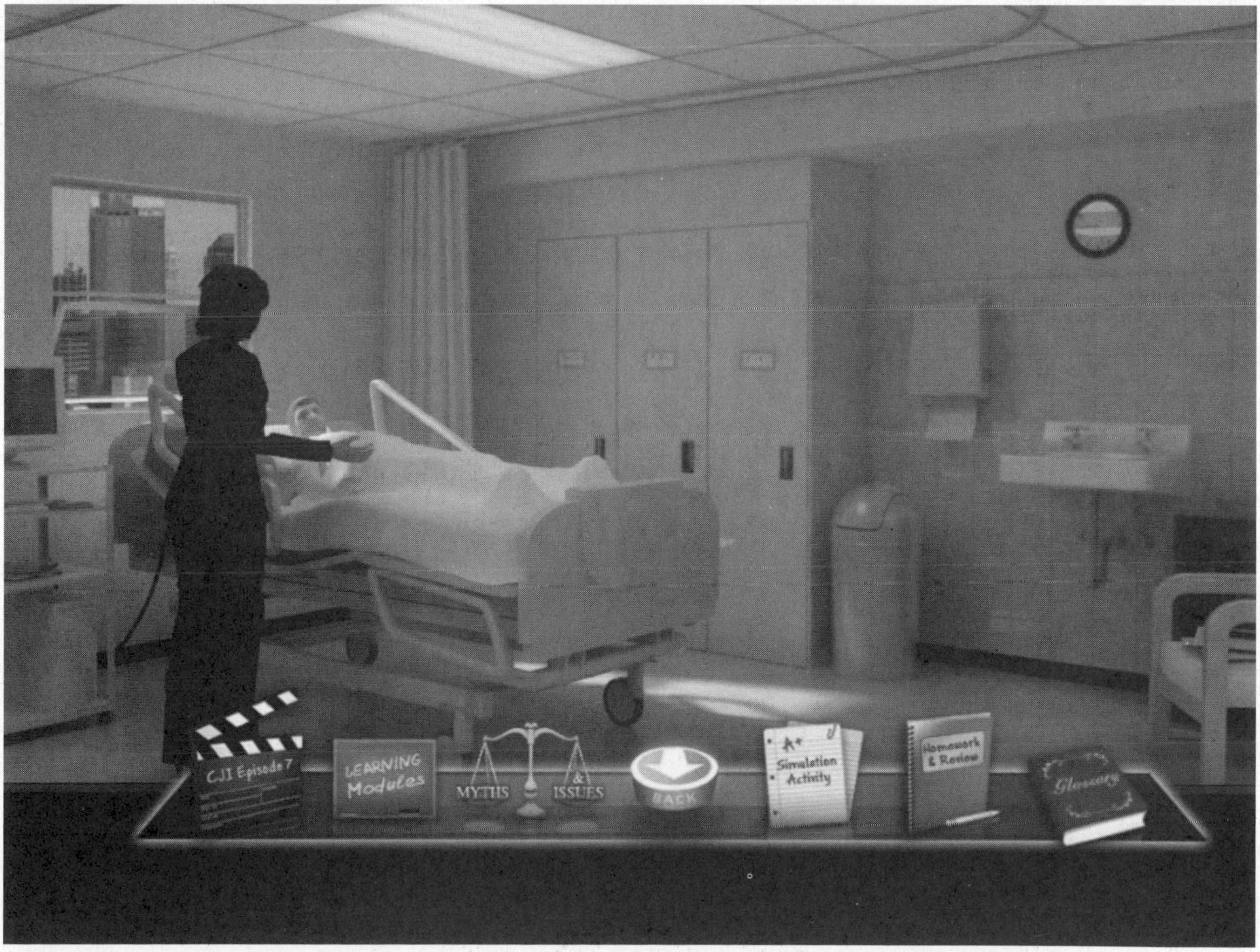

CHAPTER OUTLINE

LEARNING OBJECTIVES

After reviewing the online material and reading this chapter, you should be able to:

1. Discuss the law enforcement code of ethics and various types/levels of corruption.
2. Explain the use of force continuum in the context of the proper use of force by law enforcement.
3. Explain the concept of police civil liability and give three examples of types of misconduct that could lead to civil suits against the police.
4. Describe the elements of community policing and give examples of a community policing strategy.
5. Define terms related to policing issues and challenges.

KEY TERMS

1983 lawsuit
Bivens action
City of Canton, Ohio v. *Harris*
civil liability
community policing
deadly force
excessive force
grass eaters
Knapp Commission
less-than-lethal weapons
meat eaters
police corruption
police use of force
police working personality
Prior v. *Woods*
problem police officer
role malfeasance
suicide by cop
use of force continuum

7.0 The police: Issues and challenges

7.1 Ethics and corruption

7.1.1 Police personality and culture

POLICE WORKING PERSONALITY

All aspects of the traditional values and patterns of behavior evidenced by police officers who have been effectively socialized into the police subculture. Characteristics of the police personality often extend to the personal lives of law enforcement personnel.

- **Police working personality** is all aspects of the traditional values and patterns of behavior evidenced by police officers who have been effectively socialized into the police subculture.
  - Characteristics of the police personality often extend to the personal lives of law enforcement personnel.
  - In *Justice Without Trial: Law Enforcement in a Democratic Society* (1966), Jerome Skolnick (b. 1931) identified the process of informal socialization as it relates to law enforcement officers.
    - Typically, once in the field, a veteran officer is assigned to a rookie to "teach" him the ropes. This informal socialization process is often more important than formal training.
    - Six recognizable characteristics of police working personality:
      - Conservative
      - Authoritarian
      - Cynical
      - Suspicious
      - Hostile
      - Individualistic
  - Other researchers have added the following characteristics to Skolnick's original six:
    - Dogmatic
    - Insecure
    - Loyal
    - Efficient
    - Honorable
    - Secret
    - Prejudiced
  - Isolation and solidarity
    - Dangers of police work not only draws police together as a group, but separates them from the rest of society.
    - The element of danger contains the seeds of isolation.
    - The element of authority also helps to account for the police officer's social isolation.
  - Socialization into the police subculture appears to be an ongoing process.

- The police subculture exists because it eases the life of working police officers.
- Police subculture is more concerned with the "way one actually gets things done" than with official policies, administrative procedures, or even laws.

❖ Police personality is also brought to the job.

- A body of research suggests that the basic police personality is something that leads certain people to police work.
- People with conservative backgrounds continue to view themselves as defendants of middle-class morality.

7.1.2 Corruption is behavioral deviation from an accepted ethical standard.

- **Police corruption** is the abuse of police authority for personal or organizational gain.
- Carl Klockars, in "The Measurement of Police Integrity," *National Institute of Justice Research in Brief* (2000) claimed that:
  - ❖ Policing is an occupation that is rife with opportunities for misconduct.
  - ❖ "Policing is a highly discretionary, coercive activity that routinely takes place in private settings, out of sight of supervisors, and in the presence of witnesses who are often regarded as unreliable."
- Occupational deviance vs. abuse of authority
  - ❖ Occupational deviance is deviance that is motivated by the desire for personal benefit.
  - ❖ Abuse of authority occurs most often to further organizational goals of law enforcement.
- Categories of corrupt law enforcement officers:
  - ❖ **Grass eaters** are law enforcement officers who accept bribes or goods in exchange for not issuing tickets, making arrests, etc.
    - Grass eaters do not initiate the corrupt activity, but do not refuse it when offered.
    - Examples: taking meals for free or taking cash for not writing a ticket
  - ❖ **Meat eaters** are police officers who initiate corrupt activity such as soliciting bribes or taking a share of the drugs they confiscate to sell for their own profit, etc.
    - Examples: keeping drugs from a bust either for their own use or sale, taking goods from a store that has been broken into by thieves, or soliciting bribes from individuals involved in illegal activities to allow them to continue

POLICE CORRUPTION

The abuse of police authority for personal or organizational gain. (Carl B. Klockars et al., The Measurement of Police Integrity, *National Institute of Justice Research in Brief* [Washington, DC: NIJ, 2000], p. 1.)

GRASS EATERS

Police officers who accept bribes or goods in exchange for not issuing tickets, making arrests, etc. These officers do not initiate the corrupt activity, but do not refuse it when offered.

MEAT EATERS

Police officers who initiate corrupt activities such as soliciting bribes, taking a share of drugs they confiscate for sale and their own profit, etc.

KNAPP COMMISSION

A committee that investigated police corruption in New York City in the early 1970s.

- **Knapp Commission** was created in the early 1970s as a result of an exposé in the *New York Times* about extensive corruption in the New York City Police Department.
    - Uncovered a complex web of corruption that included protection rackets run by police officers
    - The Knapp Commission created the terms grass eaters and meat eaters.
- Mollen Commission was created to investigate police corruption in New York City in 1993 and was headed by former judge and deputy mayor Milton Mollen.
    - Officers who testified revealed that officers were:
        - Dealing drugs
        - Stealing confiscated drugs
        - Stifling investigations
        - Beating innocent people
        - Running a cocaine ring out of a police station
        - Covering up embarrassing incidents
- Specific types of corruption
    - To visualize police corruption, imagine a pyramid with each step to the top being a type of corruption, progressively becoming more serious the higher one proceeds up the pyramid.
    - Starting at the base of the pyramid and working up, they are:
        - Gratuities
            - Acceptance of small favors
            - Examples: free coffee, cigarettes, or meals
        - Playing favorites
            - Selective enforcement of the law
            - Example: not ticketing or arresting friends/family
        - Minor bribes
            - Acceptance of minor sums of money in return for favors
            - Example: accepting a $20 bill from a motorist for not writing a speeding ticket
        - Being above "inconvenient laws"
            - Violations of laws are considered too inconvenient or a nuisance by law enforcement officers.
            - Examples: speeding, smoking marijuana, driving drunk

- **Role malfeasance**
  - Acts that are illegal or harmful that relate directly to responsibilities of law enforcement officers
  - Examples: destroying evidence, offering biased testimony, protecting other corrupt law enforcement officers

ROLE MALFEASANCE
In law enforcement, this can be represented by the destruction of evidence, biased testimony, or the protection of "crooked cops."

- Major bribes
  - Accepting large sums of money in return for overlooking violations of the law
- Property crimes
  - Property crimes committed by law enforcement officers
  - Examples: burglary, theft
- Criminal enterprise
  - Law enforcement officers engaging in ongoing criminal activity
  - Examples: resale of confiscated drugs, resale of stolen property
- Denial of civil rights
  - Routinized schemes to circumvent constitutional guarantees of due process
  - Examples: planting of evidence, lying in court
- Violent crimes committed by law enforcement officers
  - Examples: physical abuse or torture of suspects, nonjustifiable homicide

7.1.3 Dangers of police work

- Violence in the line of duty
  - Law enforcement officers who die as a result of a felonious attack
    - For the years 1997 to 2006, the number of law enforcement officers feloniously killed:
      - 2006: 48
      - 2005: 55
      - 2004: 57
      - 2003: 52
      - 2002: 56
      - 2001: 70 (This figure does *not* include the 72 deaths that resulted from the events of September 11, 2001.)
      - 2000: 51

  - 1999: 42
  - 1998: 61
  - 1997: 70
- Profile of the average officer feloniously killed
  - Average age: 38 years old
  - Average length of service: 11 years
  - Gender: 45 of the 48 were male
  - Race
    - White: 38
    - Black: 5
    - Asian/Pacific Islander: 1
    - American Indiana/Alaskan Native: 1
    - Race was not reported: 3
- Circumstances under which law enforcement officers died
  - Twelve officers died in 2006 as a result of felonious attacks during arrest situations.
  - Ten of the officers were fatally assaulted when ambushed.
    - Entrapment/premeditation: 1
    - Unprovoked attacks: 9
  - Eight officers were fatally attacked when responding to disturbance calls.
    - Bar fights: 6
    - Family disputes: 2
  - Eight officers were fatally attacked while conducting traffic pursuits or stops.
    - Felony vehicle stops: 0
    - Traffic violation stops: 8
  - One officer was fatally attacked while handling, transporting, or maintaining the custody of prisoners.
  - One officer was fatally attacked while handling persons with mental illness.
  - Two officers were victims in tactical situations that included barricaded offenders, hostage taking, high-risk entry, etc.
  - Six officers were killed investigating suspicious persons/circumstances.

- Weapons
  - Forty-six of the 48 law enforcement officers who died from felonious attacks in 2006 were murdered with firearms.
    - Thirty-six were slain with handguns.
    - Eight were killed with a rifle.
    - Two were killed with a shotgun.
  - Two officers were killed by a vehicle.
- Officer fatalities by region:
  - Twenty-two officers were employed in the South.
  - Eleven officers were employed in the West.
  - Seven officers were employed in the Northeast.
  - Six officers were employed in the Midwest.
  - Two officers were employed in Puerto Rico.
- Days/time of day of officer fatalities
  - More officers (seven) died in August from felonious attacks than any other month in 2006; however, February, May, and October each had six officer fatalities.
  - Sunday was the day with the fewest officers fatally attacked (two).
  - The time period from 10:01 p.m. to midnight had the most number of officers fatally attacked, with seven.

❖ Law enforcement officers killed accidently

- Sixty-six law enforcement officers died as the result of accidents that occurred in the line of duty.
- Profile of officers killed accidentally
  - Average age: 36 years old
  - Average length of service: 10 years
  - Gender: 64 of the officers were male
  - Race
    - White: 59
    - Black: 4
    - Asian/Pacific Islander: 3
- Circumstances of the accidental deaths
  - Thirty-eight officers died in 2006 as a result of automobile accidents.

- ❒ Thirteen officers were struck and killed by vehicles.
  - Nine of the 13 officers were directing traffic/assisting motorists.
  - Four of the 13 officers were performing traffic stops or working roadblocks.
- ❒ Eight officers died as a result of motorcycle accidents.
- ❒ Four officers died as a result of accidental shootings, which includes:
  - Crossfires
  - Training sessions
  - Cleaning mishaps

- ■ Risk of disease and infected evidence
  - ❖ At times, the responsibilities of law enforcement officers place them in situations where they run the risk of contracting diseases either from individuals they have to deal with or evidence they collect.
  - ❖ Police, like firefighters and emergency medical service (EMS) personnel, are considered "first responders." They are typically the first on the scene to render service and therefore can be exposed to all sorts of dangerous situations.
  - ❖ Law enforcement officers can come into contact with diseases capable of being transmitted via blood and other bodily fluids.
    - ◆ Examples of types of diseases: hepatitis B, tuberculosis
  - ❖ Examples of possible methods of transmission of diseases:
    - ◆ From breath alcohol instruments
    - ◆ Handling of evidence of all types
    - ◆ Having blood of other individuals splatter on them
    - ◆ Fluid splattering on law enforcement officers from delivery of a baby
    - ◆ Bite attacks by infected individuals
    - ◆ Handling and removal of dead bodies, especially those that have been decomposing
  - ❖ Bloodborne Pathogens Act of 1991
    - ◆ This act requires that law enforcement officers receive the proper training related to preventing contamination by bloodborne infectious agents.
    - ◆ The act also requires law enforcement officers to undergo an annual refresher course on the subject of bloodborne contaminants.

- Stress among law enforcement officers
  - Medical research indicates that serious stress over long periods of time is generally regarded as destructive, and even life threatening.
  - As a career, law enforcement has typically been perceived as a high stress-level job.
    - Each time a law enforcement officer answers a call, he or she has no idea in advance of the actual outcome of the call, the level of force that will need to be used, or the stress that may be involved.
    - Law enforcement ranks among the top 10 stress-producing jobs in the United States, according to the American Institute of Stress.
  - In *Police Stress: Is Anyone Out There Listening?* (1986), Joseph Victor identified four sources of police stress:
    - External stress
      - There are real dangers that exist for law enforcement officers when a call for service is answered.
    - Organizational stress
      - This type of stress is generated by work responsibilities like paperwork and training requirements.
    - Personal stress
      - The relationships that exist between officers contribute to the stress that individual officers experience.
    - Operational stress
      - The total effect on officers of the need to combat daily tragedies of urban life
  - Regardless of the amount of effort law enforcement officers expend in trying to assist citizens with their problems, they become frustrated when they are unable to save people from dire circumstances.
    - An arrest may not lead to conviction.
    - The evidence submitted may not be admissible.
    - The sentences handed down may not be considered long enough even if the offender is placed in prison.
  - Suicide rate for law enforcement officers
    - Law enforcement has one of the highest suicide rates of all professions.
    - The suicide rate for law enforcement is twice that for the general population.

- Stress for law enforcement officers and their families are also of concern.
  - Family problems and stress can negatively affect the quality of a police officer's work and the overall performance of police departments.
  - The Bureau of Justice Statistics has identified six important sources of family stress:
    - Shift work and overtime: Many law enforcement agencies, mostly local departments, require officers to rotate shifts, sometimes as frequently as weekly.
    - Concern over the officer's inability or unwillingness to express feelings at home
    - Fear by the family that the spouse working as a law enforcement officer will be killed in the line of duty
    - The presence of a gun or guns in the home can be stressful for the family.
    - The officer's 24-hour role as a law officer: Most police officers are required to carry their weapon and to handle situations even when off-duty.
    - Avoidance, teasing, or harassment of the officer's children by other children because of the parent's job
  - Peer support programs for spouses and life partners and for the adolescent children of officers have been developed to address issues of stress.
- Officer fatigue. In *Evaluating the Effects of Fatigue on Police Patrol Officers: Final Report* (2000), Bryan Vila, et. al. identified factors that contribute to officer fatigue:
  - Overtime assignments
  - Shift work
  - Night school
  - Endless hours spent waiting to testify
  - Emotional and physical demands of the job
  - Trying to maintain a family and social life during irregular periods of off-duty time

POLICE USE OF FORCE

The use of physical restraint by a police officer when dealing with a member of the public. (National Institute of Justice, *Use of Force by Police: Overview of National and Local Data* [Washington, DC: NIJ, 1999].)

7.2 Types of force

7.2.1 **Police use of force** is the use of physical restraint by a police officer when dealing with a member of the public (taken from the National Institute of Justice, *Use of Force by Police: Overview of National and Local Data*, 1999).

7.2.2 Reasonable and necessary force

- What is reasonable?
- What is necessary?

7.2.3 **Use of force continuum.** Police officers generally have five types of force that escalate as follows:

- Use of authority (body language, tone of voice, etc.)
- Use of body positioning (pushing, restraining, etc.)
- Use of restraints (cuffing)
- **Less-than-lethal weapons** (use of baton, pepper spray, stun gun, etc.)
- Deadly force (gun)

USE OF FORCE CONTINUUM

Standard use of force continuum ranges from the mere physical presence of the officer up to and through the use of deadly force by the police officer.

LESS THAN LETHAL WEAPONS

Weapons designed to disable, capture, or immobilize a suspect.

7.2.4 Face-to-face contact. Matthew Durose, Erica Smith, and Patrick Lanagan, in *Contact Between the Police and the Public 2005* (2007), estimated that over 43.5 million people nationwide have face-to-face contact with law enforcement officers during a 12-month period; almost 18 million of these contacts are the result of traffic stops.

- Approximately 700,000 (1.6%) of all contacts involve the use or threat of force.
- Handcuffing is not included in the above definition of the use of force. However, when it is, the number of contact involving the use of force or threat of force increases to 1.2 million (2.5%).
- In the majority of instances when force is used, they involve weaponless tactics (the percentages add up to over 100 because some suspects had more than one form of force used against them by the law enforcement officer in the same contact).
  - The suspect was pushed or grabbed by a law enforcement officer: 78.9%
  - The suspect had a chemical sprayed in the face: 6.2%
  - The suspect was kicked or hit: 15.6%
  - The suspect had a gun pointed at him or her: 27.6%
  - Some other tactic was used by the law enforcement officer: 18%

7.2.5 Use of force by type of encounter

- International Association of Chiefs of Police
  - *Police Use of Force in America* (2001)
    - Arrests: 39%
    - Disturbance: 21%
    - Traffic stop: 14%
    - Domestic: 11%
    - Drunk/disorderly: 9%
    - Investigation: 6%

7.2.6 The force factor. In *The Force Factor: Measuring and Assessing Police Use of Force and Suspect Resistance: A Final Report* (2001), Geoffrey P. Alpert and Roger G. Dunham reported on research about police use of force.

- Their research revealed six things about police use of force:
  - Only a small percentage of the encounters involve force.
  - Use of force typically occurs when police are trying to make an arrest and the suspect is resisting.
  - Use of force appears to be unrelated to an officer's personal characteristics, such as age, gender, or ethnicity.
  - Use of force is most likely to occur when the police are dealing with suspects under the influence of alcohol or drugs, or with mentally ill individuals.
  - When injuries occur as a result of the use of force, they are unlikely to be minor.
    - In one study, researchers found that the most common injury to a suspect was a bruise or abrasion (48%).
  - A small proportion of officers are disproportionately involved in use-of-force incidents.
- Force factor is the level of force used by the police relative to the suspect's level of resistance.
  - Force factor is an important element in reducing the number of injuries to both law enforcement officers and suspects.
  - Measuring the force factor
    - Calculated by measuring the suspect's level of resistance and the officer's level of force on an equivalent scale, then subtracting the level of resistance from the level of police force
  - Alpert and Dunham's study of force factor found the level of force that officers use is closely related to the type of training that their departments emphasize.

EXCESSIVE FORCE

The application of an amount and/or frequency of force greater than that required to compel compliance from a willing or unwilling subject.

PROBLEM POLICE OFFICER

A law enforcement officer who exhibits problem behavior, as indicated by high rates of citizen complaints and use-of-force incidents as well as other evidence. (Samuel Walker, Geoffrey P. Albert, and Dennis J. Kenney, *Responding to the Problem Police Officer: A National Study of Early Warning Systems* [Washington, DC: National Institute of Justice, 2000].)

7.2.7 **Excessive force** is the application of an amount and/or frequency of force greater than that required to compel compliance from a willing or unwilling subject.

- Excessive force and **problem police officers**
  - A problem police officer is a law enforcement officer who exhibits problem behavior, as indicated by high rates of citizen complaints and use-of-force incidents as well as by other evidence.
  - The Christopher Commission
    - Formed in 1991 in response to the Rodney King beating, examines the structure and operation of the Los Angeles Police Department (LAPD)

- The commission found that 1,800 police officers were repeat offenders, and had multiple complaints against them for excessive use of force between 1986 and 1990.
  - More than 1,400 officers had only one or two complaints.
  - One hundred eighty-three LAPD officers had four or more complaints.
  - Forty-four LAPD officers had six or more complaints.
    - The 44 officers with six or more complaints had received positive performance evaluations that failed to record "sustained" complaints or discuss their significance.
  - Sixteen LAPD officers had eight or more complaints.
  - One LAPD officer had 16 complaints lodged against him by members of the public.

7.2.8 Police use of **deadly force**

DEADLY FORCE

Force likely to cause death or great bodily harm. Also, "the intentional use of a firearm or other instrument resulting in a high probability of death."

- Deadly force is force likely to cause death or great bodily harm.
  - Includes the intentional use of a firearm or other instrument resulting in a high probability of death
- Jodi M. Brown and Patrick A. Langan in *Policing and Homicide, 1976–98: Justifiable Homicide by Police, Police Officers Murdered by Felons* (2001), reported that the number of justifiable homicides by police averages nearly 400 felons each year.
- *Tennessee* v. *Garner* (1985)
  - Edward Garner, a 15-year-old suspected burglar
  - Garner was shot to death by a Memphis police officer after he refused an order to halt and attempted to climb over a chain-link fence.
  - Garner's father sued the Memphis Police Department, claiming his son's constitutional rights had been violated.
  - U.S. Supreme Court held that the use of deadly force by the police to prevent the escape of a fleeing felon could be justified only where the suspect could reasonably be thought to present a significant threat of serious injury or death to the public or to the officer, *and* where deadly force is necessary to effect the arrest.
  - Court held that the use of deadly force to prevent the escape of all felony suspects, whatever the circumstances, was constitutionally unreasonable.
- *Graham* v. *California* (1989)
  - The U.S. Supreme Court established the standard of objective reasonableness.

        - Under objective reasonableness, an officer's use of deadly force could be assessed in terms of "reasonableness at the moment."
    - Whether deadly force has been used appropriately should be judged from the perspective of a reasonable officer on the scene and not with the benefit of 20/20 hindsight.
    - The justices wrote, "the calculus of reasonableness must embody allowance for the fact that police officers are often forced to make split-second judgments—in circumstances that are tense, uncertain, and rapidly evolving—about the amount of force that is necessary in a particular situation."
- Imminent danger standard restricts the use of deadly force to only those situations where the lives of agents or others are in danger.
    - In 1995, following the fiascos at the Branch Davidian complex in Waco, Texas, and the Ruby Ridge massacre in Ruby Ridge, Idaho, in 1992, the federal government established the imminent danger standard.
    - The imminent danger standard policy adopted by the FBI includes the following elements:
        - Defense of life
            - Agents may use deadly force only when necessary; that is, only when they have probable cause to believe that the subject poses an imminent danger of death or serious physical injury to the agent or to others.
        - Fleeing subject
            - Deadly force may be used to prevent the escape of a fleeing subject if there is probable cause to believe that the subject has committed a felony involving the infliction or threatened infliction of serious physical injury or death and that the subject's escape would pose an imminent danger of death or serious physical injury to the agents or others.
        - Verbal warning
            - If feasible, and if doing so would not increase the danger to the agent or to others, a verbal warning to submit to the authority of the agent should be given prior to the use of deadly force.
        - Warning shots
            - Agents may not fire warning shots.
        - Vehicles
            - Agents may not fire weapons solely to disable moving vehicles.

- ❐ Weapons may be fired at the driver or occupant of a moving motor vehicle only when the agents have probable cause to believe that the subject poses an imminent danger of death or serious physical injury to the agents or to others and when the use of deadly force does not create a danger to the public that outweighs the likely benefits of its use.

- It is estimated that on average, 400 suspects are killed by gunfire by public law enforcement officers each year.
  - Suspects shot and wounded: 1,200
  - Suspects shot at and missed: 1,800
- **Suicide by cop** occurs when a citizen intentionally acts in such an aggressive and threatening manner to give the police officer no other option than to take the life of the citizen.
  - In "Ten Percent of Police Shootings Found to Be 'Suicide by Cop,'" *Criminal Justice Newsletter* (1998), a study of Los Angeles police officers' fatal shootings found that over 10% could be classified as "suicide by cop."
  - Three general categories of "suicide by cop"
    - Direct confrontations: suicidal subjects instigate attacks on police
    - Disturbed interventions: cases in which potentially suicidal subjects take advantage of police intervention, forcing police to kill him or her
    - Criminal interventions: cases in which criminals prefer death to capture

SUICIDE BY COP

Occurs when a citizen intentionally acts in such an aggressive and threatening manner to give the police officer no other option than to take the life of the citizen.

7.2.9 Less-than-lethal weapons are weapons designed to disable, capture, or immobilize—but not kill—a suspect. Examples:

- Stun guns
- Tasers
- Rubber bullets
- Beanbag projectiles
- Pepper spray
- Snare nets fired from shotguns
- Disabling sticky foam
- High-tech guns that fire bolts of electromagnetic energy at a target
- Microwave beams that heat the tissue of people exposed to them until they desist in their illegal or threatening behavior or lose consciousness

CIVIL LIABILITY

Holds that police officers are accountable for their behavior and protects the individual citizen from excessive or inappropriate treatment. Law enforcement departments can suffer significant financial loss when an officer fails the public trust.

CITY OF CANTON, OHIO V. HARRIS

A 1989 case of failing to properly screen, train, or supervise staff case in which the department failed to train an officer sufficiently, resulting in a medical and psychiatric emergency of a detainee.

7.3 Police liability

7.3.1 **Civil liability** holds that police officers are accountable for their behavior and protects the individual citizen from excessive or inappropriate treatment.

- Involves the potential responsibility for payment of damages or other court-ordered enforcement as a result of a ruling in a lawsuit
- Two types of civil suits
  - State
  - Federal
- Major sources of police civil liability
  - Assault
  - Battery
  - False arrest/imprisonment
  - Malicious prosecution
  - Negligence in the care of suspects in custody
  - Inappropriate use of force and deadly force
  - Racial profiling
- *Biscoe* v. *Arlington County* (1984)
  - Alvin Biscoe lost both legs when hit by a police car involved in a high-speed chase.
  - Biscoe was an innocent bystander who was waiting to cross the street when the patrol car went out of control.
  - Arlington County Police Department was found liable because they had a high-speed chase policy, which the officer driving the car violated.
  - Biscoe was awarded $5 million.
- *Kaplan* v. *Lloyd's Insurance* (1985)
  - Louisiana Police Department had a policy of prohibiting a police officer from going over 20 miles above the speed limit to give chase.
  - The officer violated the policy by going 75 mph in a 40-mph zone.
  - The police department was not held responsible, but the officer was liable.
- ***City of Canton, Ohio* v. *Harris*** (1989)
  - Geraldine Harris was arrested and taken to the Canton, Ohio, police station.
  - While at the police station, she slumped to the floor several times.
  - Officers left Ms. Harris on the floor and never called for qualified medical assistance.

- ❖ Upon release, family members took her to the local hospital where she was found to be suffering from several emotional ailments and was hospitalized for a week.
- ❖ The U.S. Supreme Court ruled "failure to train" can become the basis for legal liability on part of municipality.
- ❖ Failure to train amounts to deliberate indifference to the rights of persons with whom the police come into contact.

- *Board of County Commissioners of Bryan County, Oklahoma* v. *Brown* (1997)
    - ❖ Burns, a deputy with the Bryan Sheriff's Department, was charged with using excessive force in arresting a woman.
    - ❖ The woman sued the county for damages, claiming that Burns had been hired in spite of his criminal record.
    - ❖ Prior to being hired, Burns had pleaded guilty to various driving infractions and other misdemeanors, including assault and battery.
    - ❖ A spokesperson for the sheriff's department testified that the department admitted to receiving Burns' driving record and criminal records, but had not reviewed either in detail before the decision to hire.
    - ❖ The U.S. Supreme Court ruled that to establish liability, plaintiffs must show that the municipal action in question was not simply negligence, but was taken with deliberate indifference as to its known or obvious consequences.
    - ❖ "Only where adequate scrutiny of the applicant's background would lead a reasonable policymaker to conclude that the plainly obvious consequence of the decision to hire the applicant would be the deprivation of a third party's federally protected right can the official's failure to adequately scrutinize the applicant's background constitute deliberate indifference."
    - ❖ In conclusion, a municipality may not be held liable solely because it employs a person with an arrest record.

7.3.2 Federal cases

- 1871
    - ❖ **1983 lawsuits** (based on Title 42 passed by Congress in 1871)
    - ❖ The 1983 lawsuits are civil suits brought under Title 42, section 1983 of the U.S. Code, against anyone denying others of their constitutional rights to life, liberty, or property without due process of law.
    - ❖ The act is designed to ensure civil rights of men and women of all races.
    - ❖ The act requires due process of law before any person can be deprived of life, liberty, or property and specifically provides for redress for the denial of these constitutional rights.

1983 LAWSUIT

A civil suit brought under Title 42, Section 1983, of the U.S. Code against anyone who denies others their constitutional right to life, liberty, or property without due process of law.

PRIOR V. WOODS

A 1981 negligence case in which police officers mistook the resident of a home as a burglar and killed him.

BIVENS ACTION

A civil suit, based on the case of *Bivens* v. *Six Unknown Federal Agents*, brought against federal government officials for denying the constitutional rights of others.

- ***Prior* v. *Woods*** (1981)
  - David Prior was mistaken for a burglar and shot to death in front of his home.
  - The Prior family was awarded $5.7 million for their loss.
  - The Detroit Police Department was held responsible under a 1983 lawsuit for the wrongful death.
- ***Bivens* action** is a civil suit based upon the case of *Bivens* v. *Six Unknown Federal Agents* (1971), brought against federal government officials for denying constitutional rights of others.
  - *Bivens* action allows for lawsuits to be brought against federal law enforcement agents.
  - Lawsuits are still prevented from being filed against the federal government.
    - Federal Tort Claims Act (FTCA) grants broad immunity to federal government agencies engaged in discretionary activity.
    - Westfall Act
      - Short name for Federal Employees Liability Reform and Tort Compensation Act of 1988
      - Addresses when a federal employee is sued for a wrongful or negligent act
      - Empowers the attorney general to certify that the employee was acting within the scope of his or her office or employment at the time of the incident
      - Upon certification, the employee is dismissed from the action and the United States is substituted as defendant.
      - The case then falls under the governance of the FTCA.

7.3.3 Qualified immunity "shields law enforcement officers from constitutional lawsuits if reasonable officers believe their actions to be lawful in light of clearly established law and the information the officers possess."

- The qualified immunity doctrine's central objective is to protect public officials from undue interference with their duties and from potentially disabling threats of liability.
- *Hunter* v. *Bryant* (1991)
  - Even law enforcement officials who reasonably, but mistakenly, conclude that probable cause is present are entitled to immunity.
- *Saucier* v. *Katz* (2001)
  - Case that helped to formulate qualified immunity doctrine
  - Court established a two-pronged test for assessing constitutional violations by government agents.

        - Court hearing the case must decide whether the facts, taken in the light most favorable to the party asserting the injury, show that the defendant's conduct violated a constitutional right.
        - Court must then decide whether the right was clearly established.
            - For a right to be clearly established, "It would be clear to a reasonable [defendant] that his conduct was unlawful in the situation he confronted."

- *Idaho* v. *Horiuchi* (2001)
    - Case involved FBI sharpshooter Lon Horiuchi, who was charged with negligent manslaughter by prosecutors in Boundary County, Idaho, following a 1992 incident at Ruby Ridge, Idaho.
    - Incident began when federal agents tried to arrest Randy Weaver, a self-proclaimed separatist on weapons charges.
    - Following an initial confrontation and gun battle in which a deputy U.S. marshal was killed, a standoff between federal officials and the Weaver family ensued.
    - Agents surrounded the Weaver cabin in which the whole Weaver family and an unknown number of armed supporters had taken refuge.
    - Horiuchi, operating under rules of engagement developed by the FBI fired at an armed man, who while outside the cabin seemed to be taking aim at an approaching FBI helicopter.
    - As the man sought cover, Horiuchi fired again, just as the man entered the Weaver cabin.
    - The bullet struck Mrs. Weaver in the head and then the intended target.
    - Mrs. Weaver was holding a baby in her arms when hit in the head. Mrs. Weaver died instantly.
    - Horiuchi argued that he was attempting to protect the helicopter and that his actions had therefore been reasonable.
    - Appellate court justices questioned his story and decided the helicopter had never been in any real danger and that Horiuchi had fired into the cabin in violation of the FBI's rules of engagement.
    - Ninth U.S. Circuit Court of Appeals ruled that federal law enforcement officers are not immune from state prosecution where their actions violate state law either through malice or zeal.
    - The appellate court's decision opened the door to Horiuchi's prosecution by Idaho authorities on state manslaughter charges.

- ❖ With the election of a new district attorney in Boundary Country, the charges were dropped. The new attorney decided too much time had passed for an effective case to be made.
- ❖ Randy Weaver served 16 months in a federal facility following the incident.
- ❖ Surviving members of the Weaver family were awarded $3 million in a suit they brought against the federal government.

COMMUNITY POLICING

A collaborative effort between the police and the community that identifies problems of crime and disorder and involves all elements of the community in the search for solutions to these problems.

7.4 Community policing

7.4.1 Police–community relations (PCR) is an area of police activity that stresses the need for the community and the police to work together effectively, and emphasizes the notion that the police derive their legitimacy from the community they serve.

- Interest in police–community relations began in the 1960s and 1970s for most police departments.
- The social unrest of the 1960s in terms of civil rights marches and demonstrations against the Vietnam War helped pave the way for the demise of the legalistic style of policing and the development of police–community relations programs.
- The police during the 1960s and early 1970s were viewed by many as agents of the establishment.
- PCR represented a movement away from an exclusive police emphasis on apprehension of law violators and an increase on positive police–citizen interactions.

7.4.2 Types of police–community relations programs:

- Team policing
- Community policing

7.4.3 Team policing is the reorganization of conventional patrol strategies into an "integrated and versatile police team assigned to a fixed district."

- The idea for team policing is believed to have originated in Aberdeen, Scotland.
- Officers are assigned semi-permanently to a particular neighborhood.
- Officers are expected to become familiar with the people who live and work in the neighborhood as well as with their problems and concerns.
- Officers assigned to the neighborhood are given considerable authority in processing complaints from arrest through resolution.
- Crimes are investigated and solved at the local level.
    - ❖ Specialists are only called in if the resources needed are not available locally.

7.4.4 Community policing is a collaborative effort between the police and the community that identifies problems of crime and disorder and involves all elements of the community in the search for solutions to these problems.

- Mark H. Moore and Robert C. Trojanowicz in "Corporate Strategies for Policing," *Perspectives on Policing, No. 6* (1988) identified three generic "corporate strategies" guide in American policing.
  - Strategic policing is a type of policing that retains the traditional police goal of professional crime fighting but enlarges the enforcement target to include nontraditional kinds of criminals such as serial offenders, gangs and criminal associations, drug-distribution networks, and sophisticated white-collar and computer criminals.
    - Generally makes use of innovative enforcement techniques, including intelligence operations, undercover stings, electronic surveillance, and sophisticated forensic methods
  - Problem-solving policing (also called problem-oriented policing) is a type of policing that assumes that many crimes are caused by existing social conditions within the community and that crimes can be controlled by uncovering and effectively addressing underlying social problems.
    - Makes use of community resources such as counseling centers, welfare programs, and job training facilities
    - Attempts to involve citizens in crime prevention through education, negotiation, and conflict management
  - Encourages collaboration between the police and the community that identifies problems of crime and disorder and involves all elements of the community in the search for solutions to these problems; also called community-oriented policing
    - Evolved out of the work of George Kelling and Robert Trojanowicz
      - George Kelling, *The Newark Foot Patrol Experiment* (1981)
      - Robert Trojanowicz, "An Evaluation of a Neighborhood Foot Patrol Program," *Journal of Police Science and Administration* (1983)
      - Kelling and Trojanowicz posited that if patrol officers spent time on foot in their neighborhoods, citizens would have more positive attitudes toward police.
    - Community members and the police are expected to share responsibility for establishing and maintaining peaceful neighborhoods.

- Jerome Skolnick and David H. Bayley in *Community Policing: Issues and Practices Around the World* (1988) identified four elements of community policing:
  - Community-based crime prevention
  - The reorientation of patrol activities to emphasize the importance of nonemergency services
  - Increased police accountability to the public
  - A decentralization of command, including a greater use of civilians at all levels of police decision making
- Bureau of Justice Statistics (BJS) report (2001)
  - Showed that nearly 113,000 full-time sworn personnel regularly engaged in community policing activities
  - This number was up from 21,000 sworn officers in 1997.
- Title I of the Violent Crime Control and Law Enforcement Act of 1994
  - Known as the Public Safety Partnership and Community Policing Act of 1994
  - Purposes of act:
    - To increase number of officers interacting directly with members of the community
    - To provide additional and more effective training to officers to enhance their problem solving, service, and other skills needed in interacting with members of the community
    - To encourage the development and implementation of innovative programs to permit members of the community to assist local law enforcement agencies in the prevention of crime in the community
    - To encourage the development of new technologies to assist local law enforcement agencies in reorienting the emphasis of their activities from reacting to crime to preventing crime
- Office of Community Oriented Policing Services (COPS)
  - Established by U.S. Department of Justice as a response to the above law
  - COPS office administered the funds necessary to add 100,000 community-policing officers.
  - In 1999, the COPS office funded the 100,000 officers.
  - Congress funded another $500 million in 2000 to create an additional 50,000 community-policing officers.

- Critique of community policing
  - ❒ The range, complexity, and evolving nature of community-policing programs have made their effectiveness difficult to measure.
  - ❒ Citizen satisfaction with police performance can be difficult to conceptualize and quantify.
  - ❒ Those who study community policing have often been stymied by ambiguity surrounding the concept of community.
  - ❒ There is continuing evidence that not all police officers or police managers are ready to accept nontraditional images of police work.
    - The goals of community policing frequently conflict with standard police performance criteria leading to a perception among officers that community-policing programs are inefficient at best, and at worst, a waste of time.
  - ❒ Some researchers have warned that a police subculture is so committed to a traditional view of police work, which is so focused on crime fighting, that efforts to promote community policing can demoralize an entire department.
    - Police subculture is a particular set of values, beliefs, and acceptable forms of behavior characteristic of American police with which the police profession strives to imbue new recruits.
    - Socialization into the police subculture commences with recruit training and continues thereafter.

CHAPTER SUMMARY

➢ There are a number of factors that contribute to police corruption. Police personality and culture, including the socialization of police, affect police behavior. The characteristics of the police personality have an impact on both professional and personal life. Police corruption is the abuse of police authority for personal and organizational gain. There are various levels of police corruption, which starts with behavior like accepting gratuities and escalates to major bribes and property crimes. At the same time, the life of a police officer is filled with danger and stress. Police officers risk violence and death in the line of duty and the danger of disease from infected evidence and bloodborne pathogens. The suicide rate among police officers is the highest of any profession.

➢ Police use of force is the use of physical restraint by a police officer when dealing with a member of the public. The notion of reasonable and/or necessary force is essential to evaluating whether police force is justified. Police officers generally use five types of force that escalates as follows: use of authority, use of body positioning, use of restraints, less-than-lethal weapons, and finally, deadly force. Excessive force is the application of an amount and/or frequency of force greater than that required to compel compliance from a willing or unwilling subject. Police use of deadly force is likely to cause death or great bodily harm and involves the intentional use of a firearm or other instrument resulting in a high probability of death.

- Police liability falls into the categories of civil liability, federal cases, and qualified immunity. Civil liability, which protects individual citizens from excessive or inappropriate treatment, holds that police officers are accountable for their behavior. Qualified immunity protects law enforcement officials from lawsuits if they believe their actions are lawful in light of established law and the information the officer possesses.
- Community policing seeks all elements of the community to solve these problems. Community policing is a collaborative effort between the police and the community that identifies problems of crime and disorder. Team policing is the reorganization of conventional patrol strategies into an "integrated and versatile police team assigned to a fixed district."

ONLINE@CRIMINAL JUSTICE INTERACTIVE

Learning Modules

7.1 Ethics and Corruption
7.2 Types of Force
7.3 Police Liability
7.4 Community Policing

Myths and Issues Videos

Myth vs. Reality: Police Often Have to Confront Dangerous Situations with Deadly Force
Issue 1: Profiling
Issue 2: Police Ethics and Corruption

Simulation Activity: Use of Force

Homework and Review

In the News
Web Activity
Review Questions
Essay Questions
Flashcards

Chapter 8

The Courts: History, Structure, and Key Players

CHAPTER OUTLINE

- 8.0 The courts: History, structure, and key players
- 8.1 History and organization of the courts
  - 8.1.1 Structure of the court system
  - 8.1.2 Federal system
  - 8.1.3 State court system
- 8.2 Courtroom roles
  - 8.2.1 Ten basic roles
  - 8.2.2 Courtroom professionals
  - 8.2.3 Courtroom nonprofessionals
- 8.3 The prosecution and defense
  - 8.3.1 Distinct of prosecution and defense
  - 8.3.2 Before trial
  - 8.3.3 At trial
  - 8.3.4 After trial and conviction
- 8.4 The trial judge
  - 8.4.1 Daily administrative responsibilities
  - 8.4.2 Before trial
  - 8.4.3 At trial
- 8.5 The grand jury
  - 8.5.1 Selection process
  - 8.5.2 Role of grand jury
  - 8.5.3 Secrecy
  - 8.5.4 Investigative powers
  - 8.5.5 Rights of witnesses
- 8.6 Types of witnesses
  - 8.6.1 Eyewitness
  - 8.6.2 Defendant
  - 8.6.3 Character witness
  - 8.6.4 Expert witness

LEARNING OBJECTIVES

After reviewing the online material and reading this chapter, you should be able to:

1. Discuss the history of the courts.
2. Explain the organization of state and federal court systems in the United States.
3. Describe the roles of the primary courtroom participants in criminal trials.
4. Explain the adversarial relationship between the prosecution and defense before, during, and after trial.
5. Explain the roles and responsibilities of the trial judge.
6. Explain the role of the grand jury.
7. Compare and contrast lay witnesses and expert witnesses.
8. Define terms related to the history of, structure of, and key players in the courts.

KEY TERMS

adversarial process
bail
bailiff
change of venue
character witness
clerk of the court
community court
court administrator
court reporter
defendant
defense attorney
defense counsel
docket
expert witness
eyewitness
judge
juror
jury
lay witness
original jurisdiction
plea bargain
power of judicial review
preliminary hearing
prosecutor
prosecutorial discretion
trial *de novo*
writ of *certiorari*

8.0 The courts: History, structure, and key players

8.1 History and organization of the courts

8.1.1 Structure of the court system

- The United States has a dual-court structure that includes two systems that interface at various levels: the federal system and the state system.
- The two systems were created to maintain a certain amount of autonomy for states and separation from federal control.
  - ❖ States continue to create, enforce, and have judicial authority over legal matters based on their state constitutions and laws passed by their legislature.
  - ❖ The federal court system has jurisdiction over cases involving:
    - ◆ Federal law
    - ◆ Disputes between states
    - ◆ Claims against the United States
    - ◆ Constitutional issues
    - ◆ Treaties with other countries
    - ◆ Cases of the admiralty and maritime jurisdiction
    - ◆ Disputes between citizens of different states

8.1.2 Federal system is comprised of three tiers: U.S. district courts, U.S. courts of appeal, U.S. Supreme Court.

- History of the federal system
  - ❖ Article III of the U.S. Constitution established the federal judiciary and its jurisdiction.
    - ◆ Section 1: "The judicial Power of the United States shall be vested in one supreme Court, and in such inferior Courts as the Congress may from time to time ordain and establish . . .."
    - ◆ Section II: "The judicial Power shall extend to all Cases, in Law and Equity, arising under this Constitution, the Laws of the United States, and Treaties made, or which shall be made, under their Authority;—to all Cases affecting Ambassadors, other public Ministers and Consuls;—to all Cases of admiralty and maritime Jurisdiction;—to Controversies to which the United States shall be a Party;—to Controversies between two or more States;—between a State and Citizens of another State,—between Citizens of different States, between Citizens of the same State claiming Lands under Grants of different

States and between a State, or the Citizens thereof, and foreign States, Citizens or Subjects."

- Judiciary Act of 1789
  - In its first session, Congress addressed the organization of the federal courts with the passage of the Judiciary Act of September 1789.
  - Act represented a compromise that established a three-part system of federal courts.
    - Supreme Court (as stipulated by Article III of the U.S. Constitution)
    - District courts are responsible for:
      - Admiralty cases
      - Minor criminal cases
      - Civil suits
    - Circuit courts to serve as principal trial courts over:
      - Most federal crimes
      - Disputes between citizens of different states
      - Suits involving the government
      - Some appeals from the district courts
- Bill of Rights
  - The Bill of Rights (the first ten amendments) was ratified in 1791.
  - The defined structure of the federal judiciary was not enough to eliminate the doubt raised by many Americans.
  - James Madison presented a draft of a bill of rights that would guarantee many of the legal protections demanded by critics of the Constitution.
  - Rather than restructuring the judiciary, Madison's proposed amendments emphasized civil liberties and the rights of criminal **defendants**.

DEFENDANT
Individuals who stand accused of committing a criminal offense.

- Reorganization Act of 1801
  - Congress approved a sweeping reorganization of the nation's court system and significantly expanded federal jurisdiction.
  - Reduced the size of the Supreme Court from six justices to five
  - Eliminated the Supreme Courts justices' circuit court duties
  - Created 16 judgeships for the 6 judicial circuits
  - Jurisdiction over all cases arising under the Constitution and acts of the United States were to be presided over by the circuit courts.

- Judiciary Act of 1891
  - Created the U.S. court of appeals (originally called the circuit court of appeals) to relieve caseload burden in the Supreme Court and to handle a dramatic increase in federal filings
    - When Supreme Court was originally established, justices would travel around the country twice a year visiting circuit courts in different states.
    - Travel by Supreme Court justices was both time-consuming and difficult.
  - Nine courts of appeals, one for each judicial circuit were established.
  - The existing circuit judges and a newly authorized **judge** in each circuit were the judges of the appellate courts.

JUDGE

Ultimate authority in the courtroom. Safeguards both rights of accused and interests of the public. Determines guilt or innocence of defendant when trial is not before a jury.

- In 1893, Congress created a court of appeals of the District of Columbia.
- Judiciary Act of 1925, also known as the Certiorari Act, sought to reduce workload of the U.S. Supreme Court.
  - The majority of the Supreme Court's workload became discretionary.
    - Direct appeal to the Supreme Court was removed.
    - Appellants would file petitions for writs of *certiorari* with the Supreme Court.
      - **Writ of *certiorari*** is an order by a higher court directing a lower court to send the record in a given case for review.
      - Four of nine justices would have to agree to hear a case for the writ of *certiorari* to be approved.

WRIT OF *CERTIORARI*

A writ issued from an appellate court for the purpose of obtaining from a lower court the record of its proceedings in a particular case. In some states, this writ is the mechanism for discretionary review. A request for review is made by petitioning for a writ of *certiorari*, and the granting of review is indicated by the issuance of the writ.

- Magistrate Act of 1968 created a system of magistrates to replace U.S. commissioners, who in some form or another had served the federal judiciary since the 1790s.

- Current federal judiciary
  - U.S. Supreme Court
    - Nine justices
      - One chief justice
        - John G. Roberts, Jr. appointed by President George W. Bush on September 29, 2005.
      - Eight associate justices
        - John Paul Stevens (appointed January 1972)
        - Antonin Scalia (appointed September 1986)
        - Anthony Kennedy (appointed February 1988)

- Clarence Thomas (appointed October 1991)
- Ruth Bader Ginsburg (appointed August 1993)
- Stephen Breyer (appointed August 1994)
- Samuel Alito (appointed January 2006)
- Sonia Sotomayor (appointed August 2009)

◆ Appointed by president and confirmed by the U.S. senate.

◆ Justices serve for life.

◆ Court is located in Washington, D.C., across the street from the U.S. Capitol.

◆ **Power of judicial review** is the power of the court to review actions and decisions made by lower courts and other government agencies.

POWER OF JUDICIAL REVIEW
The power of the court to review actions and decisions made by lower courts and other government agencies.

❐ Alexander Hamilton
- *Federalist Papers* (published 1787–1788)
- Through the practice of judicial review, the Court would ensure that the "will of the whole people," as grounded in the Constitution, would be supreme over the "will of the legislature."

❐ *Marbury* v. *Madison* (1803)
- Landmark case that formed basis for judicial review.
- This case was the first time the U.S. Supreme Court declared something to be "unconstitutional."
- The decision in this case set the stage for the idea of checks and balances and established the authority of the U.S. Supreme Court.
    - Chief Justice John Marshall declared, "It is emphatically the province of the judicial department to say what the law is."

◆ The U.S. Supreme Court has "little original jurisdiction."

◆ Typically reviews transcripts of cases under its consideration.

◆ Four of the nine justices must vote to hear a case.

◆ U.S. Supreme Court issues writs of *certiorari*.

◆ U.S. Supreme Court only reviews cases that involve a substantial federal question.

❐ Of approximately 5,000 requests for review, the Court only selects about 200 to hear.

- The Court may allow a brief presentation by attorneys for each side, but Court is not required to allow presentations.
  - ❒ Each side is allotted 30 minutes for arguments before the justices.
- U.S. Supreme Court conducts trials for disputes between states.
  - ❒ Recent example:
    - New York and New Jersey were disputing the boundary line relating to Ellis Island and in which state the famous island was located.
    - Supreme Court determined in 1998 that New Jersey had jurisdiction over all portions of the island created *after* the original compact was approved (effectively, more than 80% of the island's present land).
- Court convenes the first Monday in October of each year, and adjourns, typically, in early July.
- The term is divided into sittings, when cases are heard, and time for writing and delivering opinions.
  - ❒ Typically, between 22 and 24 cases are heard at each sitting.

❖ U.S. court of appeals

- Twelve courts of appeal (based on geographic areas), often referred to as "circuit courts," review cases of U.S. District Courts and U.S. Tax Court.
  - ❒ Appointed by president, confirmed by the U.S. senate
  - ❒ Judges serve for life.
  - ❒ There are 167 appeals court judges.
  - ❒ Chief judge
    - Chief judge is the judge who has served on the court the longest and who is under 65 years of age.
    - Performs administrative duties in addition to hearing cases
    - Chief judge serves for a maximum of seven years.
  - ❒ Mandatory jurisdiction
    - U.S. court of appeals is required to hear cases brought to them from their district courts.
  - ❒ Panel of judges
    - Criminal cases on appeal are usually heard by a panel of three judges.

- ❐ Because the U.S. Constitution guarantees a right to appeal, the U.S. court of appeals has been inundated with cases.
- ❐ The U.S. Court of Appeals for the District of Columbia (often called the Twelfth Circuit) hears cases arising in the District of Columbia or concerning many departments of the federal government.
- ❐ Federal appellate courts operate under the *Federal Rules of Appellate Procedure*:
  - Each appellate court can also create its own local rules; some circuits rely on oral arguments while others require written summary dispositions.
- ❐ Appeals generally fall into three categories:
  - Frivolous appeals (These appeals are generally disposed of quickly.)
    - Appeals with little substance
    - Appeals that raise no significant new issues
  - Ritualistic appeals
    - Brought primarily because of the demand of litigants
    - Probability of reversal is negligible.
  - Nonconsensual appeals
    - Entail major questions of law and policy
    - Typically, there is considerable professional disagreement among the courts and within the legal profession.
    - Probability of reversal is highest in these types of appeals.

◆ Federal Circuit Court of Appeals, established in 1882, considered the Thirteenth Circuit Court of Appeals.

- ❐ Represents the merger of the U.S. Court of Claims and the U.S. Court of Customs and Patent Appeals
- ❐ Has nationwide jurisdiction in a variety of areas:
  - International trade
  - Government contracts
  - Patents and trademarks
  - Certain monetary claims against the U.S. government
  - Federal personnel
  - Veterans' benefits

- Appeals to the Federal Circuit Court can come from:
  - All federal district courts
  - U.S. Court of Federal Claims
  - U.S. Court of International Trade
  - U.S. Court of Appeals for Veterans Claims
  - U.S. Merit Systems Protection Board
  - Board of Contract Appeals
  - Board of Patent Appeals and Interferences
  - Trademark Trial and Appeals Board
  - U.S. International Trade Commission
  - Office of Compliance of the United States Congress
  - Government Accountability Office Personnel Appeals Board
- Breakdown of types of cases reviewed by the Federal Circuit Court:
  - Administrative law cases (55%) involve mostly personnel and veterans' claims.
  - Intellectual property cases (31%) involve mostly patents.
  - Cases involving monetary damages against the U.S. government (11%)
    - Involve mostly government contract cases, tax refund appeals, tax refunds appeals, unlawful takings, civilian and military pay cases
- U.S. district courts, authorized as part of the Judiciary Act of 1789
  - The lowest level of federal court
  - Have jurisdiction to hear nearly all categories of federal cases, including both criminal and civil
  - Ninety-four district courts
    - Each state has at least one district court with the exception of the District of Wyoming, which includes the Montana and Idaho portions of Yellowstone Park.
    - States with the greatest number of district courts: California (4), New York (4), and Texas (4).
    - In addition to states having at least one district courts, district courts are also located in the following: Puerto Rico,

District of Columbia, one in each of the U.S. territories (Guam, Virgin Islands, Northern Mariana Islands).

- Each district court also includes a U.S. bankruptcy court as a unit of the district court.
- District courts are considered the "trial" courts of the federal system.
- Considered the courts of **original jurisdiction** with two exceptions:
  - Court of International Trade hears cases involving international trade and customs issues.
  - U.S. Court of Federal Claims hears cases for monetary damages against the United States, disputes over federal contracts, unlawful taking of property by the federal government.

ORIGINAL JURISDICTION

The lawful authority of a court to hear or to act on a case from its beginning and to pass judgment on the law and the facts. The authority may be over a specific geographic area or over particular types of cases.

  - District courts cases for 2006 to 2008

	2006	2007	2008
Filings	335,868	335,655	349,969
Civil filings	259,541	257,507	267,257
Criminal filings	56,532	57,172	61,026

  - Major types of filings for 2008:
    - Prisoner petitions: 54,786
    - Personal injury/product liability: 52,110
    - Contract issues: 34,172
    - Justice system offenses: 32,132
  - There are 678 district court judges.
  - Appointed by the president, confirmed by the Senate.
  - Judges serve for life.
  - Magistrate judges
    - Serve district court system and assist federal judges.
    - Responsibilities include conducting arraignments, setting bail, issuing warrants, and trying minor offenders.

8.1.3 State court system

- Most state systems consist of three tiers:
  - Trial courts
  - Appellate courts
  - State supreme court
- History of state courts
  - Massachusetts Bay Colony in 1629
    - General Court consisted of governor, 18 assistants, and 118 elected officials.
    - Combined legislature and court made laws, held trials, and imposed sentences.
    - By 1639, Massachusetts had grown, and county courts were established.
      - General Court became court of appeals and retained original jurisdiction only in cases involving "tryalls of life, limm, or banishment" and divorce.
    - The General Court banned the observation of Christmas.
      - "For preventing disorders, arising in several places within this jurisdiction by reason of some still observing such festivals as were superstitiously kept in other communities, to the great dishonor of God and offense of others: it is therefore ordered by this court and the authority thereof that whosoever shall be found observing any such day as Christmas or the like, either by forbearing of labor, feasting, or any other way, upon any such account as aforesaid, every such person so offending shall pay for every such offence five shilling as a fine to the county." (Taken from the records of the General Court, May 11, 1659.)
      - The General Court rescinded the banning of Christmas in 1681.
  - In the 1700s, Pennsylvania began its colonial existence with the belief that "every man could serve as his own lawyer."
    - Common peacemakers served as referees in disputes.
      - Parties to a dispute could plead their case before a common peacemaker.
      - Decision of peacemaker was binding.
      - Peacemaker system ended in 1766.
  - Prior to 1776, all colonies had fully functioning courts.
    - Lack of trained lawyers made operations difficult.
    - Most colonies retained strict control over the number of individuals allowed to practice law.

- In 1645 in Virginia, law provided for the removal of "mercenary attorneys" from office and prohibited the practice of law for a fee.
- Most other colonies retained strict control over the number of authorized lawyers by requiring formal training in English law schools and appointment by the governor.
- Between 1695 and 1769, New York allowed only 41 lawyers to practice.
    - Trial of John Zenger, editor of the *New York Journal*
        - Zenger was accused of slandering Governor William Cosby.
        - Cosby threatened to disbar any lawyer who defended Zenger.
        - Andrew Hamilton, a Pennsylvania lawyer, took the case since he was immune to the governor's threats because he was from out of state.

- After 1776, most states made no distinction between *original jurisdiction* and *appellate jurisdiction*.
    - Original jurisdiction is the lawful authority of a court to hear or act upon a case from its beginning and to pass judgment on the law and the facts; authority may be over a specific geographic area or over particular types of cases.
    - Appellate jurisdiction is the lawful authority of a court to review a decision made by a lower court.

- Modern-day state court systems
    - Early 1900s, American Bar Association and American Judicature Society
        - American Bar Association and American Judicature Society began joint movement toward simplification of state court structure.
            - Reform sought to unify redundant courts that held overlapping jurisdictions.
            - Uniform model was suggested for states everywhere that would build upon:
                - A centralized court structure composed of a clear hierarchy of trial and appellate courts
                - The consolidation of numerous lower-level courts with overlapping jurisdictions
                - A centralized state court authority that would be responsible for the budgeting, financing, and management of all courts within a state

- Trial courts
  - Lower courts, or courts of limited jurisdiction, often called magistrate or district courts
    - The courts are where criminal cases begin.
    - Magistrate courts
      - Conduct arraignments.
      - Set **bail**.
      - Take pleas.
      - Conduct trial if case is minor.
        - Examples of such cases: misdemeanors, traffic violations, small claims
    - Rarely hold jury trials.
      - Usually hold what are referred to as bench trials, which are trials held only in front of a judge.
    - This level court does *not* keep detailed records of the case (transcript).
    - The case file typically includes only information on charge, plea, finding, and sentence.
  - High courts, or courts of general jurisdiction; also called superior courts, circuit courts, or county courts
    - Authorized to hear any criminal case
    - In many states, this court also provides the first level of appellate review for courts of "limited jurisdiction."
    - **Trial *de novo*** literally means a new trial.
      - Term is applied to cases that are retried on appeal, as opposed to those that are simply reviewed on the record.
      - Review of lower-court (magistrate/district court) decision by court of general jurisdiction is usually through a new trial since lower courts have no transcripts to submit for review.
- **Adversarial process** is the two-sided structure under which American criminal trial courts operate that pits the prosecution against the defense; in theory, justice is done when the most effective adversary is able to convince the judge or jury that his or her perspective on the case is the correct one.
  - Adversarial process pits interests of the state, represented by the **prosecutor**, against the defendant, represented by **defense counsel** (also called **defense attorney**).

BAIL

The money or property pledged to the court or actually deposited with the court to effect the release of a person from legal custody.

TRIAL *DE NOVO*

Literally, "new trial." The term is applied to cases that are retried on appeal, as opposed to those that are simply reviewed on the record.

ADVERSARIAL PROCESS

The two-sided structure under which American criminal trial courts operate that pits the prosecution against the defense. In theory, justice is done when the most effective adversary is able to convince the judge or jury that his or her perspective on the case is the correct one.

PROSECUTOR

Represents the government or the interests of the community in a criminal trial. Also known as district attorney, state's attorney, county attorney, commonwealth attorney, or prosecuting attorney.

DEFENSE COUNSEL (ALSO DEFENSE ATTORNEY)

A licensed trial lawyer hired or appointed to conduct the legal defense of a person accused of a crime. The Sixth Amendment of the U.S. Constitution guarantees all defendants, regardless of their financial means, the right to effective assistance of defense counsel.

- The burden of proof is on the prosecution to prove "beyond a reasonable doubt" that the defendant committed the crime.
- The adversarial process is constrained by procedural rules.

❖ Appellate courts

- Appeal is generally the request for a court with appellate jurisdiction to review the judgment, decision, or order of a lower court.
- Types of appeals courts
    - Intermediate appellate court
        - Often called the "court of appeals"
        - Thirty-nine states have an appellate court.
        - Typically, appellate courts do not conduct a new trial but instead provide a review of the official record (the transcript).
        - May allow brief oral arguments to be made and will consider written briefs submitted by both sides
        - Most lower-court convictions are affirmed upon appeal.
        - If an appeal is upheld, the case is remanded back to the lower court for retrial.
            - The lower court can choose to retry the defendant or to not retry and therefore release the defendant from prosecution of those charges.
        - The losing side in an appeal can appeal to the next level of appeal court, typically the state supreme court.
        - Appellant is the side initiating the appeal; appellee is the side opposed to the appeal.
    - High-level appellate court, often called the state supreme court
        - Considered to be the "court of last resort" at the state level
        - All states have a court of last resort.
        - A case can be appealed to the U.S. Supreme Court if it is based on a claim of violation of defendant's rights as guaranteed under federal law or the U.S. Constitution.
            - Appeals are not automatically granted; they must meet certain standards and then they need four of the nine U.S. Supreme Court justices voting to review the case.

COURT ADMINISTRATOR

A coordinator who assists with case-flow management, operating funds budgeting, and court docket administration.

DOCKET

The court schedule; the list of events comprising the daily or weekly work of a court, including the assignment of the time and place for each hearing or other item of business or the list of matters that will be taken up in a given court term. See also court calendar.

- **Court administrator** is a coordinator who assists with case-flow management, operating funds, budgeting, and court **docket** administration.
  - Court administrators manage the operational functions of the courts by:
    - Preparing, presenting, and monitoring budgets
    - Analyzing the flow of cases to determine where additional resources such as judges, prosecutors, and others may be needed and shifting those resources
    - Collecting and publishing statistics describing the operation of state courts
    - Finding ways to streamline case processing and improve court efficiency
    - Serving as a liaison for the court with the state legislature
    - Developing and coordinating requests for federal/outside funding
    - Managing court personnel, including promotions for support staff and the handling of retirement and other benefits packages for court employees
    - Creating/coordinating plans for training of judges and other court personnel
    - Assigning judges to courtrooms
    - Overseeing payments to legal counsel for indigent defendants
  - New Jersey
    - Employed the first state court administrator in 1948
- Dispute-resolution centers involve an informal hearing designed to mediate interpersonal disputes without resorting to the more formal arrangements of criminal trial courts.
  - Function is to hear victims' claims of minor wrongdoings such as passing bad checks, trespassing, shoplifting, petty theft, and to resolve the disputes.
    - Works closely with justice system
    - Currently over 200 such programs in the United States
    - Frequently staffed by volunteer mediators
    - First programs developed in the early 1970s.
      - Community Assistance Project in Chester, Pennsylvania
      - Night Prosecutor Program in Rochester, New York
    - Community mediation programs have become a central feature of today's restorative justice movement.

        - ◆ Federal government established Neighborhood Justice Centers in Los Angeles, Kansas City, and Atlanta in the 1970s.

- **Community court** movement
    - ❖ Community court is a low-level court that focuses on quality-of-life crimes that erode a neighborhood's morale, emphasizes problem-solving rather than punishment, and builds on restorative principles like community service and restitution.
    - ❖ Community courts are always official components of the formal justice system.
    - ❖ Criticisms of community court
        - ◆ They typically work only with minor offenders, thereby denying the opportunity for mediation to victims and offenders in more serious cases.
        - ◆ Defendants may see community courts as just another form of criminal sanction rather than as a true alternative to processing by the criminal justice system.

COMMUNITY COURT
A low-level court that focuses on quality-of-life crimes that erode a neighborhood's morale, emphasizes problem-solving rather than punishment, and builds upon restorative principles like community service and restitution.

For more on the history and organization of the courts, visit Criminal Justice Interactive online > The Courts: History, Structure, and Key Players > Learning Modules > 8.1 History and Organization of the Courts.

8.2 Courtroom roles

8.2.1 There are 10 basic roles associated with the courtroom during a trial and two types of individuals who participate in the courtroom:

- Courtroom professionals
    - ❖ Judge
    - ❖ Prosecuting attorney
    - ❖ Defense counsel
    - ❖ Bailiff
    - ❖ **Court reporter**
    - ❖ **Clerk of the court**
- Nonprofessionals
    - ❖ Lay witnesses
    - ❖ **Jurors**
    - ❖ Defendant
    - ❖ Spectators and the press
- The roles may also involve witnesses and a court administrator (professionals), and the victim (nonprofessional).

COURT REPORTER
Creates a written record of all that occurs during a trial. Also called court stenographer or recorder.

CLERK OF THE COURT
Maintains all records of criminal cases, issues summons, prepares the jury pool, subpoenas witnesses, marks physical evidence, and maintain custody of evidence.

JUROR
A member of a trial or grand jury who has been selected for jury duty and is required to serve as an arbiter of the facts in a court of law. Jurors are expected to render verdicts of "guilty" or "not guilty" as to the charges brought against the accused, although they may sometimes fail to do so (as in the case of a hung jury).

JURY

Determines guilt or innocence of a defendant based on the facts presented at a trial. Article II of the U.S. Constitution requires that "[t]he trial of all crimes . . . shall be by jury."

8.2.2 Courtroom professionals

- A judge is an elected or appointed public official who presides over a court of law and who is authorized to hear and sometimes to decide cases and to conduct trials.
  - Responsibilities
    - Ensures justice is served
    - Rules on matters of law
    - Makes decisions about admissibility of evidence
    - Rules on objections
    - Maintains discipline of court and disciplines anyone who challenges the order of the court
    - Sentences offenders after determination of guilt, except in capital cases
    - When there is no **jury**, the judge determines the guilt or innocence of the defendant.
    - If there is no court administrator, the chief judge also would:
      - Develop schedules for the judges of the court
      - Hire support staff
      - Oversee training programs for new judges and staff
  - Methods of judicial selection
    - Federal level: nominated by president, confirmed by senate.
    - State level
      - Two general methods
        - Popular election
        - Gubernatorial appointment
      - Both methods (popular election and gubernatorial appointment) have been criticized for allowing politics to enter into the decision making.
  - Missouri Plan, also called the merit plan of judicial selection
    - Adopted to avoid political bias in either of the selection methods
    - Combines elements of both election and appointment
    - Judicial vacancies are filled by the following method:
      - List of candidates is screened by a nonpartisan judicial nominating committee.
      - Nonpartisan committee forwards final list to an arm of governor's office who reviews and selects from the list for appointment.
      - After specified period of time, appointed judge stands for election by public.

- Judge runs unopposed.
- Public votes either to retain judge or to have someone new appointed and then process starts over.

- Qualifications of judges
  - Currently, almost all states require judges at court of general jurisdiction and appellate level to:
    - Have a law degree
    - Be licensed to practice law
    - Be a member of the state bar association
    - Many states also require new judges to attend and participate in state-sponsored training sessions.
      - Training sessions often include topics such as courtroom procedure, evidence, dispute, resolution, judicial writing, administrative record-keeping, and ethics.
      - National Judicial College located at the University of Nevada, Reno, was established in 1963 by the Joint Committee for Effective Administration of Justice to train judges from around the country.
    - Lower-court judges
      - In some jurisdictions, magistrates, district court judges, and justices of the peace are not required to have graduated from law school.
      - Forty-three states allow nonlawyers to be lower-court judges.
      - One thousand three hundred nonlawyers are serving as full-time judges around the nation without having graduated from law school.
  - Judicial misconduct
    - All states have some method for addressing complaints about judges.
    - At federal level, Judicial Councils Reform and Judicial Conduct and Disability Act (1980)
      - Specifies procedures for registering a complaint against a federal judge
      - Allows impeachment proceedings to occur in serious cases

- Depending on the jurisdiction, the prosecuting attorney may be known by any of the following: solicitor, district attorney, state's attorney, county attorney, or commonwealth attorney.
  - Prosecuting attorney represents the government or the interests of the community in a criminal trial.
  - Primary representative of the people in a criminal trial

- Typically elected to a four-year term
  - Forty-five states elect prosecutors.
  - Five states appoint prosecutors.
  - All federal prosecutors are appointed.
- Responsibilities:
  - Introduce evidence against defendant
  - Direct testimony of witnesses for the state
  - Argue in favor of conviction
  - File appeals on behalf of state to appellate court
  - Argue briefs before appellate court
  - Make presentations to parole boards to try to prevent individual from being paroled
  - Present information/evidence to grand jury
  - Decide what charges to bring against defendant
- Approximately 2,300 chief prosecutors and 24,000 assistant prosecutors
- Often work with local police to advise about possible arrests
  - While role is limited, prosecutor involvement in police investigations may help make a better case for presentation in court.
- **Prosecutorial discretion** is the decision-making power of prosecutors based on the wide range of choices available to them in the handling of criminal defendants, scheduling of cases for trial, acceptance of bargained pleas, etc. The most important form of prosecutorial discretion lies in the power to charge, or not to charge, a person with an offense.
  - Justice Robert H. Jackson (1940) stated, "The prosecutor has more control over life, liberty, and reputation than any other person in America."
  - One-third to one-half of all felony cases are dismissed by the prosecutor prior to trial or before a **plea bargain** is made.
  - Prosecutor decides which charges to file and which witnesses to call.
  - Decides whether to file multiple or separate charges against a defendant
    - Multiple charges allow presentation of a large amount of evidence and the complete sequence of events.
    - Separate charges: Try one charge at a time thereby having multiple trials causing defendant to have to defend himself or herself numerous times.
      - Also allows prosecutor to learn from earlier cases, especially if they fail to obtain a conviction in the first case.

PROSECUTORIAL DISCRETION

The decision-making power of prosecutors, based on the wide range of choices available to them, in the handling of criminal defendants, the scheduling of cases for trial, the acceptance of negotiated pleas, and so on. The most important form of prosecutorial discretion lies in the power to charge, or not to charge, a person with an offense.

PLEA BARGAIN

A negotiated agreement among the defendant, prosecutor, and court as to an appropriate plea and associated sentence in a given case. A plea bargain circumvents the trial process and dramatically reduces the time required for the resolution of a criminal case.

- Following conviction, prosecutors are usually allowed to make sentencing recommendations to the judge.
- When a defendant appeals a conviction, prosecutors may need to defend their own actions in briefs filed with appellate court.
- If a convicted individual becomes eligible for parole the prosecutor in many jurisdictions is allowed to make a recommendation to the parole board.
- *Brady* v. *Maryland* (1963)
  - U.S. Supreme Court held that the prosecution is required to disclose to the defense exculpatory evidence (evidence that clears guilt or blame) that directly relates to claims of either guilt or innocence.
- *U.S.* v. *Bagley* (1985)
  - Court ruled that prosecution must disclose any evidence that the defense requests.
  - Court reasoned that, to withhold evidence even when it does not directly relate to issues of guilt or innocence, may mislead the defense into thinking that such evidence does not exist.

- Prosecutor liability
  - *Imbler* v. *Pachtman* (1976)
    - U.S. Supreme Court ruled that "state prosecutors are absolutely immune from liability . . . for their conduct in initiating and in presenting the State's case."
  - *Burns* v. *Reed* (1991)
    - Court held that "[a] state prosecuting attorney is absolutely immune from liability for damages . . . for participating in a probable cause hearing, but not for giving legal advice to the police."
    - Cathy Burns of Muncie, Indiana, allegedly shot her sleeping sons while laboring under a multiple personality disorder.
    - Prosecutor told police that he had permission to hypnotize a defendant who then confessed to crimes while under hypnosis.
    - Defendant later petitioned U.S. Supreme Court that the evidence obtained while she was hypnotized was inadmissible and prosecutor knew this.
- Abuse of discretion
  - Considerable opportunity for abuse by prosecutors
    - Not prosecuting friends
    - Accepting guilty pleas for drastically reduced charges for personal considerations

- ❒ Overzealous prosecution to gain visibility
- ❒ Scheduling activities to intentionally make life difficult for defendants (depositions, etc.)
- ❒ Personal biases:
  - Leniency towards females
  - Discrimination against specific minority groups

- ❖ Prosecutor's professional responsibility
  - ◆ Prosecutors are subject to American Bar Association (ABA) Code of Professional Responsibility.
  - ◆ Serious violations of the code may result in a prosecutor being disbarred from the practice of law.

- ■ Defense counsel is a licensed trial lawyer hired or appointed to conduct the legal defense of a person accused of a crime.
  - ❖ The Sixth Amendment of the U.S. Constitution guarantees all defendants, regardless of their financial means, the right to effective assistance of defense counsel.
  - ❖ Role of defense counsel
    - ◆ Represent the accused as soon as possible after arrest and ensure that civil rights are not violated.
    - ◆ Participate in plea negotiations
    - ◆ Prepare adequate defense including the presentation of witnesses on behalf of the defendant:
      - ❒ Expert witnesses
      - ❒ Lay witnesses
        - Witnesses to the crime
        - **Character witnesses**
    - ◆ Argue against case presented by prosecutor.
    - ◆ Present argument at time of sentencing.
    - ◆ File appeals
  - ❖ Criminal lawyer
    - ◆ Three major categories:
      - ❒ Private attorneys
      - ❒ Court-appointed counsel
      - ❒ Public defenders
    - ◆ Defense of the poor
  - ❖ *Powell* v. *Alabama* (1932)
    - ◆ Court required that states provide defense for indigents charged with capital offenses.
  - ❖ *Johnson* v. *Zerbst* (1938)
    - ◆ Court overturned conviction of indigent federal inmate.

CHARACTER WITNESS

A witness who provides information about the quality of character or reputation of the accused or another witness.

- Court declared, "if the accused . . . is not represented by counsel and has not competently and intelligently waived his constitutional right, the Sixth Amendment stands as a jurisdictional bar to a valid conviction and sentence depriving him of his life or his liberty."
- Court established right of indigents to have counsel appointed for them in all federal cases.

❖ *Gideon* v. *Wainwright* (1963)

- Extended right to appointed counsel for indigents in all felony cases in state courts

❖ *Arginsinger* v. *Hamlin* (1972)

- Awarded right of indigents to have legal counsel in any case where a person could lose their liberty (includes misdemeanors)

❖ *In re Gault* (1967)

- Extended right to legal counsel for juveniles charged with delinquent acts
- State programs for indigent offenders
    - ❒ Court-assigned counsel
        - Fee, usually relatively low, is paid based on set state rate.
        - A roster of local attorneys willing to take cases under the established fee structure is used to select attorneys.
    - ❒ Public defender program
        - Uses full-time salaried attorneys who do nothing else professionally except represent indigent defendants.
    - ❒ Contract attorney program
        - Least widely used form of indigent defense program
        - Arrangements made with local criminal lawyers to provide counsel for indigent defendants on a contractual basis.

❖ *Anders* v. *California* (1967)

- Supreme Court found that in order to protect a defendant's constitutional right to appellate counsel, appellate courts must safeguard against the risk of accepting an attorney's negative assessment of a case where an appeal is not actually frivolous.

❖ *Smith* v. *Robbins* (2000)

- Convicted murderer Lee Robbins told his court-appointed counsel he wanted to file an appeal.

- Robbins' attorney concluded that the appeal would be frivolous and filed a brief with the state court of appeals to that effect.
- The state court of appeals agreed with the attorney's assessment and the appeal was not heard.
- The California Supreme Court denied further review of the case.
- Robbins appealed to the federal court system that he had been denied effective assistance of appellate counsel because his counsel's belief did not comply with the requirement that the brief must mention "anything in the record that might arguably support the appeal."
- A federal district court agreed with Robbins.
- The Ninth Circuit Court of Appeals agreed. The case then went to the U.S. Supreme Court.
- Supreme Court held that the procedure established in the case of *Anders* v. *California* (1967) is only one method of satisfying the Constitution's requirements for indigent criminal appeals and that the states are free to adopt different procedures as long as those procedures adequately safeguard a defendant's right to appellate counsel.

❖ *Texas* v. *Cobb* (2001)

- Raymond Cobb was arrested on charges of burglary.
- A woman and her 16-month-old daughter had disappeared from the house that had been burglarized.
- Because Cobb was indigent, counsel was appointed to represent him.
- Cobb confessed to the burglary, but denied knowledge of the disappearance of the woman and child from the home.
- While free on bond on the burglary, Cobb confessed to his father that he had killed the woman and child.
- Cobb's father contacted the police about his son, and Raymond Cobb was arrested.
- Cobb waived his *Miranda* rights and confessed to the murders.
- Raymond Cobb was convicted of capital murder and sentenced to death.
- Cobb appealed saying that his confession should not have been admitted into evidence at his trial because it was obtained in violation of his Sixth Amendment right to counsel.
- Cobb claim stemmed from the fact that counsel had been appointed for him in the burglary case.

        - Texas Court of Criminal Appeals agreed with Cobb and reversed his conviction.
        - Texas appeals court stated that once the right to counsel attaches to the offense charged, it also attaches to any other offense that is very closely related factually to the offense charged.
        - State of Texas appealed to U.S Supreme Court.
        - U.S. Supreme Court overturned the Texas appeals court and held that the Sixth Amendment right to counsel is "offense specific" and does not necessarily extend to offenses that are "factually related" to those that have actually been charged.
    - The ethics of defense
        - Four main groups of ethical standards exist for attorneys:
            - Canons of Professional Ethics
            - Mode Code of Professional Responsibility
            - Model Rules of Professional Conduct
            - Standard for criminal justice
        - The American Bar Association (ABA) Standard for Criminal Justice states in part that:
            - "The defense counsel, in common with all members of the bar, is subject to standards of conduct stated in statutes, rules, decisions of courts, and codes, canons, or other standards of professional conduct. Defense counsel has no duty to execute any directive of the accused which does not comport with law or such standards."
            - "Defense counsel should not intentionally misrepresent matters of fact or law to the court."
            - "Defense counsel should disclose to the tribunal legal authority in controlling jurisdiction [information] known to defense counsel to be directly adverse to the position of the accused and not disclosed by the prosecutor."
            - "It is the duty of every lawyer to know and be guided by the standards of professional conduct as defined in codes and canons of the legal profession applicable in defense counsel's jurisdiction."
- **Bailiff** is an armed law enforcement officer responsible for maintaining order in the court and ensuring that the rules of court are followed.
    - Charged with ensuring order in the courtroom under the direction of the judge
    - Announces the entry of the judge into the courtroom as well as the judge's exit from the courtroom

BAILIFF
An armed law enforcement officer responsible for maintaining order in the court and ensuring that the rules of court are followed.

- Calls out the names of witnesses as they are requested to appear
- Maintains control over the accused if the accused has not been released on bail
- Maintains physical custody and supervises jury during deliberations and sequestering

- Court reporter, also called court stenographer
  - Creates written record of all court proceedings including:
    - Testimony
    - Objections
    - Judge's rulings
    - Judge's instructions to the jury
    - Arguments made by attorneys
    - Results of conferences between the attorneys and the judge
  - Accurate written record is necessary if there is to be an appeal.
- Clerk of the court (also known as county clerk)
  - Maintains all records of criminal cases including pleas and motions made before and after a trial
  - Prepares jury pool and issues jury summonses
  - Subpoenas witnesses for both prosecution and defense
  - During trial, marks physical evidence for identification and maintains custody of evidence
  - Swears in witnesses
  - Some states allow clerk:
    - Power to issue warrants
    - Serve as judge of probate (overseeing wills and the administration of estates)

EXPERT WITNESS

A witness who has special knowledge and skills recognized by the court. They are allowed to express opinions and draw conclusions within their area of expertise. Types of expert witnesses include doctors, psychologists, ballistic specialists, etc.

- **Expert witness** is a witness who has special knowledge and skills recognized by the court.
  - Expert witnesses are allowed to express opinions and draw conclusions within their area of expertise.
- Court administrator provides uniform court management.
  - Major impetus toward the hiring of local court administrators came from the 1967 President's Commission on Law Enforcement and the Administration of Justice when they reported that the court system was "a system that treats defendants who are charged with minor offenses with less dignity and consideration than it treats those who are charged with serious crimes."

- ❖ Within a few years, the National Advisory Commission on Criminal Justice Standards and Goals recommended that all courts with five or more judges create a position of court administrator.
- ❖ Not all courts have a court administrator.
- ❖ Those courts not large enough to have a court administrator rely on chief judge to fulfill responsibilities.

8.2.3 Courtroom nonprofessionals

- **Lay witness** is an **eyewitness**, character witness, or other person who is not considered an expert. Lay witnesses must testify to facts alone, and may not draw conclusions or express opinions.
  - ❖ Can be compelled to testify if summoned with a subpoena
    - ◆ Subpoena is a written order issued by a judicial officer or grand jury requiring an individual to appear at a specific day and time to give testimony under oath or bring material to be used as evidence.
    - ◆ Subpoenas can require an individual to produce pertinent books, papers, records, and other items to be surrendered to the court.
  - ❖ All witnesses are subject to cross-examination.
  - ❖ Many states pay a witness to compensate for expenses or lost wages.
    - ◆ *Demarest* v. *Manspeaker et al.* (1991)
      - ❐ U.S. Supreme Court held that federal prisoners subpoenaed to testify are entitled to witness fees just as nonincarcerated witnesses would be.
  - ❖ Thirty-nine states and the federal government have laws or guidelines requiring witnesses to be notified of scheduling changes and cancellations in criminal proceedings.
  - ❖ Victim and Witness Protection Act of 1982
    - ◆ Requires the U.S. attorney general to develop guidelines to assist victims and witnesses in meeting the demands placed upon them by the justice system.

LAY WITNESS
An eyewitness, character witness, or other person who is not considered an expert.

EYEWITNESS
A witness who testifies to having actually seen or experienced some element related to the crime process that either confirms or negates the culpability of the accused.

- Jurors
  - ❖ Article II of the U.S. Constitution requires option of jury by states.
    - ◆ ". . . [t]he trial of all crimes . . . shall be by jury."
    - ◆ Most states use juries of 12 individuals and one or two alternates designated to fill in for jurors who are unable to continue due to accident, illness, or personal emergency.
      - ❐ A juror is a member of a trial or grand jury selected for jury duty and required to serve as an arbiter of the facts in a court of law.

- Jurors are expected to render verdicts of guilty or not guilty as to the charges brought against the accused, although they may sometimes fail to do so (as in the case of a hung jury).
  - Jury duty is regarded as a responsibility of citizenship.
  - Aliens, convicted felons, and citizens who have served on a jury within the past two years are excluded from jury service in most jurisdictions.
  - Names of prospective jurors are often gathered from:
    - Tax registers
    - Motor vehicle records
    - Voter registration rolls
  - Jurors must be:
    - Adults
    - Citizens
    - Speak English
    - Be a local resident
    - Have at least ordinary intelligence
  - Jury of one's peers originated in the Magna Carta (1215).

- Defendant
  - Generally, must be present at trial
    - Federal rules of criminal procedure require that a defendant "must be present at every stage of a trial . . . [except that a defendant who] is initially present may . . . be voluntarily absent after the trial has commenced."
  - *Crosby* v. *U.S.* (1993)
    - Court held that a defendant may not be tried in absentia even if he or she was present at the beginning of a trial where his or her absence is due to escape or failure to appear.
  - *Zafiro* v. *U.S.* (1993)
    - U.S. Supreme Court held that in federal courts, defendants charged with the same offenses may be tried together, even though their defenses may be very different.
  - Majority of defendants are poor, uneducated, and are members of a minority group.

- Defendants have the right to represent themselves and need not retain counsel or accept the assistance of court-appointed attorneys.
- Defendants can influence events in the courtroom by exercising their choice in:
  - Deciding whether to testify
  - Selecting and retaining counsel
  - Planning a defense strategy in coordination with their attorney
  - Deciding what information to provide to (or withhold from) the defense team
  - Deciding what plea to enter
  - Determining whether to file an appeal if convicted

- Press
  - Press plays an important role in the courtroom, keeping the public informed about proceedings, especially in well-known cases.
  - Forty-two states allow cameras in the courtroom, but in most instances the judge needs to give permission before filming can begin.
  - Most states that allow cameras prohibit filming of:
    - Jurors
    - Juveniles
    - Conferences between attorney and defendant
    - Conferences between attorney and judge
  - States that ban television or video cameras outright: Indiana, Maryland, Mississippi, Nebraska, Utah
  - *Nebraska Press Association* v. *Stuart* (1976)
    - Supreme Court ruled that trial court judges could not legitimately issue gag orders as long as the defendant's right to a fair trial and impartial jury could be ensured by traditional means (change of venue, trial postponement, and jury selection).
      - A **change of venue** is the movement of a suit or trial from one jurisdiction to another or from one location to another within the same jurisdiction.
        - A change of venue may be made in a criminal case to ensure that the defendant receives a fair trial.
      - Trial postponement allows for memories to fade and emotions to cool.
      - Jury selection and screening to eliminate biased people from the jury pool

CHANGE OF VENUE

The movement of a trial or lawsuit from one jurisdiction to another or from one location to another within the same jurisdiction. A change of venue may be made in a criminal case to ensure that the defendant receives a fair trial.

PRELIMINARY HEARING

A proceeding before a judicial officer in which three matters must be decided: (1) whether a crime was committed, (2) whether the crime occurred within the territorial jurisdiction of the court, and (3) whether there are reasonable grounds to believe that the defendant committed the crime.

- ❖ In 1986, the Supreme Court extended press access to **preliminary hearings**, which it said are "sufficiently like a trial to require public access."

- ■ Victim
  - ❖ One of the most forgotten people in the courtroom
  - ❖ Not unusual for victim to be unaware of the final outcome of a case that intimately involves them.
  - ❖ Historical background
    - ◆ Middle Ages
      - ❒ Victim or their survivors actively involved in trial.
        - • Testified
        - • Examined witnesses
        - • Challenged defense
        - • Pleaded with judge/jury for conviction
        - • Sometimes allowed/expected to carry out sentence
    - ◆ Victim involvement ended with monarchs assuming offense was against monarchy and not an individual.
  - ❖ Victims, in some instances, seem to be victimized a second time at the hands of the criminal justice system because of:
    - ◆ Uncertainties as to their role in the criminal justice process
    - ◆ A general lack of knowledge about the criminal justice system, courtroom procedure, and legal issues
    - ◆ Trial delays that result in frequent travel, missed work, and wasted time
    - ◆ Fear of the defendant or of retaliation from the defendant's associates
    - ◆ The trauma of testifying and cross-examination

For more on roles in the courtroom, visit Criminal Justice Interactive online, The Courts: History, Structure, and Key Players > Learning Modules > 8.2 Courtroom Roles.

8.3 Prosecution and defense

8.3.1 The prosecution and the defense and their distinct roles in the trial process

8.3.2 Before trial

- ■ Prosecutor is responsible for:
  - ❖ Deciding to press charges
  - ❖ Deciding what charges to press
  - ❖ Plea bargaining conditions

- ❖ Sharing evidence with defense
- Defense is responsible for:
  - ❖ Providing legal advice and support during pretrial questioning, lineups, and trial
  - ❖ Representing the defendant in plea bargaining
  - ❖ Obtaining prosecutor's evidence

8.3.3 At trial

- Prosecutor is responsible for:
  - ❖ Preparing and presenting the state's case
  - ❖ Carrying burden of providing legal guilt
  - ❖ Arguing for conviction, acting from the view that the defendant is guilty
- Defense is responsible for:
  - ❖ Representing and supporting the defendant at trial
  - ❖ Undermining the state's effort to establish guilt

8.3.4 After the trial and conviction

- Prosecutor is responsible for:
  - ❖ Making sentencing recommendations
- Defense is responsible for:
  - ❖ Seeking reduced penalties at sentencing and possibly filing appeals

For more on the prosecution and defense, visit Criminal Justice Interactive online > The Courts: History, Structure, and Key Players > Learning Modules > 8.3 The Prosecution and Defense.

For more on the relationship between the prosecution and defense, visit Criminal Justice Interactive online > The Courts: History, Structure, and Key Players > Myths and Issues Videos > Myth vs. Reality: The Courtroom Is a Level Playing Field.

For practice in understanding the appeals process from the prosecutor's point of view, visit Criminal Justice Interactive online > The Courts: History, Structure, and Key Players > Simulation Activity: State and Federal Court Systems.

8.4 The trial judge

8.4.1 Daily administrative responsibilities

- The trial judge deals with legal issues, but many judges also have the same administrative responsibilities that other middle managers deal with.

- Trial judge is responsible for:
  - Managing daily activities of court offices, including daily office routines
  - Managing staff and determining need for new staff
  - Overseeing court activities
  - Training subordinate judges

8.4.2 Before trial

- Bail/pretrial release responsibilities. The trial judge is responsible for ensuring the rights of the accused so that an appeal can be avoided.
  - Issuing search and arrest warrants
  - Bail
  - Need for bail and amount that will guarantee the defendant will return to court
  - Also determines other pretrial release issues
- Preliminary hearings
  - Determines what the essential evidence needed is to determine if a trial is justified
- Pretrial motions
  - Change of venue or other motions that set conditions of trial
- Plea bargain
  - Judge must approve any plea bargain.

8.4.3 At trial

- Oversees jury
  - Ensures that jury is impartial
  - Advises jury regarding deliberation and response
- Presides over trials
  - Rules on procedural objections and matters of law raised in court that determine admissibility of evidence
  - May disallow the evidence if it is a violation of procedures or a defendant's rights
  - May reprimand, eject, fine, or confine those who disturb the decorum of the courtroom
  - Determines sentencing decisions
    - Determines the punishment under the advisement of others and the confines of the law

For more on the roles of a trial judge, visit Criminal Justice Interactive online > The Courts: History, Structure, and Key Players > Learning Modules > 8.4 The Trial Judge.

For more on the responsibilities of a trial judge and their effect on the courts, visit Criminal Justice Interactive online > The Courts: History, Structure, and Key Players > Myths and Issues Videos > Issue 1: Assembly Line Justice: The Effect of the Backlog of Cases on the Courts.

8.5 The grand jury

8.5.1 Selection process: Both trial and grand juries are selected according to predefined procedure, usually from the voting population of the jurisdiction. A subpoena to serve on a jury requires response and participation. Candidates are screened according to the needs of the case.

8.5.2 The role of the grand jury: to determine if there is sufficient evidence to go to trial.

- Trial jury
  - Typically lasts 6 to 12 hours.
  - Serves for duration of trial.
- Grand jury
  - Consists of up to 23 jurors
  - Serves for a specific time period and may be seated on multiple grand juries during this time

8.5.3 Secrecy

- Unlike trial jurors who appear publicly at the trial, grand jurors maintain secrecy throughout the process. The accused is not presented in a grand jury investigation. Secrecy is important because it:
  - Prevents potential defendants from fleeing or destroying evidence
  - Prevents perjury or tampering with possible witnesses
  - Allows free disclosure by witnesses
  - Protects the accused, who is considered innocent at this stage

8.5.4 Investigative powers

- The grand jury investigates wrongdoing, not only the accused wrongdoers. As a result, it requires access to a board and deep pool of data. The grand jury has an array of legal powers to compel the provisions of information and evidence.
- The grand jury can require testimony and tangible evidence. Fourth Amendment protection from unreasonable search and seizure rarely applies to grand jury subpoena.

- The grand jury may offer immunity to protect against future prosecution on the acts revealed, or be limited to protecting the witness from his or her actual testimony being used in future prosecutions.
- Contempt—the failure to respond to a grand jury subpoena—can result in the application of civil and criminal responses, including fines, incarceration, and other actions.

8.5.5 Rights of witnesses

- Witnesses called before a grand jury do not have all the rights associated with trial testimony. The constitutional protection against self-incrimination does not apply to witnesses called before the grand jury. Mirandizing witnesses may not be constitutionally required, but most states require it by law.
    - The accused has no right to testify or be represented.
    - Those called to testify must present themselves.
    - Those called to testify do not have the right to counsel in the courtroom.

For more on the grand jury, visit Criminal Justice Interactive online > The Courts: History, Structure, and Key Players > Learning Modules > 8.6 The Grand Jury.

8.6 Types of witnesses

8.6.1 Eyewitness testifies as to having actually seen or experienced some element of the crime that either confirms or negates the culpability of the accused.

- Victims are powerful eyewitnesses.

8.6.2 Defendant

- May choose to testify but cannot be compelled to
- Jurors sometimes interpret silences as guilt; the defendant should not be penalized for exercising a constitutional right.

8.6.3 Character witness

- Provides information about the quality of character or reputation of the accused or of another witness

8.6.4 Expert witness

- Has a specialized knowledge or skill recognized by the court as relevant to the case under consideration. Experts may express opinions and draw conclusions within their area of expertise. Expert witnesses may be paid to testify. Some examples of expert witnesses are physicians, crime lab technicians, chemists, psychiatrists, and accountants.

- Expertise is demonstrated through education, work experience, publications, and awards.
- Problems with expert witness testimony:
  - Can be confusing to the jury
  - Nature of subject matter can be too scientific.
  - Disagreements between expert witnesses cause jury to not know whom to believe.

For more on the history and organization of the courts, visit Criminal Justice Interactive online > The Courts: History, Structure, and Key Players > Learning Modules > 8.6 Types of Witnesses.

CHAPTER SUMMARY

- The United States has a dual-court structure that consists of the federal system and the state system. The two systems were originally created to maintain autonomy of states and to balance federal control. The federal system was established by Article III of the U.S. Constitution. The Judiciary Act of 1789 established the three tiers of the federal system: U.S. district courts, U.S. court of appeals (originally called the circuit court of appeal), and the U.S. Supreme Court. The U.S. district courts are the lowest level of the federal courts and handle all categories of federal cases, both criminal and civil. The U.S. court of appeals has jurisdiction over appeals within their region, as well as the decisions of federal agencies. The Supreme Court reviews actions and decisions made by lower courts and other government agencies. The state court system also has three tiers: trial courts, appellate courts, and state supreme court. The current structure was created in the early 1900s by the American Bar Association and American Judicature Society in an effort to create a clear hierarchy and unify redundant courts. The responsibility of trial court is to conduct trials in the case of minor violations, and to conduct arraignments, set bail, and take pleas. The court of appeals handles the request for appeals and the state supreme court is considered the court of last resort at the state level.
- There are 10 basic roles associated with the courtroom during a trial. Courtroom professionals include judges, prosecuting attorneys, defense counsel, bailiffs, court reporters, and clerk of courts. Lay witnesses, jurors, defendant, and spectators and press comprise the nonprofessionals in the courtroom. A judge is responsible for ensuring justice is served by ruling on matters of law including objections, making decisions about evidence, maintaining court discipline, and sentencing offenders. A prosecuting attorney represents the government or the interests of the community at a criminal trial, while the defense conducts the legal defense of a person accused of a crime. The bailiff is a law enforcement officer responsible for maintaining order in the court, the court reporter creates a written record of all court proceedings, and the clerk of court maintains all records of criminal cases. Among the courtroom nonprofessionals are witnesses (lay witnesses, eyewitnesses, and

character witnesses); jurors, who are responsible for rendering verdicts; the victim, who is often one of the most forgotten individual in the courtroom; and the spectators and press, who keep the public informed about proceedings.

- Prosecutors and defense attorneys have distinct responsibilities before, during, and after the trial. Before the trial, the prosecutor is responsible for such tasks as determining what charges to press, plea bargaining conditions, and sharing evidence with defense, while the defense attorney provides support during pretrial activities, representing the defendant in plea bargaining and obtaining the prosecutor's evidence. During the trial, prosecutors prepare and present the state's case, providing proof of legal guilt, and arguing for conviction, while the defense attorney represents the defendant at trial and undermines the state's efforts to establish guilt. After conviction, the prosecutor makes sentencing recommendations and the defense attorney seeks reduced penalties and may file appeals.
- A trial judge deals with legal issues inside the courtroom, but also has responsibilities for the daily administration of the court. These responsibilities may include managing daily office routines, managing staff, overseeing court activities, and training subordinate judges. Before trials, judges issue search and arrest warrants, determine the amount of bail or whether bail will be set, and determine other pretrial issues. At the trial, the judge oversees the jury, presides over the trial, and makes sentencing decisions.
- A grand jury is a jury of up to 23 jurors who determine whether there is enough evidence to take the case to trial. Members of a grand jury must maintain secrecy regarding the proceedings to prevent perjury, witness tampering, and the flight of defendants. Secrecy also allows for free disclosure by witnesses and protects the accused. The grand jury has access to a wide array of legal powers to compel the provision of information and evidence.
- There are various types of witnesses in the courtroom. An eyewitness testifies about events of the crime process that they have seen and confirms or negates the culpability of the accused. The defendant may choose to testify but cannot be compelled to do so. A character witness provides information about the quality of character of reputation of the defendant or of another witness. Expert witnesses have specialized knowledge or skills related to the crime and include such persons as physicians, crime lab technicians, chemists, psychiatrists, and accountants.

ONLINE@CRIMINAL JUSTICE INTERACTIVE

Learning Modules

8.1 History and Organization of the Courts
8.2 Courtroom Roles
8.3 The Prosecution and Defense
8.4 The Trial Judge
8.5 The Grand Jury
8.6 Types of Witnesses

Myths and Issues Videos

Myth vs. Reality: The Courtroom Is a Level Playing Field
Issue 1: Assembly Line Justice: The Effect of the Backlog of Cases on the Courts
Issue 2: Specialized Courts

Simulation Activity: State and Federal Court Systems

Homework and Review

In the News
Web Activity
Review Questions
Essay Questions
Flashcards

Chapter 9

Pretrial Activities and the Criminal Trial

CHAPTER OUTLINE

9.0 Pretrial activities and the criminal trial
9.1 Post-arrest activities
- 9.1.1 Steps and legal requirements
- 9.1.2 First appearance
- 9.1.3 Pretrial motions

9.2 The bail system
- 9.2.1 Pretrial detention vs. pretrial release

9.3 The pros and cons of plea bargaining
- 9.3.1 Process is usually informal.
- 9.3.2 Negotiations between attorneys
- 9.3.3 Negotiations with defendant
- 9.3.4 Rejection
- 9.3.5 Pros—arguments for plea bargaining
- 9.3.6 Cons—arguments against plea bargaining

9.4 Steps in the trial process
- 9.4.1 Rules of evidence
- 9.4.2 Factual guilt vs. legal guilt
- 9.4.3 Adversarial system
- 9.4.4 Jury selection
- 9.4.5 Criminal trial process
- 9.4.6 Closing arguments
- 9.4.7 Judge's charges to jury

9.5 Rights at trial
- 9.5.1 The Constitution ensures fairness.
- 9.5.2 Fairness
- 9.5.3 Facts
- 9.5.4 Protection
- 9.5.5 Assertion

9.6 Jury deliberation
- 9.6.1 Unanimous verdict
- 9.6.2 Problems with the jury system
- 9.6.3 Professional jury system

LEARNING OBJECTIVES

After reviewing the online material and reading this chapter, you should be able to:

1. Describe the pretrial/post-arrest process from the time of arrest through arraignment.
2. Explain the bail process including the role of the judge, defendant, and bail bondsman.
3. Describe the plea bargain process and discuss the pros and cons of plea bargaining.
4. Describe the steps in the trial process from the trial initiation through the reading of the verdict.
5. Present four key rights of defendants when at trial.
6. Discuss the process of jury deliberation and decision making.
7. Define terms related to pretrial activities and the criminal trial.

KEY TERMS

arraignment
array
bail
bail bondsman
challenge for cause
circumstantial evidence
closing argument
direct evidence
factual guilt
first appearance
harmless error rule
hearsay
hearsay rule
legal guilt
opening statement
peremptory challenge
perjury
plea
plea bargaining
release on recognizance (ROR)
rules of evidence
scientific jury selection
sequestered jury
signature bond
Sixth Amendment
Speedy Trial Act
unsecured bond
verdict
voir dire

9.0 Pretrial activities and the criminal trial

9.1 Post-arrest activities

9.1.1 Steps and legal requirements

- The federal government, under the auspices of the U.S. Supreme Court, has established certain rights that each defendant is entitled to prior to the trial.

9.1.2 First appearance, also called "initial appearance"

- An appearance before a magistrate during which the legality of the defendant's arrest is initially assessed and the defendant is informed of the charges on which he or she is being held.
  - At this stage in the criminal justice process, **bail** may be set or pretrial release arranged.
- Defendants are brought before a judge, usually a magistrate, and the formal charges are read.
- Defendants are advised of their rights at this time.
- Defendants are provided with an opportunity to have counsel represent them if they cannot afford to employ the services of one on their own.
- Bail may be set by the magistrate at this first appearance.
- *McNabb* v. *U.S.* (1943)
  - Established any unreasonable delay in the first appearance would make a confession inadmissible if officers obtained a confession during the delay.
  - Established a 48-hour time period in which a defendant has to be brought forward for his or her first appearance.
- The **first appearance** may also involve a "probable cause" hearing.
  - Probable cause hearings are necessary when arrests are made without a warrant because such arrests do not require a prior judicial determination of probable cause.
  - During a probable cause hearing, the judge would seek to decide whether, at the time of apprehension, the arresting officer had reason to believe both of the following:
    - That a crime had been, or was being, committed
    - That the defendant was the person who committed the crime
  - *County of Riverside* v. *McLaughlin* (1991)
    - Imposed a promptness requirement upon probable cause determination for in-custody arrestees.
    - The U.S. Supreme Court held that "a jurisdiction that provides judicial determinations of probable cause within 48 hours of arrest will, as a general matter, comply with the promptness requirement."

BAIL

The money or property pledged to the court or actually deposited with the court to effect the release of a person from legal custody.

FIRST APPEARANCE

An appearance before a magistrate during which the legality of the defendant's arrest is initially assessed and the defendant is informed of the charges on which he or she is being held. At this stage in the criminal justice process, bail may be set or pretrial release arranged. Also called initial appearance.

    - The Court specified that weekends and holidays could not be excluded from the 48-hour requirement and that, depending upon the specifics of the case, delays of fewer than two days may still be unreasonable.

- Some states waive a first appearance and proceed directly to **arraignment**.

ARRAIGNMENT

Strictly, the hearing before a court having jurisdiction in a criminal case, in which the identity of the defendant is established, the defendant is informed of the charge and of his or her rights, and the defendant is required to enter a plea. Also, in some usages, any appearance in criminal court prior to trial.

9.1.3 Pretrial motions

- Motion for discovery is filed by the defense with the court asking to review all of the evidence the prosecution intends to present at trial.
  - The prosecution's evidence may include physical evidence, a list of witnesses, documents, and photographs.
- Motion to suppress evidence is a motion by the defense because the evidence was obtained illegally.
- Motion to dismiss is submitted because of:
  - The belief that the indictment or information is faulty
  - The violation of speedy trial rule has occurred.
  - A **plea** bargain with the defendant has occurred.
  - The death of an important witness or the disappearance of necessary evidence
  - The admission by the victim that the charges were fabricated
  - The success of the motion to suppress evidence that then causes the prosecution's case to be weakened or nonexistent

PLEA

In criminal proceedings, the defendant's formal answer in court to the charge contained in a complaint, information, or indictment that he or she is guilty or not guilty of the offense charged, or does not contest the charge.

- Motion for continuance asks for a delay in the start of a trial because a witness is not available, defendant is ill, or there is a change in defense counsel who now needs to familiarize himself or herself with the case.
- Motion for change of venue is based on the belief that pretrial publicity prevents it from being tried before an unbiased jury.
  - Two ways to change venue:
    - Move the trial to another location across the state.
    - Select and bring a jury from another part of the state.
- Motion for severance of offenses is a request from the defense to have the defendant tried separately on each charge.
  - Some defendants believe that when they are tried for numerous charges at once it makes them appear guilty.
- Motion for severance of defendants is a request to have separate trials when more than one defendant is being tried at the same time.
  - A motion for severance of defendants is usually filed when a defendant believes the jury may see the other defendant as guilty and then be prejudiced against the second defendant.

- Motion to determine present sanity is a method of delaying a trial.
  - A person cannot be tried, sentenced, or punished while insane.
- Motion for a bill of particulars requests the court to require the prosecutor to provide detailed information about the charges.
  - This motion is usually asked for when a defendant has been charged with more than one count of a crime or more than one crime.
- Motion for a mistrial is likely to be declared when highly prejudicial comments are made by either attorney.
  - This motion can be made at any time and by either side.
- Motion for arrest of judgment is a motion to stop proceedings after a jury has reached a verdict but before the defendant is sentenced.
- Motion for a new trial is based on discovery of new evidence after a trial has been completed and the defendant has been found guilty.

For more on post-arrest activities, visit Criminal Justice Interactive online > Pretrial Activities and the Criminal Trial > Learning Modules > 9.1 Post-Arrest Activities.

9.2 The bail system

9.2.1 Pretrial detention vs. pretrial release

- Pretrial detention: If a defendant is charged with a very serious crime, bail can be denied and defendant stays in jail until the conclusion of the trial.
- Pretrial release: The release of an accused person from custody, for all or part of the time before or during prosecution, upon his or her promise to appear in court when required.
- Early intervention program is another name for pretrial services programs that can include pretrial release.
  - Functions of early intervention programs:
    - To gather and present information about newly arrested defendants and available release options for use by judicial officers in deciding what conditions are to be set for a defendant's release prior to trial
    - To supervise defendants' release from custody during the pretrial period by monitoring their compliance with release conditions and by helping to ensure that they appear for scheduled court events
- Types of pretrial release:
  - Bail is the posting of bond (usually money) as a pledge that the defendant will appear at trial.
    - Bonds can be posted in the form of:
      - Money
      - Property

- Other valuables
- Fully secured bond
  - Requires defendant to post the full amount of bail set by the court
  - If the individual does not show, the whole amount is forfeited.
- Bail bondsman
  - Bail bondsman, also called a bondsman, is a person, usually licensed, who effects release on bail for people charged with offenses and held in custody by pledging to pay a sum of money if the defendant fails to appear in court as required.
  - The bail bondsman is in business to make money, and does so by keeping the 10 to 20% for the bail money the defendant puts up, regardless of whether or not the defendant shows up for court.
  - If the defendant fails to show up for court appearances, the bail bondsman is held responsible for the payment of the full amount of the bail to the court.
  - **Bail bondsman** often use bounty hunters to arrest and return to custody defendants who do not appear in court as required so they can avoid paying the full amount of the bail.

BAIL BONDSMAN

A person, usually licensed, whose business it is to effect release on bail for people charged with offenses and held in custody by pledging to pay a sum of money if the defendant fails to appear in court as required. Also called a bondsman.

- Alternatives to bail
  - Some studies have found that many defendants who are offered the opportunity for bail are unable to raise the money, even the 10% to 15% if they use a bail bondsman.
  - To extend the opportunity for pretrial release to a greater number of nondangerous arrestees, several states and the federal government now make available various alternatives to the cash bond:
    - **Release on recognizance (ROR)**
      - No cash is required.
      - Defendant agrees to appear.
      - Defendant usually has strong ties to the community.
        - Owns a home in the community
        - Has a job they have had for many years
        - Has numerous family members in the community
    - Property bond is a bond in which the defendant is allowed to substitute other items of value in place of the cash, including land, houses, cars, and stocks/bonds.

RELEASE ON RECOGNIZANCE (ROR)

Defendant is set free based only on a signed promise to return for further legal proceedings.

- ❒ Deposit bail is an amount of money, usually 10% of the bail that is placed with the court.
    - Bail is returned, minus a small fee, if the accused shows up for court proceedings.
    - The key to deposit bail is that the defendant works directly with the court and not a bail bondsman, thereby gets back much of what he or she posts if he or she shows up as required.
- ❒ Conditional release imposes a set of requirements on the defendant.
    - Restrictions placed on the defendant's behavior may include drug testing, avoiding specific people or places, and attendance at a regular job.
    - The defendants report to an officer of the court or to a police officer at designated times.
- ❒ Third-party custody
    - An alternative that assigns custody of the defendant to an individual or agency that promises to ensure his or her later appearance in court

UNSECURED BOND
A bond that is based upon a court-determined dollar amount of bail.

- ❒ **Unsecured bond** is based upon a court-determined dollar amount of bail.
    - Like a credit contract, it requires no monetary deposit with the court.
    - Defendant agrees in writing that failure to appear will result in the defendant having to pay bail to the court.

SIGNATURE BOND
Used only in minor offenses. No assessment of danger is made. The accused simply signs a promise to return to court.

- ❒ **Signature bond** allows release of the defendant based on a written promise to appear.
    - No particular assessment of the defendant's dangerousness or likelihood of later appearing in court involved in the decision to allow for a signature bond.
    - This type of bond is typically used in minor offenses cases.
    - A signature bond may be issued by the arresting officer on behalf of the court.

- ■ Danger laws are laws intended to prevent the pretrial release of criminal defendants judged to present a danger to others in the community.
    - ❖ Danger laws limit the right to bail for certain kinds of offenders.

- ❖ 1984 Federal Bail Reform Act
  - ◆ Allows federal judges to assess the danger of an accused individual to the community and to deny bail to individuals who are thought to be dangerous.
  - ◆ A suspect held in pretrial custody on federal criminal charges must be detained if "after a hearing . . . he is found to pose a risk of flight and a danger to others or the community and if no condition of release can give reasonable assurances against these contingencies."
- ❖ Donald E. Prior and Walter F. Smith in "Significant Research Findings Concerning Pretrial Release," *Pretrial Issues* (1982), found that 16% of defendants released before trial were rearrested, and of those, 30% were arrested more than once.
- ❖ *U.S.* v. *Montalvo-Murillo* (1990)
  - ◆ The defendant was not provided with a detention hearing at the time of the first appearance.
  - ◆ The appeals court subsequently released the defendant.
  - ◆ The U.S. Supreme Court said that the defendant has no right to freedom because of a minor statutory violation.
  - ◆ "Unless it has substantial influence on the outcome of the proceedings . . . failure to comply with the Act's prompt hearing provision does not require release of a person who should otherwise be detained."
- ❖ *U.S.* v. *Hazzard* (1984)
  - ◆ The U.S. Supreme Court held that Congress was justified in providing for denial of bail to offenders who represent a danger to the community.
  - ◆ Later cases have supported the presumption of flight, which federal law presupposes for certain types of defendants.

For more on the bail system, visit Criminal Justice Interactive online > Pretrial Activities and the Criminal Trial > Learning Modules > 9.2 The Bail System.

PLEA BARGAINING

The process of negotiating an agreement among the defendant, the prosecutor, and the court as to an appropriate plea and associated sentence in a given case. Plea bargaining circumvents the trial process and dramatically reduces the time required for the resolution of a criminal case.

9.3 The pros and cons of **plea bargaining**

9.3.1 Process is usually informal.

- ■ Most jurisdictions have their own process.
- ■ Plea bargaining generally proceeds as follows:
  - ❖ Both sides review the case and evaluate its strengths.

- ❖ Other issues may come into play:
  - ◆ The prosecutors desire to close the case.
  - ◆ The media attention to the case
  - ◆ The defense may be more or less convinced of the client's innocence.

9.3.2 Negotiations between attorneys

- When negotiations begin, the prosecutor is considering one of three actions for a guilty plea:
  - ❖ Reduction of severity of charges
  - ❖ Reduction of number of charges
  - ❖ Reduction of sentence

9.3.3 Negotiations with defendant

- Once the plea negotiations have occurred between the prosecution and defense attorneys, the defense attorney must present the agreement to the defendant and discuss the pros and cons.
- If the defendant accepts, the agreement is presented to the judge for approval.
- The judge must approve the agreement and then the conviction is noted and the sentence is issued.

9.3.4 Rejection

- Judges will sometimes reject a plea agreement or actually enter the negotiations.
- If negotiations fail, the case will go to trial.

9.3.5 Pros—arguments for plea bargaining

- Saves time and money
- Preserves resources for notorious crimes
- Reduces court caseloads and amount of resources the state must dedicate to the judicial processes
- Ensures speedy resolution of the case
- May elicit useful information about other criminal activities
- Protects all parties from the traumatic and unpredictable results of a trial
- Prevents social stigma associated with a public trial

9.3.6 Cons—arguments against plea bargaining

- May encourage prosecutors to charge at higher levels to give room for negotiations
- May compromise the dignity of the criminal justice system

- Nonguilty defendants may plead guilty rather than a risk a guilty verdict and harsher sentence.
- Pro bono attorneys may prefer to plea bargain a case rather than go to trial, reducing their financial losses.
- Penalizes defendants who seek a trial, since trail convictions may result in harsher sentences than similar cases where plea agreements are approved

For more on the pros and cons of plea bargaining, visit Criminal Justice Interactive online > Pretrial Activities and the Criminal Trial > Learning Modules > 9.3 The Pros and Cons of Plea Bargaining.

For more on the pros and cons of plea bargaining > visit Criminal Justice Interactive online > Pretrial Activities and the Criminal Trial > Myths and Issues Videos > Issue 1: The Pros and Cons of Plea Bargaining.

9.4 Steps in the trial process

9.4.1 All trials are required to follow the rules of evidence.

- Rules of evidence are rules of the court that govern the admissibility of evidence at a criminal trial or hearing.
- The rules of evidence are partially based on tradition.
- All U.S. jurisdictions have formalized **rules of evidence** in written form.
- The *Federal Rules of Evidence* govern federal court procedures.

RULES OF EVIDENCE

Court rules that govern the admissibility of evidence at criminal hearings and trials.

9.4.2 Factual guilt vs. legal guilt

- **Factual guilt**
  - ❖ Deals with the issue of whether the defendant is actually responsible for the crime of which he or she stands accused.
  - ❖ If the defendant did it, then he or she is, in fact, guilty.

FACTUAL GUILT

Guilt that deals with the issue of whether the defendant is actually responsible for the crime.

- **Legal guilt**
  - ❖ This type of guilt is established only when prosecutors present evidence that is sufficient to convince the judge or jury that the defendant is guilty as charged.

LEGAL GUILT

Guilt that is established sufficient to convince the judge or jury that the defendant is guilty as charged.

- The distinction between factual guilt and legal guilt indicates the possibility that guilty defendants may be found "not guilty," or that "not guilty" defendants may be found "guilty."

9.4.3 Adversarial system

- The adversarial system is the two-sided structure under which the American criminal trial courts operate that pits the prosecution against the defense.
- In theory, justice is done when the most effective adversary (prosecutor or defense attorney) is able to convince the judge or jury that his or her perspective on the case is the correct one.
- The adversarial system requires that advocates for both sides do their utmost within the boundaries set by law and professional ethics, to protect and advance the interests of their clients.

SPEEDY TRIAL ACT

A 1974 federal law requiring that proceedings against a defendant in a federal criminal case begin within a specified period of time, such as 70 working days after indictment. Some states also have speedy trial requirements.

- **Speedy Trial Act** requires that the prosecution must seek indictment or information within 30 days of arrest or federal charges are dismissed; one 30-day extension is granted when the grand jury is not in session.
  - ❖ The trial must begin within 70 working days after the indictment for those who plead not guilty.
    - ◆ The trial start date can be extended to 180 days if the defendant is not available or witnesses cannot be called within the 70-day limit.
  - ❖ Delays brought about by the defendant, through requests for a continuance or because of escape, are not counted in the specified time periods.
  - ❖ The Speedy Trial Act is applicable only to federal courts; most states have enacted their own speedy trial legislation.

9.4.4 Jury selection

SIXTH AMENDMENT

Guarantees the right to a speedy trial, the right to confront witnesses, and the right to an impartial jury.

- **Sixth Amendment**
  - ❖ "In all criminal prosecutions, the accused shall enjoy the right to a speedy and public trial, by an impartial jury of the State and district wherein the crime shall have been committed, which district shall have been previously ascertained by law, and to be informed of the nature and cause of the accusation; to be confronted with the witnesses against him; to have compulsory process for obtaining witnesses in his favor, and to have the Assistance of Counsel for his defence."

VOIR DIRE

Literal translation is "to see and speak the truth." Process through which prospective jurors are questioned to determine if they are unbiased and can be impartial during the trial. If jurors are found to be unacceptable during the *voir dire*, they can be excused from serving the jury.

- ***Voir dire*** is the process through which prospective jurors are questioned to determine if they are unbiased and can be impartial during the trial.
  - ❖ The literal translation is "to see and speak the truth."
  - ❖ If jurors are found to be unacceptable during the *voir dire*, they can be excused from serving on the jury.
  - ❖ Types of challenges that the prosecution and defense attorneys can log:

- Challenges to the **array**
  - Array is a list of jurors who are summoned to appear for jury duty.
  - Generally, this type of challenge is filed by the defense counsel.
  - Challenges the pool from which the jurors are to be selected, claiming it is not representative of the community or is biased in some significant way

ARRAY

List of jurors who are summoned to appear for jury duty.

- Challenges for cause
  - Either the prosecutor or the defense counsel can file a challenge for cause against any prospective juror.
  - **Challenge for cause** is based on a valid reason that the juror should be dismissed.
  - Examples of reasons for filing a challenge for cause:
    - Potential juror is a relative of someone directly associated with the case.
    - The potential juror worked for the defendant or the victim.
    - Potential juror has demonstrated some prejudice against either the defendant or victim's race or religion.
  - Most jurisdictions provide for an unlimited number of challenges for cause.
  - *Witherspoon* v. *Illinois* (1968)
    - U.S. Supreme Court determined that a juror opposed to the death penalty could be excluded from such juries if it were shown that:
      - The juror would automatically vote against conviction without regard to the evidence, or
      - The juror's philosophical orientation would prevent an objective consideration of the evidence.
  - *Mu'Min* v. *Virginia* (1991)
    - Dawud Majud Mu'Min was a Virginia inmate who was serving time for first-degree murder.
    - While accompanying a work detail outside the prison, Mu'Min committed another murder.

CHALLENGE FOR CAUSE

A challenge to a jury based on a valid reason why the juror should be dismissed.

- At the trial for the most recent murder, 8 of the 12 jurors who were seated admitted that they had heard or read something about the case.
- All eight of the jurors indicated that they had not formed an opinion in advance as to Mu'Min's guilt or innocence.
- Following his conviction, Mu'Min appealed to the Supreme Court claiming his right to a fair trial had been violated due to pretrial publicity.
- Court denied the appeal, upholding the lower court's conviction.
- Court citied the juror's claim not to be biased.

PEREMPTORY CHALLENGE
The right to challenge a potential juror without disclosing the reason for the challenge. Prosecutors and defense attorneys routinely use peremptory challenges to eliminate from juries individuals who, although they express no obvious bias, are thought to be capable of swaying the jury in an undesirable direction.

- ◆ **Peremptory challenge** is the right to challenge a potential juror without disclosing the reason for the challenge.
  - ❐ Prosecutors and defense attorneys routinely use peremptory challenges to eliminate from juries individuals who, although they express no obvious bias, are thought to be capable of swaying the jury in an undesirable direction.
  - ❐ Limitations on peremptory challenges
    - State courts limit the number of peremptory challenges each side can use.
      - The limit is intended to prevent the possibility of delaying the selection of a jury for reasons other than cause.
      - Federal courts allow each side up to 20 peremptory challenges in death penalty cases but as few as three peremptory challenges in minor criminal cases.

SCIENTIFIC JURY SELECTION
The use of correlation techniques from the social sciences to gauge the likelihood that potential jurors will vote for conviction.

❖ **Scientific jury selection** is the use of correlational techniques from the social sciences to gauge the likelihood that potential jurors will vote for conviction or for acquittal.

- ◆ Predictions are based on characteristics such as economic, ethnic, social, or personal.
- ◆ The following types of persons are usually eliminated from the jury pool based on scientific jury selection because of potential bias one way or the other:
  - ❐ Potential jurors who have any knowledge or opinions about the case
  - ❐ People who have been trained in the law or criminal justice
  - ❐ Anyone working for a criminal justice agency

- ❒ Anyone who has a family member working for a criminal justice agency
- ❒ Anyone who has a family member who works for a defense attorney
- ❒ May also result in the dismissal of highly educated or professionally successful individuals to eliminate the possibility of such individuals exercising undue control over jury deliberations

❖ **Sequestered jury** is a jury that is isolated from the public during the course of a trial and throughout the deliberation process.

- ◆ Judge will decide before the trial if the jury needs to be sequestered.
- ◆ Sequestering of a jury can include:
  - ❒ Having the jury live in a hotel under the supervision of the bailiffs
  - ❒ Forbidding the jurors to read newspaper stories about the trial
  - ❒ Forbidding the jurors to watch any television stories related to the trial
  - ❒ Forbidding the jurors to have contact with the public during the trial
  - ❒ Limiting contact with family members during the trial

SEQUESTERED JURY

A jury that is isolated from the public during the course of a trial and throughout the deliberation process.

9.4.5 The criminal trial process

- ■ Opening statement is the initial statement of an attorney (or a defendant representing himself or herself) made in a court of law to a judge, or to a judge and jury, describing the facts that he or she intends to present during trial in order to prove the case.
  - ❖ The case begins with opening statements made first by the prosecutor and then by the defense.
  - ❖ Purpose of **opening statements**
    - ◆ To advise jury of what attorneys intend to prove
    - ◆ Describe how such proof will be offered
    - ◆ Defense attorney will also try to talk about human qualities of defendant.
    - ◆ During opening statements, the attorneys can only mention the evidence they intend to present as trial progresses.

OPENING STATEMENT

The initial statement of the prosecution or the defense made in a court of law to a judge or to a judge and jury, describing the facts that he or she intends to present during trial to prove the case.

- ■ Presentation of evidence is the main part of the criminal trial.
  - ❖ Evidence is anything useful to a judge or jury in deciding the facts of a case and can take the form of:
    - ◆ Witness testimony
    - ◆ Written documents

- Videotapes
- Magnetic media
- Photographs
- Physical objects

- Prosecution presents case first, followed by defense's presentation.
- Types of evidence
  - **Direct evidence** is intended to prove a fact without having to make an inference; eyewitness testimony accounts for the majority of all direct evidence.
  - **Circumstantial evidence** is indirect evidence and requires judge or jury to make inferences and draw conclusions.
  - Real or physical evidence consists of physical material such as weapons, ransom notes, and fingerprints. Physical evidence is usually introduced via exhibits.
  - Relevant evidence is evidence that has a bearing on the case.
- Limited admissibility is evidence that can be used for a specific purpose, but it might not be accurate in other circumstances such as a photo of crime scene taken during the day, even though the crime was committed at night.
- **Harmless error rule** states that there may be no grounds for appeal, even when evidence is improperly introduced at trial.
  - Appeal has to demonstrate the substantial and injurious effect or influence the evidence had in causing jury to vote for conviction.
- Testimony of witnesses is oral evidence offered by a sworn witness on the witness stand during a criminal trial.
  - Testimony is the major means by which evidence is introduced in a trial.
  - Witnesses must be competent to testify; they must have personal knowledge of the information they are discussing and understand that their duty is to tell the truth.
- Defendants have the right not to testify.

- **Perjury** is the intentional making of a false statement as part of the testimony by a sworn witness in a judicial proceeding on a matter relevant to the case at hand.
  - Witnesses who perjure themselves are subject to impeachment, in which either the defense or the prosecution demonstrates that a witness has intentionally offered false testimony.

DIRECT EVIDENCE
Evidence that, if believed, directly proves a fact. Eyewitness testimony and videotaped documentation account for the majority of all direct evidence heard in the criminal courtroom.

CIRCUMSTANTIAL EVIDENCE
Evidence that requires a judge or a jury to make inferences and draw conclusions.

HARMLESS ERROR RULE
A rule that states that there may be no grounds for appeal, even when evidence is improperly introduced at trial.

PERJURY
The intentional making of a false statement as part of the testimony by a sworn witness in a judicial proceeding on a matter relevant to the case at hand.

- Children as witnesses
  - Thirty-seven states allow the use of videotaped testimony in criminal courtrooms, and 32 permit the use of closed-circuit television, which allows the child to testify out of the presence of the defendant.
  - *Coy* v. *Iowa* (1988)
    - Supreme Court ruled that a courtroom screen, used to shield child witnesses from visual confrontation with a defendant in a child sex-abuse case, had violated the confrontation clause of the Constitution.
  - *Maryland* v. *Craig* (1990)
    - Sandra Craig, a former preschool owner and administrator in Clarksville, Maryland, had been found guilty by a trial court of 53 counts of child abuse, assault, and perverted sexual practices, which she allegedly performed on the children under her care.
    - During the trial, four young children, none over the age of six, testified against Craig while separated from her in the judge's chambers.
    - Questioned by the prosecutor, the children related stories of torture, being buried alive, and sexual assault with a screwdriver.
    - Craig appealed, arguing her ability to communicate with her lawyer (who had been in the judge's chambers during the testimony of the children) had been impeded and that her right to a fair trial under the Sixth Amendment had been denied since she was not given the opportunity to be confronted with the witnesses against her.
    - Craig's appeal was denied.
    - Justice O'Connor, writing for the majority stated that "if the state makes an adequate showing of necessity, the State interest in protecting child witnesses from the trauma of testifying in a child-abuse case is sufficiently important to justify the use of a special procedure that permits a child witness to in such cases testify," it is acceptable.
  - *White* v. *Illinois* (1992)
    - U.S. Supreme Court ruled that in-court testimony provided by a medical provider and the child's babysitter, which repeated what the child had said to them concerning White's sexually abusive behavior, was permissible.
    - Court rejected White's claim that out-of-court statements should be admissible only when the witness is unavailable to testify at trial saying instead, "A finding

of unavailability of an out-of-court declarant is necessary only if the out-of-court statement was made at a prior judicial proceeding."

HEARSAY RULE
The long-standing precedent that hearsay cannot be used in American courtrooms. Rather than accepting testimony based on hearsay, the court will ask that the person who was the original source of the hearsay information be brought in to be questioned and cross-examined. Exceptions to the hearsay rule may occur when the person with direct knowledge is dead or is otherwise unable to testify.

HEARSAY
Something that is not based on the personal knowledge of a witness. Witnesses who testify about something they have heard, for example, are offering hearsay by repeating information about a matter of which they have no direct knowledge.

- **Hearsay rule** is the long-standing precedent that hearsay cannot be used in American courtrooms.
  - **Hearsay** is anything not based upon the personal knowledge of a witness.
    - Rather than accepting testimony based upon hearsay, the court will ask that the person who was the original source of the hearsay information be brought in to be questioned and cross-examined.
    - Exceptions to the hearsay rule:
      - Dying declaration
        - A statement made by a person who is about to die
        - When heard by a second party, it may usually be repeated in court, provided the person knows they are about to die and the statement made relates to the cause and circumstances of the impending death.
      - Spontaneous statement is a statement given in the heat of excitement before the person has time to make it up.
        - Example: A defendant who is just regaining consciousness following a crime may make an utterance that could later be repeated in court by those who heard it.
      - Out-of-court statements made by a witness, especially when they were recorded in writing or by some other means
        - Use of such statements usually requires the witness to testify that the statements were accurate at the time they were made.
        - Especially useful in drawn out court proceedings that occur long after the crime

CLOSING ARGUMENT
Each side summarizes the evidence to assist the jury in drawing conclusions favorable to their position. No new evidence is presented.

9.4.6 Closing arguments

- Closing argument is an oral summation of a case presented to a judge, or to a judge and jury, by the prosecution or by the defense in a criminal trial.
- The summation provides a review and analysis of the evidence.
  - Testimony can be quoted.
  - Exhibits can be referred to.
  - Attention drawn to inconsistencies in the evidence presented by the other side

- States vary as to the order of closing arguments; nearly all allow the defense to speak to the jury before the prosecution.
- Some jurisdictions and the Federal Rules of Criminal Procedure authorize a defense rebuttal.
    - ❖ A rebuttal is a response to a closing argument of the other side.

9.4.7 Judge's charge to jury

- After closing arguments, judge charges the jury.
- Judges remind jurors of:
    - ❖ Their duty to consider objectively only the evidence that has been presented and of the need for impartiality
    - ❖ The statutory elements of the alleged offense
    - ❖ The burden of proof, which rests upon the prosecution
    - ❖ The need for proof beyond a reasonable doubt before a jury can return a verdict of guilt
- Judges may also provide a summary of the evidence presented.
- About one-half of the states allow judges the freedom to express their own views as to the credibility of witnesses and the significance of evidence; other states only permit judges to summarize the evidence in an objective and impartial manner.
- Judge tells jury about their need to select a jury foreperson.
- After receiving charge, jury is removed from the courtroom to deliberate.
- When the jury is in deliberation, the attorneys can challenge portions of the judge's charge.

For more on steps in the trial process, visit Criminal Justice Interactive online > Pretrial Activities and the Criminal Trial > Learning Modules > 9.4 Steps in the Trial Process.

For practice with the steps in trial process, visit Criminal Justice Interactive online > Pretrial Activities and the Criminal Trial > Simulation Activity: Steps in the Trial Process.

9.5 Rights at trial

9.5.1 The Constitution ensures fairness at trial:

- Trial must proceed in a timely way.
- Trial must be guided by an objective judge.
- Evidence must be evaluated by an impartial jury.

9.5.2 Fairness

- Speedy trial
  - ❖ Speediness is a complex calculation of timing of charges, legal actions, conditions of the defendant, and availability of witnesses.
  - ❖ Lateness will result in the dismissal of charges.
- Impartial judge
  - ❖ A judge must be objective.
  - ❖ If there are any connections or biases, these must be made public and recognized.
  - ❖ If impartiality is an issue, the judge may have to excuse himself or herself from the case.
- Impartial jury
  - ❖ A jury is selected from a list presumed to be impartial and screened by defense and prosecution.
  - ❖ The jury must come to the trial with open minds to decide case on its facts.
- Right to a lawyer
  - ❖ The defendant has the right to have counsel.
  - ❖ If they cannot afford one on their own, they have the right to have counsel appointed to defend them.

9.5.3 Facts

- Public trial
  - ❖ Allowing the public to observe the trial process, a defendant is protected from a violation of rights by the state.
- Confrontation
  - ❖ The accused has right to speak on his or her own behalf.
  - ❖ The accused may directly question and challenge the accusations and evidence.
- Compulsory process
  - ❖ The accused has the right to use the power of the legal system to require that witnesses attend the trial and provide honest and truthful testimony.

9.5.4. Protection

- Double jeopardy
  - ❖ Accused cannot be retried or repunished for the same crime after he or she has been acquitted or convicted.
  - ❖ This protection may not apply to mistrials or defendant-driven bargains.

9.5.5 Assertion

- Questions the legality of the procedures by which the accused was enticed or tricked into criminal behaviors
- Right to remain silent
  - ❖ The accused does not have to testify at trial.
  - ❖ The accused does not even have to present a defense since the burden of proof rests entirely on the prosecution.

For more on rights at trial, visit Criminal Justice Interactive online > Pretrial Activities and the Criminal Trial > Learning Module > 9.5 Rights at Trial.

9.6 Jury deliberations

9.6.1 Unanimous verdict; many jurisdictions require unanimous verdict from the jury.

- A verdict is the decision of the jury in a jury trial or of a judicial officer in a nonjury trial.
- U.S. Supreme Court has ruled in *Johnson* v. *Louisiana* (1972) and in *Apodaca* v. *Oregon* (1972) that unanimous verdicts are not required in noncapital cases.
- When a jury is unable to reach a verdict it can be declared to be a "hung jury" by the judge and be dismissed.
- For juries having difficulty reaching a **verdict**, some states allow judges to recharge a jury under a set of instructions agreed upon by the Supreme Court in the 1986 case of *Allen* v. *U.S.*
  - ❖ The *Allen* charge, as it is known, urges jury to engage in vigorous deliberations and suggests to obstinate jurors that their objections may be ill founded if they make no impression upon the other jurors.

VERDICT
The decision of the jury in a jury trial or of a judicial officer in a nonjury trial.

9.6.2 Problems with the jury system

- Many jurors cannot be expected to understand modern legal complexities and to appreciate all the nuances of trial court practices.
- In highly charged cases emotions are often difficult to separate from fact.
- Jurors may suffer from inattention or be unable to understand fully the testimony of expert witnesses or the significance of technical evidence.
- Many jurors can be stressed to the breaking point if a trial takes a long time to complete (O. J. Simpson trial took approximately one year to complete).
  - ❖ Family relationships suffer as a trial drones on.
  - ❖ Small business owners face financial ruin.

9.6.3 Professional jury system

- Opponents of the jury system have argued that it should be replaced by a panel of judges or a panel of professional jurors who would both render a verdict and impose sentence.
- Professional jurors would be paid by the government as are judges, prosecutors, and public defenders.
- Professional jurors would be trained to listen objectively and would be taught the kinds of decision-making skills necessary to function effectively within an adversarial context.
- A professional jury system offers these advantages:
  - Dependability: Professional jurors could be expected to report to the courtroom in a timely fashion and be good listeners.
  - Knowledge: Professional jurors would be trained in the law.
  - Equity: Professional jurors would understand the requirements of due process and would be less likely to be swayed by the emotional content of a case.

For more on jury deliberation, visit Criminal Justice Interactive online, Pretrial Activities and the Criminal Trial > Learning Modules > 9.6 Jury Deliberation.

For more on the fairness of juries, visit Criminal Justice Interactive online > Pretrial Activities and the Criminal Trial > Myths and Issues Videos > Issue 2: A Jury of One's Peers?

CHAPTER SUMMARY

- After the arrest, there are a host of steps and legal requirements that must be adhered to for a defendant to be able to receive a fair and impartial trial. The process begins with a first appearance, sometimes called a probable cause hearing, which is an appearance before a magistrate during which the legality of an arrest is evaluated. Some states waive a first appearance and move directly to arraignment. If the case moves to trial, a number of pretrial motions may be filed, including a motion for discovery of evidence, a motion for dismissal, or a motion to suppress evidence.
- The bail system allows a defendant to be released before the trial if bail is posted. Bail is the posting of a bond (usually money) to guarantee that the defendant will appear at trial. A defendant may be released on his own recognizance with no cash required if the defendant agrees to appear in court. This kind of release usually occurs when a defendant has strong ties to his community. Danger laws are laws intended to prevent the pretrial release of criminal defendants judged to present a danger to others in the community.

- Plea bargaining is an informal process during which both sides review the case, evaluate its strengths, and negotiate a plea for a lesser charge. Once the plea has been negotiated between the defense and prosecution and presented to the defendant, it must be approved by the judge. Plea bargaining saves time and money, preserves resources, reduces court caseloads, and ensures the speedy resolution of the case. Arguments against plea bargaining include the notion that it may encourage prosecutors to charge at higher levels, that it may compromise the dignity of the criminal justice system, and that nonguilty defendants may plead guilty rather than go on trial.
- There are a number of steps that occur when a case goes to trial. A jury is selected through *voir dire*, a process through which the prospective jurors are questioned to determine if they are unbiased and can be impartial during the trial. Depending on the case, the judge may sequester the jury, isolating them from the public during the course of a trial and throughout the deliberation process. In opening statements, the jury is informed about what the attorneys intend to prove and describe how the proof will be offered. The presentation of evidence is the main part of the criminal trial. Evidence is anything useful to a judge or jury in deciding the facts. At the end of a trial, closing arguments are presented. A closing argument is an oral summation of a case presented to a judge, or to a judge and jury, by the prosecution or by the defense in a criminal trial.
- The Constitution ensures that a trial is fair by providing for a speedy trail, maintaining an impartial judge, an impartial jury, and providing the right to a lawyer. The factual portion of a trial includes a public trial, a confrontation, the compulsory process, and protection. Many states require that juries reach a unanimous verdict. When a jury cannot reach a verdict, the trial can be declared a hung jury and dismissed. When juries have difficulty reaching a verdict, some states allow judges to speak to the jury again and issue a set of instructions agreed upon by the Supreme Court. There are problems with the jury system, including the fact that many jurors cannot be expected to understand the legal system, many jurors suffer from inattention, and jurors cannot separate emotions from fact. A professional jury system, where jurors are paid by the government, has been proposed as a valid alternative to the current system.

ONLINE@CRIMINAL JUSTICE INTERACTIVE

Learning Modules

9.1 Post-Arrest Activities
9.2 The Bail System
9.3 The Pros and Cons of Plea Bargaining
9.4 Steps in the Trial Process
9.5 Rights at Trial
9.6 Jury Deliberation

Myths and Issues Videos

Myth vs. Reality: Most Cases Go to Trial
Issue 1: Plea Bargaining: The Pros and Cons of Plea Bargaining
Issue 2: A Jury of One's Peers?

Simulation Activity: Steps in the Trial Process

Homework and Review

In the News
Web Activity
Review Questions
Essay Questions
Flashcards

Chapter 10

Sentencing

CHAPTER OUTLINE

10.0 Sentencing

10.1 Sentencing

- 10.1.1 Sentencing as a risk-management strategy
- 10.1.2 Sentencing options
- 10.1.3 Imprisonment
- 10.1.4 Fines
- 10.1.5 Limits on the range of sentencing options
- 10.1.6 Philosophies of sentencing
- 10.1.7 Goals of sentencing
- 10.1.8 Retribution
- 10.1.9 Incapacitation
- 10.1.10 Deterrence
- 10.1.11 Rehabilitation
- 10.1.12 Restoration

10.2 Presentence reports

- 10.2.1 Presentence investigation report

10.3 Indeterminate and determinate sentencing

- 10.3.1 Indeterminate sentencing
- 10.3.2 Determinate sentencing

10.4 Federal sentencing guidelines

- 10.4.1 U.S. Sentencing Commission
- 10.4.2 Guidelines for sentencing
- 10.4.3 Prison terms
- 10.4.4 Length of sentence
- 10.4.5 Criminal history
- 10.4.6 Plea bargaining at the federal level

10.5 Capital punishment

- 10.5.1 History of the death penalty
- 10.5.2 Writ of *habeas corpus*
- 10.5.3 Opposition to the death penalty
- 10.5.4 Reasons for the death penalty
- 10.5.5 Courts and the death penalty

10.6 The appeals process

- 10.6.1 Appeals may be filed by the defense.
- 10.6.2 Types of appeals
- 10.6.3 Steps in appeal process
- 10.6.4 Rights in appeals process
- 10.6.5 Outcomes

10.7 Victim rights history

- 10.7.1 Grassroots resurgence for the plight of victims
- 10.7.2 President's Task Force on Victims of Crime (1982)
- 10.7.3 Thirty states had passed their own victims' rights legislation by end of 2005.
- 10.7.4 Victim and Witness Protection Act (1982)
- 10.7.5 Victims of Crime Act (VOCA) in 1984
- 10.7.6 Violent Crime Control and Law Enforcement Act (1994)
- 10.7.7 Restorative justice
- 10.7.8 The USA PATRIOT Act
- 10.7.9 Crime Victims' Rights Act (2004)
- 10.7.10 Victim's rights at the state level
- 10.7.11 Victim-impact statements

LEARNING OBJECTIVES

After reviewing the online material and reading this chapter, you should be able to:

1. Discuss five sentencing philosophies: retribution, incapacitation, deterrence, rehabilitation, and restoration.
2. Describe three categories of sentences: probation, incarceration, and unusual sanctions.
3. Explain the role of presentence reports in the sentencing process.
4. Define and contrast determinate sentencing and indeterminate sentencing.
5. Discuss the issue of capital punishment and present one common argument for and one common argument against this sentencing option.
6. Describe three types of appeals (direct, discretionary, and interlocutory) and the steps in the appeals process.
7. Discuss the history of victims' rights and explain three specific rights granted in the Crime Victims' Rights Act of 2004.
8. Define terms related to sentencing.

KEY TERMS

aggravating circumstances
Crime Victims' Rights Act (2004)
day fine
determinate sentencing
deterrence
equity
gain time
general deterrence
good time
hedonistic calculus
incapacitation
indeterminate sentencing
just desserts
mandatory sentencing
mitigating factors
presentencing investigation
presumptive sentencing
proportionality
reasonable juror
restoration
retribution
sentencing
social debt
specific deterrence
truth in sentencing
victim impact statement
voluntary/advisory guidelines
writ of *habeas corpus*

10.0 Sentencing

SENTENCING
The imposition of criminal sanction by a judicial authority.

10.1 Sentencing

10.1.1 Sentencing is a risk-management strategy designed to protect the public while serving the ends of rehabilitation, retribution, deterrence, and restoration.

10.1.2 There are four basic sentencing options currently available:

- Imprisonment
- Fines
- Probation, which can include community-based programs
- Death

10.1.3 Imprisonment

- Bureau of Justice Statistics (2005) reports:
  - ❖ State courts convicted 1,079,000 felons in 2004.
  - ❖ In 2004, 66,518 felony convictions occurred in federal courts.
  - ❖ Forty percent were sentenced to active prison terms.
  - ❖ Thirty percent received jail sentences of less than a year.
  - ❖ Twenty-eight percent were sentenced to probation.
  - ❖ Average prison sentence for those sent to state prisons is four years and nine months.
  - ❖ Felons sentenced in 2004 were likely to serve more of their sentence before release (50%) than those sentenced in 1990 (33%).
  - ❖ Those sent to jail received an average sentence of six months.
  - ❖ Average probation sentence was 41 months.
  - ❖ Fines were imposed on 33% of convicted felons.
  - ❖ Restitution was ordered in 18% of cases.

10.1.4 Fines

- One of the oldest forms of punishment; predates the Code of Hammurabi.
- Fines are advantageous because they:
  - ❖ Contribute to state treasury.
  - ❖ Deprive criminals of proceeds of criminal activity.
  - ❖ Promote rehabilitation by enforcing economic responsibility.
  - ❖ Can be collected by existing criminal justice agencies and are relatively inexpensive to collect
  - ❖ Can be made proportionate to the severity of the offense and the ability of the criminal to pay

- Fines are criticized because they:
  - Result in release of offender, but without stringent controls on their behavior.
  - Are a relatively mild forms of punishment.
  - Discriminate against the poor.
  - Are difficult to collect
- Fines are often imposed for relatively minor law violations:
  - Driving while intoxicated
  - Reckless driving
  - Disturbing the peace
  - Disorderly conduct
  - Public drunkenness
  - Vandalism
- Judges have reported using fines in more serious cases:
  - Assault
  - Auto theft
  - Embezzlement
  - Fraud
  - Sale and possession of various controlled substances
- Fines are more likely to be imposed when the offender has a clean record and the ability to pay.
- **Day fine**
  - A concept first developed in Scandinavia.
  - Based on the idea that fines should be proportionate to the severity of the offense, but also need to take into account the financial resources of the offender
  - Day fines are computed by assessing:
    - The seriousness of the offense
    - The defendant's degree of culpability
    - Prior record measured in days
  - The use of days as a benchmark for seriousness is related to the fact that if there were no fines, the offender would be spending a number of days (or months or years) in jail or prison.
  - The number of days an offender is assessed is then multiplied by the daily wages that person earns.
  - Example:
    - If two people are sentenced to a five-day fine and one defendant earns $20 per day while the other defendant earns $200 per day, the first defendant would pay $100 while the other would pay $1,000.

DAY FINE

Fines should be proportionate to the severity of the offense, while at the same time taking into account the financial resources of the offender.

- ❖ The day-fine concept has been tested in two cities in the United States—Richmond County Criminal Court in Staten Island, New York, and in the Milwaukee Municipal Court.
  - ◆ Both studies concluded the day-fine concept could be implemented in a typical American court of limited jurisdiction.

10.1.5 Limits on the range of sentencing options are generally specified by laws at the state and federal levels.

- ■ Types and limits have shifted, and will continue to shift with public opinion, prevailing philosophies, and court decisions.
  - ❖ What is legal behavior today may eventually become illegal in the future, and then may even become legal again at some time in the future.
    - ◆ Example:
      - ❒ Marijuana
        - Early in the 1900s, marijuana was legal; today, it is illegal in most states.
        - Marijuana is legal in some jurisdictions for medicinal purposes; in one California county, it is legal to grow up to five marijuana plants on one's property.
      - ❒ Speed limit
        - Many states set the speed limit at 65 mph before the federal government mandated that to receive certain types of funds the speed limit on highways had to be reduced to 55 mph.
          - The federal government claimed that the slower speed saved lives.
        - All the states that wished to receive federal highway funds complied and lowered the speed limit to 55 mph.
        - A number of years ago the federal government removed the 55-mph maximum and most states reinstated the 65-mph limit.

10.1.6 Philosophies of sentencing are interwoven with issues of religion, morals, emotions, and economics.

10.1.7 Five goals of sentencing that coincide with the five goals of the criminal justice system:

- ■ Retribution
- ■ Incapacitation
- ■ Deterrence
- ■ Rehabilitation
- ■ Restoration

10.1.8 Retribution

- Retribution is the act of taking revenge on a criminal perpetrator.
- This philosophy is based on the need for vengeance.
- Retribution represents the earliest known rationale for punishment.
  - The earliest punishments were both swift and immediate, and often without the benefit of a hearing.
- Death and exile were common punishments.
- Model of punishment that holds that offenders are responsible for their behavior
- Punishment is seen as something the offender deserves, and should even be required, by the offender's behavior.
- The goal of retribution is not deterrence; it is satisfaction.

RETRIBUTION
A goal of taking revenge on criminal perpetrator.

10.1.9 Incapacitation

- Incapacitation is the use of imprisonment or other means to reduce the likelihood that an offender will commit future offenses.
- Ancient times
  - Mutilation and amputation of extremities were used to prevent a person from committing a crime again.
- Electronic monitoring is a way of achieving incapacitation without putting a person in prison.
- Incapacitation seeks to protect innocent members of society from offenders who might do them harm.
- Incapacitation is the basis for the movement toward "warehousing."

INCAPACITATION
The use of imprisonment or other means to reduce the likelihood that an offender will commit future offenses.

10.1.10 Deterrence

- Deterrence is a goal of criminal sentencing that seeks to inhibit criminal behavior through the fear of punishment.
- The goal of deterrence is to try to prevent others from committing similar crimes.
- Deterrence is designed to demonstrate to the criminal and the public that criminal activity is not worthwhile.
- Two types of deterrence:
  - **Specific deterrence** is a goal of criminal sentencing that seeks to prevent a particular offender from engaging in repeat criminality.
    - A sentence is provided to the offender such that they will not commit a similar crime in the future.
  - **General deterrence** is a goal of criminal sentencing that seeks to prevent others from committing crimes similar to the one for which a particular offender is being sentenced by making an example of the person sentenced.

SPECIFIC DETERRENCE
A goal of criminal sentencing that seeks to prevent a particular offender from engaging in repeat criminality.

GENERAL DETERRENCE
A goal of criminal sentencing that seeks to prevent others from committing crimes similar to the one for which a particular offender is being sentenced by making an example of the person sentenced.

DETERRENCE
A goal of criminal sentencing that seeks to inhibit criminal behavior through the fear of punishment.

HEDONISTIC CALCULUS
The notion that individuals calculate whether the benefits of committing the crime outweigh the possible penalties.

- **Deterrence** is based on a "fear of the law."
- **Hedonistic calculus** is the notion that individuals calculate whether the benefits of committing the crime outweigh the possible penalties.
  - Based on the hedonistic calculus, individuals can be deterred from committing a crime by having the punishment outweigh the advantages or benefits of committing the crime.

10.1.11 Rehabilitation

- Rehabilitation is the attempt to reform a criminal offender and is intended to reduce the number of crimes being committed.
- Rehabilitation usually uses education and counseling to change behavior.
- The development of the discipline of psychology in the 1930s led to the establishment of rehabilitation as a goal for offenders.
- Sometimes referred to as the medical model.
- The emphasis by the justice system on rehabilitation ended in the 1970s.

RESTORATION
A goal of criminal sentencing that attempts to make the victim "whole again."

10.1.12 **Restoration**

- Restoration is a goal of criminal sentencing that attempts to make the victim "whole again."
- Restoration seeks to address the damage to the victim and the community.
- Crime is viewed as a violation against a person in addition to being a violation of the State.
- Restorative justice intends to address the violation of the person (the victim).
- Types of restorative programs:
  - Victim assistance programs
  - Victim compensation programs to reimburse victims for:
    - Suffering
    - Lost wages
    - Medical bills
- 1984 Federal Comprehensive Crime Control Act
  - Requires that "If sentenced to probation, the defendant must also be ordered to pay a fine, make restitution, and/or work in community service."

- Bureau of Justice Assistance
  - Identified four guidelines for people working in restorative justice:
    - Recognize that communities are victims.
      - Quality-of-life crimes damage communities.
      - If not addressed, low-level offenses erode communal order, leading to disinvestment and neighborhood decay, and creating an atmosphere in which morc serious crimes can flourish.
    - Use punishment to pay back the community.
      - Standard sentences (fines, prison) do little to make restitution for the damage caused by crime.
      - Restorative justice requires offenders to compensate neighborhoods through community service.
    - Combat punishment with help
      - Encouraging offenders to deal with their problems honors a community's ethical obligation to people who break its laws because they have lost control of their lives.
    - Gives the community a voice in shaping restorative sanctions.
      - The most effective restorative justice projects develop a dialogue with neighbors, seeking their input in developing appropriate community service projects.

For more on sentencing, visit Criminal Justice Interactive online > Sentencing > Learning Modules > 10.1 Sentencing.

For more on fines and probation, visit Criminal Justice Interactive online > Sentencing > Myths and Issues Videos > Issue 2: Alternative Sentencing.

10.2 Presentence reports

PRESENTENCING INVESTIGATION

The examination of a convicted offender's background prior to the sentencing. Presentence examinations are generally conducted by probation or parole officers and are submitted to sentencing authorities.

10.2.1 Presentence investigation report

- Presentence investigation is the examination of a convicted offender's background prior to sentencing.
  - Generally conducted by probation or parole officers and are submitted to sentencing authorities.

- Three types of presentence investigations:
  - Long form
    - Detailed written report on defendant's personal and criminal history
      - Contains the following information:
        - Personal information about defendant
        - Chronology of offenses
        - Record of defendant's previous convictions
        - Home life and family data
        - Educational background
        - Health history and current state of health
        - Military service
        - Religious preference
        - Financial condition
        - Sentencing recommendation made by probation/parole officer completing the report
  - Short form
    - Abbreviated written report summarizing the type of information most likely to be useful in the sentencing decision
  - Verbal report
    - Made by investigating officer to the court
- New York City Department of Probation
  - In 2004, the department averaged about 10 reports per probation officer per month.
  - In 1998, the department averaged over 40 reports per probation officer per month.
- Federal law mandates a presentence report in federal court.
  - If the law permits restitution, the probation officer must conduct an investigation and submit a report that contains sufficient information for the court to order restitution.
  - Areas covered by federal presentence report:
    - Identify all applicable guidelines and policy statements of the sentencing commission.
    - Calculate the defendant's offense level and criminal history category.
    - State the resulting sentencing range and the kinds of sentences available.
    - Identify any factor relevant to:
      - The appropriate kind of sentence
      - The appropriate sentence within the applicable sentencing range

- Identify any basis for departing from the applicable sentencing range.
- The defendant's history and characteristics, including:
  - Any prior criminal record
  - The defendant's financial condition
  - Any circumstances affecting the defendant's behavior that may be helpful in imposing sentence or in correctional treatment
  - Information that assesses any financial, social, psychological, and medical impact on any victim
  - When appropriate, the nature and extent of nonprison programs and resources available to the defendant
  - When the law provides for restitution, information sufficient for a restitution order

For more on presentence reports, visit Criminal Justice Interactive online > Sentencing > Learning Modules > 10.2 Presentence Reports.

10.3 Indeterminate and determinate sentencing

10.3.1 **Indeterminate sentencing**

INDETERMINATE SENTENCING
A model of criminal punishment that encourages rehabilitation through the use of general and relatively unspecific sentences (such as a term of imprisonment of from one to ten years).

- Indeterminate sentencing is a model of criminal punishment that encourages rehabilitation via the use of general and relatively unspecific sentences (such as a term of imprisonment of from one to ten years).
  - Sentences of this type typically contain a minimum and a maximum term of incarceration.
- During most of the twentieth century, rehabilitation goal was influential.
  - Rehabilitation requires that individual offenders' characteristics be closely considered in defining effective treatment strategies.
  - Judges were generally permitted wide discretion in choosing from among sentencing options.
- Judge has latitude or discretion in sentencing, setting the upper and lower limits on length of prison term.
- Allows for reduction in sentence for good behavior and progress towards rehabilitation
  - Based on the belief that convicted offenders are more likely to participate in their own rehabilitation if participation will reduce the amount of time they will have to spend in prison

- Parole is often an option under indeterminate sentence once an offender has demonstrated he or she is rehabilitated.
- Created to take into account different degrees of guilt. For example:
  - Did offender commit crime because of need for money? Just for the thrill?
  - How much harm was actually intended or caused?
  - Did victim contribute to own victimization?
  - What is the mental state of the offender?
  - What is the possibility of rehabilitation?
  - Did offender cooperate with the police, courts, etc.?
- The behavior of the inmate during the time of incarceration is the main determining factor of when an individual is released.
- Some states allow judge to only determine the maximum amount of the sentence, not the minimum; this is called a *partial determinate sentencing* model.
- States that still use the indeterminate sentencing model:
  - Georgia
  - Hawaii
  - Iowa
  - Kentucky
  - Massachusetts
  - Michigan
  - Nevada
  - New York
  - North Dakota
  - Oklahoma
  - Rhode Island
  - South Carolina
  - South Dakota
  - Texas
  - Utah
  - Vermont
  - West Virginia
  - Wyoming
- Problems/criticisms of indeterminate sentencing:
  - Inequality in sentencing
  - Allows judges' personalities and personal philosophies to produce a wide range of sentencing practices
  - Produces dishonesty in sentencing
    - Sentence given is not sentence served.

- ◆ Good time is the amount of time deducted from a prison sentence based on good behavior of the individual.
    - ❐ Most states have a mandatory good-time count, thereby reducing prison sentences dramatically.
    - ❐ Early releases have often been necessitated because of prison overcrowding.
- ◆ **Gain time** is the amount of time deducted from time to be served in prison on a given sentence for participating in special projects or programs.
- ◆ Bureau of Justice Statistics study (1999) shows that:
    - ❐ Violent offenders serve only 51% of their prison sentence before being released.
    - ❐ Property offenders serve only 46% of their prison sentence before being released.
    - ❐ Drug offenders serve only 46% of their prison sentence before being released.
    - ❐ For all felonies, the average sentence actually served is 49% before an individual is released.

❖ Sometimes produces excessive sentences as a result of public pressure/sentiment.

GAIN TIME

The amount of time deducted from the total time to be served.

10.3.2 Determinate sentencing

- Determinate sentencing, also called fixed sentencing, is a model of criminal punishment in which an offender is given a fixed term that may be reduced by good time or gain time.
- Under the determinate sentencing model, for example, all offenders convicted of the same degree of burglary would be sentenced to the same length of time behind bars.
- Disparity in sentencing under the indeterminate model brought about the development of the determinate sentence approach.
- In the 1970s, call for proportionality, equity, and social debt helped bring about the use of determinate sentences.
    - ❖ **Proportionality** is a principle that claims that the severity of sanction should be directly related to the seriousness of the crime committed.
    - ❖ **Equity** is a principle that claims similar crimes should receive similar sentences regardless of the characteristics of the offenders.
    - ❖ **Social debt** is a principle that holds that the offender's criminal history should objectively be taken into account in sentencing decisions—the more crimes previously committed, the harsher the sentence.

DETERMINATE SENTENCING

A model of criminal punishment in which an offender is given a fixed term that may be reduced by good time or gain time. Under the model, for example, all offenders convicted of the same degree of burglary would be sentenced to the same length of time behind bars. Also called fixed sentencing.

PROPORTIONALITY

A sentencing principle that holds that the severity of sanctions should bear a direct relationship to the seriousness of the crime committed.

EQUITY

A sentencing principle based on concerns with social equality that holds that similar crimes should be punished with the same degree of severity, regardless of the social personal characteristics of the offenders.

SOCIAL DEBT

A sentencing principle that holds that an offender's criminal history should objectively be taken into account in sentencing decisions.

- Elements of determinate sentencing:
  - Offenders are given a fixed sentence length.
  - Sentence can be reduced by good time.
  - All offenders convicted of the same crime receive same length of sentence.
  - Use of parole eliminated.
  - Five states have maintained their determinate sentencing models:
    - Arizona
    - California
    - Illinois
    - Indiana
    - Maine
- Two major types of determinate sentencing
  - **Presumptive sentencing**
    - This model became popular in the 1980s as states began experimenting with sentencing guidelines.
    - Model of criminal punishment that meets the following conditions:
      - Proper sentence is presumed to fall within a range of sentences authorized by sentencing guidelines.
      - Sentencing judges are expected to follow the sentencing guidelines; if they deviate, they must provide a written justification.
      - The sentencing guidelines provide for some review, usually by an appellate court, if the judge departs from the guidelines in sentencing an offender.
    - Guidelines typically developed by a sentencing commission and approved by the state legislature.
    - Differs from determinate and voluntary guidelines in three respects:
      - Presumptive guidelines are not developed by the legislature, but by a sentencing commission that often represents a diverse array of criminal justice and sometimes private interests.
      - Presumptive guidelines are explicit and highly structured, typically relying on a quantitative scoring instrument to classify the offense for which a person is to be sentenced.
      - Guidelines are not voluntary; judges have to adhere to the sentencing system or provide a written rationale for departures from them.

PRESUMPTIVE SENTENCING

A model of criminal punishment that meets the following conditions: (1) The appropriate sentence for an offender convicted of a specific charge is presumed to fall within a range of sentences authorized by sentencing guidelines that are adopted by a legislatively created sentencing body, usually a sentencing commission. (2) Sentencing judges are expected to sentence within the range or to provide written justification for not doing so. (3) There is a mechanism for review, usually appellate, of any departure from the guidelines.

- First four states to adopt sentencing guidelines:
  - Minnesota (1980)
  - Pennsylvania (1982)
  - Washington (1983)
  - Florida (1983)
- Federal government and 16 states now follow sentencing guidelines.
  - Ten of the states use presumptive guidelines while the remaining use voluntary/advisory guidelines.
    - **Voluntary/advisory guidelines** recommend sentencing parameters, but the law does not require that the judge follow them.
- Sentencing guidelines authored by legislative sentencing commissions are now the most popular form of determinate sentencing.
- Most state sentencing guidelines allow for:
  - Mitigating factors. **Mitigating factors** are things/circumstances surrounding the crime or the perpetrator that would cause a judge to lower the sentence from that specified in the guidelines. Examples:
    - Defendant has no prior record punishable by more than 60 days of imprisonment.
    - Defendant has already made partial or full restitution.
    - Person has previously had a good reputation in the community.
    - Defendant helped in the apprehension of another felon or testified truthfully on behalf of the prosecution in another case.
    - Victim was a voluntary participant or the defendant acted under strong provocation.
    - Offense was committed under duress, coercion, or threat that was not sufficient for a defense, but reduces the culpability of the defendant.
    - Defendant was suffering from a mental or physical condition that was insufficient to constitute a defense but that significantly reduces defendant's culpability.
  - **Aggravating circumstances** are those factors/circumstances surrounding/related to the crime or the perpetrator that would cause

VOLUNTARY/ADVISORY GUIDELINES
Guidelines that recommend sentencing parameters, but the law does not require that the judge follow them.

MITIGATING FACTORS
Circumstances relating to the commission of a crime that may be considered to reduce the blameworthiness of the defendant. See also aggravating circumstances.

AGGRAVATING CIRCUMSTANCES
Circumstances related to the commission of a crime that make it more grave than the average instance of that crime.

the judge to increase the sentence from that specified in the sentencing guidelines. Examples:

- Defendant induced others to participate in the commission of the offense.
- Offense was especially heinous, atrocious, or cruel.
- Defendant was armed or used a deadly weapon during crime.
- Offense was committed for hire.
- Victim was a law enforcement officer or a corrections officer who was on duty at the time of the offense or because of past exercise of official duties.
- Defendant took advantage of a position of trust.

- ◆ Criticism of determinate sentencing:
  - ❒ Overly simplistic
  - ❒ Based upon a primitive concept of culpability
  - ❒ Incapable of offering hope for rehabilitation
  - ❒ While it may reduce judge's discretion it increases the discretion of the prosecutor of the case.
  - ❒ Alleged inability to promote effective rehabilitation

❖ Mandatory sentencing is a determinate sentencing scheme that allows no leeway in the nature of the sentence required, and under which clearly enumerated punishments are mandated for specific offenses or for habitual offenders convicted of a series of crimes.

- ◆ Three-strikes law
  - ❒ Requires mandatory sentence for individuals who have been convicted of a third serious felony (the third has to be a violent felony)
  - ❒ Under the three-strikes laws much longer prison terms are imposed.
  - ❒ California's three-strikes law
    - Individuals who are convicted of a violent crime and have two prior convictions (do not have to be violent offenses) serve a minimum of 25 years in prison for the third offense (which has to be a violent felony).
    - Law doubles prison term for individuals convicted of a second violent felony.

- Three-strikes laws vary from jurisdiction to jurisdiction:
    - Some three-strikes laws stipulate that both of the prior convictions and the current one be for violent offenses.
    - Some jurisdictions require only that the prior convictions be for violent felonies.
    - Some three-strikes laws count only prior adult convictions while others permit consideration of juvenile crimes.

◆ **Truth in sentencing** is a close correspondence between the sentence imposed and the actual time served in prison prior to release.

- Comprehensive Crime Control Act (1984)
    - Federal government adopted a truth-in-sentencing policy for almost all federal offenders.
    - This act almost completely eliminated **good-time** credit at the federal level.
    - With elimination of good-time credit, there was no longer the need for parole, which was targeted for elimination in 1992, but extended until 2002.
- The Violent Crime Control and Law Enforcement Act of 1994
    - Set aside $4 billion to try to entice states to also pass "truth-in-sentencing" laws—money would be used for prison construction in those states that passed similar laws.
    - Federal government wanted states to guarantee that certain violent offenders would spend at least 85% of their prison sentence behind bars.
    - By 1999, 27 states and the District of Columbia had met the 85% requirement.
    - Four states have specific requirements that are considerably less than the 85% time served:
        - Texas and Maryland retain 50% requirements for violent offenders.
        - Nebraska and Indiana require all offenders to serve only 50% of their sentence.

TRUTH IN SENTENCING

A close correspondence between the sentence imposed on an offender and time actually served in prison. (Lawrence A. Greenfeld, *Prison Sentences and Time Served for Violence*, Bureau of Justice Statistics Selected Findings, No. 4 [April 1995].)

GOOD TIME

The amount of time deducted from time to be served in prison on a given sentence as a consequence of good behavior.

- Research on mandatory sentencing laws
  - Michael Tonry in *Sentencing Reform Impact* (1987) published by National Institute of Justice, found:
    - Justice personnel (police, prosecutors, judges) exercise discretion to avoid application of laws they consider unduly harsh.
    - Arrest rates for targeted crimes decline with the institution of mandatory sentences.
    - Dismissal and diversion rates increase at the early stages of processing with the institution of mandatory sentencing.
    - For cases not dismissed, plea bargain rates decline and trial rates increase.
    - For those convicted, sentencing delays increase.
    - **Mandatory sentencing** laws have little impact on overall probability that individuals will be imprisoned.
    - For those imprisoned, sentences are longer and more severe.
  - Research at federal level found that:
    - Blacks receive longer sentences under mandatory sentencing not because of discrimination, but because they represent a large percentage of those charged with trafficking crack cocaine.
    - Congress has to date singled out crack cocaine for especially harsh punishments.
    - Attempts have been made to change the law about crack cocaine and put it in the same category as regular cocaine.

MANDATORY SENTENCING

A structured sentencing scheme that allows no leeway in the nature of the sentence required and under which clearly enumerated punishments are mandated for specific offense or for habitual offenders convicted of a series of crimes.

For more on determinate and indeterminate sentencing, visit Criminal Justice Interactive online > Sentencing > Learning Modules > 10.3 Determinate and Indeterminate Sentencing.

For more on the three strikes and mandatory sentencing guidelines, visit Criminal Justice Interactive online > Sentencing > Myths and Issues Videos > Issue 1: "Three Strikes" and Other Mandatory Sentencing Guidelines.

10.4 Federal Sentencing Guidelines

10.4.1 U.S. Sentencing Commission

- Established under the Sentencing Reform Act of 1984, which is part of the Title II Comprehensive Crime Control Act of 1984.
- Created a nine-member U.S. Sentencing Commission
- Established minimum sentences for certain federal crimes, including drug offenses, and asked commission for a system that would permit flexibility in the face of mitigating or aggravating circumstances.
- Limited discretion of federal judges by creating the federal sentencing guidelines, which judges are required to follow
- Congress specified the purposes of sentencing to include:
  - Deterring criminals
  - Incapacitating and/or rehabilitating offenders
  - Providing "**just desserts**" in punishing criminals
- Congress specified that the degree of discretion available in any one sentencing category could not exceed 25% of the basic penalty for that category, or six months, whichever might be greater.
- Guidelines took effect November 1987, but were challenged on legal grounds.
- *Mistretta* v. *U.S.* (1989)
  - U.S. Supreme Court held that Congress had acted appropriately in establishing the Sentencing Commission and the guidelines could be applied to federal cases nationwide.
- *U.S.* v. *Booker* (2005)
  - U.S. Supreme Court ruled that the Sixth Amendment right to a trial by jury requires that the current federal sentencing guidelines be advisory, rather than mandatory.
  - Court struck down a provision in the law that made federal sentencing guidelines mandatory as well as a provision that permitted appellate review of departure from the guidelines.
  - Ruling gives federal judges discretion in sentencing offenders by not requiring them to adhere to the guidelines; rather, the guidelines can be used by judges on an advisory basis.
  - Judges now have discretion in sentencing defendants unless the offense carries a mandatory sentence (as specified in the law).

JUST DESSERTS

A model of criminal sentencing that holds that criminal offenders deserve the punishment they receive at the hands of the law and that punishments should be appropriate to the type and severity of the crime committed.

10.4.2 The guidelines use a table with 43 rows corresponding to the level of serious of crime—level 1 is least serious and level 43 is most serious.

10.4.3 Prison terms associated with each level overlap

- This intentional overlapping was designed to discourage unnecessary litigation.

10.4.4 An increase of six levels approximately doubles the length of the sentence.

10.4.5 Uses six categories of criminal history, with category 1 being the least amount of criminal history and category 6 being the greatest amount criminal history.

- Criminal histories are developed on a point scale.
  - ❖ Each prior imprisonment for more than 13 months counts as three points.
  - ❖ Prior prison term of six to thirteen months counts as two points.
  - ❖ If defendant committed current crime while on probation, parole, or work release, two points are added to the criminal history category.
  - ❖ The system allows for additional points to be added to the criminal history for other variables.
  - ❖ Thirteen points or more requires the individual be sentenced from category 6 of the criminal history.
  - ❖ Within each level, the highest criminal history has a sentence two to three times greater than the lowest criminal history for that level.
  - ❖ If an individual is classified as a career offender, he or she is automatically placed in category 6 of criminal history.
    - ◆ To be classified as a career criminal, the following three criteria need to be met:
      - ❐ At least 18 at time of offense
      - ❐ Offense is a crime of violence or trafficking of a controlled substance.
      - ❐ Defendant has at least two prior felony convictions of either a crime of violence or a controlled substance offense.
    - ◆ All three of the above criteria can be met by convictions obtained at one trial even when previous convictions are lacking.
      - ❐ *Deal* v. *U.S.* (1993)
        - Defendant Deal was convicted of six counts of carrying and using a firearm in a series of bank robberies in the Houston, Texas, area.
        - Federal district judge sentenced him to 105 years in prison as a career offender: 5 years on the first count, 20 years on each of the other counts.

- The sentences were to run consecutively.
- Deal appealed.
- Court held, "We see no reason why the defendant should not receive such a sentence, simply because he managed to evade detection, prosecution, and conviction for the first five offenses and was ultimately tried on all six in a single proceeding."

10.4.6 Plea bargaining at the federal level

- Ninety percent of all federal cases are the result of guilty pleas.
- The vast majority of these are the result of plea negotiations.
- U.S. Sentencing Commission allows for plea bargaining with following conditions:
  - The agreement should be fully disclosed in court record (unless there is some demonstrable reason why it should not).
  - Detail about original offense be included in the record.
- Thrust of federal rule about plea bargaining is to reduce the veil of secrecy that had previously surrounded the process.
  - Information on the decision-making process itself is available to victims, the media, and the public.
- *Melendez* v. *U.S.* (1996)
  - U.S. Supreme Court held that a government motion requesting that a trial judge deviate from the federal sentencing guidelines as part of a cooperative plea agreement does not permit imposition of a sentence below a statutory minimum specified by law.

10.5 Capital punishment

10.5.1 History of the death penalty

- Biblical Israel under Davidic monarchy
  - Instituted sentence of death by public stoning
  - After the person was stoned to death, the body was often impaled on a post at the city gates as a demonstration to the public.
- Greek society (200 B.C.E.)
  - Used poison to limit suffering
  - Socrates, accused of being a political subversive, died drinking poison derived from a hemlock tree.
- Romans
  - Used beheading most often
  - Arsonists were to be burned.

- ❖ False witnesses were thrown from a high rock.
- ❖ Witches were clubbed to death.
- ❖ Slaves were strangled.
- ❖ Christians and rabble were thrown to the lions or crucified.
  - ◆ Crucifixion was used as recently as 1997 in Yemen (a country at the southern tip of the Arabian peninsula).
    - ❐ Two convicted murderers were sentenced to be publicly crucified.

- ■ Dark Ages (426 A.D. to the early thirteenth century)
  - ❖ Executions institutionalized through use of ordeals.
  - ❖ Ordeals were designed to both judge and punish.
  - ❖ Suspects were submerged in cold water, boiled in oil, crushed under huge stones, forced to do battle with professional soldiers, or thrown into bonfires.
  - ❖ Belief was that those who were innocent would be protected by God and they would emerge unharmed; therefore, only the guilty would perish.
  - ❖ Under the direction of Pope Innocent III, trial by ordeal was eliminated in 1215 by decree of Fourth Lateran Council.
  - ❖ As a result of the Fourth Lateran Council, trials became the method for determining guilt.
    - ◆ Death penalty use was still widespread.
    - ◆ As recently as 150 years ago, 160 crimes were punishable in England by death.
    - ◆ In France around the time of the French Revolution, the guillotine was invented.
      - ❐ Created by Dr. Joseph-Ignace Guillotin, it was described as a "cool breath on the back of the neck" and was widely used in eliminating opponents of the revolution.
- ■ United States
  - ❖ Up until the early 1890s, hanging was the preferred mode of execution because it required few special materials.
  - ❖ In the 1980s, electrocution replaced hanging.
    - ◆ Appeal of electrocution was that it stopped the heart without visible signs of gross bodily trauma.
  - ❖ Since recordkeeping first began in 1608, estimates are that over 18,800 legal executions have taken place in the United States.
  - ❖ Currently, 38 states and the federal government have capital punishment laws.
    - ◆ Thirty-seven of the states permit execution for first-degree murder.

- New York permits execution for cases involving the murder of law enforcement officers, judges, and witnesses and their families, as well as for serial killers, terrorists, murderers for hire, and those who kill while committing another felony like robbery or rape.

- ❖ At the federal level, under the Violent Crime Control and Law Enforcement Act of 1994 and the 2001 USA PATRIOT Act, a total of 60 offenses are punishable by death.
- ❖ On July 1, 2001, there were 3,717 people were under sentence of death in the United States.
    - Male: 98.5%
    - White: 46%
    - Hispanic: 9%
    - Black: 43%
    - Other (mostly Native American): 2%
- ❖ Majority of states use lethal injection, while the second most common method is electrocution.
- ❖ Hanging, firing squad, and gas chamber methods still exist as options in some states.

10.5.2 Writ of *habeas corpus*

WRIT OF *HABEAS CORPUS*
A writ that directs the person detaining a prisoner to bring him or her before a judicial officer to determine the lawfulness of the imprisonment.

- Writ of *habeas corpus*, Latin for "you have the body," is a writ that directs the person detaining a prisoner to bring him or her before a judicial officer to determine the lawfulness of the imprisonment.
- Automatic review of death sentences delays the time between when the sentence is passed and when it is carried out.
    - ❖ Average of 10 years and 10 months between time of sentencing and execution of sentence
- *McCleskey* v. *Zandt* (1991)
    - ❖ Limited the number of appeals a condemned person may file with the court.
    - ❖ The repeated filing for the sole purpose of delay promotes disrespect for the finality of convictions and disparages the entire criminal justice system.
    - ❖ Court established a two-pronged criterion for future appeals after the first petition:
        - Must demonstrate good cause that the claim now being made was not included in the first filing.
        - Must demonstrate how the absence of that claim may have harmed the petitioner's ability to mount an effective defense.
- *Coleman* v. *Thompson* (1991)
    - ❖ Two months after *McCleskey* v. *Zandt*

- U.S. Supreme Court ruled that state prisoners could not cite "procedural default" such as a defense attorney's failure to meet state's filing deadline for appeals as the basis for an appeal in federal court.

- *Schlup* v. *Delo* (1995)
  - Court ruled that before an appeal based on claims of new evidence could be heard, "a petitioner must show that, in light of the new evidence, it is more likely than not that no reasonable juror would have found him guilty beyond a reasonable doubt."
  - "**Reasonable juror**" is a juror who "would consider fairly all of the evidence presented and would conscientiously obey the trial court's instructions requiring proof beyond a reasonable doubt."

REASONABLE JUROR
Juror who would consider all of the evidence presented fairly and obey the court's instructions requiring proof beyond a reasonable doubt.

- Antiterrorism and Effective Death Penalty Act (AEDPA) of 1996
  - Sets a one-year postconviction deadline for state inmates filing federal *habeas corpus* appeals
  - The deadline is six months for state death-row inmates who were provided a lawyer for *habeas* appeals at the state level.
  - Act also requires federal courts to presume that the factual findings of state courts are correct.
  - Does not permit the claim of state court misinterpretations of the U.S. Constitution as a basis for *habeas* relief unless those misinterpretations are "unreasonable" and requires that all petitioners must show prior to obtaining a hearing facts sufficient to establish by clear and convincing evidence that but for constitutional error, no reasonable fact finder would have found the petitioner guilty.
  - Act also requires approval by a three-judge panel before an inmate can file a second federal appeal raising newly discovered evidence of innocence.
- *Felker* v. *Turpin* (1996)
  - U.S. Supreme Court ruled that limitations on the authority of federal courts to consider successive *habeas corpus* petitions imposed by the Antiterrorism and Effective Death Penalty Act of 1996 are permissible since they do not deprive the U.S. Supreme Court of its original jurisdiction over such petition.

10.5.3 Opposition to the death penalty

- The death penalty can and has been used on innocent people.
  - Death Penalty Information Center
    - Claims that 135 people in 26 states have been freed from death row between 1973 and August 2009 after it was determined that they were innocent of the capital crime of which they had been convicted.

- Exonerations by state:
  - Florida (32)
  - Illinois (20)
  - Texas (9)
  - Louisiana (8)
  - Arizona (8)
  - Oklahoma (8)
  - North Carolina (8)
  - Pennsylvania (6)
  - Alabama (6)
  - Georgia (5)
  - Ohio (5)
  - New Mexico (4)
  - California (3)
  - Massachusetts (3)
  - Missouri (3)
  - Mississippi (3)
  - South Carolina (2)
  - Indiana (2)
  - Tennessee (2)
  - Idaho (1)
  - Kentucky (1)
  - Maryland (1)
  - Nebraska (1)
  - Nevada (1)
  - Virginia (1)
  - Washington (1)
- Exonerations by race:
  - Black (69)
  - White (52)
  - Latino (12)
  - Other (2)

❖ In 2000, then-governor of Illinois George Ryan announced that he was suspending all executions in his state indefinitely.

- DNA testing had shown that 13 Illinois death-row prisoners could not have committed the capital crimes for which they were convicted.

❖ American Bar Association (2000) formally requested states holding death-row inmates to use DNA testing to minimize risk that innocent people would be executed.

- In 2006, New Jersey voted to suspend the use of the death penalty until a state task force made its report on whether capital punishment is fairly imposed.
- Innocence Protection Act (2004)
  - Signed into law by President George W. Bush
  - Passed in recognition of the potential of DNA testing to exonerate the innocent
  - Provides federal funds to eliminate backlog of unanalyzed DNA samples in the nation's crime laboratories.
  - Facilitates access to postconviction DNA testing for those serving time in state or federal prisons or on death row.

- The death penalty is not an effective deterrent.
  - Studies of states that had eliminated the death penalty failed to show any increase in homicide rates (Decker and Kohfield, "A Deterrence Study of the Death Penalty in Illinois, 1933–1980," *Journal of Criminal Justice*, Vol. 12, No. 4, 1984; Decker and Kohfield, "An Empirical Analysis of the Deterrent Effect of the Death Penalty in Missouri," *Journal of Crime and Justice*, Vol. 10, No. 1, 1987).
  - Studies that found capital punishment served as a deterrent (Dezhbakhsh, Rubin, and Shepherd, "Does Capital Punishment Have a Deterrent Effect" New Evidence from Post-Moratorium Panel Data," Emory University Web Document, Posted January, 2001).
- The imposition of the death penalty is arbitrary and discriminatory.
- Imposition of the death penalty is far too expensive to justify its use.
- Using the death penalty reduces us to the level of the criminal.
- Human life is sacred, and killing at the hands of the state is not a righteous act but rather one that is on the same moral level as the crimes committed by the condemned.

10.5.4 Reasons for the death penalty

- Revenge: Only after execution can the survivors begin to heal psychologically.
- Just desserts: Some people deserve to die for what they did.
- Protection: Once executed, cannot commit another crime.

10.5.5 Courts and the death penalty

- *Wilkerson* v. *Utah* (1878)
  - Appeal filed that questioned shooting as a method of execution and raised Eighth Amendment claims that firing squads constituted a form of cruel and unusual punishment.

    - ❖ Supreme Court disagreed, contrasting the relatively civilized nature of firing squads with the various forms of torture often associated with capital punishment.

- *In re Kemmler* (1890)
    - ❖ U.S. Supreme Court defined cruel and unusual methods of execution as follows: "Punishments are cruel when they involve torture or lingering death; but the punishment of death is not cruel, within the meaning of that word as used in the Constitution."
- *Furman* v. *Georgia* (1972)
    - ❖ Court recognized the "evolving standard of decency."
    - ❖ Court invalidated Georgia's death penalty statute on the basis that it allowed a jury unguided discretion in the imposition of a capital sentence.
    - ❖ Majority of justices concluded that the Georgia statute, which permitted a jury to decide simultaneously issues of guilt or innocence while it weighed sentencing options allowed for an arbitrary and capricious application of the death penalty.
- *Gregg* v. *Georgia* (1976)
    - ❖ Court upheld two-step trial procedure requirements of Georgia's new capital punishment law as necessary for ensuring the separation of the highly personal information needed in a sentencing decision from the kinds of information reasonably permissible in a jury trial.
    - ❖ This case allowed the reinstatement of the death penalty.
- *Coker* v. *Georgia* (1977)
    - ❖ U.S. Supreme Court rejected a Georgia law imposing the death penalty for the rape of an adult woman.
    - ❖ Court concluded that capital punishment under such circumstances would be "grossly disproportionate" to the crime.
- *Blystone* v. *Pennsylvania* (1990) and *Boyde* v. *California* (1990)
    - ❖ Court upheld statutes that had been interpreted to dictate that death penalties must be imposed where juries find a lack of mitigating circumstances that could offset obvious aggravating circumstances.
- *Harris* v. *Alabama* (1995)
    - ❖ Supreme Court supported Alabama's law on capital punishment that allows juries to recommend sentences but judges to decide them.
- *Tullaepa* v. *California* (1995)
    - ❖ Court rejected appeal challenging California law that requires the jury to consider, among other things, the circumstances of the offense, prior violent crimes, and the defendant's age.

- *Ring* v. *Arizona* (2002)
  - A jury had found Timothy Stuart Ring guilt of felony murder occurring in the course of an armed robbery for the killing of an armored car driver in 1994.
  - Jury deadlocked on the charge of premeditated murder.
  - Under Arizona law, Ring could not be sentenced to death unless a judge made further findings in a separate sentencing hearing.
    - The death penalty could only be imposed if the judge found the existence of at least one aggravating circumstance specified by the law that was not offset by mitigating circumstances.
  - During the hearing the judge listened to an accomplice who said that Ring planned the robbery and shot the guard.
  - The judge determined that Ring was the actual killer and found the killing was for financial gain (an aggravating factor).
  - Ring was sentenced to death.
  - Ring appealed.
  - U.S. Supreme Court upheld the appeal stating "Arizona's enumerated aggravating factors operate as the fundamental equivalent of an element of a greater offense."
  - *Ring* established that juries, not judges, must decide the facts that lead to a death sentence.
    - The *Ring* ruling called into question at least 150 judge-imposed death sentences in at least five states.
- *Atkins* v. *Virginia* (2002)
  - U.S. Supreme Court ruled that executing mentally retarded people violates the Constitution's ban on cruel and unusual punishments.
  - Court following the lead of the federal government and the 18 states that had already banned such executions.
  - Atkins had an IQ that was measured at 59 (100 is "average").
- *Deck* v. *Missouri* (2005)
  - Court forbade the use of visible shackles during the penalty phase of capital trials unless special circumstances justify their use.
- *Roper* v. *Simmons* (2005)
  - U.S. Supreme Court determined that age is a bar to execution when the offender committed the crime when he was younger than 18.

For more on capital punishment, visit Criminal Justice Interactive online > Sentencing > Learning Modules > 10.4 Capital Punishment.

10.6 The appeals process

10.6.1 Appeals may be filed by the defense after adjudication.

- Some sentences such as death penalty cases may require an appeals process.

10.6.2 Types of appeals

- Direct appeal
  - ❖ When the consequences of error are so significant that appellate courts are mandated to review them as in capital punishment sentences, the appeal is called a direct appeal or an appeal of right.
- Discretionary appeal
  - ❖ This type of appeal is filed by the appellant based on specific errors in the case. The appellant may appeal if there are illegal grounds to imply that the laws were improperly applied to the facts of the case.
- **Interlocutory appeal**
  - ❖ When a judge's decision so impacts the case in progress that to wait until the end of the trial would significantly violate or damage the case

INTERLOCUTORY APPEAL
Filed when a judge's decision so impacts the case in progress that to wait to the end of the trial would significantly violate or damage the case.

10.6.3 Steps in the appeal process

- Timeliness is important. Failure to accommodate the jurisdiction's timeframe may result in the loss of the right to appeal.
- Each jurisdiction has its own procedures; for most, the first step in pursuing an appeal is to file a formal notice of appeal with the court.
- After the notice of appeal is filed:
  - ❖ The appellate represents trial transcripts.
  - ❖ Representatives of the appellant and the appellee each file a brief.
  - ❖ Usually, a three-judge panel reviews the briefs and may seek oral arguments to verbally review the contents of the brief.
- No witnesses are called. Only attorneys from each side speak to the judges. After consideration the panel will issue a written decision that includes the court's reasoning in the matter.

10.6.4 Rights in the appeal process

- Once an appeal is in motion, the government must ensure conditions for the appellant.
- Access to trial transcripts
- Appellants have access to court documents and transcripts regardless of financial resources. Transcripts are typically requested at the filing of the notice of appeal.

- Right to counsel during appeal; this does not include right to self-representation.
- Freedom from retaliation
- If a case is returned for retrial or for resentencing the new legal proceedings may not impose increased penalties because of the appeal.

10.6.5 Outcomes

- Appellate courts tend to support lower-court decisions to maintain legal consistency.
- There are two main types of errors that may occur during a trial for further consideration or action.
  - Harmless errors
  - Reversible errors
  - Harmless errors require new legal action to remedy the situation.
  - If a reversible error is identified, the court may take one of three actions:
    - The lower-court decision may be reversed. The conviction is set aside and there is no further legal action.
    - The lower-court decision may be reversed with the case being returned to the trial court for new legal proceedings to correct the errors.
    - The case may be remanded to the trial court without reversing the verdict with instructions for the court to remedy the errors.

For more on the appeals process, visit Criminal Justice Interactive online Sentencing > Learning Modules > 10.5 Appeals Process.

10.7 Victim rights history

10.7.1 Grassroots resurgence of concern for the plight of victims that began in the early 1970s caused the sentencing process to take into consideration the needs of victims and their survivors.

10.7.2 President's Task Force on Victims of Crime (1982)

- Paid attention to issue of victim and victim's rights
- Urged expansion of victim-assistance programs
- Recommended 68 programmatic and legislative initiatives for states and concerned citizens to pursue

10.7.3 Thirty states have passed their own victims' rights legislation by the end of 2005.

10.7.4 Victim and Witness Protection Act (1982)

- Requires victim-impact statements to be considered at federal sentencing hearings and places responsibility for their creation on federal probation officers

10.7.5 Victims of Crime Act (VOCA) (1984)

- Provided federal funding to help states establish victim assistance and victim compensation programs
- Victim-assistance programs today offer services in the areas of:
  - Crisis intervention
  - Follow-up counseling
  - Helping victims secure their rights under law
    - Can include helping victims to file civil suits to recoup financial losses

10.7.6 Violent Crime Control and Law Enforcement Act (1994)

- Created federal right of allocution for victims of violent and sex crimes, permitting victim to speak at sentencing hearing.
- Requires sex offenders and child molesters convicted under federal law to pay restitution to their victims and prohibits the diversion of federal victims' funds to other programs.
- Provide civil rights remedies for victims of felonies motivated by gender bias and extend "rape shield law" protections to civil cases and to all criminal cases as a bar to irrelevant inquiries into a victim's sexual history.
- A subsection titled Violence Against Women Act (VAWA) provides financial support for police, prosecutors, and victims' services in cases involving sexual violence and domestic abuse.

10.7.7 Restorative justice

- This movement helped push the emphasis on and development of victim assistance program and victim's rights.
- Restorative justice provides basis for victim-compensation programs.
- All 50 states have passed legislation providing for monetary payments to victims of crime.
  - Payments are primarily designed to compensate the victim for medical expenses and lost wages.
  - Generally, claims from victims who are significantly responsible for their own victimization are rejected.

10.7.8 The USA PATRIOT Act (2001)

- Amended the Victims of Crime Act of 1984 to make victims of terrorism and their families eligible for victim-compensation payments
- Act also created an antiterrorism emergency reserve fund to help provide compensation to victims of terrorism.

CRIME VICTIMS' RIGHTS ACT (2004)
Enunciated rights applicable to all victims of crimes such as protection from accused, timely notice of court proceedings, participation in court proceedings, conference with an attorney, timely resolution, and respect, privacy, and fairness.

10.7.9 **Crime Victims' Rights Act (2004)**

- Part of the Justice for All Act (2004)
- Grants the following rights to victims of federal crimes:
  - The right to be reasonably protected from the accused
  - The right to reasonable, accurate, and timely notice of any public proceeding involving the crime or of any release or escape of the accused
  - The right to be included in any such public proceeding
  - The right to be reasonably heard at any public proceeding involving release, plea, or sentencing
  - The right to confer with the federal prosecutor handling the case
  - The right to full and timely restitution as provided by law
  - The right to proceedings free from unreasonable delay
  - The right to be treated with fairness and with respect for the victim's dignity and privacy
- The act expressly requires federal courts to ensure that they are afforded to victims.

10.7.10 Victim's rights at the state level

- Every state has a set of legal rights for crime victims in its code of laws, often called a victims' bill of rights.
- Rights generally include:
  - To be notified of proceedings and the status of the defendant
  - To be present at certain criminal justice proceedings
  - To make a statement at sentencing or other times
  - To restitution from a convicted offender
  - To be consulted before a case is dismissed or a plea agreement entered
  - To a speedy trial
  - To keep the victim's contact information confidential
- In addition to statutory rights of victims, 32 states have adopted state victims' rights constitutional amendments.

10.7.11 Victim-impact statements

VICTIM-IMPACT STATEMENT
The in-court use of victim- or survivor-supplied information by sentencing authorities seeking to make an informed sentencing decision.

- Usually a written document that describes the losses, suffering, and trauma experienced by the victim or the victim's survivors.
- Approximately 20 states now have laws mandating citizen involvement in sentencing, and all 50 states and the District of Columbia allow for some form of submission of a victim-impact statement either at the time of sentencing or to be contained in the presentence investigation reports made by court officers.
- California study shows that fewer than 3% of victims chose to appear or testify at sentencing hearings after the state's victim rights law was passed.
- Constitutionality of victim-impact statements
  - *Booth* v. *Maryland* (1987)
    - Irvin Bronstein (78) and his wife Rose (75) were robbed and brutally murdered in their home in Baltimore, Maryland.
    - The killers were John Booth and Willie Reid, acquaintances of the Bronsteins who were caught stealing to support their heroin habits.
    - Booth decided to allow the jury to set his sentence.
    - State requires that a jury consider a victim-impact statement.
    - A victim-impact statement was used in court at the sentencing phase.
    - Statement was a powerful one describing the loss suffered by the Bronstein children as a result of their parents' murders.
    - U.S. Supreme Court overturned lower-court conviction.
    - Victim-impact statements, at least in capital cases, violate the Eighth Amendment ban on cruel and unusual punishment.
    - Use of victim-impact statement could lead to the risk that the death penalty might be imposed in an arbitrary and capricious manner.
  - *Payne* v. *Tennessee* (1991)
    - Case of double murder, a 28-year-old mother and her two-year-old daughter in Millington, Tennessee
    - Another child was severely wounded and witnessed the death of his mother and sister.
    - Prosecution claimed that Tyrone Payne, a 20-year-old retarded man, had killed the mother and child after the woman resisted his sexual advances.

- Grandmother read victim-impact statement in court about boys having continuing nightmares.
- Tennessee Supreme Court upheld conviction.
- U.S. Supreme Court also upheld conviction.
- Reasoning: A victim-impact evidence is simply another form or method of informing sentencing authority about the specific harm caused by the crime.
- This decision represented an about-face by the Supreme Court from its 1987 decision in *Booth* v. *Maryland* (1987)

For more on victim rights history, visit Criminal Justice Interactive online > Sentencing > Learning Modules > 10.6 Victim Rights History.

CHAPTER SUMMARY

- Sentencing is a risk-management strategy that is intended to protect the public while creating an opportunity for rehabilitation, retribution, deterrence, and restoration. Imprisonment, fines, probation, and death are the four basic sentencing options available. Fines are one of the oldest forms of punishment and have the advantage of contributing to state treasury and depriving criminals of proceeds of criminal activity. The disadvantages of fines include the fact that they are difficult to collect and that they discriminate against the poor. Limits on the range of sentencing options are specified by the laws at the state and federal levels. The philosophies of sentencing are interwoven with such issues as religion, morals, emotions, and economics. There are five goals of sentencing: retribution, incapacitation, deterrence, rehabilitation, and restoration. Retribution is the act of taking revenge on a criminal perpetrator. Incapacitation is the use of imprisonment or other means to reduce the likelihood that an offender will commit future offenses. Deterrence is a goal of criminal sentencing that seeks to inhibit criminal behavior through fear of punishment. Rehabilitation is the attempt to reform a criminal offender. Restoration is a goal of criminal sentencing that makes the victim "whole again."
- A presentence report is an examination of a convicted offender's background prior to sentencing. Presentence reports are normally conducted by probation and parole officers and are submitted prior to sentencing. There are three kinds of presentence reports. The long form is a detailed written report on the defendant's personal and criminal history. The short form is an abbreviated written report summarizing the type of information most likely to be useful in the sentencing decision. A verbal report is made by the investigating officer directly to the court.
- There are two types of sentencing: determinate and indeterminate. Determinate sentencing, also called fixed sentencing, is a model of criminal punishment in which an offender is given a fixed term that may be reduced by good time or gain time. All offenders convicted of the same crime receive the same length of sentence. Indeterminate sentencing is a model of criminal punishment that

encourages rehabilitation through the use of general and relatively unspecific sentences. Indeterminate sentencing is based on the belief that convicted offenders are more likely to participate in their own rehabilitation if that reduces the amount of time they will have to be incarcerated. Sentences of this type typically contain a minimum and a maximum term of incarceration and allow for reduction in sentence for good behavior and progress towards rehabilitation.

- Capital punishment has been used throughout history and has involved such activities as beheading, burning at the stake, boiling in oil, and poisoning. Up until the 1890s in the United States, hanging was the preferred mode of execution because it required few special materials.
- In the 1980s, electrocution replaced hanging. Today, the majority of states that permit capital punishment use lethal injection. At the federal level, under the Violent Crime Control and Law Enforcement Act of 1994 and the 2001 USA PATRIOT Act, a total of 60 offenses are punishable by the death penalty. Opposition to the death penalty includes the contention that the death penalty can and has been used on innocent people, that the death penalty is not an effective deterrent, and that the death penalty reduces society to the level of the killer.
- The U.S. Sentencing Commission was established under the Sentencing Reform Act of 1984. The commission established minimum sentences for certain federal crimes, including drug offenses, and permitted flexibility in the face of mitigating or aggravating circumstances.
- Congress specified the purposes of sentencing to include deterring criminals, incapacitating and/or rehabilitating offenders, and providing "just desserts" in punishing criminals
- These guidelines took effect November 1987, but they were challenged on legal grounds. The Supreme Court struck down a provision in the law that made federal sentencing guidelines mandatory. The ruling gives federal judges discretion in sentencing offenders by not requiring them to adhere to the guidelines; rather, the guidelines can be used by judges on an advisory basis. At the federal level, 90% of all cases are the result of guilty pleas, the majority of which are the result of plea negotiations.
- Appeals may be filed by the defense after adjudication. Some sentences, such as death penalty cases, may require an appeals process. A direct appeal is made when the consequences of an error are so significant that appellate courts are mandated to review them. A discretionary appeal is filed by the appellant based on specific errors in the case. An interlocutory appeal is filed when a judge's decision so impacts the case in progress that to wait to the end of the trial would significantly violate or damage the case. While each jurisdiction has its own procedures, for most, the first step in pursuing an appeal is to file a formal notice of appeal with the court. After the notice of appeal is filed, the appellate represents trial transcripts, then the representatives of the appellant and a panel of judges review the briefs and may seek oral arguments. Once an appeal is in motion, the government must ensure conditions for the appellant including access to trial transcripts and court documents.
- Victim-impact statements are usually written documents that describe the losses, suffering, and trauma experienced by the victim or the victim's survivors. Approximately 20 states now have laws mandating citizen involvement in sen-

tencing, and every state allows for some form of submission of a victim-impact statement either at the time of sentencing or to be contained in the presentence investigation reports made by court officers.

ONLINE@CRIMINAL JUSTICE INTERACTIVE

Learning Modules

10.1 Sentencing
10.2 Presentence Reports
10.3 Determinate and Indeterminate Sentencing
10.4 Capital Punishment
10.5 The Appeals Process
10.6 Victim Rights History

Myths and Issues Videos

Myth vs. Reality: When Does "Life in Prison" Mean "Life in Prison"?
Issue 1: "Three Strikes" and Other Mandatory Sentencing Guidelines
Issue 2: Alternative Sentencing

Simulation Activity: Sentencing

Homework and Review

In the News
Web Activity
Review Questions
Essay Questions
Flashcards

Chapter 11

Corrections: History and Institutions

CHAPTER OUTLINE

LEARNING OBJECTIVES

After reviewing the online material and reading this chapter, you should be able to:

1. Describe the history of prisons focusing on nine prison eras.
2. Describe the historical evolution of women's prisons.
3. Compare and contrast prisons and jails.
4. Describe the roles and responsibilities of the following categories of prison staff: administrative, security, treatment and programs, and services.
5. Discuss issues related to prison privatization.
6. Define terms related to corrections history and institutions.

KEY TERMS

ADMAX
Ashurst-Sumners Act
Auburn system
brank
Brideswill
community-based treatment era
contract system
ducking stool
Elmira Reformatory
halfway house
Hawes-Cooper Act
industrial era
just desserts era
justice model
lease system
lex talionis
mark system
mass prison era
penitentiary era
Pennsylvania System
piece-price system
pillory
PRIDE
private prisons
privatization
public-account system
public works
punitive era
reformatory era
state-use system
stocks
three-strikes rule
treatment era
Walnut Street Jail
warehouse era
workhouse

11.0 Corrections: History and institutions

11.1 History of prisons

11.1.1 History of punishments

LEX TALIONIS

Taken from Hammurabi's Code, approximately 210 B.C.E., that delineated both crimes and punishments. The law of retaliation, based on the concept of an "eye for an eye, a tooth for a tooth."

- ***Lex talionis*** is taken from Hammurabi's Code, approximately 210 B.C.E., which delineated both crimes and punishments.
  - The law of retaliation, based on the concept of an "eye for an eye, a tooth for a tooth."
- Flogging
  - Most widely used form of punishment in England through the Middle Ages
    - Russian knot was a whip fashioned out of leather thongs tipped with fishhook-like wires.
    - Cat o' nine tails made of at least nine strands of leather or rope
  - American colonists and those who settled the Western frontier used the practice of flogging.
  - Delaware—last officially sanctioned flogging in the United States was on June 16, 1952.
  - In 1994, Michael Fay, an American from Ohio, was convicted of spray-painting parked cars in Singapore and was caned on the bottom of his feet.
- Mutilation
  - Amputation has been part of some societies:
    - Removing the hand(s) of a thief
    - Blinding spies
    - Castration of rapists
    - Removing the tongues of blasphemers
    - Breaking the fingers of thieves
  - In England during the eleventh century, mutilation took the form of blinding, cutting off of ears, and ripping out tongues of individuals who poached on the King's land. Iran and Saudi Arabia still use mutilation.
- Branding
  - Served to readily identify individuals who had been convicted of some offense
  - Romans, Greeks, French, and British used branding.
  - In 1829, British Parliament outlawed branding as a form of punishment.
  - In the United States, branding was common in the colonies.

- First offenders were often branded on their hands.
- Repeat offenders were branded on the forehead.
- Rarely were women branded; instead, they were shamed and forced to wear marks on their clothing.

- In Nathaniel Hawthorne's *The Scarlet Letter*, the main character was required by law to wear a red letter "A," which stood for adultery.
- Public humiliation
    - Stocks and pillory
        - **Stocks** is a wooden structure in which a person is placed in a sitting position with his or her hands locked in front of them while the head remained free.
        - **Pillory** is a wooden structure that closed over the person's head and hands and forced the offender to remain standing.
        - Stocks and pillories were usually located in a public square so that the punishment could include humiliation.
            - Retribution was a prerogative of the community.
            - Members of the community could register their displeasure with the offender(s) by:
                - Spitting on the offender
                - Throwing rotten eggs at the offender
                - In serious cases, rocks were thrown at the offenders, which could result in the death of the offender.
    - **Brank** is a birdcage-like contraption that fit over the head of the offender. A door on the front by the mouth was fitted with a razor blade that went into the mouth of the offender when the door was closed.
    - **Ducking stool** is a see-saw device onto which an offender was tied, and it was then lowered into a lake or river. Offender was turned upside down like a duck looking for food.
- **Workhouses** were an early form of imprisonment; its purpose was to foster good work habits in the poor.
    - Based on the belief that poverty was caused by laziness
    - **Brideswill** was the first workhouse to open in England (1557).
        - Nicknamed "Brideswill," which became the synonym for workhouse
    - In 1576, the English Parliament supported the notion that every country should have a workhouse.

STOCKS
Wooden structures in which a person is placed in a sitting position with his or her hands locked in front of them and the head remaining free.

PILLORY
Wooden structure that closed over a person's head and hands and forced the offender to remain standing.

BRANK
A birdcage-like contraption that fit over the head of the offender.

DUCKING STOOL
A see-saw device onto which an offender was tied, lowered into a river, and then turned upside down.

WORKHOUSES
Residences that were intended to foster good work habits in the poor and homeless.

BRIDESWILL
The first workhouse, opened in England in 1557; the term became synonymous for workhouse.

- Workhouses did not incarcerate criminals; only vagrants and the economically disadvantaged.
- Workhouses were designed to reinforce the value of hard work.

- Exile
  - Practice of sending offenders out of the country
  - Hebrews sent a goat carrying the sins of man into the desert to be exiled (scapegoating).
  - The French sent offenders to Devil's Island.
  - Russia sent dissidents to Siberia.
  - England sent offenders to the American colonies beginning in 1618.
    - Program was known as "transportation."
    - American Revolution put an end to transportation of offenders to the United States.
    - The British started putting offenders on ships anchored in harbors of England.
    - In 1787, England began sending offenders to Australia.

11.1.2 Early prisons

- The first prison began some time during the Middle Ages.
- Debtor's prisons existed in Europe during the 1400s and 1500s.
- Papal Prison Hospice of San Michele, a residential school for delinquent boys, opened in 1704.
- Maison de Force opened in 1773 in Ghent, Belgium, and stressed reformation over punishment.
- Near the end of 1700s, prisons began to be used in the United States.
- **Penitentiary era** (1790–1825)
  - Philadelphia (1790)
    - **Walnut Street Jail** was converted to a prison by the Quakers.
      - Goal of Quakers was to provide religion and humanity to those imprisoned.
      - Offenders, it was hoped, would make amends with society and accept responsibility for their misdeeds.
      - Offenders were provided with the opportunity to do penance:
        - Study of the Bible was the primary method.
      - Offenders were held in solitary confinement.

PENITENTIARY ERA (1790–1825)

Separate and silent system; sought penance in total solitude, and used handicrafts to help maintain sanity. Also called Pennsylvania System.

WALNUT STREET JAIL

A prison established by the Quakers to provide religion and humanity to those imprisoned by allowing them to do penance.

- Offenders wore a hood when they entered the prison and were taken to their cells.
    - The hood prevented them from seeing other inmates as well as being seen.
    - Hood was also worn when they were released from prison.
    - The intent was for the offenders to not have any contact with or knowledge of each other.
- Exercise was allowed, but only in small high-walled yards attached to each of the cells to prevent any contact between inmates.
- Handicrafts were introduced allowing inmates to work in their cells.
- Inmates figured out a way to communicate with one another, even though all these precautions had been taken.
    - The sanitary system for the cells was a trough filled with water that ran across the back of the cells.
    - The trough was connected through all the cells in that particular line.
    - The trough was built on an angle so that when necessary, the lower end could be opened and the water and waste released.
    - Once water was completely removed, the lower end would be reclosed and the water refilled from the top end.
    - In between the emptying and filling, the inmates could communicate with one another through the then-empty trough.
- Style became known as the **Pennsylvania system**.
    - Characteristics:
        - Solitary confinement
        - Individual cells
        - Encouraged rehabilitation
        - Massive physical structure with impenetrable walls
    - Prisons that used the Pennsylvania system:
        - Western Penitentiary, Pittsburgh, Pennsylvania (1826)
        - Eastern Penitentiary, Cherry Hill, Pennsylvania (1829)

PENNSYLVANIA SYSTEM

A system of imprisonment that featured solitary confinement, individual cells, encouraged rehabilitation, and massive physical ssructure with impenetrable walls.

- Other states began to model their prison system after Pennsylvania:
  - Vermont
  - Massachusetts
  - Maryland
  - New York

MASS PRISON ERA (1825–1876)
An era in which the Auburn system dominated, a system in which inmates ate, lived, and worked together in enforced silence.

- **Mass prisons era** (1825–1876)
  - New York State Prison at Auburn
    - Introduced "congregate" but silent style of prison.
    - Offenders ate, lived, and worked together in enforced silence.
    - Inmates worked together in group workshops.
    - Corporal punishment was used with offenders who violated rules.
      - Whipping and hard labor were used to maintain the rule of silence.
  - Style became known as the **Auburn system**.
    - From 1825 onward, most of the prisons built in the United States followed the Auburn system.

AUBURN SYSTEM
A style of prison in which individuals ate, lived, and worked together in enforced silence.

REFORMATORY ERA (1876–1890)
An era characterized by the use of indeterminate sentences and believed in rehabilitation.

- **Reformatory era** (1876–1890)
  - Model was based on the use of the indeterminate sentences and belief in rehabilitation, especially for youthful offenders.
  - Movement emerged as a result of the work of two individuals:
    - Captain Alexander Maconochie
      - Warden of Norfolk Island Prison off the coast of Australia in the 1840s
      - "Doubly condemned"
        - Prisoners who had been "transported" to Australia and had also committed a crime while in Australia were sent to Norfolk Island; hence, "doubly condemned."
      - When Maconochie arrived at Norfolk Island, conditions were atrocious:
        - Disease was rampant.
        - Fights among inmates left many dead and more injured.
        - Sanitary conditions were practically non-existent.
      - **Mark system**
        - A system developed by Maconochie by which prisoners could earn credits to buy their freedom.
        - A negative behavior caused marks to be lost.

MARK SYSTEM
A system that allowed prisoners to earn credits toward freedom by exhibiting positive behavior.

        - Mark system constituted the first "early release" program and led to recognition of the indeterminate sentence as a useful tool in the reformation of offenders.
        - Based on the number of marks an inmate earned, prisoner could be moved to less and less secure facilities, and eventually be released.
        - Maconochie became known as "father of parole" because of similarities between his system and that of later day parole.
    - ❐ In 1844, Maconochie was removed as warden because he was considered to be too lenient with prisoners.
- ◆ Sir Walter Crofton was named head of the Irish Prison System in 1854. He adapted Maconochie's program and called it "ticket of leave."
    - ❐ Set up four-stage program:
        - Entry stage: Offender is placed in solitary confinement and given simple, unmotivating work.
        - Second stage: Offenders worked on fortifications at Spike Island in Dublin where they were housed.
        - Field unit stage: Offenders worked on public service projects in the community under the supervision of unarmed guards.
        - Ticket of leave stage: Offenders were allowed to live and work in the community under the occasional supervision of a "moral instructor."
    - ❐ Crofton believed reintegration into the community was necessary for the success of rehabilitation.

❖ **Elmira Reformatory** and birth of parole

- ◆ Opened in Elmira, New York, in 1876
- ◆ Zebulon Brockway was appointed warden.
    - ❐ Brockway, the former superintendent of the Detroit House of Corrections, was a leading advocate of the indeterminate sentence.
    - ❐ He was the former superintendent of the Detroit House of Corrections.
- ◆ New York had passed an indeterminate sentencing bill that made possible early release for inmates who earned it.
- ◆ Elmira accepted only first-time offenders between the ages of 16 to 30.

ELMIRA REFORMATORY

Zebulon Brockway as warden of the Elmira Reformatory tried to humanize prison life and make a prisoner more fit for society. Merged ideas of reformation, early release, and supervision by nonpolice agents into the earliest form of parole in the United States.

- System of graded stages was introduced.
  - Offenders were required to meet goals in education, behavior, and other goals as appropriate.
  - Education/schooling was mandatory.
- Training in a trade such as telegraphy, tailoring, plumbing, and carpentry was available.
- Movement proved to be a failure.
- Many offenders returned to life of crime once released.
- Although a failure, the Elmira Reformatory established principles that remain with us today, including:
  - Indeterminate sentencing
  - Parole
  - Trade training
  - Education
  - Primacy of reformation

INDUSTRIAL ERA (1890–1935)

Prisoners served as cheap labor while learning a trade. States were able to generate income from labor, and there was great potential for exploitation of the workers.

- **Industrial era** 1890–1935)
  - Goal of this prison era was to maximize use of the offender's labor during imprisonment.
  - The industrial movement began in northeastern United States, which already had developed a large industrial base.
  - Prison facilities were characterized by thick, high walls, stone or brick buildings, guard towers, and smokestacks rising from within.
  - Types of industries:
    - Northern prisons
      - Smelted steel
      - Manufactured furniture
      - Molded tires
    - Southern prisons
      - Used prisoners for farm labor
      - Public works projects to rebuild after the Civil War
      - Used prisoners to replace the slaves who had received their freedom
  - Types of offender labor systems:
    - **Contract system**
      - Private businesses paid for the rental of inmate labor.
      - Private businesses provided the raw materials and supervised the manufacturing process inside of the prisons.

CONTRACT SYSTEM

A system in which private businesses paid for inmate labor and supervised the manufacturing.

- **Piece-price system**
  - Goods were produced for private businesses inside of the prison under the supervision of prison authorities.
  - Prisons were paid according to the number and quality of the goods they produced.

PIECE-PRICE SYSTEM
A system in which goods were produced for private businesses under prison supervisions.

- **Lease system**
  - Prisoners were taken outside the prison to work sites under the supervision of armed guards.
  - Once at the place of work, private businesspeople would take over the supervision and employed the prisoners.

LEASE SYSTEM
A system in which prisoners are taken outside of prison to work under the supervision of armed guards.

- **Public-account system**
  - Industries were owned entirely by prisons; private businesses were eliminated.
  - Prisons handled the manufacture of goods from beginning to end.
  - Finished goods were sold on the free market.

PUBLIC-ACCOUNT SYSTEM
A system in which industries are owned entirely by prisons and the prisons handle the manufacture of goods from beginning to end. The finished goods are sold on the free market.

- **State-use system**
  - Prisons manufactured goods only for use by the prison or other government agencies.
  - Prisons could not compete on the free market because of their inexpensive labor advantage and lack of need for the goods.
  - Examples of things manufactured under the state-use system:
    - License plates
    - Hunting/fishing licenses
    - Furniture
    - Cleaning supplies

STATE-USE SYSTEM
A system in which prisons manufacture goods only for use by the prison or other government agencies.

- **Public works**
  - Examples of types of work:
    - Prisoners maintained public roadways.
    - Cleaned public parks
    - Maintained and restored public buildings

PUBLIC WORKS
Structures (such as highways, parks, and schools) built at government expense for public use.

- Industrial prisons
  - Examples:
    - San Quentin (California)
    - Sing Sing (New York)
    - Auburn Prison (New York)
    - Illinois State Penitentiary at Statesville (Illinois)

HAWES-COOPER ACT

An act that required prison-made goods conform to the regulations of states through which they were shipped.

- **Hawes-Cooper Act** (1929) required that prison-made goods conform to regulations of the states through which they were shipped
  - States could outlaw the manufacture of free-market goods in their own prisons, which could then prevent the shipment of prison-made goods from other states.
  - This act came about as a result of the labor movement—complaints that industries could not compete with the cheap prison labor in the manufacture of goods.

ASHURST-SUMNERS ACT

Federal legislation of 1935 that effectively ended the industrial prison era by restricting interstate commerce in prison-made goods.

- **Ashurst-Sumners Act** (1935)specifically prohibited the interstate transportation and sale of prison-made goods where state laws forbade them.
  - This legislation was brought on, in part, because of the results of the Depression, which influenced most states to pass laws against their prisons producing goods for the free market.
  - Ashurst-Sumners Act effectively ended the industrial prison era.
- Most prison industries today operate under a state-use model.
  - State prisons can manufacture goods for:
    - Use exclusively in the prison system itself
    - Use by other state agencies
    - Use by the state to sell on the open market (license plates)
- Federal prison industry
  - Established in 1934
  - UNICOR (Federal Prison Industries, Inc.)
  - A 1994 study of inmates who participated in UNICOR:
    - Showed better adjustment
    - Were less likely to be revoked at the end of their first year in the community
    - Were more likely to find employment in the halfway house and community

PRIDE ACT

Designed to reauthorize and improve the program of block grants to states, this Act temporarily assists families in need and improves access to child care.

- **PRIDE Act** (1981) (*P*rison *R*ehabilitative *I*ndustries and *D*iversified *E*nterprises, Inc.) was funded by private-sector businesses.
  - Florida became first state to experiment with the wholesale transfer of its correctional industry program from public to private control. PRIDE

industries include sugarcane processing, construction, and automobile repair.

- ❐ Other states have since followed suit.

- ◆ National task force on prison industries (1986)
  - ❐ Report established five principles to help guide renewal of prison industries:
    - Private sector should be involved in prison industries.
    - Practices and regulations that impede the progress of prison industries should be changed.
    - Prison industries should provide meaningful and relevant work opportunities for inmates.
    - Prison industries should operate in a businesslike manner.
    - Prison industries should reduce inmate idleness.
- ◆ *P*rison *I*ndustry *E*nhancement *C*ertification *P*rogram (PIECP)
  - ❐ Originally authorized under the Justice System Improvement Act of 1979
  - ❐ Crime Control Act of 1990 authorizes continuation of the program indefinitely.
  - ❐ Program is administered by the Bureau of Justice Assistance.
  - ❐ Exempts certified state and local departments of corrections from normal federal restrictions on the sale of inmate-made goods in interstate commerce
  - ❐ Allows private industry to establish joint ventures with state and local correctional agencies to produce goods using inmate labor
  - ❐ As of 2005, 37 state and 4 county-based certified correctional industry programs operate in the United States managing at least 175 business partnerships with private industry.

- **Punitive era** (1935–1945)
  - ❖ With a moratorium on prison industries created by the Ashurst-Sumners Act (1935), prisons reverted back to custody and security as their main goals.
  - ❖ Large maximum-security institutions evolved.
  - ❖ Prisons were built in rural locations with the "out of sight, out of mind" mentality.

PUNITIVE ERA (1935–1945)

Prison was to be used for punishment while education, treatment, and work were luxuries. Maximum-security prisons were built in isolated places. Under this system there was an increase in riots and escape attempts.

- ❖ Belief was that inmates owed a debt to society.
- ❖ Innovations were rare during this period.

TREATMENT ERA (1945–1967)
Based on the medical model. Classification and treatment led to rehabilitation. Therapy, training, and education were provided. Treatments included extensive sensory deprivation and neurosugeries.

- **Treatment era** (1945–1967)
  - ❖ Development of behavioral techniques in the 1930s and 1940s ushered in the concept of treatment in prisons.
  - ❖ Offenders came to be viewed as "clients."
  - ❖ Treatment was based on the "medical model."
    - ◆ Medical model is a therapeutic framework for handling offenders that viewed offenders as "sick" and who could be "cured."
  - ❖ Individual and group therapy treatment programs evolved.
  - ❖ Types of therapy programs used:
    - ◆ Behavior therapy
    - ◆ Chemotherapy
    - ◆ Neurosurgery
    - ◆ Sensory deprivation
    - ◆ Aversion therapy
  - ❖ Behavior therapy
    - ◆ Structured to provide rewards for approved behavior while punishing undesirable behavior
    - ◆ Rewards can include:
      - ❒ Better housing
      - ❒ Canteen privileges
      - ❒ TV privileges
  - ❖ Chemotherapy
    - ◆ Use of drugs, especially tranquilizers to modify behavior
  - ❖ Neurosurgery
    - ◆ Used to control aggressive behavior and destructive urges
    - ◆ Frontal lobotomies were part of this form of therapy.
  - ❖ Sensory deprivation
    - ◆ Denial of stimulation that could cause outbursts by isolating prisoners in a quiet, secluded environment
  - ❖ Aversion therapy
    - ◆ Drugs and electric shock used to teach prisoners to associate negative behavior with pain and displeasure. For example, child abusers were shown pictures of naked children and given an electric shock to the groin area.

COMMUNITY-BASED TREATMENT ERA (1967–1980)
Era focused on resocialization in supervised community settings since community programs were believed to be more effective than incarceration.

- **Community-based treatment era** (1967–1980)
  - ❖ A sentencing approach that relies on the resources of the community instead of the prison; the movement was also called deinstitutionalization, diversion, and decarceration.

- ❖ Basic underlying assumption: Rehabilitation could not occur in isolation from the community to which inmates must eventually return.
- ❖ Jerome Miller
  - ◆ In 1972, he was director of Youth Services for Massachusetts.
  - ◆ Closed all reform schools and placed juveniles offenders in community group homes.
- ❖ **Halfway house** is a temporary living situation designed to provide a way for newly released offender to ease into living in the outside world.
  - ◆ When in the halfway house, the offender is still under the control of the justice system.
  - ◆ Individuals typically live at the house but they are allowed to go to work or school during the day and return to the halfway house during the evening and on weekends.
  - ◆ Halfway in
    - ❒ Individuals who have been placed on probation; one condition of their probation is that they live in the halfway house.
  - ◆ Halfway out
    - ❒ Individuals who have been paroled from an institution; one of the conditions of their parole is that they reside in the halfway house until they are ready for full release.
  - ◆ Prerelease guidance centers
    - ❒ Federal community facilities, first opened in 1961.
    - ❒ The first two facilities were opened in Los Angeles and Chicago.
    - ❒ Focus was on juveniles and youthful offenders.
  - ◆ President's Commission on Law Enforcement and the Administration of Justice (1967)
    - ❒ Recommended the use of community-based facilities to re-establish relationships between the offender and family, work, and other social agencies
  - ◆ A typical residential facility houses 15 to 20 residents and operates under the supervision of a director supported by a handful of counselors.
    - ❒ The environment is nonthreatening.
    - ❒ Residents are generally free to come and go during the workday.
    - ❒ The facility looks more like a motel or house than a jail or prison.

HALFWAY HOUSES

Temporary living situations provide a way for newly released offender to "ease in" to living in the outside world. When in the halfway house, the offender is still under the control of the justice system.

        - Fences and walls are nonexistent.
        - Transportation is provided to and from work, and to educational programs.
        - The facility usually keeps a portion of the wages earned by residents to help defray the costs of room and board.

- Work-release programs are prison programs that temporarily release prisoners into the community to meet job responsibilities.
    - Prisoners are usually housed in minimum-security prisons, but go to work during the day and return to the facility at night.
    - In 1913, Wisconsin passed the first work-release legislation.
    - In 1957, North Carolina established a comprehensive work-release program that spurred the work-release movement.
    - In 1965, the Federal Prisoner Rehabilitation Act was created as a work-release program for federal prisoners.
    - As work-release programs grew, study release was initiated.
        - A study-release program allows inmates to attend local colleges and technical schools during the day and return to the facility at night.
- Open institutions are prison institutions that encourage two-way interaction between the prison and the community.
    - Prisoners are encouraged and given opportunities to become involved in the community.
    - Community members are given the opportunity to volunteer time in the prison.
        - Training is provided by the institution.
        - Training is provided to citizens who wish to sponsor inmates on day trips into the community for recreation, meals, and the like.
    - Some programs experimented with conjugal visits.
        - Based on a merit system, conjugal visits allowed visits between male inmates and their spouses in motel-like environments built on the prison grounds.
        - California was one of the first to allow conjugal visits but did not allow them for those who have been convicted of rape or sex offenses, recently disciplined inmates, or sentenced to death or life without parole.

- Co-ed facilities
  - Federal Bureau of Prisons
    - In 1971, the bureau began experimenting with co-ed prisons.
    - Pleasanton Youth Center in California became one of the first to house both men and women.

WAREHOUSING ERA (1980–1995)
A movement in the 1980s that represented a return to incarceration because increased recidivism and ongoing criminality by offenders in the community-based programs led to a loss of faith in treatment and rehabilitation. Mandatory minimum sentences, truth-in-sentencing legislation, and goal of protecting society rather than treating the offender became the focus.

- **Warehousing era** (1980–1995)
  - Public disappointment with the community-based model and high rates of recidivism has led to the warehousing era.
  - Recidivism
    - Recidivism is the commission of another crime by an individual who has previously been convicted of a crime.
    - The new crime may or may not be of the same type as the previous crime, and are committed at the local, state, or federal level.
    - *Annual Report 1987*, Bureau of Justice Statistics (1988)
      - Nearly 70% of young adults paroled from prison in 22 states were rearrested for a serious crime one or more times within six years of release.
      - This group committed an estimated 36,000 new felonies within six years of release, including:
        - Murders: 324
        - Rapes: 231
        - Robberies: 2, 291
        - Violent assaults: 3,053
      - Forty-six percent of the recidivists would have been in prison at the time of their readmission to prison if they had served the maximum term to which they had originally been sentenced.
      - Those with six or more previous arrests were rearrested 90% of the time following release.
      - The length of time that a parolee has served in prison had no consistent impact on recidivism rates.
  - Robert Martinson in "What Works: Questions and Answers about Prison Reform," *Public Interest* (1974), surveyed 231 research studies that evaluated correctional treatment programs between 1945 and 1967.
    - None of the 231 programs appeared to substantially reduce recidivism.
    - "Nothing-works doctrine" developed in the 1970s casting doubt on the treatment model.

- Timothy A. Hughes, Doris J. Wilson, and Allen J. Black in *Trends in State Parole* (2001), found that in 1990, murderers served, on average, 92 months in prison before release. In 2000, it had increased to 106 months for the crime of murder.
  - From 1990 to 2000, actual time served in prison before release for the crime of rape increased 27%, while it increased by 35% for drug offenders.
- Paige Harrison and Allen J. Beck in *Prisoners in 2006*, Bureau of Justice Statistics (2007), found that between 1980 and 2007, the state and federal prison populations more than quadrupled from 329,000 inmates to more than 1.5 million.
- American Bar Association study (1992) found that overcrowding was directly attributed to systemwide emphasis on drug-related offenses.
  - There was a 2.2% drop of per capita rate of reported crime during the 1980s, while there was a 110% increase in the incarceration rate.
- In 1992, 40 states and the District of Columbia were operating under court order to reduce overcrowding.
  - Nine state prison systems had come under court control.
    - Alaska
    - Florida
    - Kansas
    - Louisiana
    - Mississippi
    - Nevada
    - Rhode Island
    - South Carolina
    - Texas
- Methods used by states to reduce overcrowding:
  - Construction of temporary tent cities within prison walls
  - Implementation of a policy of early release for less dangerous inmates and mandatory diversion programs for first-time nonviolent offenders
  - Use of sentence rollbacks to reduce the sentences of selected inmates by a fixed amount, usually 90 days.
  - Early parole
  - By 2000, 34 states and the District of Columbia had shifted some of their correctional burden to local jails.
- Dimensions of overcrowding
  - Prison overcrowding can be measured along a number of dimensions, including:
    - Space available per inmate
    - How long inmates are confined in cells or housing units per day

- Living arrangements (single versus double bunking)
- Type of housing (segregation facilities, tents)

- Prisons have developed three types of prison capacity (the size of the correctional population an institution can effectively hold):
  - Rated capacity is the number of inmates a prison can handle according to the judgment of experts.
  - Operational capacity is the number of inmates a prison can effectively accommodate based upon management considerations.
  - Design capacity is the number of inmates a prison was intended to hold when it was built or modified; design capacity typically shows the highest amount of overcrowding.
- *Rhodes* v. *Chapman* (1981) considered the issue of double bunking along with other alleged forms of deprivation at the Southern Ohio correctional facility.
  - The facility, built in 1971, was substantially overcrowded according to the original housing plans on which it was constructed.
  - The facility was designed to house one inmate per cell; the cells were small (only 63 square feet of floor space on average). The facility was housing 2,300 inmates, 1,400 who were double-celled.
  - Kelly Chapman, an inmate serving time for armed robbery and prison escape, claimed that his portion of the cell was too small.
  - Thirty-six states joined the case in support of the Ohio practice of double-celling.
  - The American Medical Association and the American Public Health Association supported Kelly Chapman's position.
  - The U.S. Supreme Court, reasoning that overcrowding is not necessarily dangerous if other services are adequate, held that prison housing conditions may be "restrictive and even harsh," for they are part of the penalty that offenders pay for their crimes.
- Overcrowding combined with other negative conditions may lead to findings against the prison system. The following conditions should be met:
  - The prisons' meeting of basic human needs
  - The adequacy of the facility's staff
  - The program opportunities available to inmates
  - The quality and strength of the prison management

JUST DESSERTS ERA (1995–PRESENT)

New "get tough" and zero-tolerance initiatives increased mandatory sentences for violent crimes. Shift from deterrence to punishment with incarceration being a natural consequence for committing crimes. Also includes a reduced use of parole.

JUSTICE MODEL

A contemporary model of imprisonment based on the principle of just desserts.

- **Just desserts era** (1995–Present)
  - **Justice model** is a contemporary model of imprisonment in which the principle of just desserts forms the underlying social philosophy.
  - Imprisonment is seen as fully deserved and a proper consequence of criminal behavior.
  - A return to punishment as the root purpose of imprisonment
  - Chain gang
    - Alabama became the first state, in 1995, to reinstitute the chain gain, but discontinued it in 1996 as a result of a lawsuit.
      - The chain gang was designed for parole violators.
      - Prisoners served up to 90 days on chain gangs working 12-hour shifts.
      - Prisoners even remained chained while using the portable toilet.
      - Shotgun-toting guards oversaw prisoners who were chained together by the ankles while they worked the state's roadsides picking up trash, clearing brush, and filling ditches.
  - Arizona and Florida reestablished chain gangs as a result of Alabama's lead.
    - Florida' Department of Corrections continues to use restricted labor squads (its name for chain gangs) at seven correctional institutions.
      - In 1998, 179 close-custody inmates were assigned to these work squads.
      - Inmates are shackled at the ankles, but not connected to each other.
  - Virginia
    - Abolished parole in 1995 and increased the length of sentences for certain violent crimes by as much as 700%
    - Planned the building of a dozen new prisons.
  - Corrections Compendium (1995)
    - Survey reported that 28 states showed a decrease in prisoner privileges during the preceding 12 months.
      - Examples of reduced privileges:
        - Personal property allowed
        - Restrictions on outside purchases
        - Restrictions on packages from home
        - Elimination of cable TV
        - Abolished family visits
        - No more special occasion banquets

- "Penal Austerity: Perceived Utility, Desert, and Public Attitudes Toward Prison Amenities," *American Journal of Criminal Justice* (2001) by Brandon K. Applegate, was completed using a Florida sample.
  - Survey respondents widely supported the elimination of:
    - Prison pornography, including magazines (82.9%)
    - Curtailment of cable television (78.4%)
    - Ban on boxing and martial arts (75.5%)
    - Reduced availability of books (8.5%)
    - Elimination of job training and basic literacy programs (9%)
    - Cancellation of psychological counseling programs (5.5%)
    - End supervised family visits (7%)
- Other get-tough initiatives
  - **"Three-strikes" rules** are statutes that require mandatory sentences (sometimes life in prison without the possibility of parole) for offenders convicted of a third felony.
    - Such mandatory sentencing enhancements are aimed at determining known and potentially violent offenders, and are intended to incapacitate convicted criminals through long-term incarceration.
    - Three-strikes laws have been enacted in 24 states, and are being considered in other states.
    - Federal government requires life imprisonment for federal criminals convicted of three violent felonies or drug offenses.

THREE-STRIKES RULE

Statutes that require mandatory sentences for offenders convicted of a third felony.

For more on the history of prisons, visit Criminal Justice Interactive online > Corrections: History and Institutions > Learning Modules > 11.1 History of Prisons.

11.2 History of women's prisons

11.2.1 Overview

- In the earliest days of America, criminals, both men and women, were punished with public humiliation and corporal punishment.
- Colonies began to adopt to trade punitive responses for reform and rehabilitation.
- By the latter part of the sixteenth century, Pennsylvania Quakers had developed the concept of penitentiaries.

- Women and men were held in the same facilities, but segregated during daytime activities.
- Women were supervised by men.
  - This put them at considerable risk for sexual assault.

- Today, women's prisons offer the same things men's prisons offer:
  - Work education and vocational programs
  - Rigid scheduling
  - Tight security
- One primary difference: Women's prisons offer considerable resources in programs designed to maintain parent-child relationships.

11.2.2 Women's prisons

- In 1816, Quaker Elizabeth Fry lobbied for prison reforms in England.
  - Formed the Ladies Society for Promoting the Formation of Female Prisoners
- Fry addressed the special needs of women prisoners, particularly the importance of sex segregation, female guards, and reduced physical labor.
- In 1825, Fry's ideas were adopted in the United States, resulting in similar reforms.
  - The New York House of Refuge provided a separate building for female juveniles who were supervised by female staff.
- Vocational training in domestic sciences began to evolve, although the solitary system discouraged communal activities and allowed for hard physical labor.
- In 1863, Zebulon Brockway opened the Detroit House of Correction.
  - This facility had a separate unit for women, female guards, and an increased emphasis on education and preparation to return to society.
  - Women were housed in homelike cottages, in small family-like groups of approximately 30.
  - Matrons served as role models for inmates.
- In 1873, Indiana Reformatory for Women and Girls opened as the first U.S. prison for females only. Other states soon followed suit.
- Prisons trained women in traditionally female professions.
  - Gender stereotyping in training opportunities continued into the 1980s, even while women's roles in the outside world had expanded beyond those limitations.

- Today, women's prisons are now organized and managed much like men's prisons with:
  - Increased physical security
  - A wider array of vocational training programs
  - Special housing to hold disorderly and violent offenders
  - Programs related to parenting

For more on the history of women's prisons, visit Criminal Justice Interactive online > Corrections: History and Institutions > Learning Modules > 11.2 History of Women's Prisons.

11.3 Prisons and jails

11.3.1 Prisons

- There are 126 federal prisons and over 1,400 state prisons.
- Prison populations
  - Bureau of Justice Statistics
    - Total number of prisoners held in federal or state prisons:
      - 2008: 1,540,805
      - 2003: 1,440,655
      - 2001: 1,381,892
      - 1997: 1,182,169
    - Estimated number of federal and state prisoners per 100,000 U.S. residents:
      - 2008: 509
      - 2007: 506
    - Number of federal and state prisoners by gender for 2008:
      - Women: 115,779
      - Men: 1,494,805
    - Number of federal and state prisoners by race for 2008:
      - Black males per 100,000 black males: 4,777
      - Hispanic males per 100,000 Hispanic males: 1,760
      - White males per 100,000 white males: 1,760
    - Percent of state prisoners by offense category for different years:
      - Violent crimes
        - 2005: 53%
        - 2003: 49%
        - 2001: 46%
        - 1997: 47%

        - Property crimes
            - 2005:19%
            - 2003: 19%
            - 2001: 24%
            - 1997: 23%
        - Drug crimes
            - 2005: 20%
            - 2003: 20%
            - 2001: 23%
            - 1997: 22%
    - Prisoners serving life sentences in 2008
        - U.S. prisoners serving life sentences: 1 out of 10
        - Inmates held in prisons: 140,610 out of 1,540,805
            - Inmates who were serving life sentences in 1984: 34,000
        - Sixty-six percent of prisoners serving life sentences are Hispanic or Black.
        - In New York state, only 16.3% of those serving life sentences are white.
    - Seven states, plus the federal prison system, do not allow for the possibility of parole for those serving life sentences.
        - States that do not permit parole for those serving life sentences:
            - Illinois
            - Iowa
            - Louisiana
            - Maine
            - Pennsylvania
            - South Dakota
            - West Virginia
    - Juveniles serving life sentences in 2008:
        - Juveniles who were serving life sentences: 6,897
        - Juveniles who were serving these sentences without the possibility of parole: 1,755
        - Of the total number of juveniles serving life sentences, 2,623 of them were in California.
- Profile of typical state system:
    - One high-security prison for long-term, high-risk offenders
    - One or more medium-security institution for offenders who are not high risk
    - One institution for adult women

- One or two institutions for young adults (generally under the age of 25)
- One or more specialized mental hospital-type security prisons for mentally ill prisoners
- One or more open-type institutions for low-risk, nonviolent inmates
- One out of every four state institutions is a large, maximum-security prison with a population approaching 1,000 inmates.
- Typical state prison is small with less than 500 inmates.
- Community-based facilities average around 50 residents.

- Profile of prisoners
  - Low level of formal education
  - Socially disadvantaged background
  - Lack of significant vocational skills
  - Most have served time in a juvenile facility.
- Security levels of state prisons
  - Supermax
    - These are "control-unit" prisons, or units within prisons.
    - The most secure levels of custody at the state level. Examples:
      - Wisconsin Secure Program Facility
      - Red Onion in West Virginia
      - Tamms in Illinois
      - Ohio State Penitentiary
  - Maximum-security level
    - High level of security, characterized by:
      - High fences/walls of concrete
      - Barriers between the living area and outer perimeter
        - Electric perimeters
        - Laser motion detectors
        - Electronic and pneumatic locking systems
        - Metal detectors
        - X-ray machines
        - Television surveillance
      - Thick walls
      - Secure cells
      - Gun towers
      - Armed guards
      - Radio communication between staff
      - Computer information systems

- All death-row inmates are placed in maximum-security prisons.
  - Spend most of their day in single cells
  - Often permitted only a brief shower once a week under close supervision
- Most states have at least one maximum-security prison.

❖ Medium-security level
- Similar in design to maximum-security facilities; however, they allow prisoners more freedom
  - Permitted to associate with other prisoners
  - Can go to prison yard, use exercise room, and use library
  - Can shower and use bathroom facilities under less supervision
- "Count" is the process of counting number of inmates during the course of the day.
  - Counts take place at set times and at random.
  - All other business of prison stops until the count is verified.
  - Counts are usually taken four times a day.
- Generally smaller than maximum-security facilities
- Tend to have barbed wire at the top of fences instead of large stone walls of maximum-security institutions
- Cells and living quarters tend to have more windows and are often located closer to the perimeter of the institution.
- Generally more prison programs
- Housing can be dormitory style but still most often are individual cells.

❖ Minimum-security level
- Prisoners tend to be housed in dormitory-style units.
- Prisoners are usually free to walk around most of the facility.
- Some of the newer facilities provide for private rooms that prisoner can personally decorate.
- Access to canteen
- Often wear uniforms of a color different from inmates of a higher custody facility; sometimes allowed to wear their own clothes
- Work under only general supervision and have access to recreational, educational, and skills training programs on the prison grounds
- Guards are unarmed and gun towers do not exist.

- Fences, if they do exist, are usually low and sometimes even unlocked.
- Counts are usually not taken; prisoners are kept track of through administrative work schedules.
- Extensive visitation and furlough privileges
- Own restraint is the primary force keeping prisoners in the institution.

- Federal prison system
  - In 1895, Leavenworth Federal Prison opened in Leavenworth, Kansas, and became the first federal prison for civilians.
    - Facility had expanded to hold 1,200 prisoners by 1906.
  - In 1906 in Atlanta, Georgia, second federal prison opened.
  - McNeil Island Prison in Washington was opened in the early 1900s.
  - In 1927, the first prison for women was opened in Alderson, West Virginia. This is where Martha Stewart was incarcerated.
  - In 1930, the Federal Bureau of Prisons was created.
    - Federal Bureau of Prisons was charged with providing progressive and humane care for federal inmates.
    - Centralized administration of the 11 federal prisons that were in operation at the time
  - In 1933, in Springfield, Missouri, the Medical Center for Federal Prisoners opened with a 1,000-bed capacity.
  - In 1934, Alcatraz began operations.
  - In 1984, the Sentencing Reform Act was passed. The act established determinate sentencing, abolished parole at the federal level, and reduced good time.
  - The number of federal prisons grew as a result of the Sentencing Reform Act of 1984.
    - From 1980 to 1989 the federal inmate population more than doubled from just over 24,000 to almost 58,000.
    - During the 1990s, the federal inmate population again more than doubled, reaching approximately 136,000.
    - Today, the federal system serves an inmate population of more than 207,000 at 126 institutions.
  - Federal security levels
    - Minimum security
      - Also known as Federal Prison Camps (FPCs)
      - Have dormitory housing
      - A relatively low staff-to-inmate ratio

- Limited or no perimeter fencing
- Work and program oriented
- Many are located adjacent to large institutions or on military bases.
- Inmates help serve the labor needs of the larger institution or base.
- Examples: Elgin Air Force Base, Florida; Maxwell Air Force Base, Florida; Alderson, West Virginia
- Fifty-five of these facilities house 35% of federal prison population.

◆ Low security
- Also known as Federal Correctional Institutions (FCIs)
- Have double perimeters
- Employ vehicle patrols around perimeters
- Mostly dormitory or cubicle housing
- Strong work and program components
- Staff-to-inmate ratio in these institutions is higher than in minimum-security facilities.
- Examples: Butner, North Carolina; Danbury, Connecticut
- Forty-one such facilities, with 28% of federal prison inmate population

◆ Medium security
- FCIs and USPs (U.S. penitentiaries) designated to house medium-security inmates.
- Have strengthened perimeters
    - Often have double fences with electronic detection systems
- Mostly cell-type housing
- A wide variety of work and treatment programs
- An even higher staff-to-inmate ratio than low-security FCIs, and even greater internal controls
- Examples: Terminal Island, California; Lompoc, California; Seagoville, Texas
- Twenty-six medium-security facilities
- Twenty-three percent of the federal prison population

◆ High security
- Also known as U.S. penitentiaries (USPs)
- Have highly secured perimeters that may feature walls or reinforced fences
- Multiple- and single-occupant cell housing

- Highest staff-to-inmate ratio
- Close control of inmate movement
- Armed patrol
- Examples: Atlanta, Georgia; Lewisburg, Pennsylvania; Terre Haute, Indiana; Leavenworth, Kansas
- Eight high-security facilities, approximately 13% of the federal prison population

- **Administrative maximum (ADMAX)**
  - Ultra-maximum-security prison
  - Only one exists, in Florence, Colorado.
    - Has an underground entrance that is heavily guarded
    - In an effort to reduce escape attempts, there are small windows only allowing a view upward to the sky so inmates cannot tell where in the building their cells are.
  - Holds mob bosses, spies, terrorists, murderers, and escape artists
  - Dangerous prisoners are confined to cells 23 hours per day.
  - Prisoners are not allowed to associate with one another.
  - One percent of the federal prison population

ADMAX

Administrative maximum. The term is used by the federal government to denote ultra-high-security prisons.

- Federal correctional facilities exist as single institutions or as federal correctional complexes.
  - Allenwood, Pennsylvania is an example of a federal correctional complex.
    - Consists of:
      - A U.S. penitentiary
      - A federal prison camp
      - Two federal correctional institutions: one low security; one medium security

11.3.2 Jails

- Originally were locally operated for short-term confinement
  - Intended to hold suspects following arrest and awaiting trial, typically sentenced to up to a year in a local facility.
- Current uses
  - Receive individuals pending arraignment and those awaiting trial, conviction, or sentencing.
  - Readmit probation, parole, and bail-bond violators and absconders.
  - Temporarily detain juveniles, the mentally ill, and others pending transfer to appropriate facilities.

- Hold individuals for the military, for protective custody, for contempt, and for the courts as witness.
- Release convicted inmates to the community upon completion of their sentence.
- Transfer inmates to federal, state, or other authorities.
- House inmates for federal, state, or other authorities because of overcrowding in their facilities.
- Operate community-based programs with day reporting, home detention, electronic monitoring, or other types of supervision.

- Jail statistics
  - Jail profile
    - There are 3,365 jails operating in the United States.
    - Approximately 207,000 jail employees
    - On average, inmate cost is around $15,000 per year per inmate.
    - Most jails (66%) are designed to house 50 or less inmates.
    - Six percent of the jails hold over 50% of the prisoners.
      - The 50 largest jails hold almost 30% of all inmates.
        - Los Angeles County jail is the largest jail in the United States, and in 2008, it had a daily average population of 22,349 inmates, which put it at 87% capacity.
        - New York City jail is the second largest, with a daily average population of 19,554 inmates, which put it at 71% capacity.
        - Los Angeles and New York City together held 5.33% of all jail inmates.
        - States with more than one jurisdiction among the nation's 50 largest jails:
          - California (10)
          - Florida (9)
          - Texas (6)
          - Georgia (4)
          - Pennsylvania (2)
          - Tennessee (2)
  - 2008 Bureau of Justice midyear report
    - There were 785,556 inmates being held in the nation's local jails, up from 780,174 at midyear 2007, and 672,723 in 2003.

- In addition to those individuals held in jails, jails supervise individuals outside of the jail facilities (72,852):
    - ❒ Weekender programs: 12,325
    - ❒ Electronic monitoring: 13,539
    - ❒ Home detention: 498
    - ❒ Day reporting: 5,758
    - ❒ Community service: 18,475
    - ❒ Other pretrial supervision: 12,452
    - ❒ Other work programs: 5,808
    - ❒ Treatment programs: 2,259
    - ❒ Other: 1,739
- Jails reported adding 14,911 beds during the previous 12 months, bringing capacity to 828,413.
    - ❒ Ninety-five percent of the rated capacity was occupied at midyear 2008.
- The number of jail inmates per 100,000 U.S. residents was 258 in 2008.
- Gender
    - ❒ Almost 9 out of every 10 jail inmates were adult males.
    - ❒ Using a one-day count in 2008, the breakdown of jail inmates was as follows:
        - There were 678,677 adult male inmates in 2008 compared to 615,618 in 2003.
        - There were 99,175 adult female inmates in 2008 compared to 49,857 in 2003.
        - There were 7,703 juvenile inmates in 2008 compared to 7,248 in 2003.
    - ❒ Pregnancy is a problem for jails.
        - Approximately 4% of female inmates are pregnant at the time they are admitted to jail.
        - In urban areas, approximately 10% of the female population in jails is reported to be pregnant on any given day.
        - A few hundred children are born to women in jail each year.
        - Jailed mothers are typically separated from the children they give birth to in jail because the jail is not equipped to handle a newborn.

        - Drug abuse is a significant problem of women in jail.
            - Over 30% of women admitted to jail have a substance abuse problem.
    - Race
        - Using a one-day count in 2008, the breakdown of jail inmates was as follows:
            - White/non-Hispanic: 333,300
            - Black/non-Hispanic: 308,000
            - Hispanic: 128,500
        - Blacks were three times more likely than Hispanics and five times more likely than whites to be in jail.
- Jail overcrowding
    - Many of the jails in existence today are old, outdated, understaffed, and in general, poorly funded.
    - In the 1990s there was a strong movement to improve jails, mostly with an emphasis on building new jails and increasing capacity as a response to overcrowding.
    - Causes of jail overcrowding:
        - Inability of jail inmates to make bond
        - Unnecessary delays between arrest and final case disposition
        - Unnecessary limited access to vital information about defendants that could be useful in facilitating court-ordered pretrial release
        - Limited ability of justice system to handle cases expeditiously due to a lack of resources (judges, prosecuting attorneys, etc.)
        - Inappropriate attorney delays
        - Unproductive statutes that require that specified nonviolent offenders be jailed (shoplifters, DUIs, minor drug offenses)

For more on prisons and jails, visit Criminal Justice Interactive online > Corrections: History and Institutions > Learning Modules > 11.3 Prisons and Jails.

For more on rehabilitation in prisons and jails, visit Criminal justice Interactive online > Corrections: History and Institutions > Myths and Issues Videos > Myth vs. Reality: The Correctional System Rehabilitates Offenders.

11.4 Prison employees

11.4.1 Many jobs within a prison structure

- Many of the jobs are the same as in any large residential organizations, hospitals, retirement homes, and universities.
- Every service and commodity required by staff or inmates must be brought into prison.
- No matter what the daily responsibilities of a prison employee are, there is constant potential for danger.
- The environment is rigidly managed.

11.4.2 Categories of prison jobs

- Administrative
  - Manages the bureaucratic activities of the prison complex. The jobs include:
    - Warden
    - Department heads
    - Computer specialists
    - Financial managers
    - Human resources
- Security
  - Provides the security systems that ensure the safety of inmates, employees, and the community. Jobs include:
    - Deputy wardens
    - Staff trainers
    - Security supervisors
    - Correctional officers
- Treatment and programs
  - Treatment and programs staff provide educational, training, psychological, and other programs and services to inmates. Jobs include:
    - Therapists and counselors
    - Teachers and trainers
    - Recreation staff
    - Case managers
    - Chaplains
- Services
  - Services staff operate the departments that organize, administer, and implement systems to address the direct physical needs of inmates. Jobs include:
    - Health services
    - Facilities management

- Food services
- Inmate labor and industries
- Landscape management

For more on prison employees, visit Criminal Justice Interactive online > Corrections: History and Institutions > Learning Modules > 11.4 Prison Employees.

For more on prison employees, visit Criminal Justice Interactive online > Corrections: History and Institutions > Simulation Activity: Prison Operations.

11.5 Correctional systems

11.5.1 **Private prisons**

PRIVATE PRISONS

Prison facilities operated for local and state governments by private enterprise for profit.

- History of private prisons
  - Private prisons are prison facilities operated for local and state governments by private enterprise for a profit.
  - The first for-profit prison in the United States, San Quentin in California, opened in 1852.
    - Originally operated as a private enterprise; after a number of major scandals, it was turned over to state control.
  - **Privatization** movement
    - The movement toward the wider use of private prisons
    - Began in the 1980s mostly as a response to the increased number of incarcerations as a result of the "war on drugs."
  - In 1984, the Corrections Corporation of America (CCA) awarded contract to take over a facility in Hamilton County, Tennessee.
    - This was the first time that any government in the United States had contracted out the complete operation of a jail to a private company.

PRIVATIZATION

The movement toward the wider use of private prisons.

- Private prisons today
  - Today there are a number of major corporations that are involved in the operation of private prisons. Examples:
    - Cornell Corrections: 70 facilities, 15 states, 20,192 capacity
    - Corrections Corporation of America (CCA): 64 facilities, 19 states, 75,000 capacity
    - Correctional Services Corporation (CSC): 63 facilities, 21 states and Puerto Rico , 13, 000 capacity
    - GEO Corporation (formerly Wackenhut Corporation): 60 facilities, 14 states and other countries, 60,000 capacity

- ❖ Growth of the number of inmates under private prison care in the United States:
    - ◆ In 1986, there were 2,620 prisoners in private prisons.
    - ◆ In 1997, there were over 74,000 prisoners in private prisons.
    - ◆ In 2001, there were over 87,000 prisoners in private prisons.
    - ◆ In 2007, there were over 113,000 prisoners in private prisons.
    - ◆ In midyear 2008,there were 126,249 prisoners held in private facilities: 32,712 were federal prisoners, 93,537 were state prisoners.
    - ◆ Prisoners held in private prisons represented 7.8% of all prisoners incarcerated midyear 2008: 16.3% of all federal prisoners were being held in private prisons, 6.6% of all state prisoners were being held in private prisons.
    - ◆ By 2007, 32 states , the District of Columbia, and the federal government had prisoners in private facilities.
    - ◆ *Richardson* vs. *McKnight* (1997)
        - ❒ Issue of whether or not prison guards employed by private firms are entitled to qualified immunity from lawsuits by prisoners charging a violations of Section 1983 of Title 42 of the U.S. Code (1983 lawsuits)
            - • Section 1983: prohibits anyone from depriving another of their civil rights
        - ❒ Supreme Court found that "while government-employed prison guards may have enjoyed a kind of immunity defense arising out of their status as public employees at common law . . .. There is no conclusive evidence of an historical tradition of immunity for private parties carrying out these functions."

11.5.2 Issues regarding prison privatization

- ■ Efficiency
    - ❖ Private organizations can provide better services for less cost, but, a prison is a very dangerous place to cut back on staff and services.
        - ◆ If saving money takes precedence over maintaining staff qualifications and treatment availability, rehabilitation will suffer and recidivism will rise.
- ■ Quality of services
    - ❖ Food, living conditions, and access to treatment are key to the quality of life of an inmate and affects prison staff.

- Cost-management could ultimately result in:
  - Poorer security
  - Increased danger for staff
  - May cost society in the form of poor rehabilitation
- Accountability
  - Oversight is found less often in private companies.
    - Human rights and civil rights of inmates are at risk.
    - If rights are violated, it is unclear who is legally culpable.

For more on correctional systems, visit Criminal Justice Interactive online > Corrections: History and Institutions > Learning Modules > 11.5 Correctional Systems.

For more on private versus public prisons, visit Criminal Justice Interactive online > Corrections: History and Institutions > Myths and Issues Videos > Issue 1: Prison: Public and Private.

CHAPTER SUMMARY

- The history of prisons can be divided into nine distinct eras. Early prisons developed during the Middle Ages, some of which stressed reformation over punishment. Prisons in the United States developed in the late 1700s by the Quakers, whose goal was to provide religion and humanity to those imprisoned. The mass prisons era (1825–1876) was characterized by a silent style of prison, where offenders ate, lived, and worked together in enforced silence. The reformatory era (1876–1890) was a movement based on the use of indeterminate sentencing and belief in rehabilitation, especially for youthful offenders. During the industrial era (1890–1935), the goal of imprisonment was to maximize the use of offender's labor during imprisonment. In the punitive era (1935–1945), large maximum prisons evolved and security and custody was emphasized. The treatment era (1945–1967) ushered in the use of behavioral techniques as treatment in prison. During 1967 to 1980, community-based treatment, a sentencing approach that relies on the resources of the community instead of prison, developed. The warehousing era (1980–1995) followed, brought about by public disappointment with the community-based model that led to an increase in incarcerations. The just desserts era (1995–present) is a contemporary model of imprisonment in which the principle of just desserts forms the underlying social philosophy.
- In the earliest days in the United States, men and women were held in the same facilities, but segregated during daytime activities. Because the women were supervised by men, they were at great risk for sexual assault. In part because of the lobbying of Quaker Elizabeth Fry who stressed the special needs of women,

separate facilities for women developed, which trained women in domestic sciences. Today's women's prisons are organized and managed much like men's prisons, with the exception that most women's prisons have programs related to parenting.

- Today, there are 126 federal prisons and over 1,400 state prisons. One out of every four state institutions is a large maximum-security prison, with a population approaching 1,000 inmates. These prisons are characterized by high levels of security, including electric perimeters, laser motion detectors, and electron and pneumatic locking systems. Medium-security prisons are similar in design to maximum-security facilities, but they allow prisoners more freedom, including the ability to associate with others and to obtain entry to the prison yard, library, and exercise room. In minimum-security prisons, prisoners tend to be housed in dormitory-style units and are usually free to walk around most of the facility. Federal security facilities also range from minimum to high security and exist as single instructions or as federal correctional complexes. Jails are locally operated for short-term confinement and are intended to hold suspects following arrest and awaiting trial, and individuals typically sentenced to up to a year in a local facility. In addition to those individuals held in jails, jails supervise individuals outside of jail facilities that have been sentenced to other programs, such as electronic monitoring, community service, and treatment programs. Many of today's jails are old, outdated, understaffed, and overcrowded due to underfunding.
- There are many jobs within the prison structure, but each of them requires that the employee face the constant potential of danger. Administrative positions generally involve managing the bureaucratic activities of the prison complex and include such jobs as warden, department heads, financial managers, and computer specialists. Security staff provides security systems that ensure the safety of employees, inmates, and the community, and include such jobs as deputy wardens, staff trainers, and correctional officers. Treatment and programs staff provide educational training and psychological or other services to inmates, and includes counselors, teachers, and chaplains. The services staff operates the departments that organize, administer, and implement systems, and includes health and food services, facilities management, and landscape management.
- Private prisons have existed in the United States since the mid-1800s, but the privatization movement really took hold in the 1980s as a result of the increased number of incarcerations. Today there are a number of major corporations that are involved in the operation of private prisons. There are several concerns that have arisen regarding privatizations. Private prisons may be able to provide better services for less, but their safety may be compromised in the process. Cost management could also result in diminished services in the areas of food, living conditions, access to treatment, and security. Finally, because of potential lack of oversight, the human and civil rights of the inmates are at risk.

ONLINE@CRIMINAL JUSTICE INTERACTIVE

Learning Modules

11.1 History of Prisons
11.2 History of Women's Prisons
11.3 Prisons and Jails
11.4 Prison Employees
11.5 Correctional Systems

Myths and Issues Videos

Myth vs. Reality: The Correctional System Rehabilitates Offenders
Issue 1: Prison: Public and Private
Issue 2: The Prison Building Boom and Crime: The Chicken and Egg Syndrome

Simulation Activity: Prison Operations

Homework and Review

In the News
Web Activity
Review Questions
Essay Questions

Chapter 12

Corrections in the Community

CHAPTER OUTLINE

12.0 Corrections in the community

12.1 The value of probation and parole

- 12.1.1 Incarceration is not always the answer to criminal behavior.
- 12.1.2 Sentencing options
- 12.1.3 The advantages of probation and parole
- 12.1.4 Disadvantages of parole and probation

12.2 Objectives and conditions of probations

- 12.2.1 Probation
- 12.2.2 History of probation
- 12.2.3 The use of probation
- 12.2.4 Probation revocation

12.3 Special supervision programs

- 12.3.1 Indeterminate sanctions

12.4 History of parole

- 12.4.1 Parole
- 12.4.2 History of parole

12.5 Parole board

- 12.5.1 Parole boards
- 12.5.2 Statutory decrees
- 12.5.3 Extent of parole
- 12.5.4 Parole conditions

12.6 Court cases related to probation and parole

- 12.6.1 U.S. Supreme Court cases

LEARNING OBJECTIVES

After reviewing the online material and reading this chapter, you should able to:

1. Define the terms "probation" and "parole" and discuss their value to the criminal justice system and society.
2. Describe the objectives and common conditions of probation/parole.
3. Describe the following special supervision programs: work release, halfway houses, electronic monitoring, and community service.
4. Explain the history of the parole system in the United States.
5. Discuss the role of the parole board in the parole process.
6. Define terms related to corrections in the community.

KEY TERMS

Bearden v. *Georgia*
community service
Comprehensive Crime Control Act
electronic monitoring
Elmira Reformatory
Escoe v. *Zerbst*
Gagnon v. *Scarpelli*
Greenholtz v. *Nebraska*
Griffin v. *Wisconsin*
home confinement
indeterminate sanctions
intensive supervision
Irish system
Kelly v. *Robinson*
mark system
Mempa v. *Rhay*
Minnesota v. *Murphy*
Mixed sentencing
Morrissey v. *Brewer*
National Probation Act
Parole
Parole board
Parole conditions
Pennsylvania Board of Probation and Parole v. *Scott*
Probation
Probation revocation
revocation hearing
shock incarceration
shock probation
split sentences
statutory decree
U.S. v. *Knight*
Young v. *Harper*

PROBATION

The supervised release of an offender instead of incarceration, although often with a suspended sentence held as motivation for the offender.

PAROLE

Refers to a conditional release from prison before the completion of the sentence. The parolee must comply with certain conditions of behavior.

12.0 Corrections in the community

12.1 The value of probation and parole

12.1.1 Incarceration is not always the answer to criminal behavior.

12.1.2 Sentencing options (not available in other countries)

- **Probation** is the supervised release of an offender instead of incarceration.
- **Parole** refers to a conditional release from prison before the completion of the sentence.
- Probation and parole are similar in many ways:
  - Both involve close supervision of an offender while he or she lives in the community.
  - Both require certain behaviors from the offender, such as checking in with authorities, participation in treatment, or other behavioral indications of social responsibility.

12.1.3 The advantages of probation and parole

- Lower cost: It is less expensive to keep a person in the community than incarcerated.
- Increased employment
  - Quality jobs are not available in institutions.
  - Offenders who are released are able to contribute to the "free" economy when they are employed outside of prison.
    - They pay taxes.
    - They stimulate the local economy by spending money.
- Restitution: When an offender works, he or she can participate in court-ordered restitution.
  - Restitution is the payment of money or providing services to the victim of a crime or the community.
- Community support: Participation in family and community activities helps to tie offender back into the community.
  - Probation avoids separating members of families, while parole reunites family members separated from each other by a prison sentence.
- Reduced risk of criminal sanctions: Prisons can teach offenders new crimes; keeping a person in the community helps to take the focus away from criminal activity.
- Increased use of community services: Probation/parole can provide psychological counseling such as job training, psychological and substance-abuse counseling, support groups, financial services, church outreach groups, and social services.

- Increased opportunity for rehabilitation
  - Probation/parole serves as an incentive to rehabilitate an offender.
  - Staying out of prison is often encouragement to an individual to not commit other offenses.

12.1.4 Disadvantages of parole and probation

- Relative lack of punishment
- Increased risk to the community
  - When a convicted offender is released to the community on probation or parole, it poses a risk to the community.
    - Potential for commission of another crime exists.
    - Individuals can abscond.
- Increased social costs
  - Increased risk of new crimes
  - Potential of increased expenses for those who do not meet their obligations: additional child support, welfare costs, housing expenses, legal aid, and indigent health care.

For more on the objectives and conditions of parole, visit Criminal Justice Interactive online > Corrections and the Community > Learning Modules > 12.1 The Value of Probation and Parole.

12.2 Objectives and conditions of probation

12.2.1 Probation

- Certain requirements of behavior are required to maintain freedom.
  - Conditions of probation can include:
    - Obtaining and keeping a job
    - Not frequenting bars
    - Restitution
    - Going to school
  - By violating probation, the offender can have his or her probation revoked and be placed in prison to serve their sentence.

12.2.2 History of probation

- England in the 1300s
  - English courts established the practice of "binding over for good behavior."
  - Offenders were placed in the custody of willing citizens.

- Boston in the 1850s
  - John Augustus (1784–1859), a bootmaker, was generally recognized as the world's first probation officer.
    - Attended sessions of criminal court and volunteered to take home carefully selected offenders as an alternative to prison.
    - In 1841, Augustus went to the police court in Boston and convinced them to let him take a drunk home instead of to jail.
      - Augustus paid the fine and court costs of $3.76.
      - The offender was to return to court after three weeks.
      - Augustus found the offender a job and made him sign a pledge to stop drinking.
      - When the offender and Augustus returned to court, the offender was sober, neatly dressed, and had a job.
      - The court began to allow Augustus to take home other offenders.
    - Eventually, Augustus branched out to take home all sorts of offenders.
    - John Augustus was the first to use the term probation, which comes from the Latin word "probare," meaning "to prove, to test."
    - In 1843, Augustus added helping children to his roster.
    - When Augustus died in 1859, he had helped over 2,000 people.
    - Only four caused difficulties, for whom Augustus had to forfeit bail.
  - In 1878, Massachusetts authorized the mayor of Boston to hire a probation officer.
  - In 1880, every city in Massachusetts had a probation officer.
  - In 1890, every court in Massachusetts had a probation officer.
  - In 1897, Missouri established probation officer positions.
  - In 1898, Vermont began establishing probation officer positions.
  - In 1899, Rhode Island followed with probation officers.
  - In 1925, all 48 states had probation legislation.
    - **National Probation Act** (1925) allowed federal judges to appoint federal probation officers.
    - Federal Probation Service was established to serve the U.S. Courts.

NATIONAL PROBATION ACT

An act that allowed federal judges to appoint federal probation officers.

12.2.3 The use of probation

- Probation is the most commonly used form of sentencing.
- As of the end of 2007:
  - There were 4,293,163 individuals on probation in the United States.
    - There were 23,450 individuals on probation at the federal level.
      - This represented a 4.1% decrease from 2006.
    - There were 4,269,713 individuals on probation at the state level.
      - This represented a 1.9% increase from 2006.
      - Georgia had the largest number of individuals on probation, with 435,361.
        - There were 6,144 individuals on probation per 100,000 adult residents.
      - New Hampshire had the fewest number of individuals on probation, with 4,650.
        - There were 454 individuals on probation per 100,000 adult residents.
- In 1998, 3.2 million individuals were on probation nationwide.
- Adults on probation at the end of 2007:
  - Gender
    - Female: 699,230 (23%)
    - Male: 2,282,672 (77%)
    - Unreported: 1,311,261
  - Race
    - White: 1,450,333 (55%)
    - Black: 761,036 (29%)
    - Hispanic: 352,376 (13%)
    - American Indiana/Alaskan Native: 23,896 (1%)
    - Asian/Native Hawaiian/other Pacific Islander: 19,483 (1%)
    - Of two or more races :12,069
    - Unknown or not reported: 1,667,197
  - Type of offense
    - Felony: 1,479,166 (47%)
    - Misdemeanor: 1,593,989 (51%)
    - Other infractions: 82,390 (3%)
    - Unknown or were not reported: 1,137,618

  - Most serious offense
    - Violent crime: 17%
      - Domestic violence: 66,843
      - Other violent offenses: 315,971
    - Property crime: 545, 559 (24%)
    - Drug offense: 593,544 (27%)
    - Driving while intoxicated and other traffic offenses: 18%
      - Driving while intoxicated or under the influence: 331,710
      - Other traffic offenses: 82,195
    - Other offenses: 301,612 (13%)
    - Unknown or not reported: 2,055,729
  - Entering probation, by type of sentence
    - Without incarceration: 620,840
    - With incarceration: 207,386
    - Probation through a deferred sentence, pretrial supervision, after a bench warrant was served, a reinstatement of their original sentence, placement in a drug court program, and other types of offenses: 39,955
    - Unknown or not reported: 1,315,146
- Adults leaving probation by type of exit, 2007:
  - Adults who left probation by the end of 2007: 2,122,681
    - Released having completed their probation: 982,072
    - Incarcerated with a new sentence: 56,335
    - Incarcerated under their current sentence: 124,032
    - Incarcerated for other or unknown reasons: 75,462
    - Absconded: 52,030
    - Discharged to a warrant or detainer: 13,648
    - Released from supervision (includes those who failed to meet all conditions of supervision, some with only financial conditions, and some early terminations and expirations of sentence): 177,441
    - Transferred to another probation agency: 11,122
    - Died: 8,999
    - Released from supervision because they were deported, released through a legislative mandate, had their sentence dismissed or overturned by the court through an appeal, had their sentence closed administratively or deferred, and other types of exits: 83,574
    - Unknown or not reported: 537,966

- Two types of conditions are applied to probationers.
  - Standard (also called general)
  - Special (also called specific)
- Standard conditions are conditions that apply to all probationers.
  - Define limits on movement.
  - Help probation department to control probationers
  - Examples of conditions that can apply to all probationers, depending on the jurisdiction:
    - Obey all laws—municipal, county, state, and federal.
    - Stay away from the victim.
    - Pay a fine.
    - Regular reporting to the probation officer
    - No use or possession of controlled substances except those prescribed by a doctor
    - Submit to testing of breath, urine, or blood for controlled substances or alcohol use if the probationer has a history of substance abuse or if there is suspicion that the probationer has used illegal substances.
    - Participate in a substance abuse evaluation as directed by the supervising officer and follow recommendations of the evaluator if there are reasonable grounds to believe there is a history of substance abuse.
    - Remain within the jurisdiction of the court until written permission to leave is granted by the supervising officer.
    - If physically able, find and maintain gainful employment, approved schooling, or a full-time combination of both.
    - Change neither employment nor residence without prior permission from the supervising officer.
    - Permit the supervising officer to visit the probationer or the probationer's work site or residence, and to conduct a walk-through of the common areas and the rooms in the residence.
    - Consent to the search of person, vehicle, or premises upon request of a representative of the supervising officer if the supervising officer has reasonable grounds to believe that evidence of a violation will be found, and submit to fingerprinting or photographing, or both when requested.
    - Promptly and truthfully answer all reasonable inquiries by the supervising officer or other representatives of a county community corrections agency.

- Do not possess weapons, firearms, or dangerous animals.
- If under supervision for, or previously convicted of, a sex offense, and if recommended by the supervising officer, successfully completing a sex offender treatment program approved by the supervising officer and submitting to polygraph examinations at the direction of the supervising officer.
- Participate in a mental health evaluation as directed by the supervising officer and follow the recommendation(s) of the evaluator.
- If required to report as a sex offender, report with the Department of State Police, a chief of police, a county sheriff, or the supervisory agency when supervision begins, within 10 days of a change of residence, and once each year within 10 days of the probationer's date of birth.

- Special conditions
  - Apply to specific cases.
  - Objectives of special conditions
    - Designed to meet the needs of individual probationers
  - Conditions that may be added to a general list that are mandated by a judge, given the offender and the crime characteristics
  - Examples of some specific conditions:
    - Surrender driver's license.
    - Successfully pass a G.E.D. test.
    - Complete community service.
    - Required to be home after dark.
    - Avoid certain neighborhoods or intersections (for drug-related offenses).
    - Some jurisdictions have special condition packages that they add depending on the crime. Examples of three special condition packages:
      - Substance Abuse Package (taken from the Clackamas County, Oregon, Community Corrections Conditions of Probation)
        - Obtain a substance abuse evaluation as directed by the probation officer, follow through with any treatment recommendations, including inpatient treatment, and comply with all follow-up treatment.
        - Not use or possess alcoholic beverages (including "near beer"), illegal drugs or narcotics, and shall notify the probation

officer of any medical prescriptions given by a doctor

- Do not enter or frequent any establishment whose primary income is derived from the sale of alcoholic beverages.
- Shall not frequent places where narcotics are used, sold, or kept
- Shall not possess any narcotics paraphernalia, including smoking devices, and shall not associate with any person known to use, sell, or possess any illegal drugs or narcotics
- Submit to monitored testing at the direction of the probation officer and at the defendant's own expense.
- Take Antabuse if medically able, and at the direction of the probation officer
- Not to drive without a valid license and insurance and shall be subject to the requirements of the Guardian Interlock System according to DMV policies for a hardship license
- If the crime of conviction is a DUII, you must attend a DUII Victim's Panel within 60 days of this judgment.
- Attend Alcoholics/Narcotics Anonymous meetings at the direction of the probation officer
- Submit defendant's person, residence, vehicle, or property to search by the probation officer at any time without benefit of a search warrant when the probation officer has reasonable grounds to believe that such a search will reveal evidence of a violation of this probation

❒ Sex Offender Package (taken from the Clackamas County, Oregon, Community Correction Conditions of Probation)

- Have no contact with any female or male under the age of 18, unless authorized by your probation officer
- Consent to and cooperate with polygraph examinations and penile plethysmograph assessments when deemed necessary by the therapist and/or the probation officer (plethysmograph measures changes in

the volume of organs or other body parts, particularly those changes resulting from blood flow)

- Be financially responsible for all counseling costs incurred by the victim(s)
- Consent to the sharing of assessment and treatment information between public and private agencies, agents, and persons who are deemed essential in assessing, monitoring, and mediating treatment for sexual deviancy problems
- Not possess or use at any time any type of pornography including, but not limited to written, telephonic, computer-based pictures, videotapes or audiotapes, and cannot frequent establishments associated with the sex industry
- Enter and complete a sex offender treatment program as directed by the probation officer
- Consent to, and cooperate with, any plan deemed necessary by the probation officer and/or therapist to maintain and monitor offense-free behavior for the duration of this probation
- Not be involved in any organizations which would place defendant in direct contact with children, i.e., Boy Scouts, Girl Scouts, 4-H, Big Brother or Big Sister programs, Sunday school teaching, etc.
- Not frequent or visit places that exist primarily for the enjoyment of children, i.e., circuses, amusement parks, zoos, etc.
- Must register as a sex offender pursuant to Oregon Revised Statutes
- Submit to blood testing for DNA purposes and HIV testing with release of information to the victims(s)
- Submit defendant's person, residence, vehicle, or property to search by the probation officer at any time without the benefit of a search warrant when the probation officer has reasonable grounds to believe that such a search will reveal evidence of a violation of this probation

❒ Financial Crimes Package (taken from the Clackamas County, Oregon, Community Corrections Probation Guidelincs)

- Advise current and any future employer, including temporary agencies, of this probation and the nature of the crime
- Provide probation officer with employment information and allow communication between employer and probation officer for purposes of monitoring compliance with probation conditions.
- Do not accept any employment which includes the handling of money, i.e., cash, checks, credit cards, or bank cards, accounts payable, without obtaining permission from your probation officer and making a full disclosure to the employer
- Do not change employment or job duties without prior permission of the probation officer and report any changes in supervisor to the probation officer immediately
- Permit the probation officer to visit your place of employment
- Provide complete personal financial records, i.e., tax records, household income and expenses, bank statements, etc., to the probation officer upon request
- Prior to engaging in any financial transaction over $200.00, must obtain permission from the probation officer
- Must submit to polygraph examination at your own expense upon request of parole/probation officer pertaining to employment and financial matters only
- Submit defendant's person, residence, vehicle or property to search by the probation officer at any time without benefit of a search warrant when the probation officer has reasonable grounds to believe that such a search will reveal evidence of a violation of this probation

12.2.4 **Probation revocation** is a court order in response to a violation of conditions of probation, taking away a person's probationary status, and usually withdrawing the conditional freedom associated with that status.

PROBATION REVOCATION

A court order taking away a convicted offender's probationary status and usually withdrawing the conditional freedom associated with that status in response to a violation of the conditions of probation.

- The California Penal Code permits a trial court to revoke probation:
  - ❖ "If the interests of justice so require and the court, in its judgment, has reason to believe . . . that the person has violated any of the conditions of his or her probation, has become abandoned to improper associates or a vicious life, or has subsequently committed other offenses, regardless whether he or she has been prosecuted for such offense."

REVOCATION

The administrative act of determining that the parolee or probationer has failed to comply with behavioral expectations during release. Revocation results in the rescinding of a suspended sentence for a probationer, or the return to incarceration of a parolee.

- **Revocation** proceedings have very specific requirements and steps that must be followed before probation can be revoked.
- Steps in the revocation process:
  - ❖ Written notice of the claimed violation must be provided to the probationer.
  - ❖ The evidence against the probationer must be disclosed.
  - ❖ The probationer must have an opportunity to be heard in person and to present witnesses and documentary evidence.
  - ❖ Probationer has the right to confront and cross-examine adverse witnesses.
  - ❖ The probation revocation hearing must be before a neutral and detached hearing body like a court.
  - ❖ A written statement by the fact-finder as to the evidence relied on and the reasons for revoking probation

For more on the objectives and conditions of parole, visit Criminal Justice Interactive online > Corrections and the Community > The Value of Probation and Parole > Learning Modules > 12.2 Objectives and Conditions of Parole.

For practice determining the appropriate conditions for probation/parole, visit Criminal Justice Interactive online > Corrections and the Community > Simulation Activity: Determining Conditions for Probation and Parole.

12.3 Special supervision programs

12.3.1 Indeterminate sanctions

INDETERMINATE SANCTIONS

The use of less, or nontraditional sentences in lieu of imprisonment; sometimes called "alternative sentencing" strategies.

- Are the use of less or nontraditional sentences in lieu of imprisonment; sometimes called "alternative sentencing" strategies
- Provides sentencing options besides the traditional choices of prison and probation
- Advantages of indeterminate sanctions:
  - ❖ They are less expensive to operate per offender than imprisonment.
  - ❖ They are "socially cost-effective" because they keep the offender in the community, thus avoiding the breakup of

the family and the stigmatization that accompanies imprisonment.

- ❖ They provide flexibility in terms of resources, time of involvement, and place of service.

- **Split sentencing** is a sentence explicitly requiring the convicted offender to serve a period of confinement in a local, state, or federal facility, followed by a period of probation.
  - ❖ Split sentences are frequently given to minor drug offenders and serve notice that continued law violations may result in imprisonment for much longer periods.

SPLIT SENTENCE

A sentence explicitly requiring the convicted offender to serve a period of confinement in a local, state, or federal facility, followed by a period of probation.

- **Shock probation/parole** is the practice of sentencing offenders to prison, allowing them to apply for probationary release, and enacting such release in surprise fashion.
  - ❖ The offender usually does not know that he or she will be released, and expects to serve a long sentence in prison.
  - ❖ Shock probation lowers the cost of confinement, maintains community and family ties, and may be an effective rehabilitative tool.

SHOCK PROBATION

The practice of sentencing offenders to prison, allowing them to apply for probationary release, and enacting such release in surprise fashion. Offenders who receive shock probation may not be aware that they will be released on probation and may expect to spend a much longer time behind bars.

- Parole (discussed in detail in Section 12.1)
- **Shock incarceration** is a sentencing option that makes use of boot camp-type prisons to impress on convicted offenders the realities of prison life.
  - ❖ Usually used for first-time offenders
  - ❖ Military-type boot camp involving strict discipline, physical training, and hard labor
  - ❖ Programs last from 90 to 180 days.
  - ❖ Georgia (1983) was the first state to create a shock incarceration program.
  - ❖ Approximately 30 states operate boot camps.
  - ❖ Despite their growth in popularity in the 1990s, more recent research has shown correctional boot camps to have at best, mixed results.
    - ◆ "Correctional Boot Camps: Lessons From a Decade of Research," *National Institute of Justice* (2003)
      - ❐ Findings
        - Participants reported positive short-term changes in attitudes and behaviors; they also had better problem-solving and coping skills.
        - With few exceptions, these positive changes did not lead to reduced recidivism.
        - The boot camps that did produce lower recidivism rates offered more treatment services, had longer sessions, and included more intensive postrelease supervision.

SHOCK INCARCERATION

A sentencing option that makes use of "boot camp"-type prisons to impress on convicted offenders the realities of prison life.

- Not all programs with these features had successful results.
- Under a narrow set of conditions, boot camps can lead to small relative reductions in prison populations and correctional costs.

MIXED SENTENCING

A sentence that requires that a convicted offender serve weekends (or other specified periods of time) in a confinement facility (usually a jail) while undergoing probationary supervision in the community.

COMMUNITY SERVICE

A sentencing alternative that requires offenders to spend at least part of their time working for a community agency.

- **Mixed sentencing** and community service is a sentence that requires that a convicted offender serve weekends (or other specified periods of time) in a confinement facility (usually a jail) while undergoing probationary supervision in the community.
  - **Community service** is a sentencing alternative that requires offenders to spend at least part of their time working for a community agency.
  - Community service is compatible with most other forms of innovations in probation and parole.
  - Community service participants are usually minor criminals, drunk drivers, and youthful offenders.
  - Authorities rarely agree on what community service activities are supposed to accomplish.
  - Examples of community service:
    - Washing police cars
    - Cleaning graffiti off of walls
    - Refurbishing public facilities
    - Cleaning school buses

INTENSIVE SUPERVISION

A form of probation that requires frequent face-to-face contact with a probation officer.

- **Intensive supervision** is a form of probation that requires frequent face-to-face contact with a probation officer.
  - Georgia (1982) was the first state to use intensive supervision.
    - Program involves:
      - Five face-to-face contacts per week
      - Mandatory curfew
      - Required employment
      - Weekly check of local arrest records
      - Routine, unannounced alcohol and drug testing
      - A required number of house of community service
      - Automatic notification of probation officers via the State Criminal Information Network when intensive probation supervision clients are arrested
      - Caseloads of probation officers are much lower than the national average.
      - Officers work as a team, with one probation officer and two surveillance officers supervising about 40 probationers.

- **Home confinement** and electronic monitoring
  - House arrest is a situation in which individuals ordered confined to their homes are sometimes monitored electronically to ensure they do not leave during the hours of confinement. Absence from the home during working hours is often permitted.
  - Offenders may leave home only in a medical emergency or to go to a job or to buy household essentials.
  - Used with pregnant women, geriatric offenders with special needs, and/or terminally ill offenders
  - **Electronic monitoring**
    - Electronic bracelets now have computer chips that must be inserted into a modem on a phone to verify their presence in the home during random phone calls at all hours of the day.
  - Estimates show that traditional home confinement programs cost about $1,500 to $7,000 per offender per year, while electronic monitoring increases the cost by at least $1,000.
  - Critics argue that house arrest may endanger the public and that it may provide little or no actual punishment.
- Individual innovations by judges
  - A common theme is that of "public shaming."
    - Example: having shoplifters wear cardboard signs declaring themselves to be shoplifters while they walk in front of the store in which they were caught

HOME CONFINEMENT
Individuals ordered confined to their homes and are sometimes monitored electronically to ensure they do not leave during the hours of confinement. Absence from the home during working hours is often permitted.

ELECTRONIC MONITORING
A monitoring system that uses devices attached to a probationer or parolee that can provide documentation of the offender's location.

For more on the special supervision program, visit Criminal Justice Interactive online > Corrections and the Community > Learning Modules > 12.3 Special Supervision Programs.

For more on community-based programs, visit Criminal Justice Interactive online > Corrections and the Community > Myths and Issues Videos > Myth vs. Reality: Community-Based Sentences Provide for Close Monitoring and Supervision.

12.4 History of parole

12.4.1 Parole

- Conditions are set for parole status, and violation of conditions can result in the offender having their parole revoked and being returned to prison.

12.4.2 History of parole

- Parole is a French term that means "word," as in giving one's word of honor or promise.

- Captain Alexander Maconochie
  - Warden of Norfolk Island Prison, approximately 1,000 miles off the coast of Australia in the 1840s
  - Prisoners who had been transported to Australia and had also committed a crime while in Australia were sent to Norfolk Island; hence, they were considered to have been "doubly condemned."
  - When Maconochie arrived at Norfolk Island, conditions were atrocious:
    - Disease was rampant.
    - Fights among inmates left many dead and more injured.
    - Sanitary conditions were practically nonexistent.
  - **Mark system** was a system developed by Maconochie; prisoners could earn credits to buy their freedom.
    - Accomplishing tasks was more important than time served for determining release.
    - A negative behavior caused marks to be lost.
    - Mark system constituted the first "early release" program and led to recognition of the indeterminate sentence as a useful tool in the reformation of offenders.
    - Inmates they could be moved to less and less secure facilities and eventually be released based on the number of marks they earned.
  - Maconochie became known as "father of parole" because of similarities between his system and that of later day parole.

MARK SYSTEM

The first early release program, the mark system led to recognition of the indeterminate sentence as a useful tool in the reformation of offenders.

- Sir Walter Crofton was named head of the Irish Prison System in 1854.
  - Adapted Maconochie's program; after a period of strict imprisonment, Crofton began transferring offenders to "intermediate prisons" where they could accumulate marks based on work performance, behavior, and educational improvement.
- In 1870, at National Prison Association meeting in Cincinnati, a paper by Crofton was read.
  - Specific references to the **Irish system** were incorporated into the Declaration of Principles along with other such reforms as indeterminate sentencing and classification for release based on a mark system.
- Parole in the United States
  - **Elmira Reformatory** opened in New York in 1876.
    - Zebulon Brockway, a leading advocate of indeterminate sentencing, was appointed warden.

IRISH SYSTEM

Penal Servitude Act passed by Parliament in 1853 allowed the release of well-behaved felons. Sir Walter Crofton adopted ideas from Norfolk Island and the "ticket of leave" concept into the Irish prison system.

ELMIRA REFORMATORY

Zebulon Brockway, as warden of the Elmira Reformatory, tried to humanize prison life and make a prisoner more fit for society. Merged ideas of reformation, early release, and supervision by nonpolice agents into the earliest form of parole in the United States.

- Brockway established a two-prong system for managing prison populations and preparing inmates for release.
  - Indeterminate sentencing
  - Parole supervision
- System of graded stages was introduced.
  - Offenders required to meet goals in:
    - Education
    - Behavior
    - Other goals as appropriate
  - Education/schooling was mandatory.
- Training in a trade was available, such as:
  - Telegraphy
  - Tailoring
  - Plumbing
  - Carpentry
- New York had passed an indeterminate sentencing bill, which made it possible for the early release of inmates who had earned it.
- The Elmira Reformatory accepted only first-time offenders who were between the ages of 16 and 30.
- Upon admission they were placed in the second grade of classification.
- After six months of good behavior, they were promoted to first grade.
  - If they misbehaved, they could be reduced to the third grade, and they would then have to start working their way back up.
- Continued good behavior while in first grade could result in release.
- Once released, the offender stayed under the jurisdiction of the authorities for six months.
- Volunteer guardians met with the released offender on the first day of each month.
- Movement proved to be a failure.
- Many offenders returned to life of crime once released.
- Although a failure, the Elmira Reformatory established principles that remain with us today.
  - Indeterminate sentencing
  - Parole
  - Trade training
  - Education

- Primacy of reformation
    - In 1907, New York became the first state to adopt all components of a parole system.
    - In 1942, all states and the federal government had adopted systems of parole.

- History of federal parole
    - In 1910, parole at the federal level began after legislation was passed.
        - Parole boards were established at three federal penitentiaries.
        - Each parole board consisted of:
            - The warden of the institution
            - The physician of the institution
            - The superintendent of prisons of the Department of Justice in Washington, D.C.
    - In 1930, a single, centralized board of parole was created.
        - Board consisted of three members, serving full time, appointed by the attorney general
    - In 1945, attorney general ordered Board of Parole to report directly to him.
    - In 1948, attorney general increased size of Board of Parole to five members because of the increase in federal prison population.
    - In 1950, Board of Parole is increased to eight members appointed by the president with advice and consent of the senate.
        - Members served six-year terms.
        - Board of Parole placed under the Department of Justice for administrative purposes.
    - In 1976, Parole Commission and Reorganization Act (1976) was retitled Board of Parole as United States Parole Commission.
        - Established it as an independent agency within the Department of Justice.
        - Nine commissioners appointed by the president with the advice and consent of the senate.
        - Six-year terms
        - Parole commission was required to establish specific guidelines for parole decision making and written reasons for parole denial, and an administrative appeal process.

COMPREHENSIVE CRIME CONTROL ACT

An act that provided for the abolition of the Parole Commission.

- In 1984, **Comprehensive Crime Control Act** of 1984 was passed, establishing the United States Sentencing Commission.

- ❖ Act provided for the abolition of the parole commission on November 1, 1992 (five years after the sentencing guidelines were to take effect).

- In 1987, the initial set of sentencing guidelines took effect.
  - ❖ Federal defendants sentenced for offenses committed after November 1, 1987 were to serve determinate sentences and are not eligible for parole consideration.
- In 1990, the Judicial Improvement Act of 1990 was passed, extending the life of the parole commission until November 1, 1997.
  - ❖ The original phaseout (in 1992) did not adequately provide for persons sentenced under the law in effect prior to November 1, 1987 who had not yet completed their sentences.
  - ❖ Elimination of, or reduction in, parole eligibility for such cases would raise a serious *ex post facto* issue.
- In 1996, the Parole Commission Phaseout Act of 1996 was passed, extending the life of the parole commission for the same reason as the Judicial Improvement Act of 1990.
  - ❖ Parole commission was extended to November 1, 2002.
- In 2002, the 21st Century Department of Justice Appropriations Authorization Act of 2002 extended the life of the parole commission until November 1, 2005.
- The status of the parole commission is still unresolved today.

For more on the history of parole, visit Criminal Justice Interactive online > Corrections and the Community > Learning Modules > 12.4 History of Parole.

12.5 Parole board

12.5.1 **Parole boards**

- Board members are typically appointed by the governor or the state.
- Grant paroles based on a review of each case
- Considered "discretionary" parole

12.5.2 **Statutory decree**

- Mandatory parole
- Automatic after offender serves a certain amount of their sentence minus the time for good behavior and other special considerations

12.5.3 Extent of parole

- Number of individuals on parole as of the end of 2007: 824,365
  - ❖ Federal level: 92,673
  - ❖ State level: 731,692

PAROLE BOARD

A state paroling authority. Most states have parole boards that decide when an incarcerated offender is ready for conditional release. Some boards also function as revocation hearing panels. Also called parole commission.

STATUTORY DECREE

Mandatory parole, that automatically goes into effect after the offender serves a certain amount of their sentence minus the time for good behavior and other special considerations.

- Gender
  - Female: 96,944 (12%)
  - Male: 690,462 (88%)
- Race
  - White: 322,501 (42%)
  - Black: 287,640 (37%)
  - Hispanic: 148,557 (19%)
  - American Indian/Alaska Native: 7,727 (1%)
  - Asian/Native Hawaiian/other Pacific Islander: 5,590 (1%)
- Type of offense
  - Violent: 180,501 (26%)
  - Property: 168,954 (24%)
  - Drug: 254,472 (37%)
  - Public order: 49,725 (7%)
  - Other: 38,569 (6%)
- Parolees returned to incarceration: 183,253
  - Federal level: 10,573
  - State level: 172,680
- Adults leaving parole, by type of exit
  - Completed parole: 214,604
  - Returned to prison or jail: 183,253
    - With a new sentence: 47,357
    - With parole revocation: 129,609
    - Other: 6,287
  - Parolees who failed to meet all conditions of supervision, including some with only financial conditions remaining whose cases may have been turned over to a business office, and other types of unsatisfactory expirations of sentence: 8,834
  - Other: 71,356
    - Parolees who had absconded: 53,981
    - Parolees who had died: 4,975
    - Parolees who had transferred to another jurisdiction: 2,948
    - Others: 9,452
  - Unknown: 4,133
- Adults entering parole, by type of sentence
  - Under discretionary model of parole board: 152,018
  - Under mandatory model: 241,027
  - By reinstatement (persons returned to parole after serving time in a prison because of a parole violation): 40,647

- ❖ Other (includes parolees who were sentenced by a judge to a fixed period of incarceration based on a determinate statute, immediately followed by a period of supervised release; transferred from another state; released temporarily to parole; released from a boot camp; released through a conditional or mental health release to parole; absconders who were returned to parole supervision; on pretrial supervision; sentenced to community supervision for life because of a sex offense; and others): 55,494
- ❖ Unknown or not reported: 16,779

12.5.4 **Parole conditions** are the general and specific limits imposed upon an offender who is released on parole.

PAROLE CONDITIONS

Parole conditions are the general and specific limits imposed upon an offender who is released on parole.

- General conditions tend to be fixed by state statute.
- Special conditions are mandated by the parole board; background of the offender is taken into consideration.
- Conditions for parole are similar to those placed on offenders on probation.
- General conditions include (taken from State of Oregon Board of Parole and Post Supervision):
  - ❖ Pay supervision fees, fines, restitution or other fees ordered by the Board.
  - ❖ Not use or possess controlled substances except pursuant to a medical prescription
  - ❖ Submit to testing of breath or urine for controlled substance or alcohol use if the offender has history of substance abuse or if there is a reasonable suspicion that the offender has illegally used controlled substances.
  - ❖ Participate in a substance abuse evaluation as directed by the supervising officer and follow the recommendations of the evaluator if there are reasonable grounds to believe there is a history of substance abuse.
  - ❖ Remain in the State of Oregon until written permission to leave is granted by the Department of Corrections or a county community corrections agency.
  - ❖ If physically able, find and maintain gainful full-time employment, approved schooling, or a full-time combination of both.
  - ❖ Change neither employment nor residence without prior permission from the Department of Corrections or a county community corrections agency.
  - ❖ Permit the supervision officer to visit the offender or the offender's residence or work site and to conduct a walk-through of the common areas and of the rooms in the residence occupied by or under the control of the probationer.
  - ❖ Consent to the search of person, vehicle or premises upon the request of a representative of the supervising officer if

the supervising officer has reasonable grounds to believe that evidence of a violation will be found, and submit to fingerprinting or photographing, or both, when requested by the Department of Corrections or a county community corrections agency for supervision purposes.

- ❖ Obey all laws, municipal, county, state and federal
- ❖ Promptly and truthfully answer all reasonable inquiries by the Department of Corrections or a county community corrections agency.
- ❖ Not possess weapons, firearms, or dangerous animals
- ❖ Report as required and abide by the direction of the supervising officer

- Special conditions include (taken from State of Oregon Board of Parole and Post Supervision):
  - ❖ Offender shall be evaluated by a mental health evaluator and follow all treatment recommendations.
  - ❖ Offender shall continue to take any psychiatric or psychotropic medication that was prescribed prior to or at the time of release from custody until otherwise directed by a physician.
    - ◆ At the direction of the parole officer, the offender shall undergo a psychiatric evaluation and take any medications recommended.
    - ◆ The offender shall comply with a medication monitoring program at the request of the parole officer.
  - ❖ Offender shall have no contact with minor females and shall not frequent any places where minors are likely to congregate (e.g., playgrounds, school grounds, arcades) without prior written approval from their supervising officer.
  - ❖ Offender shall have no contact with minor males and shall not frequent any places where minors are likely to congregate (e.g., playgrounds, school grounds, arcades) without prior written approval from their supervising officer.
  - ❖ Offender shall submit to random polygraph tests as part of a sex offender surveillance program.
  - ❖ Offender shall enter and complete or be successfully discharged from a recognized and approved sex offender treatment program which may include polygraph and/or plethysmograph testing
    - ◆ Offender shall abide by a prohibition of sexually deviant materials, activities or behavior that the offender may use for the purpose of deviant sexual arousal, unless otherwise allowed by the Parole Officer in writing.
  - ❖ Offender shall pay court ordered restitution to the clerk of the court of the county of sentencing.

- ❖ If required to report as a sex offender, report with the Department of State Police, a Chief of Police, a County Sheriff or the Supervising Agency: when supervision begins, within 10 days of a change in residence and once a year within 10 days of the person's date of birth
- ❖ Offender shall not possess or use intoxicating beverages.
- ❖ Other: Special Conditions may be imposed that are not listed above when the Board of Parole and Post Prison Supervision determines that such conditions are necessary.
- ❖ Offender shall have no contact direct or indirect with those listed:
- ❖ Consent to search of computer or other electronic equipment upon the request of the supervising officer, or their representative, if the supervising officer has reasonable grounds to believe that evidence of a violation will be found

■ Sex Offender Package (taken from State of Oregon Board of Parole and Post Supervision):

- ❖ Agreement to comply with any curfew set by the board, the supervisory authority or the supervising officer
- ❖ A prohibition against contacting a person under 18 years of age without the prior written approval of the board, supervisory authority or supervising officer
- ❖ A prohibition against frequenting, without the prior written approval of the board, supervisory authority or supervising officer, a place where persons under 18 years of age regularly congregate
- ❖ A prohibition against working or volunteering at a school, day care center, park, playground or other place where persons under 18 years of age regularly congregate
- ❖ Entry into and completion of or successful discharge from a sex offender treatment program approved by the board, supervisory authority or supervising officer
    - ◆ The program may include polygraph and plethysmograph testing.
    - ◆ The person is responsible for paying for the treatment program.
- ❖ A prohibition against any contact with the victim, directly or indirectly, unless approved by the victim, the person's treatment provider and the board, supervisory authority or supervising officer
- ❖ Unless otherwise indicated for the treatment required under subparagraph (e) of this paragraph, a prohibition against viewing, listening to, owning or possessing any sexually stimulating visual or auditory materials that are relevant to the person's deviant behavior

- ❖ Agreement to consent to a search of the person or the vehicle or residence of the person upon the request of a representative of the board or supervisory authority if the representative has reasonable grounds to believe that evidence of a violation of a condition of post-prison supervision will be found
- ❖ Participation in random polygraph examinations to obtain information for risk management and treatment
    - ◆ The person is responsible for paying the expenses of the examinations.
    - ◆ The results of a polygraph examination under this subparagraph may not be used in evidence in a hearing to prove a violation of post-prison supervision.
- ❖ Maintenance of a driving log and a prohibition against driving a motor vehicle alone unless approved by the board, supervisory authority or supervising officer
- ❖ A prohibition against using a post-office box unless approved by the board, supervisory authority or supervising officer

For more on the parole board, visit Criminal Justice Interactive online > Corrections and the Community > Learning Modules > 12.5 The Role of Parole Boards.

12.6 Court cases related to probation and parole

12.6.1 U.S. Supreme Court cases that provide the legal framework for probation and parole supervision

GRIFFIN* v. *WISCONSIN

A 1987 Supreme Court case that ruled that probation officers may conduct searches of a probationer's residence without the need for either a search warrant or probable cause.

- ■ *Griffin* v. *Wisconsin* (1987)
    - ❖ Supreme Court ruled that probation officers may conduct searches of a probationer's residence without the need for either a search warrant or probable cause.
    - ❖ "A probationer's home, like anyone else's, is protected by the Fourth Amendment's requirement that searches to be 'reasonable.'" However, "a State's operation of a probation system . . . presents 'special needs' beyond normal law enforcement that may justify departures from the usual warrant and probable cause requirements."
    - ❖ Probation, the Court concluded, is similar to imprisonment because it is a "form of criminal sanction imposed upon an offender after determination of guilt."

PENNSYLVANIA BOARD OF PROBATION AND PAROLE* v. *SCOTT

A 1998 Supreme Court case in which the court declined to extend exclusionary rule to apply to searches by parole officers, even where such searches yield evidence of parole violations.

- ■ *Pennsylvania Board of Probation and Parole* v. *Scott* (1998)
    - ❖ The Supreme Court declined to extend exclusionary rule to apply to searches by parole officers, even where such searches yield evidence of parole violations.
    - ❖ "The Court has repeatedly declined to extend the [exclusionary] rule to proceedings other than criminal trials . . .. The social costs of allowing convicted criminals who violate

their parole to remain at large are particularly high . . . and are compounded by the fact that parolees . . . are more likely to commit future crimes than are average citizens."

- *U.S.* v. ***Knights*** (2001)
  - Mark James Knights was a California probationer who had signed a standard probation form agreeing to waive his constitutional protection against warrantless searches as a condition of probation.
  - The form did not limit such searches to probation officers, but instead required that Knights submit to a search at any time with or without a search warrant or reasonable cause, by any probation or law enforcement officer.
  - When Knights came under suspicion for setting a fire that caused $1.5 million in damages, police officers searched his home without a warrant.
  - The search uncovered evidence that implicated Knights in the arson.
  - A federal district court granted a motion by Knights' attorneys to suppress the evidence because the search was for police investigatory purposes, rather than for probationary purposes.
  - The Ninth Circuit Court affirmed the lower court's decision.
  - The U.S. Supreme Court overturned the Ninth Circuit Court's decision.
  - The U.S. Supreme Court held that the warrantless search of Knights' residence "supported by reasonable suspicion and authorized by a probation condition, satisfied the Fourth Amendment . . . as nothing in Knights' probation condition limits searches to those with a 'probationary purpose.'"
  - The Supreme Court decision expanded the search authority normally reserved for probation and parole officers to police officers under certain circumstances.
- Revocation hearing cases
  - **Revocation hearing** is a hearing held before a legally constituted hearing body (such as a parole board) to determine whether a parolee or probationer has violated the conditions and requirements of his or her parole or probation.
  - Most frequent violations for which revocation occurs:
    - Failure to report as required to a probation or parole officer
    - Failure to participate in a stipulated treatment program
    - Alcohol or drug abuse while under supervision
  - ***Escoe* v. *Zerbst*** (1935)
    - U.S. Supreme Court held that probation "comes as an act of grace to one convicted of a crime" and that the

U.S.* v. *KNIGHTS

A 2001 Supreme Court case in which the court stated that the warrantless search, "supported by reasonable suspicion and authorized by a probation condition, satisfied the Fourth Amendment."

REVOCATION HEARING

A hearing before a legally constituted hearing body to determine whether a parolee or probationer has violated the conditions and requirements of his or her parole or probation.

ESCOE* v. *ZERBST

A 1935 Supreme Court case in which the court held that probation "comes as an act of grace to one convicted of crime," and that revocation of probation with hearing or notice to the probationer is acceptable practice.

revocation of probation without hearing or notice to the probationer is acceptable practice.

- This decision has been greatly modified by the case of *Mempa* v. *Rhay* (1967).

MEMPA* v. *RHAY

A 1967 Supreme Court case in which the court held that in probation revocation decisions, both notice and a hearing were required.

❖ ***Mempa* v. *Rhay*** (1967)

- Mempa, at age 17, had been convicted of riding in a stolen car and was placed on probation in 1959.
- Some months later, Mempa was accused of a burglary and a hearing was held at which Mempa admitted to the burglary.
- Mempa's probation was revoked and he was sent to prison.
- Mempa was not given privilege of having an attorney present when his probation was revoked, nor was he given the chance to present evidence or testimony on his behalf.
- U.S. Supreme Court held that in probation revocation decisions, both notice and a hearing were required.
- The probationer was also granted the opportunity to be represented by counsel before a deferred prison sentence could be imposed.

MORRISSEY* v. *BREWER

The 1972 Supreme Court case that held that revocation procedure for parolees require written notice, evidence of violation, and an impartial detached body at hearing. The parolee will have a chance to appear, the right to cross-examine witness, and receive written statement of the outcome of revocation.

❖ ***Morrissey* v. *Brewer*** (1972)

- Relates to revocation proceedings regarding parolees
- U.S. Supreme Court held that revocation proceedings for parolees require the following:
  - ❒ Written notice specifying alleged violation be given to parolee
  - ❒ Evidence of violation be disclosed
  - ❒ An impartial, detached body be responsible for the parole revocation hearing
  - ❒ The parolee have a chance to appear and offer a defense, including:
    - Testimony
    - Documents
    - Witnesses
  - ❒ The right to cross-examine witnesses against him be provided to parolee
  - ❒ Written statement of outcome of revocation hearing be provided to parolee, including the testimony considered and reasons for revoking parole if that is the decision

GAGNON* v. *SCARPELLI

A 1973 Supreme Court decision that established that probationers were entitled to two hearings: preliminary hearing and a more comprehensive hearing, prior to making the final revocation decision.

❖ ***Gagnon* v. *Scarpelli*** (1973)

- John Gagnon had pleaded guilty to armed robbery in Wisconsin and was sentenced to 15 years in prison, which was suspended in favor of seven years' probation.

- A day after beginning probation in Cook County, Illinois, he was arrested while committing a burglary.
- After being advised of his rights, he confessed to the burglary.
- Gagnon's probation was revoked without a hearing.
- U.S. Supreme Court held, citing its own decision in *Morrissey* v. *Brewer* (1972), that probationers were entitled to two hearings:
    - A preliminary hearing to determine whether or not there is probable cause
    - A somewhat more comprehensive hearing prior to making the final revocation decision
    - Gagnon was indigent and had requested an attorney be appointed. Supreme Court ruled that an indigent offender on probation was entitled to be provided an attorney if they claimed:
        - They had not committed the alleged violation.
        - They had substantial mitigating evidence to explain their violation.
    - Court made clear that revocation hearings were not a stage in the criminal prosecution process, but were a simple adjunct to it.

❖ ***Young* v. *Harper*** (1997)

YOUNG v. HARPER

A Supreme Court decision that ruled that "an inmate who has been released under a program to relieve prison crowding cannot be reincarcerated without getting a chance to show at a hearing that the conditions of the program have been met and is entitled to remain free."

- Former Oklahoma inmate Ernest E. Harper, who had been released in 1990 after serving 15 years in prison for murder
- Harper was released under a program governed by a formula requiring the release of a certain number of inmates as the state's prison system approached capacity.
- Months after being released, Harper received a call from his parole officer at 5:30 A.M., telling him to report back to prison by 10:00 A.M.
- Although Harper had been living according to the rules of the program under which he had been released, state officials argued that Harper was still a prisoner and said that they were only changing the conditions of his confinement by "recalling" him to an institution.
- U.S. Supreme Court disagreed.
- Court ruled that "an inmate who has been released under a program to relieve prison crowding cannot be reincarcerated without getting a chance to show at a hearing that he has met the conditions of the program and is entitled to remain free."
- U.S. Supreme Court extended *Morissey* and *Gagnon* in its ruling in this case.

GREENHOLTZ* v. *NEBRASKA

A 1979 Supreme Court decision that established that parole boards do not have to specify the evidence used in deciding to deny parole.

- *Greenholtz* v. *Nebraska* (1979)
  - U.S. Supreme Court established that parole boards do not have to specify the evidence used in deciding to deny parole.
  - Court indicated that reasons for parole denial might be provided in the interest of helping inmates prepare themselves for future review, but that to require the disclosure of evidence used in the review hearing would turn the process into an adversarial proceeding.

BEARDEN* v. *GEORGIA

A 1983 Supreme Court decision that indicated that probation could not be revoked because of failure to pay a fine and make restitution if it could be shown that the defendant was not responsible for the failure.

- ***Bearden* v. *Georgia*** (1983)
  - Bearden had pleaded guilty to burglary and had been sentenced to three years' probation.
  - One of the conditions of his probation required that he pay a fine of $250 and make restitution payments totaling $500.
  - Bearden successfully made the first two payments but then lost his job.
  - His probation was revoked and he was imprisoned.
  - U.S. Supreme Court indicated that probation could not be revoked because of failure to pay a fine and make restitution if it could be shown that the defendant was not responsible for the failure.
  - U.S. Supreme Court also indicated that alternative forms of punishment must be considered and shown to be inadequate before the defendant can be incarcerated.

KELLY* v. *ROBINSON

A 1986 Supreme Court decision that held that an individual cannot avoid having to make restitution by filing bankruptcy.

- ***Kelly* v. *Robinson*** (1986)
  - U.S. Supreme Court held that an individual cannot avoid having to make restitution by filing for bankruptcy.
  - Kelly was convicted of receiving illegal welfare payments and was ordered to make restitution of $100 per month.
  - Kelly filed for bankruptcy immediately after receiving the sentence and listed the court ordered payments as a debt.
  - Bankruptcy Court discharged the debt.
  - U.S. Supreme Court ruled that fines and other financial penalties ordered by criminal courts are not capable of being voided by bankruptcy proceedings.

MINNESOTA* V. *MURPHY

A 1984 Supreme Court decision that held that a probationer's incriminating statements made to a probation officer may be used as evidence if the probationer did not specifically claim a right against self-incrimination.

- ***Minnesota* v. *Murphy*** (1984)
  - Marshall Murphy was sentenced to three years' probation in 1980 on a charge of "false imprisonment" stemming from an alleged attempted sexual attack.
  - One condition of his probation required him to be entirely truthful with his probation officer "in all matters."

- Some time later, Murphy admitted to his probation officer that he had confessed to a rape and murder in conversations with his counselor.
- Murphy was convicted of first-degree murder, partially on the basis of the statements made to his probation officer.
- On appeal, Murphy's lawyers argued that Murphy should have been advised of his right against self-incrimination during his conversations with his probation officer.
- The Minnesota Supreme Court agreed with Murphy's lawyers.
- The U.S. Supreme Court disagreed with the Minnesota Supreme Court.
- U.S. Supreme Court ruled that a probationer's incriminating statements made to a probation officer may be used as evidence if the probationer did not specifically claim a right against self-incrimination.
- The burden of invoking the Fifth Amendment privilege against self-incrimination in this case lay with the probationer.

CHAPTER SUMMARY

- Incarceration is not the only right answer to criminal behavior. The United States provides sentencing options that are not always available in other countries. Probation is the supervised release of an offender instead of incarceration. Parole is the conditional release from prison before the completion of the sentence. There are a number of advantages to probation and parole. These include lower cost, increased employment of inmates after release, restitution opportunities, and community support that assists reentry. The disadvantages of parole and probation include the fact they are perceived as lacking punishment and that they represent a risk to the community. There may also be increased social costs including increased risk of new crimes and potential increased expenses for those who do not meet their parole or probation obligations.
- Probation requires certain conditions of behavior in order for the offender to maintain freedom. If the defendant violates these conditions, probation can be revoked and he or she can be placed in prison. There are two types of conditions applied to probationers. Standard conditions define limits on movement and apply to all probationers. Special conditions apply to specific cases and provide a program that is designed to meet the needs of individual probationers. If either category of conditions is not met, revocation proceedings, with very specific requirements and steps, are held before probation can be revoked.
- Special supervision programs use nontraditional sentences in lieu of imprisonment. They are less expensive than imprisonment and are socially cost-effective because they keep the offender in the community. Shock probation/parole is the practice of sentencing offenders to prison, allowing them to apply for probationary

release, and enacting such release in a surprise fashion. Shock probation lowers the cost of confinement, maintains community and family ties, and is seen as an effective rehabilitative tool. Shock incarceration is a sentencing option usually reserved for first-time offenders that makes use of boot camp-type prisons to impress on convicted offenders the realities of prison life. Community service is a sentencing alternative that requires offenders to spend at least part of their time working for a community agency. Intensive supervision is a form of probation that requires frequent face-to-face contact with a probation officer. Home confinement orders individuals confined to their homes and sometimes monitor them electronically.

- The history of parole dates back to the 1840s when Captain Alexander Maconochie established the mark system in a prison on Norfolk Island outside of Australia. This represented the first early-release program. Sir Walter Crofton, named head of the Irish prison system in 1854, adapted this program and introduced the program to the United States at a meeting of the National Prison Association. Parole in the United States was established by Zebulon Brockway, who developed a system of graded stages for prisoner release. Federal parole began in 1910 and parole boards were established to determine conditions. In 1984, the Comprehensive Crime Control Act was passed, establishing the United States Sentencing Commission as a substitute for the parole commission. However, the existence of the parole commission has been extended several times and its existence is still unresolved today.
- Parole boards are made up of members typically appointed by the governor or the state. Board members grant paroles based on review of each case. A statutory decree mandates parole for an offender after a certain amount of time is served, minus time for good behavior. Conditions for parole are similar to those placed on probation and can include prohibition of controlled substances, participation in substance abuse evaluation, and limits on movement.
- There are a number of landmark court cases related to probation and parole. In *Griffin* v. *Wisconsin*, the Court ruled that probation officers may conduct searches of a probationer's residence without the need for either a search warrant or probable cause. In *Pennsylvania Board of Probation and Parole* v. *Scott*, the Court declined to extend exclusionary rule to apply to searches by parole offices, even where such searches yield evidence of parole violations. In *U.S.* v. *Knights*, the Court expanded the search authority normally reserved for probation and parole officers to police officers under certain circumstances. Revocation hearing cases include *Escoe* v. *Zerbst*, which indicated that revocation of probation without hearing or notice to the probationer is acceptable practice; *Mempa* v. *Rhay*, which determined that both notice and hearing were required in revocation proceedings; and *Morrissey* v. *Brewer*, which set specific requirements for revocation hearings.

ONLINE@CRIMINAL JUSTICE INTERACTIVE

Learning Modules

12.1 The Value of Probation and Parole
12.2 Objectives and Conditions of Parole
12.3 Special Supervision Programs
12.4 History of Parole
12.5 The Role of Parole Boards

Myths and Issues Videos

Myth vs. Reality: Community-Based Sentences Provide for Close Monitoring and Supervision
Issue 1: Skyrocketing "Reentry" and Its Impact on the Community
Issue 2: Not in My Neighborhood, Well, Then Again, Maybe Yes!

Simulation Activity: Determining Conditions for Probation and Parole

Homework and Review

In the News
Web Activity
Review Questions

Chapter 13

Life Behind Bars

CHAPTER OUTLINE

LEARNING OBJECTIVES

After reviewing the online material and reading this chapter, you should able to:

1. Discuss the legal rights of inmates.
2. Explain the challenges presented by dealing with special offenders behind bars (juveniles, drug offenders, mentally ill offenders, and aging offenders).
3. Describe four types of prison programs: educational/vocational, mental health/substance abuse, employment, and recreation.
4. Discuss challenges to successful prisoner reentry.
5. Define terms related to life in prison.

KEY TERMS

Beard v. *Banks*
Block v. *Rutherford*
Booth v. *Churner*
Bounds v. *Smith*
chivalry factor
civil death
Civil Rights of Institutionalized Persons Act (CRIPA) of 1980
Cruz v. *Beto*
deprivation model
Dettmer v. *Landon*
Edwards v. *Balisok*
Estelle v. *Gamble*
Farmer v. *Brennan*
Guajardo v. *Estelle*
Hands-off doctrine
Helling v. *McKinney*
Hill v. *Blackwell*
Holt v. *Sarver*
Houchins v. *KQED, Inc.*
Hudson v. *Palmer*
importation model
In re Caulk
In re Harrell
Johnson v. *Avery*
Jones v. *North Carolina Prisoners' Labor Union, Inc.*
Lewis v. *Casey*
Mallery v *Lewis*
McNamara v. *Moody*
Newman v. *Alabama*
Pell v. *Procunier*
Pennsylvania Department of Corrections v. *Yeskey*
Ponte v. *Real*
prisonization
Prison Litigation Reform Act of 1996
prison subculture
Procunier v. *Martinez*
Ruiz v. *Estelle*
Sandin v. *Conner*
Smith v. *Coughlin*
Taylor v. *Sterrett*
total institutions
Vitek v. *Jones*
Wilson v. *Seiter*
Wolff v. *McDonnell*

13.0 Life behind bars

13.1 Legal rights of inmates

13.1.1 Hands-off doctrine

HANDS-OFF DOCTRINE
A policy of nonintervention with regard to prison management that U.S. courts tended to follow until the late 1960s.

- Hands-off doctrine is a policy of nonintervention with regard to prison management that U.S. courts tended to follow until the late 1960s.
- It was believed that those managing the prisons were both appropriate and professional in their behavior and did not need the intervention of the courts.
- For the past 50 years, the "hands-off" doctrine has languished, as judicial intervention in prison administration has dramatically increased.

CIVIL DEATH
The legal status of prisoners in some jurisdictions who are denied the opportunity to vote, hold public office, marry, or enter into contracts by virtue of their status as incarcerated felons.

- **Civil death** is the legal status of prisoners in some jurisdictions who are denied the opportunity to vote, hold public office, marry, or enter into contracts by virtue of their status as incarcerated felons.
  - While civil death is primarily of historical interest, some jurisdictions still limit the contractual opportunities available to inmates.
    - In some jurisdictions this includes the right to enter into a marriage contract.
  - Sentencing Project (2000)
    - Reported that 3.9 million American citizens were barred from voting because of previous felony convictions

HOLT v. _SARVER_
A 1969 Supreme Court decision that declared the entire Arkansas prison system to be so inhumane as to be in violation of the Eighth and Fourteenth Amendments' prohibition against cruel and unusual punishment.

- Landmark case that brought an end to the "hands-off" doctrine
  - ***Holt* v. *Sarver*** (1969)
    - Inmates of two racially segregated units of the Arkansas prison system brought a 1983 suit against Roger Sarver, the commissioner of corrections and the Arkansas Board of Corrections, challenging conditions of confinement.
    - Jack Holt, Jr. was appointed to represent the inmates.
    - The principal complaints put forward by the petitioners were that confinement in isolation cells constituted cruel and unusual punishment, as did being denied medical attention, and that penitentiary authorities failed to protect prisoners from inmate-on-inmate assaults.
    - The Court found that "the prolonged confinement of numbers of men in the same cell under the described conditions was hazardous to health and offended

modern sensibilities and, in the court's estimation, amounted to cruel and unusual punishment. The state also failed its constitutional duty to take precautions for inmates' safety."

- The commissioner was ordered to report to the Court in 30 days the steps being taken to resolve the problems.
- The Court did not approve the commissioner's report.
- Complaints continued, and five more inmates filed suit that were consolidated into one suit with the original three, to become *Holt* v. *Sarver II* (1970).
- Judge Henley declared the entire Arkansas prison system to be so inhumane as to be in violation of the Eighth and Fourteenth Amendments' prohibition against cruel and unusual punishment.
- The judge found that the state was "unable to protect the inmates from harm and possible death."
- Henley found that racial discrimination was being practiced at the prisons.
- Judge Henley noted that, unlike other cases that challenged certain practices and abuses as they affected individual Arkansas convicts, this case constituted "an attack on the System itself," the first time that an entire penitentiary system was challenged in any court.
- The case was the turning point in the history of court intervention in the management of American prisons.
- The decision marked the end of the "hands-off" era of the federal judiciary toward prisoners and the beginning of an era of prisoners' rights.
    - *Holt* v. *Sarver* inspired the 1980 movie *Brubaker* starring Robert Redford.

13.1.2 Legal basis of prisoners' rights

- ***Pell* v. *Procunier*** (1974)
    - U.S. Supreme Court established a "balancing test" that defined a guideline generally applicable to all prison operations.
        - Balancing test is a principle developed by the courts and applied to the corrections arena by *Pell* v. *Procunier* (1974). It attempts to weigh the rights of an individual, as guaranteed by the Constitution, against the authority of states to make laws or to otherwise restrict a person's freedom in order to protect the state's interests and its citizens.
    - "Prison inmate retains those First Amendment rights that are not inconsistent with his status as a prisoner or with the legitimate penological objectives of the correctional system."

PELL* v. *PROCUNIER
A 1974 Supreme Court case that established a balancing test that defined guidelines generally applicable to all prison operations.

- Inmates have rights, much the same as people who are not incarcerated, provided that the legitimate needs of the prison for security, custody, and safety are not compromised.

CIVIL RIGHTS OF INSTITUTIONALIZED PERSONS ACT (CRIPA) OF 1980

Guaranteed the slaves the right to have access to federal courts when civil rights are violated.

- **Civil Rights of Institutionalized Persons Act (CRIPA) of 1980**
  - Applies to all:
    - Adult and juvenile state jails
    - Adult and juvenile local jails
    - Detention centers
    - Prisons
    - Mental hospitals
    - Other care facilities for physically challenged or chronically ill
  - Allows the attorney general of the United States to institute civil action when "egregious or flagrant conditions exist which deprive such persons of any rights, privileges, or immunities secured or protected by the Constitution or laws of the United States."
- American Correctional Association (1987)
  - Reports that most prisoner lawsuits are based on:
    - Eighth Amendment against cruel and unusual punishment
    - Fourteenth Amendment against the taking of life, liberty, or property without the due process of law

13.1.3 Conditional rights of prisoners

CRUZ* v. *BETO

1972 Supreme Court case that confirmed that an inmate's religious choice need not be limited to a conventional or traditional one to be allowed.

- Religious freedom
  - The right to assemble for religious services and groups
    - ***Cruz* v. *Beto*** (1972)
      - Established that prisoners must be given a "reasonable opportunity" to pursue their faith, even if it differs from traditional forms of worship.
      - Meeting facilities must be provided for religious use when those same facilities are made available to other groups of prisoners for other purposes.
      - No group can claim exclusive use of a prison area for religious reasons.
      - Right to assemble for religious purposes can be denied to inmates who use such meetings to plan escapes or who take the opportunity to dispense contraband.

- ***Smith* v. *Coughlin*** (1984)
    - ❒ Inmates have rights, much the same as people who are not incarcerated, provided that the legitimate needs of the prison for security, custody, and safety are not compromised.
- ***Dettmer* v. *Landon*** (1985)
    - ❒ Federal court held that a prisoner who claimed to practice witchcraft must be provided with the artifacts necessary for his worship.
        - Included were such items as sea salt, sulfur, quartz clock, incense, candles, and white robe without hood.
    - ❒ Fourth Circuit Court partially overturned the above decision in 1986.
        - Court recognized the Church of Wicca as a valid religion but held that concerns over prison security could preclude inmates' possession of dangerous items of worship.
- ***Hill* v. *Blackwell*** (1985)
    - ❒ Prison regulations prohibiting the wearing of beards, even those grown for religious purposes, were held acceptable for security considerations.

❖ Summary of religious freedoms for inmates:

- Right of assembly for religious services and groups
- Right to attend services of other religious groups
- Right to receive visits from ministers
- Right to correspond with religious leaders
- Right to observe religious dietary laws
- Right to wear religious insignia

■ Freedom of communication and visitation

❖ Right to meet with members of the press

- *Pell* v. *Procunier* (1974)
    - ❒ Supreme Court upheld lower-court decision that denied prisoners the opportunity to hold special meetings with members of the press.
    - ❒ Court held that media interviews could be conducted through regular visitation arrangements or through correspondence.
- ***Houchins* v. *KQED, Inc.*** (1978)
    - ❒ News personnel cannot be denied correspondence with prisoners, but they have no constitutional right to interview prisoners or to inspect correctional facilities beyond the visitation opportunities available to others.

SMITH* v. *COUGHLIN

A 1984 Supreme Court case that established that prisoners have rights, much the same as people who are not incarcerated, provided that the legitimate needs of the prison for security, custody, and safety are not compromised.

DETTMER* v. *LANDON

A 1985 Supreme Court case that held that a prisoner who claimed to practice witchcraft must be provided with the artifacts necessary for his worship.

HILL* v. *BLACKWELL

A Supreme Court case that established that the prison regulations prohibiting the wearing of beards, even those grown for religious purposes, were held acceptable because of security considerations.

HOUCHINS* v. *KQED, INC.

A 1978 Supreme Court case that established that news personnel cannot be denied correspondence with prisoners, but they have no constitutional right to interview prisoners or to inspect correctional opportunities available to others.

- Right to receive publications directly from the publisher
  - *Luparar* v. *Stoneman* (1974)
    - Prisoners have no inherent right to publish newspapers or newsletters for use by other prisoners, although many prisons allow such activity and some even fund such publications.
  - ***Mallery* v. *Lewis*** (1983)
    - Court ruled that magazines that depict deviant sexual behavior can be banned.
    - Prisons cannot ban nude pictures of inmate's wives and girlfriends.
  - ***Beard* v. *Banks*** (2006)
    - Supreme Court ruled that prison officials in Pennsylvania could prohibit the state's most violent inmates from receiving magazines, photographs, and newspapers sent to them in the mail.
    - Pennsylvania Department of Corrections prohibited all inmates classified as disruptive and problematic and who are housed in the Long-Term Segregation Unit (LTSU) in LaBelle, Pennsylvania, from receiving newspapers or magazines from all sources.
    - Inmates in LTSU are kept in their cells 23 hours a day with no access to television or radio, although they can read religious literature.
    - Visits from friends and family were limited to one per month.
    - Pennsylvania prison officials argued that prohibiting newspapers and magazines was necessary to prevent fires from being started and for providing incentives for improved behavior.
    - Supreme Court agreed, reporting "prison officials have imposed the deprivation only upon those with serious prison behavior problems, and those officials, relying on their professional judgment, reached an evidence-based conclusion that the policies help to further legitimate prison objectives."
- Right to communicate with nonprisoners
  - ***Procunier* v. *Martinez*** (1974)
    - Court ruled that a prisoner's mail may be censored if it is necessary to do so for security purposes.
  - ***McNamara* v. *Moody*** (1979)
    - Court upheld the right of prisoner to write vulgar letters to his girlfriend in which he made disparaging remarks about prison staff.

MALLERY* v. *LEWIS

A 1983 Supreme Court case that ruled that magazines that depict deviant sexual behavior can be banned in prisons.

BEARD* v. *BANKS

A 2006 Supreme court case that ruled that prison officials in Pennsylvania could prohibit the state's most violent inmates from receiving magazines, photographs, and newspapers sent to them in the mail.

PROCUNIER* v. *MARTINEZ

Case that ruled that a prisoner's mail could be censored for security purposes.

MCNAMARA* v. *MOODY

Case that upheld the right of prisoners to write vulgar letters to girlfriends since such action did not affect the security of the prison.

- ❒ Court said that while letters may be embarrassing to prison officials, they did not affect the security of the prison.

- ■ Legal assistance
  - ❖ Right of access to the courts
    - ◆ *Bounds* v. *Smith* (1977)
      - ❒ Right of prisoners to petition the court was recognized
      - ❒ It is the duty of the state to assist prisoners in the preparation and filing of legal papers.
    - ◆ ***Lewis* v. *Casey*** (1996)
      - ❒ Court overturned part of *Bounds* v. *Smith* case.
      - ❒ Prisoners are not guaranteed the "wherewithal to file any and every type of legal claim, but requires only that they be provided with the tools to attack their sentences . . . and to challenge the conditions of their confinement."
  - ❖ Right to visits from attorneys
    - ◆ ***In re Harrell*** (1970)
      - ❒ Right to meet with counsel for reasonable lengths of time
  - ❖ Right to mail communications with attorneys
    - ◆ ***Guajardo* v. *Estelle*** (1977)
      - ❒ Prison must provide stamps.
    - ◆ ***Bounds* v. *Smith*** (1977)
      - ❒ Inmates have right to correspond with their attorneys.
    - ◆ ***Taylor* v. *Sterrett*** (1976)
      - ❒ Letters can be opened and inspected for contraband (but not read) in the presence of the inmate.
  - ❖ Right to communicate with legal assistance organizations
  - ❖ Right to consult with "jailhouse lawyers"
    - ◆ ***Johnson* v. *Avery*** (1968)
      - ❒ Prisoners have the right to consult with "jailhouse lawyers" for advice when assistance from trained professionals is not available.
  - ❖ Right to assistance in filing legal papers, which should include one of the following:
    - ◆ Access to an adequate law library
    - ◆ Paid attorneys
    - ◆ Paralegal personnel or law students

LEWIS* v. *CASEY

A case that overturned Bounds v. Smith, and claimed that prisoners are not guaranteed to file any and every type of legal claim, but requires that they be provided with the tools to attack their sentences and conditions of confinement.

IN RE HARRELL

A 1970 Supreme Court case that allowed inmates to meet with counsel for a reasonable length of time.

GUAJARDO* v. *ESTELLE

A 1977 Supreme Court case that mandated that the prison must provide stamps.

BOUNDS* v. *SMITH

A 1977 Supreme Court case that mandated that inmates have the right to correspond with their attorneys.

TAYLOR* v. *STERRETT

A 1976 Supreme Court case that stated that letters can be opened and inspected for contraband, but not read, in the presence of the inmate.

JOHNSON* v. *AVERY

A 1969 Supreme Court case that affirmed that inmates must have full access to the legal system, and may also have legal assistance, including consultation with other inmates.

RUIZ v. ESTELLE

A 1982 Supreme Court ruling that found the Department of Corrections lacking in its medical treatment programs.

NEWMAN v. ALABAMA

A 1972 Supreme Court case that found that prison medical services were inadequate.

HELLING v. MCKINNEY

A 1993 Supreme Court case that indicated prison officials are responsible for correcting environmental conditions of prison life that pose a threat to inmate health.

- Medical treatment
  - Right to sanitary and healthy conditions
    - ***Ruiz* v. *Estelle*** (1982)
      - Court found Department of Corrections lacking in its medical treatment programs.
      - Court continued to monitor progress of the Department of Corrections while it improved:
        - Record keeping
        - Physical facilities
        - General medical care
    - ***Newman* v. *Alabama*** (1972)
      - Prison medical services were found to be inadequate.
      - Problems included:
        - Not enough medical personnel
        - Poor physical facilities for medical treatment
        - Poor administrative techniques for dispersal of medications
        - Poor medical records
        - Lack of medical supplies
        - Poorly trained or untrained prisoners who provided some medical services and performed minor surgeries.
        - Medically untrained personnel who determined the need for treatment
    - ***Helling* v. *McKinney*** (1993)
      - Court gave an indication that environmental conditions of prison life that pose a threat to prisoner health may have to be corrected.
      - Nevada inmate William McKinney claimed that exposure to secondary cigarette smoke circulating in his cell was threatening his health in violation of the Eighth Amendment's prohibition of against cruel and unusual punishment.
      - U.S. Supreme Court ordered that a federal district court provide McKinney with the opportunity to prove his allegations, and held that "an injunction cannot be denied to inmates who plainly prove an unsafe, life-threatening condition on the ground that nothing yet has happened to them."
      - Court gave notice to prison officials that they are responsible not only for "inmates' current serious health problems," but also for maintaining environmental conditions under which health problems might be prevented from developing.

- Right to medical attention for serious physical problems
  - ***Estelle* v. *Gamble*** (1976)
    - Specified prison officials' duty to provide for inmates' medical care
    - Court concerned itself with "deliberate indifference" on part of staff toward a prisoner's need for serious medical attention.
      - Deliberate indifference is the wanton disregard for thc health of inmates.
  - ***Farmer* v. *Brennan*** (1994)
    - Court clarified concept of deliberate indifference by holding that it required both actual knowledge and disregard of risk of harm.
    - Dee Farmer, a preoperative transsexual with obvious feminine characteristics had been incarcerated with other males in the federal prison system.
    - While mixing with other inmates, Farmer was beaten and raped by a fellow prisoner.
    - Farmer sued correctional officials claiming they had acted with deliberate indifference to his safety because they knew the prison was a violent environment and that Farmer would be particularly vulnerable to sexual attack.
    - The U.S. Court of Appeals for the Seventh Circuit agreed with Farmer.
    - U.S. Supreme Court sent Farmer's case back to lower court for rehearing after clarifying what it said was necessary to establish deliberate indifference.
    - "Prison officials have a duty under the Eighth Amendment to provide humane conditions of confinement. They must ensure that inmates receive adequate food, clothing, shelter, and medical care and must protect prisoners from violence at the hands of other prisoners . . .."
    - " . . . a constitutional violation occurs only where . . . the official has acted with 'deliberate indifference to inmate health or safety.'"
    - "A prison official may be held liable under the Eighth Amendment for acting with 'deliberate indifference' to inmate health or safety only if he knows that inmates face a substantial risk of serious harm and disregards that risk by failing to take reasonable measures to abate it."

ESTELLE* v. *GAMBLE

A 1976 Supreme Court case that established inmates' rights to medical treatment while incarcerated.

FARMER* v. *BRENNAN

A 1994 Supreme Court case that clarified the concept of deliberate indifference by holding that it required both actual knowledge and disregard of risk of harm.

PENNSYLVANIA DEPARTMENT OF CORRECTIONS v. YESKEY

A Supreme court case that established that the Americans with Disabilites Act applies to prisons and prison inmates.

- *Pennsylvania Department of Corrections* v. *Yeskey* (1998)
  - In May, 1994, Ronald Yeskey was sentenced to serve 18 to 36 months in a Pennsylvania correctional facility.
  - Sentencing court recommended that Yeskey be placed in Pennsylvania's Motivational Boot Camp for first-time offenders (successful completion of six-month program would have led to his release on parole).
  - Yeskey was refused admission because of his medical history of hypertension.
  - Yeskey sued Pennsylvania Department of Corrections alleging that his exclusion violated the Americans with Disabilities Act (ADA) of 1990, Title II, which prohibits a "public entity" from discriminating against a qualified individual with a disability on account of that disability.
  - Supreme Court held that the ADA applies to prisons and prison inmates.
- Right to needed medications
- Right to treatment in accordance with "doctor's orders"
  - *In re Caulk* (1984)
    - Court held that prisoners can be forced to take medications in an emergency situation against their will.

IN RE CAULK

A 1984 Supreme Court case that held that prisoners can be forced to take medications in an emergency situation against their will.

- Protection
  - Right to food, water, and shelter
  - Right to protection from foreseeable attack
  - Right to protection from predictable sexual attack
  - Right to protection against suicide
- Institutional punishment and discipline
  - An absolute right against corporal punishment (unless sentenced to such punishments)
  - Right to due process prior to punishment, including: notice of charges, a fair and impartial hearing, an opportunity for defense, a right to present witnesses and a written decision
  - *Jones* v. *North Carolina Prisoners' Labor Union, Inc.* (1977)
    - Court held that prisons must establish some formal opportunity for the airing of prisoner grievances.
    - Today, a large number of states have an established grievance procedure whereby a prisoner files a

JONES v. NORTH CAROLINA PRISONERS' LABOR UNION, INC.

A 1977 Supreme Court decision that held that prisons must establish some formal opportunity for the airing of prisoner grievances.

complaint with the local authorities and receives a mandated response.

- ❒ Modern grievance procedures range from the use of a hearing board composed of staff members and inmates to a single staff appointee charged with the resolution of complaints.

❖ ***Wolff* v. *McDonnell*** (1974)

- ◆ Case involved a prisoner deprived of previously earned good-time credits because of misbehavior.
- ◆ Court established that "good-time" credits were a form of "state-created right(s)" which, once created, could not be "arbitrarily abrogated."
- ◆ Established that sanctions could not be levied against prisoners without due process
- ◆ Where written prison regulations governing hearings exist, the courts have held that prisoners going before disciplinary hearing boards are entitled to:
  - ❒ Notice of the charges brought against them
  - ❒ The chance to organize a defense
  - ❒ An impartial hearing
  - ❒ The opportunity to present witnesses and evidence on their behalf
  - ❒ A written statement of the hearing board's conclusions

WOLFF v. MCDONNELL

A 1974 Supreme Court case that established that sanctions could not be levied against prisoners without due process.

❖ ***Ponte* v. *Real*** (1985)

- ◆ Supreme Court held that prison officials must provide an explanation to inmates who are denied the opportunity to have a desired witness at their hearing.

PONTE v. REAL

A 1985 Supreme Court ruling that held that prison officials must provide an explanation to inmates who are denied the opportunity to have a desired witness at their hearing.

❖ ***Vitek* v. *Jones*** (1980)

- ◆ Extended the requirement of due process to inmates about to be transferred from prisons to mental hospitals

VITEK v. JONES

A 1980 Supreme Court ruling that extended the requirement of due process to inmates about to be transferred from prisons to mental hospitals.

■ Privacy

❖ *U.S.* v. *Ready* (1978), *Katz* v. *U.S.* (1967), and *Hudson* v. *Palmer* (1984)

- ◆ All addressed right to privacy for prisoners.
- ◆ Court held that inmates cannot have a reasonable expectation to privacy when incarcerated.

❖ ***Hudson* v. *Palmer*** (1984)

- ◆ Palmer was a prisoner in Virginia, and Hudson was a correctional officer.
- ◆ Palmer claimed that Hudson had destroyed some of his property following a cell search.

HUDSON v. PALMER

A 1984 Supreme Court case that ruled that prison officials need to be able to conduct thorough and unannounced searches and that these searches preclude a prisoner privacy in personal possessions.

- Palmer's complaint centered on the lack of due process that accompanied the destruction
- Court disagreed with Palmer and ruled that prison officials need to be able to conduct thorough and unannounced searches, and that these searches preclude a prisoner privacy in personal possessions.

BLOCK v. RUTHERFORD

A 1984 Supreme Court case that established that prisoners do not have a right to be present during a search of their cells.

❖ *Block* v. *Rutherford* (1984)

- Court established that prisoners do not have a right to be present during a search of their cells.

■ Return to hands-off doctrine?

WILSON v. SEITER

A 1991 Supreme Court case that set the most recent standard to measure cruel and unusual punishment—the test of deliberate indifference.

❖ *Wilson* v. *Seiter* (1991)

- A 1983 suit brought against Richard P. Seiter, director of the Ohio Department of Rehabilitation and Correction, and Carl Humphreys, warden of the Hocking Correctional Facility in Nelsonville, Ohio
- Pearly L. Wilson, an incarcerated felon at Hocking, alleged that a number of the conditions of his confinement constituted cruel and unusual punishment in violation of the Eighth and Fourteenth Amendments.
- Wilson specifically cited overcrowding, excessive noise, insufficient locker storage space, inadequate heating and cooling, improper ventilation, unclean and inadequate rest rooms, unsanitary dining rooms and food preparation, and housing with mentally and physically ill inmates.
- Wilson asked for a change in prison conditions and sought $900,000 in compensatory and punitive damages.
- U.S. Supreme Court denied Wilson's claim noting that no constitutional violations existed because the conditions cited by Wilson were not the result of malicious intent on the part of officials.
- Court established standard that all future challenges to prison conditions by inmates that are brought under the Eighth Amendment must show "deliberate indifference" by the officials responsible for the existence of those conditions before the Court will hear the complaint.

SANDIN v. CONNER

A 1995 Supreme Court case provided further clarification to due process required in disciplinary action.

❖ *Sandin* v. *Conner* (1995)

- Demont Conner, an inmate at the Halawa Correctional Facility in Hawaii, was serving an indeterminate sentence of 30 years to life for numerous crimes, including murder, kidnapping, robbery, and burglary.
- Conner filed a lawsuit alleging that prison officials had deprived him of procedural due process when a hearing committee refused to allow him to

present witnesses during a disciplinary hearing and then sentenced him to segregation for alleged misconduct.

- A federal appellate court agreed with Conner, concluding that an existing prison regulation that instructed the hearing committee to find guilt in cases where a misconduct charge is supported by substantial evidence meant that the committee could not impose segregation if it did not look at all the evidence available to it.
- U.S. Supreme Court overturned the appellate court decision.
- Supreme Court held that the prison regulations are not designed to confer rights on inmates, but are meant only to provide guidelines to prison staff members.

13.1.4 Prison Litigation Reform Act of 1996 (PLRA)

PRISON LITIGATION REFORM ACT OF 1996 (PLRA)
An act that (1) requires inmates to exhaust their prison's grievance procedure before filing a lawsuit; (2)requires judges to screen all inmate complaints against federal government and to immediately dismiss those deemed frivolous or without merit ,(3) prohibits prisoners from filing a lawsuit for mental or emotional injury unless they can also show there has been physical injury, and (4) requires inmates to pay court filing fees.

- Increasing number of petitions per year concerning inmate problems were being filed with the courts:
  - In 1961, there were about 2,000 petitions.
  - In 1975, there were about 17,000 petitions.
  - In 1996, there were 68,235 civil rights lawsuits in federal courts nationwide.
- Many of the lawsuits were frivolous in nature:
  - Inmate sued because he was afraid he would become pregnant as a result of homosexual relations and the prison would not provide him with birth control.
  - Inmate sued because he received only one roll with dinner.
  - Inmate sued because he was not allowed to attend religious services in the nude.
  - Inmates sued claiming religious freedom, and demanded that members of the Church of the New Song (CONS) be provided steak and Harvey's Bristol Cream Sherry every Friday in order to celebrate communion.
- In 1996, the federal Prison Litigation Reform Act (PLRA) became law.
  - A clear legislative effort to restrict inmate filings to worthwhile cases and to reduce number of suits brought by state prisoners in federal courts
  - Elements of act:
    - Requires inmates to exhaust their prison's grievance procedure before filing a lawsuit.
    - Requires judges to screen all inmate complaints against federal government and to immediately dismiss those deemed frivolous or without merit.

- Prohibits prisoners from filing a lawsuit for mental or emotional injury unless they can also show there has been physical injury.
- Requires inmates to pay court filing fees.
  - Prisoners who do not have the needed funds can pay the filing fee over a period of time through deductions to their prison commissary accounts.
- Limits the award of attorneys' fees in successful lawsuits brought by inmates.
- Revokes the credits earned by federal prisoners towards release if they file a malicious lawsuit.
- Mandates that court orders affecting prison administration cannot go any further than necessary to correct a violation of a particular inmate's civil rights.
- Makes it possible for state officials to have court orders lifted after two years unless there is a new finding of a continuing violation of federally guaranteed civil rights.
- Mandates that any court order requiring the release of prisoners due to overcrowding be approved by a three-member court before it can become effective.

EDWARDS v. BALISOK

A 1997 Supreme Court case that held that prisoners cannot sue for monetary damages for loss of good time until they sue in state court and get their disciplinary conviction set aside.

- ***Edwards* v. *Balisok*** (1997)
  - Supreme Court made it harder to successfully challenge prison disciplinary convictions.
  - Court held that prisoners cannot sue for monetary damages for loss of good time until they sue in state court and get their disciplinary conviction set aside.

BOOTH v. CHURNER

A 2001 Supreme Court case that held that an inmate seeking only monetary damages must complete any prison administrative process capable of addressing the inmate's complaint and providing some form of relief before filing his or her grievance with a federal court, even if the process does not make specific provisions for monetary relief.

- ***Booth* v. *Churner*** (2001)
  - U.S. Supreme Court held that under the PLRA, an inmate seeking only monetary damages must complete any prison administrative process capable of addressing the inmate's complaint and providing some form of relief before filing his or her grievance with a federal court, even if the process does not make specific provisions for monetary relief.

For more on the legal rights of inmates, visit Criminal Justice Interactive online > Life behind Bars > Learning Modules > 13.1 The Legal Rights of Inmates.

For more on legal rights of inmates, visit Criminal Justice Interactive online > Myths and Issues Videos > Issue 1: Should Prisoners Have Rights?

13.2 Prison life

13.2.1 The concept of total institutions

- Hans Reimer, in "Socialization in the Prison Community," *Proceedings of the American Prison Association* (1937), wrote about his experience of voluntarily serving three months in prison as an incognito participant observer.
  - The work of Reimer helped to pave the way for future research on prisons as total institutions.
- Other research that focused on male maximum-security institutions:
  - Donald Clemmer, *The Prison Community* (1940)
  - Gresham Sykes, *The Society of Captives* (1958)
  - Richard Cloward and Donald R. Cressey, *Theoretical Studies in Social Organization of the Prison* (1960)
  - Donald R. Cressey, *The Prison: Studies in Instructional Organization and Change* (1961)
- Total institutions is a term coined by Erving Goffman (1922–1982) after he studied prisons and mental hospitals.
  - Total institution is a place where people work, play, eat, sleep, and recreate together on a daily basis.
  - **Total institutions** are small societies with distinctive values and styles of life.
  - Residents are cut off from the larger society, either forcibly or willingly.
  - Residents are pressured to fulfill rigidly prescribed behavioral roles.
  - Examples of total institutions:
    - Prisons
    - Concentration camps
    - Camps
    - Mental hospitals
    - Seminaries
- Two social structures exist in prisons.
  - The formal/official structure consists of rules and procedures put in place by the wider society and enforced by the prison staff.
  - Informal/unofficial structure, called prison subculture, is represented by the values and behavioral patterns characteristic of prison inmates.
    - More powerful than formal/official structure
    - Prison subculture has been found to be surprisingly consistent across the country.

TOTAL INSTITUTIONS
Small societies in which residents are cut off from larger society and are pressured to fulfill prescribed behavioral roles.

PRISONIZATION
The process whereby newly institutionalized offenders come to accept prison lifestyles and criminal values. Although many inmates begin their prison experience with only a few values that support criminal behavior, the socialization experience they undergo while incarcerated leads to a much greater acceptance of such values.

- Subcultures develop independently of plans of the prison administrators.
- The prisons subculture includes values, roles, and even special language.
- **Prisonization** is the process whereby newly institutionalized offenders come to accept prison lifestyles and criminal values.
  - Although many inmates begin their prison experience with only a few values that support criminal behavior, the socialization experience they undergo while incarcerated leads to a much greater acceptance of such values.

- Gresham Sykes (b. 1922) and Sheldon Messinger (1925–2003), in *The Inmate Social System* (1960), recognized five elements of the prison code:
  - Don't interfere with the interests of other inmates; "never rat on a con."
  - Don't lose your head; play it cool and do your own time.
  - Don't exploit inmates; don't break your word—be right.
  - Don't whine; be a man.
  - Don't be a sucker; don't trust the guards or staff.
- Stanton Wheeler (1930–2007), in *Socialization in Correctional Communities* (1961), examined concept of prisonization in Washington State Reformatory.
  - Found that the degree of prisonization experienced by inmates tends to vary over time and is reflected in a U-shaped curve
    - Represents the levels of inmate commitment to the prison norms and values
    - When an inmate first enters prison, conventional values are of major importance. (New inmates are considered to be at the top left of the "U.")
    - As time passes, the inmate adopts the prison lifestyle and conventional values become less important. (The inmate is now considered to be at the bottom of the "U.")
    - About six months prior to their release, conventional values reestablish their importance. (Inmate is considered to be at the top right of the "U.")
- Prison argot (language)
  - Male prison slang
    - Ace duce: best friend
    - Badge (or bull, hack, "the man," or screw): a correctional officer

- Banger (or burner, shank, or sticker): a knife
- Billys: white men
- Boneyard: conjugal visiting area
- Cat-j (or j-cat): a prisoner in need of psychological or psychiatric therapy or medication
- Cellie: cellmate
- Chester: child molester
- Dog: homeboy or friend
- Fag: a male inmate who is believed to be a "natural" or "born" homosexual
- Featherwood: a peckerwood's (see below) woman
- Fish: a newly arrived inmate
- Gorilla: an inmate who uses force to take what he wants from others
- Homeboy: a prisoner from one's hometown or neighborhood
- Ink: tattoos
- Lemon squeezer: an inmate who has an unattractive girl
- Man walking: a phrase used to signal that a guard is coming
- Merchant: one who sells when he should give
- Peckerwood: a white prisoner
- Punk: a male inmate who is forced into a submissive or feminine role during homosexual relations
- Rat: an inmate who squeals
- Schooled: knowledgeable in the ways of prison life
- Shakedown: a search of a cell or of a work area
- Tree jumper: rapist
- Turn out: to rape or make into a punk
- Wolf: a male inmate who assumes the aggressive masculine role during homosexual relations

❖ Women's prison slang

- Cherry: a female inmate who has not yet been introduced to lesbian activities
- Fay broad: a white female inmate
- Femme (or mommy): a female inmate who plays the female during lesbian relations
- Safe: the vagina, especially when used for hiding contraband
- Stud broad (or daddy): a female inmate who assumes the role of a male during lesbian relations

- In *Who Rules The Joint* (1982), Charles Stastny and Gabrielle Tyrnauer traced the evolution of prison subculture through a study of the Washington State Penitentiary.
    - "It is no longer meaningful to speak of a single inmate culture or even subculture . . .. [I]t was clear that the unified, oppositional convict culture, found in the sociological literature on prisons, no longer existed." (p 135)
    - Four clearly distinguishable subcultures
        - Official
            - Promoted by staff
            - Impacts lives of inmates primarily through the creation of an inmate subculture
        - Traditional
            - Participants spend much of their time lamenting the decline of the convict code among younger prisoners.
        - Reform
            - Unique to Washington State Penitentiary
                - Result of brief experiment with inmate self-government during the 1970s
                    - Inmate participation in civic-style clubs
                    - Citizen involvement in daily activities of the prison
                    - Banquets
                    - Inmate speaking tours
        - Revolutionary
            - Built upon radical political rhetoric of the disenfranchised
- Functions of prison society
    - Two models:
        - **Deprivation model**
        - **Importation model**
    - Deprivation model is a prison subculture that is an adaptation to the deprivation.
        - It becomes a way of dealing with the psychological, social, physical, and sexual needs of individuals who live in a highly controlled environment.
        - In *Society of Captives* (1958), Gresham Sykes (b. 1922) identified things prisoners are deprived of:
            - Liberty
            - Goods and services
            - Heterosexual relationships

DEPRIVATION MODEL

Prison subculture is an adaption to the deprivation.

IMPORTATION MODEL

Inmates bring with them to prison the specific values, roles, and behaviors from the outside world.

            - Autonomy
            - Personal security
        - A **prison subculture** develops to respond to deprivations.
    - Importation model
        - Inmates bring with them to prison the specific values, roles, and behaviors from the outside world.
        - When an inmate is confined, these external elements shape the inmate's social world.
    - The permanent social arrangement (structural dimensions) of the prison helps to shape the subculture of the prisoners.
    - In *The Prison Community* (1940), Donald Clemmer identified structural dimensions of inmate society:
        - Prisoner/staff dichotomy
        - The three general classes of prisoners
        - Work gangs and cellhouse groups
        - Racial groups
        - Type of offense
        - The power of inmate "politicians"
        - Degree of sexual abnormality
        - The record of repeat offenses
        - Personality differences due to prison socialization
    - Clemmer's nine elements help to define an inmate's position in the inmate "pecking order" and create expectations of the appropriate role for that person.
        - Prison roles serve to satisfy the needs for power, sexual performance, material possessions, individuality, and personal pleasure, and to define the status of one prisoner relative to another.
        - Prison roles also provide for a redistribution of wealth inside the prison.

PRISON SUBCULTURE

The values and behavioral patterns characteristic of prison inmates. Prison subculture has been found to be surprisingly consistent across the country.

- Homosexuality in prison
    - Older prisoners looking for sexual partners will often provide protection for new, first-time prisoners, as well as things like candy, cigarettes, drugs, and money.
    - In exchange for these items the older inmate expects to receive some "payback," often in the form of sexual favors.
    - In Gresham Sykes's study of prison argot (language), *Society of Captives* (1958), a number of terms surfaced describing homosexual activity:
        - Wolf
            - Aggressive men who assumed the masculine role in homosexual relations

    - Committed to their heterosexual identity and participate in homosexuality only because of prison conditions
  - Punk
    - Those forced into submitting to the female role by wolves
    - As with the "wolves," these individuals are committed to their heterosexual identity and participate in homosexuality only because of prison conditions.
  - Fag
    - Describes a special category of men who have a natural proclivity toward homosexual activity and effeminate mannerisms
    - Generally engaged in homosexual lifestyles before their entry into prison and continued to emulate feminine mannerisms and styles of dress once incarcerated
- Prison rape
  - Rape in prison is often the result of gang activity, or of prisoners working together to overpower the victim.
  - A large proportion of sexual aggressors are characterized by:
    - Low education
    - Poverty
    - Having grown up in a broken home headed by their mother
    - A record for violent offenses
  - Victims of prison rape tend to be:
    - Physically slight
    - Young
    - White
    - Nonviolent offenders
    - From suburban or rural areas
  - Lee Bowker, in *Prison Victimization* (1980), contends that most sexual aggressors do not consider themselves to be homosexuals.
    - Sexual release is not the primary motivation for the sexual attack.
    - Many aggressors must continue to participate in gang rapes in order to avoid becoming victims themselves.
    - The aggressors have themselves suffered much damage to their masculinity in the past.

- Victims of prison sexual assault:
  - Live in fear
  - May feel constantly threatened
  - Can turn to self-destructive activities
  - Question their masculinity
  - Undergo personal devaluation
  - Sometimes turn to violence

- Prison lifestyles and inmate types
  - John Irwin, in *The Felon* (1970), described his experience as an inmate after having been convicted of a felony.
    - Irwin claims that prison lifestyles are adaptations to the prison environment.
  - Types of prisoners:
    - The mean dude
      - Quick to fight
      - Give no quarter
      - Other inmates know that the mean dude is better left alone.
      - The mean dude receives frequent write-ups for violations and spends much of his time in solitary confinement.
      - The prison subculture supports the role of the mean dude in two ways:
        - By expecting prisoners to be tough
        - By type of wisdom that says "only the strong survive"
    - The hedonist
      - Builds their lives around limited pleasures that can be found within the prison
      - Smuggling contraband, drug running, gambling, and homosexuality are the main foci for hedonists.
      - This type tends to live only for the "now."
    - The opportunist
      - Takes advantage of positive experiences prison has to offer, such as:
        - Schooling
        - Trade programs
        - Counseling
        - Other self-improvement activities
      - The "do-gooders" of the prison
      - Generally well-liked by the prison staff

- Other types of prisoners shun the opportunist.
- These types may be religious.

- The retreatist
  - These are prisoners who attempt some form of psychological retreat from the realities of imprisonment.
  - Retreatists often become heavily involved in drug and alcohol use, and they even attempt suicide.
  - Depression and mental illness mark the retreatist personality.
- The legalist
  - A "jailhouse lawyer," this prisoner fights confinement through the law.
  - Since many prisoners are facing many years of confinement, their only means of release is through the courts.
- The radical
  - This individual views himself as a political prisoner.
  - Society is viewed as the oppressor who forced criminality on the prisoner through an unequal distribution of power.
- The colonist
  - These individuals view the prison as their home.
  - Colonists have many friends on the inside.
  - Typically, colonists hold either positions of power or respect (sometimes both) among their fellow prisoners.
  - The colonist does not look forward to leaving prison, and when he is released, he has been known to commit a new crime so he lands back in prison.
- The religious
  - These prisoners have a very strong religious faith and they may be "born-again" Christians, committed Muslims, or even satanists or witches.
  - The religious frequently attend services and form prayer groups.
- The gang-bangers
  - These individuals are affiliated with prison gangs.
  - They depend upon the gang for defense and protection.
  - Gang-bangers display gang signs, gang tattoos, and use their gang affiliation to obtain goods and services from both inside and outside of the prison.

- The realist
  - This prisoner sees incarceration as a natural consequence of criminal activity.
  - It is just an unfortunate part of "doing criminal business."
  - The realist usually knows the inmate code and does not get into trouble.
  - They are able to adjust to living on the outside when released.

13.2.2 Women in prison

- Number of female prisoners sentenced to more than one year under the jurisdiction of state or federal correctional authorities as of June 30, 2008:
  - There are 106,410 female prisoners, representing 6.9% of all sentenced prisoners.
    - Incarcerated at the federal level: 11,602
    - Incarcerated at the state level: 94,808
  - Imprisonment rate
    - Total rate: 69 per 100,00 U.S. residents
    - Federal rate: 8 per 100,000 U.S. residents
    - State rate: 62 per 100,000 U.S. residents
- Estimated number of women held in state or federal prisons or local jails midyear 2008:
  - Total number of women held: 207,700
    - By race:
      - White: 94,500 (48%)
      - Black: 67,800 (35%)
      - Hispanic: 33,400 (17%)
    - By age:
      - 18 to 19: 5,500 (3%)
      - 20 to 24: 38,800 (19%)
      - 25 to 29: 32,000 (15%)
      - 30 to 34: 35,400 (17%)
      - 35 to39: 38,800 (19%)
      - 40 to 44: 32,600 (16%)
      - 45 to 49: 18,200 (9%)
      - 50 to 54: 8,000 (4%)
      - 55 to 59: 3,300 (2%)
      - 60 to 64: 1,300 (1%)
      - 65 or older: 800 (0.004%)

- Estimated number of inmates held in state or federal prisons, or in local jails, per 100,000 U.S. residents midyear 2008:
  - Total rate for women held: 135 per 100,000 U.S. residents
    - White: 93 per 100,000 U.S. residents
    - Black: 349 per 100,000 U.S. residents
    - Hispanic: 147 per 100,000 U.S. residents
- For women in state prisons:
  - Nearly one in three women in state prisons reported committing their offenses to support a drug addiction.
    - Drug-related offenses include:
      - Larceny
      - Burglary
      - Fraud
      - Prostitution
      - Embezzlement
      - Robbery
  - More than 65% of women in state prisons reported being mothers of children under 18.
  - A 2004 federal government study found 73% of women in state prisons either had symptoms of a clinical diagnosis of mental illness and/or were receiving treatment from a mental health professional in the past year.
  - About 40% of women in state prisons were employed.
  - Nearly 30% of women in state prisons were receiving public assistance before arrest.
    - About 37% had incomes of less than $600 per month prior to arrest.

CHIVALRY FACTOR

Based upon the archaic cultural stereotype that depicted women as helpless or childlike compared to men, which allegedly lessened the responsibility of female offenders in the eyes of some male judges and prosecutors, resulting in fewer prison sentences for women involved in criminal activity.

- **Chivalry factor** is based upon the archaic cultural stereotype that depicted women as helpless or childlike compared to men, which allegedly lessened the responsibilities of female offenders in the eyes of some male judges and prosecutors, resulting in fewer prison sentences for women involved in criminal activity.
  - For the past 40 years, the chivalry factor has been in serious decline.
    - The gender of convicted offenders, for the most part, no longer affects sentencing practices insofar as it may be tied to other social variables.

13.2.3 Profile of a woman prisoner

- *The Female Offender: What Does the Future Hold?* American Correctional Task Force on the Female Offender (1990)
  - Average age of offender is between 29 and 30.
  - Fifty-seven percent are black or Hispanic.

    - Most come from single-parent homes.
    - Half of the inmates have other family members in prison.

- Mary J. Clement, in the *National Survey of Programs for Incarcerated Women* (1991), found that:
    - Half of the inmates are high-school dropouts.
    - Thirty-four percent left school because they were bored or pregnant.
    - Fifty-five percent have been arrested an average of two to nine times.
    - Sixty-five percent have run away from home between one and three times.
    - Thirty-nine percent report drug use makes them feel better emotionally.
    - Twenty-eight percent have attempted suicide at least once.
    - Sixty-two percent were single parents with one to three children prior to imprisonment.
    - One-quarter of women entering prison has either recently given birth or is pregnant.
        - A large proportion of children are released by their imprisoned mothers into foster care or put up for adoption.
- Mary K. Shilton, in *Resources for Mother-Child Community Corrections* (2001), found:
    - Eighty percent of women entering prison are mothers.
        - Eighty-five percent of those who are mothers had custody of their children at the time of their prison admission.
    - One-quarter of women entering prison had recently given birth or were pregnant when admitted.
    - In 2000, more than 1.5 million children had mothers who were confined in prison or jail.
    - The number of women in prison who were parents of minor children more than doubled during the 1990s.
- Types of female inmates
    - Esther Heffernan, in *Making It in Prison* (1972), identified three types of women prisoners.
        - Square
            - These individuals have few experiences with criminal lifestyles.
            - They tend to sympathize with the values and attitudes of conventional society.
            - They represent a small number of prisoners.

- Cool
  - These individuals are more likely to be career offenders.
  - They tend to keep to themselves.
  - "Cools" are generally supportive of prisoner values.
- Life
  - These individuals are familiar with a life of crime.
  - Many of them have repeat arrests for prostitution, drug use, and theft.
  - They are typically full participants in the economic, social, and family arrangement of prison.
    - Family arrangements in prison allow women to achieve status and find meaning in their lives.
    - Seventy-one percent of women in prison are involved in prison families.

13.2.4 Profile of women's prisons

- American Correctional Association Report (1990), while somewhat dated, provides us with some useful information.
  - Most women's prisons are located in small towns with a population of 25,000 or less.
  - Most of the prisons were not designed to house women.
  - The number of women being sent to prison is on the rise.
  - Most facilities that house women also house men.
  - Most facilities do not have programs specifically designed for women.
  - There are very few major disturbances or escapes at women's prisons.
  - Substance abuse among female prisoners is very high.
  - There are few work assignments available to women.
  - Most women in prison have less than a high-school education.

13.2.5 Violence in women's prisons

- Violence is only used to settle questions of dominance and subordination when other manipulative strategies fail.
- Task Force on the Female Offender (1990) recommended these changes in women's prisons to reduce violence:
  - Make substance abuse programs available to women prisoners.
  - Provide programs for women prisoners to develop literacy skills.

- ❖ House female prisoners in buildings separate from male prisoners.
- ❖ Develop programs for keeping children in the facility to "fortify the bond between mother and child."
- ❖ Build institutions specifically to house women.

For more on life in prison, visit Criminal Justice Interactive online > Life behind Bars > Learning Modules > 13.2 Prison Life: Two Perspectives.

For more on life in prison, visit Criminal Justice Interactive online > Life behind Bars > Simulation Activity: Life in Prison.

13.3 Special offenders

13.3.1 AIDS-infected inmates

- In 2006, the American prison system had an HIV infection rate nearly five times that of the general, nonprison population.
- Between 2005 and 2006, the number of HIV-positive prisoners decreased 3.1% from 22,676 to 21,980, while the overall prison custody population grew 2.2% during the same period.
- At yearend 2006, 1.6% of male inmates and 2.4% of female inmates in state and federal prisons were known to be HIV-positive or to have AIDS.
- Three states house nearly half (49%) of all inmates known to be infected with HIV or to have AIDS in state prisons at yearend 2006:
  - ❖ New York (4,000)
  - ❖ Florida (3,412)
  - ❖ Texas (2,693)
- New York continued to see a large decrease (down 440) in the number of HIV/AIDS cases.
- The overall rate of confirmed AIDS cases among the prison population (0.46%) was more than 2.5 times the rate in the U.S. general population (0.17%).
- During 2006, 167 inmates in state and federal prisons died from AIDS-related causes, down from 203 in 2005.
  - ❖ Florida reported the largest number of AIDS-related deaths (28) followed by New York (14), Pennsylvania (13), Georgia (10), and Louisiana (10).
- Gender and HIV/AIDS at yearend 2006
  - ❖ Males: 19,842
  - ❖ Females: 2,138

- Confirmed cases of AIDS
  - There were 5,674 confirmed cases of AIDS at yearend 2006.
    - State prisons: 5,018
    - Federal prisons: 656
- Testing of inmates for HIV
  - Twenty-one states reported testing all inmates for HIV at admission in 2006.
  - Forty-seven states and the federal system reported testing inmates if they have HIV-related symptoms of if they requested an HIV test.
  - Forty states and the federal system test inmates after they are involved in an incident in which an inmate is exposed to a possible HIV transmission.
  - Sixteen states and the federal system test inmates who belong to specific "high-risk" groups.
  - States that test all inmates for HIV upon their release:
    - Missouri
    - Alabama
    - Florida
    - Texas
    - Nevada
  - States that test all inmates while in custody:
    - North Dakota
    - Idaho
    - Nevada
  - States that randomly test:
    - New York
    - Nevada
    - Arkansas
    - Oregon
    - Federal system
- Prisons have used strategies to try to reduce the spread of the HIV virus.
  - Testing and segregating prisoners who are infected with the disease
  - Education programs that teach both inmates and staff about the dangers of high-risk behavior and suggest ways to avoid HIV infection
- HIV-positive and AIDS-confirmed inmates pose special problems for institutions.
  - Mass screening and inmate segregation can be extremely expensive.

- ❖ Confidentiality becomes a problem, especially when inmates who test positive are segregated.
- ❖ Civil liability may result if inmates are falsely labeled as infected, or if an inmate is known to be infected and is not prevented from spreading the disease.
- ❖ In order to try to prevent the spread of the disease, many state prisons have denied HIV-positive inmates:
  - ◆ Jobs
    - ❒ Example: A 1994 federal appeals court upheld a California prison policy that bars inmates who are HIV-positive from working in food-service jobs.
  - ◆ Educational opportunities
  - ◆ Visitation privileges
  - ◆ Conjugal visits
  - ◆ Home furloughs
- ❖ Policies of segregation have raised charges that infected inmates are routinely discriminated against and denied equal treatment in ways that have no accepted medical basis.
  - ◆ In 2001, the Mississippi Department of Corrections ended its policy of segregating HIV-positive prisoners from other inmates in educational and vocational programs.

13.3.2 Geriatric offenders

- ■ The number of "geriatric" inmates in state or federal prisons or local jails has been increasing in part because of:
  - ❖ The general aging of the American population, which is reflected inside prisons
  - ❖ New sentencing policies such as "three strikes"
  - ❖ The prison-building boom that took place in the 1980s and 1990s, creating more space and reducing the need for early release
  - ❖ Reduction or termination of the use of parole
- ■ Many inmates who enter prison when they are young will grow old behind bars.
- ■ The estimated number of inmates held in state or federal prisons, or in local jails, by age as of June 30, 2008:
  - ❖ 50 to 54: 104,900
  - ❖ 55 to 59: 53,500
  - ❖ 60 to 64: 23,000
  - ❖ 65 or older: 18,300

- Of the total number of estimated prisoners, the number of females as of June 30, 2008:
    - 50 to 54: 8,000
    - 55 to 59: 3,300
    - 60 to 64: 1,300
    - 65 or older: 800
- As the inmate population becomes "gray," they need special care for their handicaps and physical impairments:
    - Eye glasses
    - Dental care
    - Medical care
    - Assistance with daily activities
    - Medical equipment
        - Walkers
        - Canes
        - Wheelchairs
        - Oxygen tanks
- Inmates may suffer from dementia, cancer, or heart disease.
    - A 1997 *New York Times* article by Fox Butterfield describes the situation of a 59-year-old male inmate who suffers from Alzheimer's and can no longer recall his age or why he was sent to prison.
    - Some large prisons have set aside special sections to care for elderly inmates who suffer from these "typical" disorders, as the number of inmates requiring round-the-clock care is expected to increase dramatically.

13.3.3 Medical problems

- Based on a 2004 Bureau of Justice Statistics survey:
    - An estimated 44% of state inmates and 39% of federal inmates reported a current medical problem other than a cold or virus.
    - Arthritis (15% state inmates; 12% federal inmates) and hypertension (state 14% state inmates; federal 13% federal inmates) were the two most commonly reported medical problems.
    - Among inmates who reported a medical problem, 70% of state and 76% of federal inmates reported seeing a medical professional because of the problem.
    - More than 8 in 10 inmates in state and federal prisons reported receiving a medical examination or blood test since admission.
    - Almost all state and federal inmates reported being tested for TB (95% state inmates; 96% federal inmates).

- More than one-third (36% of state inmates; 24% federal inmates) reported having an impairment.
- Sixteen percent of state inmates and 8% of federal inmates reported having multiple impairments.
- Female inmates in both state and federal prisons were more likely to report a current medical problem than male inmates, but were equally likely to report a dental problem.
- Male and female inmates in state and federal prisons were equally likely to report having at least one of six impairments:
  - Learning
  - Speech
  - Hearing
  - Vision
  - Mobility
  - Mental impairment
- Female inmates (11%) in state prisons were more likely to report a mental impairment than were male inmates (6%).

- Medical care of inmates can be very costly to both the state and federal governments.
  - Most facilities employ the services of nurses and doctors who either visit the prison or work regularly in a prison.
  - Dentists are either on staff or visit prisons regularly.
- More serious medical problems are often addressed by transporting the inmate to a local hospital and guarding him or her during treatment.
- Inmates who require long-term rehabilitation present additional difficulties for prison administration.

13.3.4 Mental illness

- Some mentally ill inmates are neurotic or have personality problems that increase tension in prison.
- Some inmates have serious psychological disorders that may have escaped diagnosis at trial, or did not provide a legal basis for the reduction of criminal responsibility.
- Some inmates develop psychiatric symptoms while in prison.
- A 2004 survey of inmates in state and federal correctional facilities and local jails found the following:
  - Those with any mental problem:
    - State offenders: 56%
    - Federal offenders: 45%
    - Jailed offenders: 64%

- Forty-three percent of state offenders and 54% of jailed offenders reported symptoms that met the criteria for mania.
    - About 23% of state offenders and 30% of jailed offenders reported symptoms of major depression.
- An estimated 15% of state offenders and 24% of jailed offenders reported symptoms that met the criteria for a psychotic disorder.
- Nearly 25% of both state prisoners and jail inmates who had a mental health problem had served three or more prior incarcerations compared to 20% of those who did not have a mental health problem.
- Female inmates had higher rates of mental health problems than male inmates.
    - State prisons
        - Females: 73%
        - Males: 55%
    - Federal prisons
        - Females: 61%
        - Males: 44%
    - Local jails
        - Females: 75%
        - Males: 63%
- Prison and jail inmates who had a mental health problem, by age:
    - State prisons
        - 24 or younger: 63%
        - 24 to 34: 58%
        - 35 to 44: 56%
        - 45 to 54: 51%
        - 55 or older: 39.6%
    - Federal prisons
        - 24 or younger: 58%
        - 25 to 34: 48%
        - 35 to 44: 40%
        - 45 to 54: 42%
        - 55 or older: 36%
    - Local jails
        - 24 or younger: 70%
        - 25 to 34: 65%

            - 35 to 44: 62%
            - 45 to 54: 53%
            - 55 or older: 52%
    - Prisoners who had a mental health problem and had received treatment since admission:
        - Over one in three state prisoners
        - One in four federal prisoners
        - One in six jail inmates
- Bureau of Justice Statistics (2000) survey of public and private state-level facilities (excluding jails) found that:
    - Fifty-one percent of such institutions provide 24-hour mental health care.
    - Seventy-one percent provide therapy and counseling by trained mental health professionals as needed.
    - Sixty-six percent of facilities have programs to help released inmates obtain community mental health services.
    - Thirteen percent of state prisoners were receiving some type of mental health therapy at the time of the survey.
    - Ten percent were receiving psychotropic medications, including:
        - Antidepressants
        - Stimulants
        - Sedatives
        - Tranquilizers
    - The Bureau of Justice Statistics reports that at the state level:
        - Twelve facilities are devoted exclusively to the care of mentally ill inmates.
        - Psychiatric confinement was reported by 143 prisons as being one specialty among other functions that they perform.
- *Washington* v. *Harper* (1990)
    - U.S. Supreme Court ruled that mentally ill inmates could be required to take antipsychotic drugs, even against their wishes.
    - The ruling stipulated that this requirement would apply when the inmate is dangerous to himself or others, and the treatment is in the inmate's medical interest.

- Paula M. Ditton, in *Mental Health and Treatment of Inmates and Probationers* (1999), found that the nation's prisons and jails hold an estimated 283,800 mentally ill inmates (16% of those confined) and that 547,800 such offenders are on probation.
  - ❖ Forty percent of mentally ill inmates receive no treatment at all.

For more on special offenders, visit Criminal Justice Interactive online > Life behind Bars > Learning Modules > 13.3 Special Offenders.

For more on the aging of the prison population, visit Criminal Justice Interactive online > Life behind Bars > Myths and Issues Videos > Issue 2: Our Graying Prison Population.

13.4 Prison programs

13.4.1 Prison programs improve recidivism.

13.4.2 Activities are productive and positive for inmates.

13.4.3 Educational and vocational training

- GED classes and vocational training
  - ❖ Criticized as an excessive luxury
  - ❖ Some state and federal prisons have mandatory education programs to address literacy.
  - ❖ Grant programs to pay for college courses are no longer available to inmates.
  - ❖ Specific training in trades (carpentry, food services, etc.) have been effective in reducing recidivism.
  - ❖ Training improves marketability and the potential for successful employment upon release.

13.4.4 Mental health and substance abuse

- Inmates may suffer from chronic mental illness.
- Most exhibit some symptoms of emotional and/or psychological instability.
- Inmates, even those without a diagnosed mental illness, can benefit from counseling.
- Ethical issues include the notion that an inmate has the right to refuse treatment, including medication.

13.4.5 Employment

- Federal work programs engage inmates in productive activities.
- Daily activities needed to keep any large, complex organization running—food preparation, housekeeping, facilities maintenance, or garden, farm, and landscape work.

- Provide real-life experiences; the opportunity to develop work discipline and new skills
- Small income
- Improves morale, reduces negative behaviors, and may reduce recidivism.

13.4.6 Recreation

- Organized leisure activities full time use inmate energies, and promote self-discipline and self-esteem
  - ❖ Reduce tension
  - ❖ Preclude explosion of energies in the form of riots or fights
- Some activities have been banned or restricted including weight lifting, resources, and paid television programming.
- Physical activity programs transform health and have a positive effect on the aging of prison population.

For more on prison programs, visit Criminal Justice Interactive online > Life behind Bars > Learning Modules > 13.4 History of Prisons.

13.5 Prison staff

13.5.1 Staff roles

- Warden
- Correctional officer
- Counselor
- Psychologist
- Program director
- Instructor
- Physician
- Area supervisor

13.5.2 Correctional officers

- Concerned foremost with custody and control
- Correctional officers undergo a socialization process that helps them to function by the official and unofficial rules of the prison.
- Types of correctional officers:
  - ❖ The "dictator"
    - ◆ Uses prison rules to enforce his own brand of discipline
    - ◆ These guards are bullies and may have sadistic personalities.

- Some dictators use false bravado to hide their fear of prisoners.
- These correctional officers are the ones most likely to be targeted for vengeance by prisoners.

- The "friend"
  - Tries to fraternize with the prisoners by trying to be "one of the guys."
  - These are usually the young and inexperienced officers.
- The "turnkey"
  - Cares little for what goes on in the prison setting
  - This type of correctional officer may be close to retirement or he may have become alienated from his job for various reasons such as low pay, a view that inmates are worthless, monotony of the job, etc.
  - The term "turnkey" comes from prison language that refers to a person who is there just to open and shut doors, and cares about nothing more than just getting through the day.
- The "climber"
  - Typically, a young officer who is interested in promotion
  - Often, these correctional officers are involved in additional schooling to advance themselves.
  - This type of officer has many ideas and often turns a blind eye toward inmates and their problems.
- The "reformer"
  - A do-gooder among correctional officers
  - This type of correctional officer tends to lend a sympathetic ear to the personal needs of prisoners.
  - The "reformer" correctional officer is motivated by personal ideals.
    - Some of these officers are very religious.
  - Prisoners see these officers as naïve, but harmless.

- Professionalization of correctional officers
  - Historically, a low-status job that required minimal education and offered few opportunities for career development.
  - States have been improving the position of correctional officer.
    - Currently, training is provided in most states. Examples:
      - New York state requires:
        - Six weeks of classroom-based instruction
        - Forty hours of rifle practice
        - Six weeks on-the-job training

- ◆ Psychological screening of applicants
  - ❐ Starting to be used in some states:
    - New York
    - New Jersey
    - Ohio
    - Pennsylvania
    - Rhode Island

13.5.3 Correctional officers at the federal level

- ■ Bureau of Prisons' Career Development Model (1982)
  - ❖ Established five sequential phases for development of career correctional officers based on psychological personality inventory
  - ❖ Model seeks to identify skills, abilities, and interests.
  - ❖ Phases of model
    - ◆ Phase I—career assessment
    - ◆ Phase II—career path development
    - ◆ Phase III—career enhancement and management development
    - ◆ Phase IV—advanced management and development
    - ◆ Phase V—senior executive service development

13.6 Prison riots

13.6.1 The explosive decade of prison riots (1970s–1980s)

- ■ Attica Prison, Attica, New York, September 1971
  - ❖ Resulted in 43 dead; 80 were wounded
- ■ New Mexico Penitentiary, Santa Fe, New Mexico, 1980
  - ❖ Riot resulted in 33 inmates dying, many as a result of mutilation or torture.
  - ❖ Intent was to eliminate informers and rats.
  - ❖ Two hundred prisoners were beaten and sexually assaulted.
  - ❖ The whole prison facility was virtually destroyed.
- ■ Atlanta Federal Penitentiary, Atlanta, Georgia, 1987
  - ❖ Lasted 11 days
  - ❖ Prisoners had to be relocated while prison was rebuilt.
  - ❖ Riot caused by dissatisfaction of Cuban inmates, most of who had arrived on the Mariel boatlift.
    - ◆ Mariel boatlift involved some of Cuba's most violent and problematic prisoners that Fidel Castro decided to release and ship to the United States.

- State Correctional Institution at Camp Hill, Pennsylvania, 1989
  - Lasted two nights
  - More than 100 injured
  - Prison mostly destroyed
  - At the time of the riot, prison was 45% over capacity of 2,600 prisoners.

13.6.2 Prison riots (1990s to present)

- Southern Correctional Facility, Lucasville, Ohio, 1993
  - Lasted 11 days
  - Nine prisoners and 1 correctional officer died (hung by inmates).
  - Inmates demanded:
    - Televising of parade of 450 inmates at the close of the riot
    - No retaliation by officials
    - Review of medical staffing and care
    - Review of mail and visitation rules
    - Review of commissary prices
    - Better enforcement against what the inmates called "inappropriate supervision."
- Riots occurred in October, 1995, throughout the federal prison system.
  - Riots were related to inmate grievances over perceived disparities in federal drug sentencing policies and the possible loss of weight-lifting equipment.
  - Within a few days, there was a nationwide lockdown of 73 federal prisons.
- Pelican Bay State Prison, California, February, 2000
  - Riot between 200 black and Hispanic prisoners
  - One inmate was killed.
  - Fifteen inmates were wounded.
- Torrance County Detention Facility, Estancia, New Mexico, November, 2000
  - A privately run facility
  - Thirty-two inmates took 12 correctional officers hostage.
  - Two correctional officers were stabbed and seriously injured.
  - Eight additional correctional officers were beaten.
  - Riot was stopped after an emergency response team used tear gas.

- San Quentin Prison, California, 2005
  - ❖ Forty-two inmates were injured when a fight broke out during breakfast between Hispanic and white prisoners.
  - ❖ Riot occurred in a section of the prison housing 900 inmates who were under lockdown because of previous fighting.
- New Castle Correctional Facility, New Castle, Indiana, 2007
  - ❖ A two-hour disturbance
  - ❖ Two injured staff members
  - ❖ A number of fires were set at the facility.

13.6.3 Causes of riots

- Possible causes:
  - ❖ Insensitive prison administration and neglected inmate demands. Examples:
    - ◆ Call for "fairness" in disciplinary hearings
    - ◆ Request for better food
    - ◆ More recreational opportunities
  - ❖ Violent lifestyle of prisoners when on the street carried over and maintained in prison.
  - ❖ Dehumanizing prison conditions
    - ◆ Overcrowding
    - ◆ Lack of ability for individual expression
  - ❖ Riots regulate inmate society and redistribute power balances among inmate groups.
    - ◆ Riots allow for opportunity to "cleanse" the prison population of informers and rats.
    - ◆ Riots allow for struggles among power brokers and ethnic groups to be resolved.
  - ❖ "Power vacuums" created
    - ◆ Changes in prison administration create power vacuums.
    - ◆ Transfer of influential inmates to other prisons
    - ◆ Court-ordered injunctions that change the daily prison routine. Examples:
      - ❒ Court-ordered end to "building tender" system in Texas prisons
        - "Building tenders" were tough prisoners who were given free reign by prison administrators in keeping other prisoners in line.
      - ❒ Gangs developed in Texas prisons to fill the power vacuum created by disbanding of "building tender" system.

- Gang membership in 1992 was estimated at over 1,200.
  - Examples of gangs:
    - Texas Syndicate
    - Aryan Brotherhood of Texas
    - Mexican Mafia (sometimes known as La Eme, Spanish for the letter M)
    - Aryan Warriors
    - Black Gangster Disciples
    - Black Guerrilla Family
    - Confederate Knights of America
    - Nuestra Familia (Hispanic)

13.6.4 Stages in prison riots and control

- Vernon Fox, in *Prison Riots in a Democratic Society* (1982), identified five phases of prison riots:
  - Explosion
    - Tend to involve binges
      - Excessive use of alcohol
      - Excessive use of drugs
      - Extensive sexual activity
    - Buildings are burned.
    - Facilities are wrecked.
    - Old grudges between inmates are settled.
  - Organization (into inmate-led groups)
    - Leadership changes tend to occur.
    - New leaders emerge who can organize inmates to confront authorities.
    - Bargaining strategies develop.
  - Confrontation (with authorities)
  - Termination (through negotiation or physical confrontation)
  - Reaction and explanation (usually by investigative commission)

13.7 Prison reentry

13.7.1 Housing

- Many inmates have lost government benefits such as federal or state housing subsidies.
- Must rely on friends and family
- Only other option may be living on the streets.

13.7.2 Employment

- Criminal record eliminates many professions and labor jobs.
- Vocational skills and work experiences gained while in prison may be of limited value in the outside world.

13.7.3 Social network

- Reinstating and developing new ties can be overwhelming.
- Distance of time and space weakens old relationships.
- Change of status may create rifts in strong relationships.
- Inmate may be out of practice with social skills and suffer guilt and anxiety.

For more on prison reentry, visit Criminal Justice Interactive online > Life behind Bars > Learning Modules > 13.5 Prisoner Reentry.

CHAPTER SUMMARY

- Until the late 1960s the Courts maintained a hands-off doctrine of intervention in regard to prison management. For the past 50 years, the Courts have intervened more aggressively in prison administration and have established the stricter adherence to and interpretation of the legal rights of inmates. *Holt* v. *Sarver* brought the official end to the hands-off doctrine, during which the Supreme Court declared the entire Arkansas prison system to be so inhumane that it violated the Eighth and Fourteenth Amendments' prohibition against cruel and unusual punishment. The conditional rights for inmates that have been established by the Court include the right to religious freedom, freedom of communication and visitation, the right to legal assistance, and the right to medical attention. The Prison Litigation Reform Act of 1996 identifies the process an inmate must go through to file a formal grievance against the prison system.
- Prisons are considered a "total institution," an institution in which people work, play, eat, sleep, and recreate together on a daily basis. Total institutions are small societies with distinctive values and styles of life. Prisonization is the process by which newly institutionalized offenders come to accept prison lifestyles and criminal values. Prison has its own language, or argot, that is specific to male and female prisoners. There are two models of prison society. The deprivation model is a prison subculture that is an adaptation to the deprivation. In the importation model, inmates bring with them to prison the specific values, roles, and behaviors from the outside world. Homosexuality is part of the prison subculture and may involve older prisoners who will provide protection or other items to newer prisoners in exchange for sexual favors. Rape is also a characteristic of prison life and it is often the result of prisoners working together to overpower the victim. The number of women being sent to prison is on the rise, with women inmates representing almost 7% of prisoners serving sentences of more than a year. Most

women's prisons were not designed to house women and many do not have programs designed specifically for women.

- Special offenders in prison are of a particular challenge. Prisons have to develop special testing procedures, educational programs, and segregation policies for AIDS-infected patients. Geriatric offenders are increasing in prison because of the general aging of the population and the institution of the "three-strikes" rule. These inmates may suffer from dementia or diseases and ailments associated with old age. Medical issues for the general prison population are also an issue. A significant percentage of inmates may have mental impairment or psychological disorders.
- Prison programs improve recidivism and are productive and positive for inmates. Programs may include educational and vocational programs, mental and substance abuse education, employment, and recreation.
- Prison staff includes correctional officers, many of who have their own distinct style of management. Historically, the position of correctional officer has been a low-status job that required minimal formal education, but states are now providing training and psychological screening of applicants. At the federal level, the Bureau of Prisons' Career Development Model established in 1982, developed five sequential phases for the career of correctional officers based on psychological personality inventory.
- Prison riots exploded during the 1970s and 1980s, resulting in deaths and destruction of facilities. The prison riots at Attica in New York were one of the most damaging riots of the decade. During the 1990s, the Southern Correctional Facility in Lucasville, Ohio, had an 11-day riot in which nine prisoners died and one correctional officer was hung by inmates. At the federal level, riots occurred in October 1996 throughout the system. There are several possible causes for prison riots: insensitive prison administration and neglected inmate demands, violent lifestyle of prisoners when on the street that carries over to prison, dehumanizing prison conditions, and power vacuums in prison administration that occur when daily routines are changed.
- Entering society after prison is challenging for offenders. Housing may be difficult to obtain, as many inmates have lost government benefits such as federal or state housing. A criminal record often eliminates many employment opportunities. Reinstating and developing new social ties can also be overwhelming.

ONLINE@CRIMINAL JUSTICE INTERACTIVE

Learning Modules

13.1 The Legal Rights of Inmates
13.2 Prison Life: Two Perspectives
13.3 Special Offenders
13.4 History of Prisons
13.5 Prisoner Reentry

Myths and Issues Videos

Myth vs. Reality: The Death Penalty, a Cost-Effective Solution
Issue 1: Should Prisoners Have Rights?
Issue 2: Our Graying Prison Population

Simulation Activity: Life in Prison

Homework and Review

In the News
Web Activity
Review Questions

Chapter 14

The Juvenile Justice System

CHAPTER OUTLINE

LEARNING OBJECTIVES

After reviewing the online material and reading this chapter, you should be able to:

1. Describe the four major processes in the juvenile justice system: intake, adjudication, disposition, and post-adjudication.
2. Discuss the differences between the adult and juvenile justice systems.
3. Explain the history of the juvenile court.
4. Define five types of juvenile offenders: noncriminal, irresponsible, situational, drug and alcohol, and chronic.
5. Compare and contrast the legal rights of juveniles and adults.
6. Discuss issues related to the transfer of juveniles to the adult criminal justice system.
7. Define terms related to the juvenile justice system.

KEY TERMS

abused children
adjudicatory hearing
Breed v. *Jones*
delinquent children
dependent children
detention hearing
discretionary waiver
disposition
Ex parte Crouse
Illinois v. *Montanez*
In re Gault
In re Winship
intake
juvenile justice system
juvenile petition
Kent v. *U.S.*
mandatory waiver
McKeiver v. *Pennsylvania*
neglected children
opportunity theory
parens patriae
patria potestas
preliminary hearing
presumptive waiver
reform school
Schall v. *Martin*
social disorganization
social ecology
status offender
status offense
undisciplined child

14.0 The juvenile justice system

14.1 How juveniles are processed

14.1.1 The current juvenile justice process

- The current juvenile justice process has evolved from the early days as a result of changes in the attitudes of society, laws, and landmark Supreme Court decisions.
- Jurisdiction of juveniles is related to the age of the juvenile.
    - Most states (37) and the District of Columbia define a juvenile as someone who has not reached their eighteenth birthday.
        - Alabama
        - Alaska
        - Arizona
        - Arkansas
        - California
        - Colorado
        - Delaware
        - District of Columbia
        - Florida
        - Hawaii
        - Idaho
        - Indiana
        - Iowa
        - Kansas
        - Kentucky
        - Maine
        - Maryland
        - Minnesota
        - Mississippi
        - Montana
        - Nebraska
        - Nevada
        - New Jersey
        - New Mexico
        - North Dakota
        - Ohio
        - Oklahoma
        - Oregon

- Pennsylvania
- Rhode Island
- South Dakota
- Tennessee
- Utah
- Vermont
- Virginia
- Washington
- West Virginia
- Wyoming

- Ten states use the age of 17.
  - Georgia
  - Illinois
  - Louisiana
  - Massachusetts
  - Michigan
  - Missouri
  - New Hampshire
  - South Carolina
  - Texas
  - Wisconsin
- Three states use the age of 16.
  - Connecticut
  - New York
  - North Carolina

- Waiver to adult court
  - All 50 states have judicial waiver provisions that allow for juveniles who commit serious crimes to be bound over to criminal court.
  - Approximately 2% of all juveniles are bound over to adult criminal courts.
  - Juveniles who commit violent crimes or who have prior records are among the most likely to be transferred to adult criminal court.
  - Types of waivers
    - **Discretionary waiver** is a waiver in which discretion is given to juvenile court judges to transfer jurisdiction in individual cases involving minors so as to allow prosecution in adult criminal courts.
      - The most popular form of waiver, used by 47 states and the District of Columbia

DISCRETIONARY WAIVER
A waiver in which discretion is given to juvenile court judges to transfer jurisdiction in individual cases involving minors so as to allow prosecution in adult criminal courts.

- ❐ Most discretionary waiver statutes specify some minimum criteria similar to those outlined in *Kent* v. *U.S.* (1966) that must be met before the court may consider the transfer. (See Section 14.4, Juvenile's Legal Rights, for detailed discussion of this case.)
- ❐ The juvenile court must conduct a hearing at which the parties are entitled to present evidence related to the waiver issue.
- ❐ The prosecution bears the burden of proof in a discretionary waiver hearing.
- ❐ Many state laws specify that the juvenile court shall or must transfer certain interests if the public interests require it or unless there are good reasons not to.
- ❐ The number of delinquency cases judicially waived peaked in 1994 at 13,000 cases.
  - Since 1994, the number of cases judicially waived declined 47% to 6,900 cases in 2005.
  - Of the 6,900 cases judicially waived in 2005:
    - Crimes against persons: 51%
    - Crimes against property: 27%
    - Drug crimes: 12%
    - Public order crimes: 10%
  - In terms of age, of the 6,900 cases judicially waived in 2005:
    - Fifteen or younger: 15%
    - Sixteen or older: 85%
  - In terms of race, of the 6,900 cases judicially waived in 2005:
    - White: 57%
    - Black: 39%
    - Other: 4%

MANDATORY WAIVER

A waiver that provides for transfer of juvenile cases to adult criminal court that meet certain age, offense, or other criteria.

- ◆ **Mandatory waiver**, also called statutory waiver, used by 14 states, provides for transfer of juvenile cases to adult criminal court that meet certain age, offense, or other criteria.
  - ❐ For cases that meet the required criteria, the case originates in the juvenile court; however, the juvenile court has no role other than to confirm that the statutory requirements for mandatory transfer are met.
  - ❐ In true mandatory waiver jurisdictions, the juvenile court is called upon only to determine that there is probable cause to believe a juvenile of

the requisite age committed an offense falling within the mandatory waiver law.

- **Presumptive waiver**, used by 12 states and the District of Columbia, shifts the burden of proof to the juvenile to show that the juvenile should not be transferred to adult court.
  - Some states require in this type of waiver that the juvenile not only has the burden of proof at the waiver hearing, but must present "clear and convincing evidence" that a waiver is not justified.

PRESUMPTIVE WAIVER
A waiver that shifts the burden of proof to the juvenile to show that the juvenile should not be transferred to adult court.

14.1.2 How the system works

- Intake and detention hearings
  - An intake hearing is the first step in decision making regarding a juvenile whose behavior or alleged behavior is in violation of the law or could otherwise cause a juvenile court to assume jurisdiction.
    - Juveniles come to the attention of police or social agencies either through arrest or juvenile petitions often filed by parents, teachers, school administrators, neighbors, etc.
      - **Juvenile petition** is a document filed in juvenile court alleging that a juvenile is a delinquent, a status offender, or a dependent and asking that the court assume jurisdiction over the juvenile or that the alleged delinquent be transferred to a criminal court for prosecution as an adult.
    - Three-quarters of all referrals to juvenile court come directly from law enforcement authorities.
    - Detention hearings are conducted by a juvenile court judge or by an officer of the court such as a juvenile probation officer who has been given the authority to make intake decisions.
      - Detention hearings investigate whether the juvenile is a candidate for confinement and represents a "clear and immediate danger to himself or herself and/or others."
      - One in five juvenile cases involves detention prior to adjudication.
    - Possible **intake** outcomes:
      - Dismissal
      - Diversion; can be diverted to:
        - Job-training programs
        - Mental health facilities
        - Drug-treatment programs
        - Educational counseling

JUVENILE PETITION
A document filed in juvenile court alleging that a juvenile is a delinquent, a status offender, or a dependent and asking that the court assume jurisdiction over the juvenile or that an alleged delinquent be transferred to a criminal court for prosecution as an adult.

INTAKE
The first step in decision making regarding a juvenile whose behavior or alleged behavior is in violation of the law or could otherwise cause a juvenile court to assume jurisdiction.

- Other community service agencies
  - National Center for Juvenile Justice estimates that more than half of all juvenile cases disposed of at intake are handled informally and are dismissed or diverted to a social service agency.

❒ Detention

PRELIMINARY HEARING

A proceeding before a judicial officer in which three matters must be decided: (1) whether a crime was committed, (2) whether the crime occurred within the territorial jurisdiction of the court, and (3) whether there are reasonable grounds to believe that the defendant committed the crime.

DETENTION HEARING

Circumstances are examined to determine if detention is necessary for the safety of the public, or if there are good reasons to release the arrestee until trial. In juvenile justice usage, a hearing by a judicial officer of a juvenile court to determine whether a juvenile is to be detained, is to continue to be detained, or is to be released while juvenile proceedings are pending.

- **Preliminary hearing** is a hearing at which the purpose is to determine if there is probable cause to believe the juvenile committed the alleged act.
  - May be held in conjunction with **detention hearing**
  - The juvenile is advised of his or her rights at this hearing.
  - For serious offenders, the case may be transferred to adult criminal court.
  - Transfer hearings are held in juvenile court and focus on:
    - Applicability of transfer status to the case under consideration
    - Whether juvenile is amenable to treatment through available resources in juvenile system
- Adjudication is a courtroom stage at the juvenile level that is similar in substance to a criminal hearing or trial.
  - Juveniles do not have right to jury trial (*McKeiver* v. *Pennsylvania*, 1971).
    - Some states do provide for juveniles to have a trial by jury.
  - Emphasis is on privacy.
  - An **adjudicatory hearing** tends to be less formal than a criminal trial.
  - Juvenile hearings are normally completed in a matter of hours or days instead of the days or weeks of an adult criminal trial.
  - Proof beyond a reasonable doubt is required in delinquent cases; however, in status offenses, only a preponderance of evidence is required.
  - The focus of the adjudicatory hearing is still supposed to be on the child's best interests.

ADJUDICATORY HEARING

The fact-finding process wherein the juvenile court determines whether there is sufficient evidence to sustain the allegations in a petition.

DISPOSITION

The final stage in processing of adjudicated juveniles in which a decision is made on the form of treatment or penalty that should be imposed.

- **Disposition** is the final stage in processing of adjudicated juveniles, in which a decision is made on the form of treatment or penalty that should be imposed.
  - The judge typically has wider range of dispositions than do judges in adult criminal cases.
  - Because rehabilitation is still the official primary objective, the judge is likely to select the "least restrictive alternative."

- Approximately 62% of all adjudicated delinquency cases are placed on formal probation.
- Eleven percent of adjudicated delinquency cases order juveniles to pay restitution or a fine, to participate in some form of community service, or to enter a treatment or counseling program.
- In 1996, 24% of adjudicated cases resulted in the juvenile being placed outside the home in a residential facility; in 4% of adjudicated cases, the case was then dismissed or the juvenile was otherwise released.

- Secure institutions for juveniles
  - OJJDP reported in 2003:
    - There were 104,400 young people were being held under custodial supervision in the United States for:
      - Personal crimes like murder, rape, or robbery: 25%
      - Property crimes: 29%
      - Drug offenses: 9%
      - Public order offenses (including weapons offenses): 23%
      - Status offenses: 4%
      - Probation and parole violations: 14%
  - OJJDP reported in 1998:
    - There were 125,800 young people were being held under custodial supervision in the United States for:
      - Personal crimes like murder, rape, or robbery: 33.4%
      - Property crimes: 30.2%
      - Drug offenses: 8.8%
      - Public order offenses (including weapons offenses): 9.2%
      - Status offenses: 6.5%
      - Probation and parole violations: 11.9%
  - Characteristics of juveniles in confinement
    - Sickmund, Sladky, and Kang (2008)
      - *Census of Juveniles in Residential Placement Databook* (2006)
        - Males: 85%
        - Black: 40%
        - Hispanic: 20%
        - Institutionalized for having committed a status offense such as truancy, running away, or violating curfew: 5%

- In residential facilities for a serious personal or property offense: 44%
- Charged or adjudicated for homicide or murder: 1%

❒ *Census of Juveniles in Residential Placement Databook* (1997)

- Male: 87%
- Black: 40%
- Hispanic: 19%
- Institutionalized for having committed a status offense such as truancy, running away, or violating curfew: 7%
- In residential facilities for a serious personal or property offense: 42%
- Charged or adjudicated for homicide or murder: 2%

■ Post-adjudicatory review

❖ Federal court precedents have not established a clear right to appeal from juvenile court; however, many states do have such statutory provisions.

■ Dissatisfaction with today's system

❖ Belief that a chronic few are committing the majority of delinquent offenses has caused focus on three areas:

◆ Lessening the degree of privacy that surrounds juvenile proceedings

❒ In 1995, Pennsylvania opened juvenile court proceedings to the public for juveniles 14 years of age and older who have been charged with felonies.

◆ Increasing penalties associated with certain kinds of delinquent acts.

❒ OJJDP has developed a monetary and direct victim service restitution program for juvenile courts called RESTTA (Restitution Education, Specialized Training, and Technical Assistance Program).

- Program provides local juvenile courts with the information needed to make restitution a meaningful part of the dispositional process.
- Reducing diversionary opportunities for habitual, violent, and serious offenders

❒ OJJDP now calls for a systemwide strategy of intervention—treatment and rehabilitation for serious, violent, and chronic juvenile offenders that combines accountability and sanctions with increasingly intensive community-based intervention, treatment, and rehabilitation services for repeat offenders.

For more on how juveniles are processed, visit Criminal Justice Interactive online > The Juvenile Justice System > Learning Modules > 14.1 How Juveniles are Processed.

14.2 The differences between the adult and the juvenile justice system

14.2.1 Juvenile system vs. adult system

I. Juvenile System	Adult System
A. focus on delinquency	focus on criminality
B. limits rights of juveniles against unreasonable searches	provides for comprehensive rights against unreasonable searches of person, home and possession
C. provides rights against self-incrimination	provides rights against self-incrimination
D. focuses on interests of the child	assumes innocence until proven guilty
E. helping context	adversarial setting
F. petitions or complaints legitimize apprehension	arrest warrants form the basis of most arrests
G. provide for right to an attorney	provide for right to an attorney
H. closed hearing and no right to jury trial	public trial and right to jury trial
I. protection and treatment are the goals	punishment and reformation are the goals
J. specific right to treatment	no right to treatment
K. sealed records; may be destroyed at a specific age	public record of trial and judgment
L. release into parental custody	possibility of bail or release on recognizance
M. separate facilities at all levels	possible incarceration in adult correctional facility

14.2.2 The two systems, two very different approaches/philosophies:

- The juvenile justice system philosophy includes the following, when compared to the adult criminal justice system:
  - ❖ A reduced concern with legal issues of guilt or innocence and an emphasis on the child's best interests
  - ❖ An emphasis on treatment rather than punishment
  - ❖ Privacy and protection from public scrutiny through the use of sealed records and laws against publishing the names of juvenile offenders

- The use of techniques of social science in dispositional decision making rather than sentence determined by a perceived need for punishment
- No long-term confinement, with most juveniles being released from institutions by their twenty-first birthday regardless of the offense
- Separate facilities for juveniles
- Broad discretionary alternatives at all points in the process

For more on the differences between the adult and the juvenile justice system, visit Criminal Justice Interactive online > The Juvenile Justice System > Learning Modules > 14.2 Differences between Adult and Juvenile Justice System.

14.3 History of the juvenile court

14.3.1 The history of the juvenile justice system

JUVENILE JUSTICE SYSTEM

Government agencies that function to investigate, supervise, adjudicate, care for, or confine youthful offenders and other children subject to the jurisdiction of the juvenile court.

- **Juvenile justice system** refers to the agencies of the government that are involved in the investigation, supervision, adjudication, care for, or confinement of individuals, typically under the age of 18.

14.3.2 Early times

- About 753 B.C.E.
- Roman law
  - Children had membership in their family, but the father had absolute control over children.

PATRIA POTESTAS

Literally, power of father in Latin.

PARENS PATRIAE

A common law principle that allows the state to assume a parental role and to take custody of a child when he or she becomes delinquent, is abandoned, or is in need of care that the natural parents are unable or unwilling to provide.

    - ***Patria postestas*** (literally, power of father in Latin) extended to issues of life and death for all members of the family including slaves, spouses, and children.
    - ***Parens patriae*** is the common law principle that allows state to take custody of a child when he or she becomes delinquent, is abandoned, or is in need of care that the natural parents are unable or unwilling to provide.
      - Originally, the King was considered the father of the country and thus had parental rights over all his citizens.
- The laws of King Æthelberht were written around 600 A.D.
  - The earliest legal document written in the English language
  - Made no special allowances for the age of the offender
  - Children were imprisoned alongside adults; no segregated juvenile facilities existed.
- Middle ages
  - Church strongly influenced conception of children.
  - Church view at this time was that children under the age of 7 had not yet reached the age of reason, and could not be held liable for spiritual offenses.

- ❖ English law adopted the church perspective that children under 7 could not be held liable for violations.
- ❖ English law dictated that individuals between 7 and 14 were to be accorded a special status as juveniles.
- ❖ They could only be tried as adults if it could be demonstrated that they fully understood the nature of their criminal acts.
- ❖ Adulthood began at 14 (people could marry at 14).

- ■ Juveniles in early America
  - ❖ Puritan influence, with a heavy emphasis on obedience and discipline, was dominant in the early colonial period.
    - ◆ Frequent use of jails and prisons for both juveniles and adults
    - ◆ Laws reflected the teachings of the bible and provided for severe punishments, which was consistent with Puritan beliefs, that unacknowledged social evils might bring the wrath of God down on the entire colony.
    - ◆ Example of Massachusetts law in the 1600s:
      - ❒ "If a man have a stubborn or rebellious son of sufficient years of understanding, viz. sixteen, which will not obey the voice of his father or the voice of his mother, and that when they have chastened him will not harken to them, then shall his father and mother, being his natural parents, lay hold on him and bring him to the magistrate assembled in Court, and testify to them by sufficient evidence that this their son is stubborn and rebellious and will not obey their voice and chastisement, but lives in sundry notorious crime. Such a son shall be put to death." (Taken from Charles E. Springer, *Justice For Juveniles,* 2nd printing, Office of Juvenile Justice and Delinquency Prevention, 1987.)
  - ❖ Enlightenment period in Europe during the 1600s and 1700s had influence on justice system in the colonies.
    - ◆ Focused on human potential and generally rejected previously held supernatural explanations in favor of scientific ones.
    - ◆ At same time, thinking was changing; there was growth in the industrialized economy and a move away from farming.
    - ◆ Reassessment of place of children in society
    - ◆ Children were recognized as the only true heirs to the future, and society became increasingly concerned about their well-being.

- Institutional era
  - The 1800s saw rapid social changes in America.
  - Population was growing rapidly and industrial era was in full swing.
  - Children took on new value as source of cheap labor
  - On the farms, children worked side by side with parents.
  - Children fueled assembly lines and proved invaluable to shop owners whose businesses needed cheap labor.
  - Parents were gratified by the income-producing opportunities available to their children.
  - House of refuge
    - In 1823, a report by the Society for the Prevention of Pauperism in the City of New York called for the development of "houses of refuge" to save children from lives of crime and poverty; society also cited problems caused by locking up children with mature criminals.
    - In 1824, the Society for the Prevention of Pauperism established the first house of refuge in New York City.
      - Intended for only those children who could still be "rescued."
      - House served mostly young thieves, vagrants, and runaways.
      - Houses of refuge became very popular and it was not long before overcrowding developed and living conditions deteriorated.

EX PARTE CROUSE

A court decision that clarified the power that states had in committing children to institutions.

    - In 1838, ***Ex parte Crouse*** clarified the power that states had in committing children to institutions.
      - Mary Ann Crouse had been committed to the Philadelphia House of Refuge over her father's objections.
      - The commitment was made based on allegations made by girl's mother that she was incorrigible.
      - The father petitioned for Mary's release on grounds that she had been denied right to jury trial.
      - The father's petition was rejected by court.
      - The court position was based on state's interest in assisting children, and the court denied that punishment or retribution played a part in Mary's treatment.
      - The court built their decision around doctrine of *parens patriae*, an English judicial concept.
        - ". . . may not the natural parents, when unequal to the task of education, or unworthy of it, be superseded by the *parens patriae*, or common guardianship

of the community"? (Sanford Fox, "Juvenile Justice Reform: An Historical Perspective" in Fox's *Modern Juvenile Justice: Cases and Materials*, West Publishers, 1972, p. 27.)

- In the middle 1800s, the child-savers movement began.
  - An ideological framework combining Christian principles with strong emphasis on worth of individual
  - A social perspective, which held that children were to be guided and protected (Anthony Platt, *The Child Savers: The Invention of Delinquency*, University of Chicago Press, 2nd edition, 1977)
  - **Reform school** is a product of child-savers movement and embodied the atmosphere of a Christian home.
    - Chicago Reform School opened in the 1860s, providing an early model for reform schools.
      - Focused primarily on predelinquent youths who showed tendencies toward more serious criminal involvement.
    - Reform school movement emphasized traditional values and hard work.
      - Several reform schools built in rural areas; many of them were farms.
      - A few programs tried to relocate problem children to the vast open expanses of the western states.
    - Criticisms of reform schools
      - Anthony Platt, in *The Child Savers*, states "if institutions sought to replicate families, would it not have been better to place the predelinquents directly in real families"?
      - Reform schools soon became overcrowded.
      - What began as a meaningful attempt to help children ended in routinized institutional procedures devoid of the reformer's original zeal.
- *The People of the State of Illinois, ex rel. Michael O'Connell* v. *Robert Turner* (1870)
  - Daniel O'Connell had been committed to the Chicago Reform School under an Illinois law that permitted confinement for "misfortune."
    - Youngsters classified as "misfortunate" had not necessarily committed any offense.
  - Because O'Connell had not been convicted of crime, the Illinois Supreme Court ordered him released.

REFORM SCHOOL
An institution for juveniles that emphasizes traditional values and hard work.

- Court reasoned that the power of the state under ***parens patriae*** could not exceed the power of natural parents, except in punishing crime.
- *O'Connell* case is remembered for lasting distinction it made between criminal and noncriminal acts committed by juveniles.

- Juvenile court era
  - In the 1870s, Massachusetts passed legislation requiring separate hearings for juveniles.
  - In 1877, New York passed a law requiring separate hearings and prohibiting contact between juvenile and adult offenders.
  - In 1898, Rhode Island enacted juvenile court legislation.
  - In 1899, Colorado created the first comprehensive piece of legislation to adjudicate problem children.
  - In 1899, Illinois passed a codification of Illinois law that became the model for juvenile court statutes.
    - Illinois Juvenile Court Act created a juvenile court, separate in form and function from adult criminal courts.
      - To avoid stigma of criminality, the law applied the term *delinquent* rather than *criminal* to young adjudicated offenders.
        - A delinquent child is a child who has engaged in activity that would be considered a crime if the child were an adult.
    - Act specified that the best interests of the child were to guide juvenile court judges in decisions.
      - Judge was to serve as advocate for the child.
      - Concerns with guilt or innocence took second place to the betterment of the child.
      - Strict adherence to due process requirements of adult prosecutions was not deemed necessary.
    - Emphasized reformation in place of retribution.
  - In 1938, Juvenile Court Act (federal level) was passed, and it included many of the features of the Illinois statute.
  - In 1945, every state had legislation focusing on juveniles.
  - Juvenile court movement based on five principles:
    - The state is the "higher or ultimate parent" of all children.
    - Children are worth saving and nonpunitive procedures should be used.
    - Children should be nurtured and at same time protected from the stigmatizing impact of formal proceedings.

- Justice for children needs to be individualized.
- Noncriminal procedures are necessary in order to give primary consideration to the needs of the child.
  - Denial of due process could be justified in face of constitutional challenges because the court acted not to punish, but to help.

❖ Categories of children in juvenile justice system used by most states around the 1930s; not all states use all of these categories in these ways today:

- ***Delinquent* children** are those who violated the criminal law, and if adults, would be charged with the offense.
- ***Undisciplined* children** are children said to be beyond parental control, as evidenced by their refusal to obey legitimate authority; they need state protection.
- ***Dependent* children** are typically those who had no parents or guardians to care for them or had been abandoned or placed for adoption in violation of the law.
- ***Neglected* children** are those who were not receiving proper care from their parents or guardians.
- ***Abused* children** include those who suffered physical abuse at the hands of their custodians; expanded to include emotional and sexual abuse.
- **Status offenders** is a special category of offenders that embraces laws written only for children (i.e., truancy, vagrancy, runaway, incorrigibility, and curfew).
  - **Status offense** is an act or conduct that is declared by statute to be an offense, but only when committed by or engaged in by a juvenile, and that can be adjudicated only by a juvenile court.

For more on the history of juvenile justice court, visit Criminal Justice Interactive online > The Juvenile Justice System > Learning Modules > 14.3 History of the Juvenile Justice Court.

14.4 Juveniles' legal rights

14.4.1 ***Kent* v. *U.S.*** (1966)

- U.S. Supreme Court case that ended the "hands-off" era in juvenile justice.
- Focused on long-accepted concept of *parens patriae* and signaled beginning of Court's systematic review of all lower-court practices involving delinquency hearings.

DELINQUENT CHILD

A child who has engaged in activity that would be considered a crime if the child were an adult. The term delinquent is used to avoid the stigma associated with the term criminal.

UNDISCIPLINED CHILD

A child who is beyond parental control, as evidenced by his or her refusal to obey legitimate authorities, such as school officials and teachers.

DEPENDENT CHILD

A child who has no parents or whose parents are unable to care for him or her.

NEGLECTED CHILD

A child who is not receiving the proper level of physical or psychological care from his or her parents or guardians, or who has been placed up for adoption in violation of the law.

ABUSED CHILD

A child who has been physically, sexually, or mentally abused. Most states also consider a child who is forced into delinquent activity by a parent or guardian to be abused.

STATUS OFFENDER

A special category of offenders that embraces laws written only for children.

STATUS OFFENSE

An act or conduct that is declared by statute to be an offense, but only when committed by or engaged in by a juvenile, and that can be adjudicated only by a juvenile court.

KENT* v. *U.S.

A 1967 Supreme Court case that established the following rights for juveniles being transferred to adult court: (1) Right to a transfer hearing, (2) right to be present at a waiver hearing, (3) right to have attorney review reports, and (4) judge must state the reasons for transfer.

- Facts of case:
    - Morris Kent, Jr., age 14 years, was arrested in Washington, D.C., in 1959 and charged with several house burglaries and attempted purse snatching.
    - Placed on probation and released to mother's custody.
    - In September of 1961, a person entered woman's apartment in Washington D.C., raped her, and took her wallet.
    - Fingerprints matching Kent's were left behind.
    - Kent, 16 at the time, still under the juvenile court jurisdiction, was taken into custody and interrogated.
    - Kent volunteered information about the crime and spoke about other offenses.
    - After the interrogation, Kent's mother retained counsel.
    - Kent was kept in custody for another week, during which time psychological and psychiatric evaluations were conducted.
    - The results of the exams indicated that Kent was a victim of severe psychopathology.
    - The juvenile court judge, without consulting Kent, his mother, or his lawyer, remanded Kent to the adult court.
    - Kent was tried in the adult court on eight counts of burglary.
    - Kent was found guilty on six counts of burglary and robbery and sentenced to 5 to 15 years on each count.
    - Kent's lawyers appealed to the Supreme Court based on a lack of hearing at the juvenile court level before transfer to adult court took place.
    - The Supreme Court agreed with Kent's attorneys and ordered adequate hearings for juveniles being considered for transfer to adult court.
        - At such hearings juveniles are entitled to representation by attorneys who must have access to records.
    - *Kent* is especially important because it was first time the court recognized need for at least minimal due process in juvenile court hearings.

IN RE GAULT

A 1967 Supreme Court case that confirmed a juvenile's right to due process during confinement.

14.4.2 *In re Gault* (1967)

- Gerald Gault and a friend, Ronald Lewis, were taken into custody on June 8, 1964 by the sheriff of Gila County, Arizona, based on neighbor's complaint that the boys had telephoned her and made lewd remarks.
- When Gault was taken into custody, he was already on probation for having been in the company of another boy who had stolen a wallet from a lady's purse.
- Gault's parents were at work when he was picked up, and the sheriff left no notice that he had been taken into custody.

- When Gault's parents returned home after work they eventually learned from Ronald Lewis's parents that he had been taken into custody.
- Gerald's parents learned that there was to be an initial hearing, when it would be held and where, but were not told the nature of the complaint against Gault, nor could they learn the identity of the complainant, who was not present at the initial hearing.
- At the hearing, Gault was not represented by counsel.
- Gault admitted dialing the number, but said he gave the phone to Ronald Lewis who made the statements.
- Judge ordered a second hearing based on evidence.
- At a second hearing, Mrs. Gault requested the complainant be present to identify Gault's voice. The request was refused.
- Gault was adjudicated delinquent and remanded to the State Industrial School until his twenty-first birthday.
- Gault's family appealed based on six issues:
  - Notice of charges: Gault was not given notice to prepare a reasonable defense to the charges against him.
  - Right to counsel: Gault was not notified of his right to an attorney or to have attorney present at hearing.
  - Right to confront and cross-examine witnesses: Complainant can be required to be present at hearing.
  - Protection against self-incrimination: Gault was never advised he had the right to remain silent, nor was he advised his testimony could be used against him.
  - Right to transcript: Gault's attorney was not provided a copy of the transcript to prepare appeal.
  - Right to appeal: At the time of the case, Arizona did not give right to appeal to juveniles.
- The U.S. Supreme Court held for Gault based on four issues related to due process:
  - Notice of charges
  - Right to counsel
  - Right to confront/cross-examine witnesses
  - Protection against self-incrimination
- Right to transcript and right to appeal was not upheld.

IN RE WINSHIP

A 1970 Supreme Court case that required that a juvenile adjudication be based not on a preponderance of evidence, but on the stricter standard of proof, beyond a reasonable doubt. This is the same standard used in adult criminal cases.

14.4.3 *In re Winship* (1970)

- Winship, a 12-year-old boy, was charged with illegally entering a locker and stealing $112.
- A New York family court judge found Winship delinquent.

- Judge acknowledged to those in court that the evidence in the case might not be sufficient to establish Winship's guilt beyond a reasonable doubt.
- New York law at this time only required a preponderance of the evidence.
- Winship was sent to a training school for 18 months, subject to extensions until his eighteenth birthday.
- Winship's attorney appealed based on lower court's standard of evidence.
- U.S. Supreme Court upheld appeal, establishing proof beyond a reasonable doubt as standard in juvenile proceedings of delinquency.
- ". . . the constitutional safeguard of proof beyond a reasonable doubt is as much required during the adjudicatory stage of a delinquency proceeding as are those constitutional guards applied in *Gault*. . . . We therefore hold . . . that where a 12 year old child is charged with an act of stealing which renders him liable to confinement for as long as six years, then as a matter of due process...the case against him must be proved beyond a reasonable doubt."
- Court still allowed a preponderance of evidence in juvenile cases where juvenile is charged with a status offense.

MCKEIVER* v. *PENNSYLVANIA
A 1971 Supreme Court case that denied juveniles the right to a jury trial.

14.4.4 *McKeiver* v. *Pennsylvania* (1971)

- Joseph McKeiver, age 16, was charged with robbery, larceny, and receiving stolen property—all felonies in Pennsylvania.
- McKeiver had been involved with 20 to 30 boys who chased three other juveniles and took 25 cents from them.
- McKeiver had no prior arrests and had been employed.
- McKeiver's attorney requested a jury trial, and the request was denied.
- McKeiver was adjudicated delinquent and committed to a youth development center.
- McKeiver's attorney appealed to the U.S. Supreme Court.
- U.S. Supreme Court denied appeal, holding that jury trials for juveniles were not mandated by the Constitution.
- ". . . the imposition of the jury trial on the juvenile court system would not strengthen greatly, if at all, the fact finding function, and would contrarily, provide an attrition of the juvenile court's assumed ability to function in a unique manner. It would not remedy the defects of the system. . . . If the jury trial were to be injected into the juvenile court system as a matter of right, it would bring with it into the system

the traditional delay, the formality, and the clamor of the adversary system and, possibly, the public trial. . . . If the formalities of the criminal adjudicative process are to be superimposed upon the juvenile court system, there is little need for its separate existence."

- Even today, approximately 12 states provide the opportunity for a jury trial for juveniles.

14.4.5 ***Breed* v. *Jones*** (1975)

BREED v. JONES
A 1975 Supreme Court case that ruled that, if a juvenile is to be waived to adult court, the transfer must occur prior to a juvenile adjudicatory hearing.

- In 1971 Jones, age 17, was charged with committing a robbery while armed with a deadly weapon.
- At the adjudicatory hearing, Jones was found delinquent.
- At "dispositional hearing," Jones was found to be unfit for treatment as a juvenile.
- Jones was transferred to adult criminal court and subsequently found guilty of robbery in the first degree.
- Jones was committed to the California Youth Authority.
- Jones's attorney appealed to the Supreme Court based on issue of double jeopardy because he had already been adjudicated in juvenile court.
- U.S. Supreme Court upheld the appeal of Jones, pointing to the fact that the double jeopardy clause speaks in terms of "potential risk of trial and conviction—not punishment," and concluded that two separate adjudicatory processes were sufficient to warrant a finding of double jeopardy.
- Jones's original convictions were overturned, paving way for him to be returned to juvenile court.
- By the time the litigation against Jones was completed, he was beyond the age of juvenile court jurisdiction and was released from custody.
- *Jones* case severely restricted conditions under which transfers from juvenile to adult court may occur.

14.4.6 ***Schall* v. *Martin*** (1984)

SCHALL v. MARTIN
A 1984 Supreme Court case that upheld the right of state to put juveniles in preventive detention, but imposed procedural requirements

- Gregory Martin, age 14, was arrested in New York City and charged with robbery and weapons possession.
- Martin was detained for two weeks in a secure detention facility until his hearing.
- Martin was adjudicated a delinquent.
- Appealed to Supreme Court claiming that his detention had effectively denied his rights under the Fourteenth Amendment
- U.S. Supreme Court upheld constitutionality of New York statute.

- Court ruled that states have a legitimate interest in preventing future delinquency by juveniles thought to be dangerous.
- Pretrial detention of juveniles based on "serious risk" does not violate the principle of fundamental fairness required by due process.
- While Court upheld right of state to put juveniles in preventive detention, it did impose procedural requirements upon the detaining authority:
    - ❖ Cannot be imposed without prior notice
    - ❖ Cannot be imposed without an equitable detention hearing
    - ❖ Cannot be imposed without a statement by judge setting forth the reason(s) for detention

ILLINOIS* v. *MONTANEZ

The U.S. Supreme Court's refusal to hear this case upholding a lower court's decision that a concerned adult needs to be present during interrogation or the confession is inadmissible.

14.4.7 *Illinois* v. *Montanez* (1996)

- Eyewitness saw Montanez and two female companions laughing as Montanez forced a young male member of a rival gang into a men's room at Humboldt Park.
- Witness said a "noise like a firecracker" was heard, and saw Montanez emerge from the bathroom alone.
- Witness also saw the two other girls kill a second rival gang member and then Montanez kick the body; all three girls ran off.
- Dead were Jimmy Cruz and Hector Reyes, members of the Latin Kings. Both had been shot in the back of the head at close range.
- Police arrested Montanez, said to be the chief of the Maniac Latin Disciples, and her two companions.
- Montanez was charged as an adult and rights were read to her.
- Montanez refused a lawyer and made incriminating statements to police during the course of an eight-hour late-night interrogation.
- Her mother, who was in another part of the police station when Montanez was interrogated, was not allowed to be present during the questioning.
- Montanez's confession was admitted as evidence and she was convicted of homicide.
- Illinois Court of Appeals reversed lower court, holding that since the mother, a "concerned adult" was not allowed to be present during the interrogation, the confession is inadmissible.
- U.S. Supreme Court refused to hear the case, thereby upholding the Illinois Court of Appeals decision.

For more on juvenile's legal rights, visit Criminal Justice Interactive online > The Juvenile Justice System > Learning Modules > 14.4 Juvenile's Legal Rights.

14.5 Types of juvenile offenders

14.5.1 Noncriminal youths

- Typically come from disrupted families
- Status offenders
    - ❖ Youths who commit crimes that apply only to minors, such as truancy, running away, and violating curfew
- Dependent and neglected
    - ❖ Children who have been abandoned or neglected by their parents

14.5.2 Irresponsible offenders

- Youths who violate the law, but do not recognize the concept of crime or lack the emotional capacity to control their behavior
- Naive offenders
    - ❖ Commit illegal acts but lack the ability to form the criminal mind
    - ❖ Often are impulsive risk takers
- Emotionally disturbed
    - ❖ Children with severe psychological problems that cause uncontrollable actions or persistent behavior problems

14.5.3 Situational offender

- Commit crimes by taking advantages of event.
- Don't consider themselves delinquents.
- Property offenders
    - ❖ Participate in minor vandalism that may escalate to increasing damage and even assault.
- Violent offenders
    - ❖ Commit violent acts in response to the emotions of anger or pressure.

14.5.4 Drug and alcohol

- Recreational drug users who experiment with alcohol and various types of drugs
- Addicts
    - ❖ Individuals who are addicted to drugs and alcohol

14.5.5 Chronic offenders

- Sex offenders
    - ❖ Ranges from ogling to violent assault
    - ❖ Often had sexual experience at early age
    - ❖ Come from disrupted families.

- Prostitution
    - Often under direction of powerful adult
    - Difficult to leave after becoming involved
- Street gang members
    - Gangs create a sense of belonging.
    - Gangs create the illusion of safety.
    - Leaving a gang may risk death.

14.5.6 *Statistical Briefing Book* (2007)

- Estimated number of arrests for juveniles in 2007
    - Arrests in 2007: 2,180,500
        - This represented a 20% decrease from the number arrested in 1998.
    - Violent crime index offenses:
        - Number of arrests
            - Murder and non-negligent manslaughter: 1,350
            - Forcible rape: 3,580
            - Robbery: 34,490
            - Aggravated assault: 57,650
        - Percent arrested by gender for violent crime index offenses:
            - Female: 17%
            - Male: 83%
    - Property crime index offenses:
        - Number of arrests
            - Burglary: 81,900
            - Larceny-theft: 300,300
            - Motor-vehicle theft: 26,600
            - Arson: 7,200
        - Percent arrested by gender for property crime index offenses
            - Female: 35%
            - Male: 65%
    - Vandalism: 111,800 arrests, of which 13% were females
    - Drug abuse violations: 195,700 arrests, of which 16% were females
    - Liquor law violations: 141,000 arrests, of which 37% were female
    - Curfew and loitering: 143,000 arrests, of which 31% were female
    - Runaways: 108,900 arrests, of which 56% were female

    - Youths younger than age 15 accounted for 28% of all juvenile arrests for violent crime index offenses in 2007, and 31% of all property crime index offenses.

14.5.7 *Juvenile Offenders and Victims: 2006 National Report*

- Percent of youths reported engaging in criminal behavior by age 17
    - Suspended from school
        - Youths: 33%
        - Males: 42%
        - Females: 24%
        - Whites: 28%
        - Blacks: 56%
        - Hispanics: 38%
    - Ran away from home
        - Youths: 18%
        - Males: 17%
        - Females: 20%
        - Whites: 18%
        - Blacks: 21%
        - Hispanics: 17%
    - Belonged to a gang
        - Youths: 8%
        - Males: 11%
        - Females: 6%
        - Whites: 7%
        - Blacks: 12%
        - Hispanics: 12%
    - Vandalized
        - Youths: 37%
        - Males: 47%
        - Females: 27%
        - Whites: 39%
        - Blacks: 33%
        - Hispanics: 34%
    - Theft of less than $50
        - Youths: 43%
        - Males: 47%
        - Females: 38%
        - Whites: 44%
        - Blacks: 38%
        - Hispanics: 41%

- Theft of more than $50
  - Youths: 13%
  - Males: 16%
  - Females: 10%
  - Whites: 12%
  - Blacks: 15%
  - Hispanics: 14%
- Assaulted with the intent to seriously hurt the victim
  - Youths: 27%
  - Males: 33%
  - Females: 21%
  - Whites: 25%
  - Blacks: 36%
  - Hispanics: 28%
- Sold drugs
  - Youths: 16%
  - Males: 19%
  - Females: 12%
  - Whites: 17%
  - Blacks: 13%
  - Hispanics: 16%
- Carried a handgun
  - Youths: 16%
  - Males: 25%
  - Females: 6%
  - Whites: 16%
  - Blacks: 15%
  - Hispanics: 15%

14.5.8 *Monitoring the Future: National Results on Adolescent Drug Use* (2008)

- Juveniles who admitted to use of any illicit drug:
  - Twelfth graders: 37%
  - Tenth graders: 27%
  - Eighth graders: 14%
- Juveniles who admitted use of any illicit drug other than marijuana in the past 12 months:
  - Twelfth graders: 18%
  - Tenth graders: 11%
  - Eighth graders: 7%
  - Twenty-eight percent of eighth graders have tried some illicit drug other than marijuana.

- Marijuana
    - Eighth graders who have tried marijuana: 15%
        - Used marijuana in the prior month: 5.8%
- Alcohol use
    - Tried alcohol
        - Twelfth graders: 72%
        - Tenth graders: 58%
        - Eighth graders: 39%
            - Thirty-nine percent of eighth graders report having tried alcohol (more than just a few sips).
            - Eighteen percent of eighth graders say they have been drunk at least once.
    - Occasions of heavy drinking
        - Defined as five or more drinks in a row, at least once in the prior two week period
        - Twelfth graders: 25%
        - Tenth graders: 16%
        - Eighth graders: 8%
- Cigarette smoking
    - Eighth graders who have tried cigarettes: 21%
    - Eighth graders who have smoked in the prior month: 6.8%
    - Eighth graders (male) who have tried smokeless tobacco: 4%
- Inhalants
    - Eighth graders who reported inhalant use in just the past month: 4.1%

For more on how juveniles are processed, visit Criminal Justice Interactive online > The Juvenile Justice System > Learning Modules > 14.5 Types of Juvenile Offenders.

14.6 Explanation of delinquency

14.6.1 Social ecology

SOCIAL ECOLOGY
A criminological approach that focuses on the misbehavior of lower-class youth and sees delinquency primarily as the result of social disorganization.

- In 1920s, Clifford Shaw and Henry McKay, both on faculty in the Department of Sociology at the University of Chicago, studied the misbehavior of lower-class youths.
    - Delinquency is primarily the result of social disorganization.
- Social disorganization is a condition that exists when a group is faced with social change, uneven cultural development, maladaptiveness, disharmony, conflict, and lack of consensus.
    - Geographic areas characterized by economic deprivation had high rates of population turnover, which were seen as contributors to social disorganization.

SOCIAL DISORGANIZATION

A condition said to exist when a group is faced with social change, uneven development of culture, maladaptiveness, disharmony, conflict, and lack of consensus.

OPPORTUNITY THEORY

A perspective that sees delinquency as the result of limited legitimate opportunities for success available to most lower-class youths.

- **Social disorganization** weakened otherwise traditional societal controls, such as family life, church, jobs, and schools.

- Chicago Area Project in the 1930s was the first large-scale delinquency prevention program.
  - It grew out of the work of Shaw and McKay's research.
  - Created self-help centers staffed by community volunteers.
    - Centers offered variety of counseling services, educational programs, camps, recreational activities, and discussion groups.
    - Programs were intended to reduce social disorganization by bringing members of community together.

14.6.2 Opportunity theory

- Delinquency, as described by Lloyd E. Ohlin and Richard A. Cloward, in *Delinquency and Opportunity: A Theory of Delinquent Gangs* (1960)
  - Delinquency is the result of lack of legitimate opportunities for most lower-class youths.
  - Most serious delinquents face limited opportunities due to their inherent alienation from middle-class institutions.
  - Mobilization for Youth was a federally funded program based on delinquency and opportunity theory.
    - Program was designed to increase chances for legitimate success among lower-class youths, and included skills training, job placement services, employment programs, midnight basketball, keeping schools open in evenings for study sessions, etc.
- Delinquent boys
  - Albert K. Cohen, in *Delinquent Boys, The Culture of the Gang* (1955), claimed that delinquency, especially gang-related activity, is a response to the frustration of the lower-class youths' experience when they find they cannot share in the rewards of the middle-class lifestyle.
  - Vengeance and protest are major motivators among deprived youths.
- Techniques of neutralization
  - Gresham Sykes and David Matza, in "Techniques of Neutralization: A Theory of Delinquency," *American Sociological Review* (1957), recognized the role of choice in delinquent behavior.
  - Identified five components applied by delinquents in the following order:
    - Denial of responsibility
    - Denial of injury

        - Victim deserved what he got.
        - Condemning the condemners
        - Appeal to a higher loyalty

- Drift
    - David Matza, in *Delinquency and Drift* (1964), presented the concept that juveniles are not delinquent all of the time.
    - A delinquent typically "drifts" between conformity and law violation, and will choose violating the law when the social norms can be denied or explained away.
- Cohort analysis
    - Cohort is a group of individuals sharing similarities of age, place of birth, or residence.
    - Cohort analysis is a social science technique by which cohorts are tracked over time in order to identify unique and observable behavioral traits that characterize them.
    - Marvin Wolfgang's study in the 1960s found that a small group of individuals committed a majority of the crime.
        - The juveniles who commit these crimes are called the "chronic few."
        - Males born in Philadelphia in 1945 were studied until they reached the age of 18.
        - Eighteen percent of the cohort accounted for 52% of all arrests.
        - A follow-up study found that the seriousness of offenses among the cohort increased in adulthood, but that the actual number of offenses decreased as the cohort aged.
    - Wolfgang's cohort research has been criticized for the lack of a second cohort, or control group, against which the experiences of the cohort under study could be compared.

14.6.3 Program on causes and correlates of juvenile delinquency

- A study by the Office of Juvenile Justice and Delinquency Prevention
- The study was begun in 1986 with results reported in 1994 and 1995.
- Used data on 4,000 youths from three different projects:
    - Denver Youth Survey
    - Pittsburgh Youth Study
    - Rochester Youth Development Study
- The survey sampled high-risk juveniles for serious delinquency and drug use.

- Findings:
  - "The more seriously involved in drugs a youth was, the more seriously that juvenile was involved in delinquency."
  - "Greater risks exist for violent offending when a child is physically abused or neglected early in life."
  - "Students who were not highly committed to school had higher rates of delinquency."
  - "Poor family life exacerbates delinquency and drug use."
  - Affiliation with street gangs and illegal gun ownership are both predictive of delinquency.
  - Three separate developmental paths were identified:
    - Authority conflict pathway
      - Juveniles begin at around 3 to 4 years of age demonstrating "stubborn behavior," followed by defiance and authority avoidance—truancy, staying out late, or running away—around age 11.
    - Covert pathway
      - Begins with minor covert acts such as frequent lying and shoplifting, usually around age 10. Typically involves property damage such as firestarting or vandalism around age 11 or 12, followed by more serious forms of delinquency.
    - Overt pathway
      - Around age 11 or 12, minor aggression such as annoying others and bullying, which escalates into physical fighting and violence
  - Factors that help a juvenile so they do not become delinquent:
    - Commitment to school
    - Achievement in school
    - Continuance of education (no dropping out)
    - High levels of parental supervision
    - High levels of attachment to parents
    - Association with conventional peers, and peers approved by their parents

CHAPTER SUMMARY

- The current juvenile process has evolved from the early days as a result of changes in the attitudes of society, laws, and landmark Supreme Court decisions. Most states define juveniles as someone who has not reached their eighteenth birthday, but some states use the ages of 16 or 17. All 50 states have a judicial waiver provision that allows for juveniles who commit serious crimes to be bound over to criminal court. The system generally begins with an intake hearing in which a juvenile's behavior or alleged behavior is evaluated to determine whether or not it is in violation of the law. A preliminary hearing follows, at which point it is determined whether there is probable cause to believe the juvenile committed the alleged act. Disposition is the final stage in adjudicating juveniles, in which a decision is made on the form of treatment or a penalty is imposed. Although federal court has not set precedent regarding appeal, most states do have statutory provisions. Many claim that the juvenile system serves a group of chronic few offenders and suggest that the emphasis on privacy be lessened, that penalties should be increased for certain delinquent acts, and that diversionary opportunities for habitual, violent, and serious offenders be reduced.

- ➢ The adult system and the juvenile system are different in process and philosophy. The juvenile system emphasizes the child's best interests and treatment rather than punishment. Treatment relies on the techniques of social science. There is no long-term confinement and the juvenile is kept in facilities separate from adults. The system protects a juvenile's right to privacy and the court has broad discretionary alternatives at all points in the process.

- ➢ In the middle ages, English law adopted the notion that children under 7 could not be liable for violations and that individuals between the ages of 7 and 14 be given special status as juveniles. Children could be tried as adults only if they fully understood the nature of their criminal act. In early America, the Puritans, who emphasized obedience and discipline, influenced the way that juveniles were handled in regard to the law. Jails and prisons were used frequently for both adults and juveniles. The 1800s saw rapid social changes in America, and reform schools developed as a way to treat juvenile offenders. The juvenile court era followed, which emphasized advocacy for the child, and reformation instead of retribution. By 1945, every state had legislation focusing on juveniles. The juvenile court movement emphasized five principles: (1)The state is the ultimate parent of all children, (2) children are worth saving and nonpunitive procedures should be used, (3) children should be nurtured and protected from the stigmatizing impact of formal proceedings, (4) justice for children should be individualized, and (5) noncriminal procedures are necessary in order to give primary consideration to the needs of the child.

- ➢ A series of court decisions have created the case law around juvenile's legal rights. *Kent* v. *U.S.* established the right to a transfer hearing, right to be present at a waiver hearing, and the right to have an attorney review reports. *In re Gault* confirmed a juvenile's right to due process during confinement. *In re Winship* required that a juvenile adjudication be based not on a preponderance of evidence, but on the stricter standard of proof beyond a reasonable doubt. *McKeiver* v. *Pennsylvania* denied juveniles the right to a jury trial. *Breed* v. *Jones* established that if a juvenile is waived to adult court, the transfer has to occur prior to an adjudicatory hearing. *Schall* v. *Martin* established procedural requirements upon any authority that detained juveniles.

- ➢ There are generally five categories of juvenile offenders. Noncriminal youths typically come from disrupted families and include status offenders, who commit crimes that apply only to minors, and dependent and neglected youths, delinquents who have been abandoned or neglected by their parents. Irresponsible offenders are youths who violate the law, but do not recognize the concept of crime or lack the emotional capacity to control their behavior. They include naive offenders and those who are emotionally disturbed. Situational offenders don't generally consider themselves delinquents and commit crimes by taking advantage of some event. They include property offenders, who participate in minor vandalism, and violent offenders, who commit violent acts in response to the emotions of anger or pressure. Drug and alcohol offenders participate in drug and alcohol abuse either recreationally or because they are addicted. Chronic offenders include sex offenders, prostitutes, and street gang members.

- Explanations of delinquency include theories based in the social ecology research that suggest that delinquency is the result of social disorganization. Opportunity theory posits that delinquency results from the lack of legitimate opportunities for most lower-class youths. Techniques of neutralization identify the role of choice in delinquent behavior. Drift suggests that a delinquent typically drifts between conformity and violation of the law.

ONLINE@CRIMINAL JUSTICE INTERACTIVE

Learning Modules

14.1 How Juveniles are Processed
14.2 Differences between Adult and Juvenile Justice System
14.3 History of the Juvenile Justice Court
14.4 Juvenile's Legal Rights
14.5 Types of Juvenile Offenders

Myths and Issues Videos

Myth vs. Reality: Juvenile Boot Camps are an Effective Way of Treating Offenders
Issue 1: "Net Widening" with Regard to Juveniles
Issue 2: Transfer of Juveniles to Criminal Court and Juveniles in Adult Correctional Facilities

Simulation Activity: This section does not include a simulation.

Homework and Review

In the News
Web Activity
Review Questions
Essay Questions

Glossary

1983 lawsuit A civil suit brought under Title 42, Section 1983, of the U.S. Code against anyone who denies others their constitutional right to life, liberty, or property without due process of law.

abused child A child who has been physically, sexually, or mentally abused. Most states also consider a child who is forced into delinquent activity by a parent or guardian to be abused.

acquittal The defendant is found to be not guilty and set free. The verdict is final and uncontestable.

actus reus An act in violation of the law. Also called *guilty act*.

adjudication The process by which a court arrives at a decision regarding a case. Also called *resultant decision*.

adjudication hearing See **adjudicatory hearing**.

adjudicatory hearing The fact-finding process wherein the juvenile court determines whether there is sufficient evidence to sustain the allegations in a petition.

ADMAX Administrative maximum. The term is used by the federal government to denote ultra-high-security prisons.

administration of justice The performance of any of the following activities: detection, apprehension, detention, pretrial release, post-trial release, prosecution, adjudication, correctional supervision, or rehabilitation of accused persons or criminal offenders. Adapted from U.S. Code, Title 28, Section 20.3 (2[d]). Title 28 of the U.S. Code defines the term administration of criminal justice.

administrative law Law made and enforced by administrative/regulatory agencies either at the federal or state levels.

adverserial system The two-sided structure under which American criminal trial courts operate that pits the prosecution against the defense. In theory, justice is done when the most effective adversary is able to convince the judge or jury that his or her perspective on the case is the correct one.

aggravated assault The unlawful, intentional inflicting, or attempted or threatened inflicting, of serious injury upon the person of another. While aggravated assault and simple assault are standard terms for reporting purposes, most state penal codes use labels like first-degree and second-degree to make such distinctions.

aggravating circumstances Circumstances relating to the commission of a crime that make it more grave than the average instance of that crime. See also **mitigating circumstances**.

alibi A statement or contention by an individual charged with a crime that he or she was so distant when the crime was committed, or so engaged in other provable activities, that his or her participation in the commission of that crime is impossible.

alternative sentencing The use of court-ordered community service, home detention, day reporting, drug treatment, psychological counseling, victim–offender programming, or intensive supervision in lieu of other, more traditional sanctions, such as imprisonment and fines.

Americans with Disabilities Act Prohibits discrimination based on disability in a wide range of venues, including employment, accommodations, public services, and transportation.

anarchist criminology Seeks to demythologize the concepts behind the criminal justice system and the legal order on which it is based.

anomie A socially pervasive condition of normalessness. Also, a disjunction between approved goals and means.

anticipatory warrant Search warrants issued on the basis of probable cause to believe that evidence of a crime, while not presently at the place described, will likely be there when the warrant is executed.

appeal of right See **direct appeal**.

arraignment Strictly, the hearing before a court having jurisdiction in a criminal case in which the identity of the defendant is established, the defendant is informed of the charge and of his or her rights, and the defendant is required to enter a plea. Also, in some usages, any appearance in criminal court prior to trial.

array List of jurors who are summoned to appear for jury duty.

arrest The act of taking an adult or juvenile into physical custody by authority of law for the purpose of charging the person with a criminal offense, a delinquent act, or a status offense, terminating with the recording of a specific offense. Technically, an arrest occurs whenever a law enforcement officer curtails a person's freedom to leave.

arson The burning or attempted burning of property, with or without the intent to defraud. Some instances of arson result from malicious mischief, some involve attempts to claim insurance monies, and some are committed in an effort to disguise other crimes, such as murder, burglary, or larceny.

Articles of Confederation Ratified in 1781, represents the first governing document of the United States. States retained control of all government functions specified in the Articles of Confederation.

Ashurst-Sumners Act Federal legislation of 1935 that effectively ended the industrial prison era by restricting interstate commerce in prison-made goods.

assault An unlawful attack by one person upon another. Historically, assault meant only the attempt to inflict injury on another person; a completed act constituted the separate offense of battery. Under modern statistical usage, however, attempted and completed acts are grouped together under the generic term *assault*.

asset forfeiture See **forfeiture**.

Assize A series of ordinances initiated by King Henry II to improve procedures in criminal law.

atavism A condition characterized by the existence of features thought to be common in earlier stages of human evolution.

attachment Element of the bond of Hirschi's social control theory. This is important for creating conformity even when those others are deviant themselves.

attendant circumstances The facts surrounding an event.

Auburn system A form of imprisonment developed in New York State around 1820 that depended on mass prisons, where prisoners were held in congregate fashion and required to remain silent. This style of imprisonment was a primary competitor with the Pennsylvania system. See also **mass prison era**.

bail The money or property pledged to the court or actually deposited with the court to effect the release of a person from legal custody.

bail bondsman A person, usually licensed, whose business it is to effect release on bail for people charged with offenses and held in custody, by pledging to pay a sum of money if the defendant fails to appear in court as required. Also called *bondsman*.

bailiff An armed law enforcement officer responsible for maintaining order in the court and ensuring that the rules of court are followed.

balancing test A principle, developed by the courts and applied to the corrections arena by *Pell* v. *Procunier* (1974), that attempts to weigh the rights of an individual, as guaranteed by the Constitution, against the authority of states to make laws or to otherwise restrict a person's freedom in order to protect the state's interests and its citizens.

Beard* v. *Banks A 2006 Supreme court case that ruled that prison officials in Pennsylvania could prohibit the state's most violent inmates from receiving magazines, photographs, and newspapers sent to them in the mail.

Bearden* v. *Georgia A 1983 Supreme Court decision that indicated that probation could not be revoked because of failure to pay a fine and make restitution if it could be shown that the defendant was not responsible for the failure.

bed capacity See **design capacity**.

behavioral conditioning A psychological principle that holds that the frequency of any behavior can be increased or decreased through reward, punishment, and association with other stimuli.

belief Element of the bond of Hirschi's social control theory. Constitutes the acknowledgment of society's rules as being fair.

Bell* v. *Wolfish 1979 Supreme Court case that determined that routine strip searches were not unreasonable in prison.

Bill of Rights The first ten amendments to the U.S. Constitution. Drafted by James Madison as a response to concerns that the U.S. Constitution did not include a declaration of individual rights. U.S. Constitution identified what a government could do, but said nothing about what it could *not* do. Bill of Rights was ratified in 1791.

Biological School A perspective on criminological thought that holds that criminal behavior has a physiological basis.

biosocial theory Biological characteristics of an individual are only one part in the equation of behavior—other parts are the physical and social environment.

***Bivens* action** A civil suit, based on the case of *Bivens* v. *Six Unknown Federal Agents*, brought against federal government officials for denying the constitutional rights of others.

blended sentence A juvenile court disposition that imposes both a juvenile sanction and an adult criminal sentence on an adjudicated delinquent. The adult sentence is suspended on the condition that the juvenile offender successfully completes the term of the juvenile disposition and refrains from committing any new offense. Howard N. Snyder and Melissa Sickmund, *Juvenile Offenders and Victims: 2006 National Report* (Washington, DC: Office of Juvenile Justice and Delinquency Prevention, 2006).

Block* v. *Rutherford A 1984 Supreme Court case that established that prisoners do not have a right to be present during a search of their cells.

blood feud Term from the middle ages, in which a kinsman avenges the death of a family member by killing the murderer. Blood feuds were eventually replaced by the victim's family receiving monetary compensation instead of retaliating.

bobbies The popular British name given to members of Sir Robert (Bob) Peel's Metropolitan Police Force.

body types These theories suggest that certain physical features may result in a propensity to crime.

bond to the moral order Part of Hirschi's theory of social control that describes the ties that exists between individuals and the dominant, middle-class values of society.

bondsman A person, usually licensed, whose business it is to effect release on bail for people charged with offenses and held in custody, by pledging to pay a sum of money if the defendant fails to appear in court as required. Also called *bail bondsman*.

booking A law enforcement or correctional administrative process officially recording an entry into detention after arrest and identifying the person, the place, the time, the reason for the arrest, and the arresting authority.

Booth* v. *Churner A 2001 Supreme Court case that held that an inmate seeking only monetary damages must complete any prison administrative process capable of addressing the inmate's complaint and providing some form of relief before filing his or her grievance with a federal court, even if the process does not make specific provisions for monetary relief.

born criminal Lombroso considered this as physical inferiorities that characterized a biological throwback.

Bounds* v. *Smith A 1977 Supreme Court case that mandated that inmates have the right to correspond with their attorneys.

Bow Street Runners An early English police unit formed under the leadership of Henry Fielding, magistrate of the Bow Street region of London.

Brandon* v. *Allen 1981 failure to follow protocol case, in which an off-duty officer interrupted teens parked in a car, beat the boy, and shot the car when they drove away.

brank A birdcage-like contraption that fit over the head of the offender.

Breed* v. *Jones 1975 Supreme Court case that ruled that, if a juvenile is to be waived to adult court, the transfer must occur prior to a juvenile adjudicatory hearing.

Brideswill The first workhouse, opened in England in 1557; the term became synonymous for workhouse.

brief A document that outlines the facts of the case, the arguments of the party, and precedence-setting cases that relate to the errors being presented.

Bureau of Justice Statistics A U.S. Department of Justice agency responsible for the collection of criminal justice data, including the annual National Crime Victimization Survey.

burglary By the narrowest and oldest definition, trespassory breaking and entering of the dwelling house of another in the nighttime with the intent to commit a felony.

Burkholder* v. *City of Los Angeles 1982 case exercising poor judgment, in which an officer killed a nonaggressive man who was on drugs.

capable guardian A person, who if present, could prevent the occurrence of the crime.

capital offense A criminal offense punishable by death.

capital punishment The death penalty. Capital punishment is the most extreme of all sentencing options.

Carmelo* v. *Miller 1978 unnecessary roughness case, in which off-duty officers arrested and beat a suspect.

carnal knowledge Sexual intercourse, coitus, or sexual copulation. Carnal knowledge is accomplished "if there is the slightest penetration of the sexual organ of the female by the sexual organ of the male."

case law The body of judicial precedent, historically built on legal reasoning and past interpretations of statutory laws, that serves as a guide to decision making, especially in the courts.

caseload The number of probation or parole clients assigned to one probation or parole officer for supervision.

certiorari See **writ of *certiorari***.

chain of command The unbroken line of authority that extends through all levels of an organization, from the highest to the lowest.

challenge for cause A challenge to a jury based on a valid reason why the juror should be dismissed.

change of venue The movement of a trial or lawsuit from one jurisdiction to another or from one location to another within the same jurisdiction. A change of venue may be made in a criminal case to ensure that the defendant receives a fair trial.

character witness A witness who provides information about the quality of character or reputation of the accused or another witness.

charge to jury The judge provides the jury with a set of instructions to guide and assist their deliberation process. Minimally, the judge will tell the jury to select a foreman and objectively consider all the evidence presented. Judge may summarize the statutory elements of the alleged offense and the "reasonable doubt" standard or summarize evidence presented, or may even give his or her own opinions as to credibility of evidence or other details of the case.

Chicago School A sociological approach that emphasizes demographics (the characteristics of population groups) and geographics (the mapped location of such groups relative to one another) and that sees the social disorganization that characterizes delinquency areas as a major cause of criminality and victimization.

chivalry factor Based upon the archaic cultural stereotype that depicted women as helpless or childlike compared to men, which allegedly lessened the responsibility of female offenders in the eyes of some male judges and prosecutors, resulting in fewer prison sentences for women involved in criminal activity.

choice theory A theory that posits that individuals participate in crime after examining the advantages and disadvantages associated with the commission of the crime. See also rational choice theory.

circumstantial evidence Evidence that requires interpretation or that requires a judge or jury to reach a conclusion based on what the evidence indicates. From the proximity of the defendant to a smoking gun, for example, the jury might conclude that she pulled the trigger.

City of Canton, Ohio* v. *Harris 1989 failure to properly screen, train, or supervise staff case in which the department failed to train an officer sufficiently, resulting in a medical and psychiatric emergency of a detainee.

civil death The legal status of prisoners in some jurisdictions who are denied the opportunity to vote, hold public office, marry, or enter into contracts by virtue of their status as incarcerated felons. While civil death is primarily of historical interest, some jurisdictions still limit the contractual opportunities available to inmates.

civil law The branch of modern law that governs relationships between parties.

civil liability Holds that police officers are accountable for their behavior and protects the individual citizen from excessive or inappropriate treatment. Law enforcement departments can suffer significant financial loss when an officer fails the public trust.

Civil Rights Act of 1871 Guaranteed the slaves the right to have access to federal courts when civil rights are violated.

Civil Rights of Institutionalized Persons Act (CRIPA) of 1980 Guaranteed the slaves the right to have access to federal courts when civil rights are violated.

Classical School An eighteenth-century approach to crime causation and criminal responsibility that grew out of the Enlightenment and that emphasized the role of free will and reasonable punishments. Classical thinkers believed that punishment, if it is to be an effective deterrent, has to outweigh the potential pleasure derived from criminal behavior.

classification system A system used by prison administrators to assign inmates to custody levels based on offense history, assessed dangerousness, perceived risk of escape, and other factors.

clearance The event in which a known occurrence of a Part I offense is followed by an arrest or another decision that indicates that the crime has been solved.

clearance rate A traditional measure of investigative effectiveness that compares the number of crimes reported or discovered to the number of crimes solved through arrest or other means (such as the death of the suspect).

clerk of the court Maintains all records of criminal cases, issues summons, prepares the jury pool, subpoenas witnesses, and marks physical evidence and maintains custody of evidence.

closing arguments Each side summarizes the evidence to assist the jury in drawing conclusions favorable to their position. No new evidence is presented.

codes A collection of laws systematically organized.

codification The act or process of rendering laws in written form.

comes stabuli A nonuniformed mounted law enforcement officer of medieval England. Early police forces were small and relatively unorganized but made effective use of local resources in the formation of posses, the pursuit of offenders, and the like.

commitment Hirschi's idea that the emotional investment one builds up in conventional activities and pursuits of achievement will bond them to nondelinquent behavior

common law Law originating from usage and custom rather than from written statutes. The term refers to an unwritten body of judicial opinion, originally developed by English courts, that is based on nonstatutory customs, traditions, and precedents that help guide judicial decision making.

community corrections The use of a variety of officially ordered program-based sanctions that permit convicted offenders to remain in the community under conditional supervision as an alternative to an active prison sentence. Also called community-based corrections.

community-based era (1967–1980) Era focused on resocialization in supervised community settings since community programs were believed to be more effective than incarceration.

community court A low-level court that focuses on quality-of-life crimes that erode a neighborhood's morale, that emphasizes problem-solving rather than punishment, and that builds upon restorative principles like community service and restitution.

community policing A collaborative effort between the police and the community that identifies problems of crime and disorder and involves all elements of the community in the search for solutions to these problems.

community service A sentencing alternative that requires offenders to spend at least part of their time working for a community agency.

Comprehensive Crime Control Act An act that provided for the abolition of the Parole Commission.

concentric zones A conception of the city (Chicago) as a series of distinctive circles radiating from the central business district used to describe differences in crime rates.

concurrence The coexistence of (1) an act in violation of the law (*actus reus*) and (2) a culpable mental state (*mens rea*).

concurrent sentences Two or more sentences imposed at the same time after conviction for more than one offense, and served at the same time. Also, a new sentence for a new conviction, imposed upon a person already under sentence for a previous offense, served at the same time as the previous sentence.

conditional release The release by executive decision of a prisoner from a federal or state correctional facility who has not served his or her full sentence and whose freedom is contingent on obeying specified rules of behavior.

conditions of parole (probation) The general and special limits imposed on an offender who is released on parole (or probation). General conditions tend to be fixed by state statute, while special conditions are mandated by the sentencing authority (court or board) and take into consideration the background of the offender and the circumstances of the offense.

conflict theory A theoretical approach that holds that crime is the natural consequence of economic and other social inequities. Conflict theorists highlight the stresses that arise among and within social groups as they compete with one another for resources and for survival. The social forces that result are viewed as major determinants of group and individual behavior, including crime.

conformity Striving for socially-approved goals and following normal means of achieving them. Most people adapt this way; if not, according to Merton, the very existence of society would be threatened.

consecutive sentences Two or more sentences imposed at the same time, after conviction for more than one offense, and served in sequence with the other sentence. Also, a new sentence for a new conviction, imposed upon a person already under sentence for a previous offense, which is added to the previous sentence, thus increasing the maximum time the offender may be confined or under supervision.

constable First appeared in England after the Norman conquest of 1066. Meaning "Count of the Stable," those who held the position were responsible for maintaining the weapons of the townsfolk. Eventually became responsible for maintaining the "King's peace."

constitutive criminology The study of the process by which human beings create an ideology of crime that sustains the notion of crime as a concrete reality.

containment theory The aspects of the social bond and of the personality that act to prevent individuals from committing crimes and engaging in deviance.

contract system A system in which private businesses paid for inmate labor and supervised the manufacturing.

conviction The defendant is found to be guilty of at least one of the charges.

Cooper* v. *Pate 1964 case in which Supreme Court determined the conditions under which inmates could practice their religion while incarcerated.

Community-Oriented Policing (COP) A philosophy that promotes organizational strategies that support the systematic use of partnerships and problem-solving techniques to proactively address the immediate conditions that give rise to public safety issues.

Community Oriented Policing and Problem Solving (COPPS) Uses scientific methods to determine effective policing behaviors while identifying ways to meet community needs.

corporate crime A violation of a criminal statute either by a corporate entity or by its executives, employees, or agents acting on behalf of and for the benefit of the corporation, partnership, or other form of business entity.

corpus delicti The facts that show that a crime has occurred. The term literally means "the body of the crime."

corrections A generic term that includes all government agencies, facilities, programs, procedures, personnel, and techniques concerned with the intake, custody, confinement, supervision, treatment, and presentencing and predisposition investigation of alleged or adjudicated adult offenders, youthful offenders, delinquents, and status offenders.

corruption See police corruption. The abuse of police authority for personal or organizational gain.

court administrator A coordinator who assists with case-flow management, operating funds budgeting, and court docket administration.

court calendar The court schedule; the list of events comprising the daily or weekly work of a court, including the assignment of the time and place for each hearing or other item of business or the list of matters that will be taken up in a given court term. Also called *docket*.

court reporter Creates a written record of all that occurs during a trial. Also called *court stenographer* or *recorder*.

courtroom workgroup The professional courtroom actors, including judges, prosecuting attorneys, defense attorneys, public defenders, and others who earn a living serving the court.

crime Conduct in violation of the criminal laws of a state, the federal government, or a local jurisdiction, for which there is no legally acceptable justification or excuse.

crime-control model A criminal justice perspective that emphasizes the efficient arrest and conviction of criminal offenders.

Crime Index An inclusive measure of the violent and property crime categories, or Part I offenses, of the Uniform Crime Reports. The Crime Index has been a useful tool for geographic (state-to-state) and historical (year-to-year) comparisons because it employs the concept of a crime rate (the number of crimes per unit of population). However, the addition of arson as an eighth index offense and the new requirements with regard to the gathering of hate-crime statistics could result in new Crime Index measurements that provide less-than-ideal comparisons.

crime prevention The anticipation, recognition, and appraisal of a crime risk and the initiation of action to eliminate or reduce it.

crime rate The number of offenses reported for each unit of population. Typically reported as the number of crimes per 100,000 residents.

Crime Victims' Rights Act of 2004 Enunciated rights applicable to all victims of crimes such as: protection from accused, timely notice of court proceedings, participation in court proceedings, confer with an attorney, timely resolution, and respect, privacy and fairness.

criminal homicide (UCR/NIBRS) The act of causing the death of another person without legal justification or excuse.

criminal intelligence Information compiled, analyzed, and/or disseminated in an effort to anticipate, prevent, or monitor criminal activity. Office of Justice Programs, *The National Criminal Intelligence Sharing Plan* (Washington, DC: U.S. Department of Justice, 2005), p. 27.

criminal justice In the strictest sense, the criminal (penal) law, the law of criminal procedure, and the array of procedures and activities having to do with the enforcement of this body of law. Criminal justice cannot be separated from social justice because the kind of justice enacted in our nation's criminal courts is a reflection of basic American understandings of right and wrong.

criminal justice funnel A visual representation of the number of crimes and offenders who proceed through the criminal justice system.

criminal justice system The aggregate of all operating and administrative or technical support agencies that perform criminal justice functions. The basic divisions of the operational aspects of criminal justice are law enforcement, courts, and corrections.

criminal law The branch of modern law that concerns itself with offenses committed against society, its members, their property, and the social order. Also called *penal law*.

criminal negligence Behavior in which a person fails to reasonably perceive substantial and unjustifiable risks of dangerous consequences.

criminal procedure Rules and laws intended to guard against discrimination in the application of justice for those accused of a crime. The U.S. Constitution through the Fourth, Fifth, Sixth, and Eighth Amendments provide the foundations for basic criminal procedure. The part of the law that specifies the methods to be used in enforcing substantive law.

criminal subculture The primary focus would be on profit-making activities, and violence would be minimal; criminal "trades" would be practiced under the loose supervision of organized crime.

criminology The scientific study of the causes and prevention of crime and the rehabilitation and punishment of offenders.

critical criminology See **radical criminoloogy**.

Cruz* v. *Beto 1972 Supreme Court case that confirmed that an inmate's religious choice need not be limited to a conventional or traditional one to be allowed.

cultural deviance A theoretical perspective that posits that in neighborhoods where disorganization exists lower-class cultures will develop.

curtilage a legal term describing the enclosed area of land around a dwelling.

D.A.R.E. Drug Abuse Resistance Education program founded in 1983 in Los Angeles, California. A police officer led series of classroom lectures for school children grades kindergarten through 12th.

dark figure of crime Crime that is not reported to the police and that remains unknown to officials.

day fine Fines should be proportionate to the severity of the offense, while at the same time taking into account the financial resources of the offender.

deadly force Force likely to cause death or great bodily harm. Also, "the intentional use of a firearm or other instrument resulting in a high probability of death."

deconstructionist theory One of the emerging approaches that challenges existing criminological perspectives to debunk them, and that works toward replacing them with concepts more applicable to the postmodern era.

defendant Individuals who stand accused of committing a criminal offense.

defense attorney A licensed trial lawyer hired or appointed to conduct the legal defense of a person accused of a crime and to represent him or her before a court of law. See **defense counsel**.

defense counsel A licensed trial lawyer hired or appointed to conduct the legal defense of a person accused of a crime. The Sixth Amendment of the U.S. Constitution guarantees all defendants, regardless of their financial means, the right to effective assistance of defense counsel. See also **defense attorney**.

defensible space theory The belief that an area's physical features may be modified and structured so as to reduce crime rates in that area and to lower the fear of victimization that residents experience.

deliberate indifference A wanton disregard by correctional personnel for the well-being of inmates. Deliberate indifference requires both actual knowledge that harm is occurring and having disregard of the risk of harm. A prison official may be held liable under the Eighth Amendment for acting with deliberate indifference to inmate health or safety only if he or she knows that inmates face a substantial risk of serious harm and disregards that risk by failing to take reasonable measures to abate it.

delinquency In the broadest usage, juvenile actions or conduct in violation of criminal law, juvenile status offenses, and other juvenile misbehavior.

delinquent A juvenile who has been adjudged by a judicial officer of a juvenile court to have committed a delinquent act.

delinquent act An act committed by a juvenile for which an adult could be prosecuted in a criminal court, but for which a juvenile can be adjudicated in a juvenile court or prosecuted in a court having criminal jurisdiction if the juvenile court transfers jurisdiction. Generally, a felony- or misdemeanor-level offense in states employing those terms.

delinquent child A child who has engaged in activity that would be considered a crime if the child were an adult. The term delinquent is used to avoid the stigma associated with the term criminal.

dependent child A child who has no parents or whose parents are unable to care for him or her.

deposit bail An amount of money, usually 10% of the bail, that is placed with the court. Bail is returned, minus a small fee if the accused shows up for court proceedings. If the individual does not show, the whole amount is forfeited.

deprivation model Prison subculture is an adaption to the deprivation.

design capacity The number of inmates a prison was intended to hold when it was built or modified. Also called *bed capacity*.

detention hearing Circumstances are examined to determine if detention is necessary for the safety of the public, or if there are good reasons to release the arrestee until trial. In juvenile justice usage, a hearing by a judicial officer of a juvenile court to determine whether a juvenile is to be detained, is to continue to be detained, or is to be released while juvenile proceedings are pending.

determinate sentencing A model of criminal punishment in which an offender is given a fixed term that may be reduced by good time or gain time. Under the model, for example, all offenders convicted of the same degree of burglary would be sentenced to the same length of time behind bars. Also called *fixed sentencing*.

deterrence A goal of criminal sentencing that seeks to inhibit criminal behavior through the fear of punishment.

Dettmer* v. *Landon A 1985 Supreme Court case that held that a prisoner who claimed to practice witchcraft must be provided with the artifacts necessary for his worship.

differential association A theory developed by Edwin Sutherland that states that crime is learned in primary groups.

differential identification Daniel Glaser's addition to differential association suggests the degree and strength of identification with another person is key to learning values.

differential reinforcement Key to C. Ray Jeffery's learning theory, which says people have different conditioning histories and therefore, learn differently.

digital criminal forensics The lawful seizure, acquisition, analysis, reporting, and safeguarding of data from digital devices that may contain information of evidentiary value to the trier of fact in criminal events.

diminished capacity A defense based on claims of a mental condition that may be insufficient to exonerate the defendant of guilt but that may be relevant to specific mental elements of certain crimes or degrees of crime. Also called *diminished responsibility*.

direct appeal When consequences of error are so significant that appellate courts are mandated to review them, as in capital punishment sentences. Also called *appeal of right*.

direct evidence Evidence that, if believed, directly proves a fact. Eyewitness testimony and videotaped documentation account for the majority of all direct evidence heard in the criminal courtroom.

direct patrol A police-management strategy designed to increase the productivity of patrol officers through the scientific analysis and evaluation of patrol techniques.

direct-supervision jail A temporary confinement facility that eliminates many of the traditional barriers between inmates and correctional staff. Physical barriers in direct-supervision jails are far less common than in traditional jails, allowing staff members the opportunity for greater interaction with, and control over, residents. Also, new-generation jail; podular direct jail.

discretion The ability of an individual to use personal/professional judgment in handling a situation. For example, a police officer can choose to warn an individual or arrest an individual. If the officer arrests the individual, the officer often has the ability to decide what offense with which to charge the individual. A prosecutor has the ability to decide which cases he or she will take to trial and which he or she will dismiss.

discretionary appeal This type of appeal is filed by the appellant based on specific errors in a case. The appellant may appeal if there are legal grounds to imply the laws were improperly applied to the facts of the case.

discretionary parole Boards grant parole based on their member's assessment of the offender or his or her capability of being successful in the outside world.

discretionary release The release of an inmate from prison to supervision that is decided by a parole board or other authority.

discretionary waiver A waiver in which discretion is given to juvenile court judges to transfer jurisdiction in individual cases involving minors so as to allow prosecution in adult criminal courts.

disposition The final stage in processing of adjudicated juveniles, in which a decision is made on the form of treatment or penalty that should be imposed.

dispositional hearing The final stage in the processing of adjudicated juveniles in, which a decision is made on the form of treatment or penalty that should be imposed on the child.

dispute-resolution center An informal hearing place designed to mediate interpersonal disputes without resorting to the more formal arrangements of a criminal trial court.

diversion The official suspension of criminal or juvenile proceedings against an alleged offender at any point after a recorded justice system intake, but before the entering of a judgment, and referral of that person to a treatment or care program administered by a nonjustice or private agency. Also, release without referral.

docket The court schedule; the list of events comprising the daily or weekly work of a court, including the assignment of the time and place for each hearing or other item of business or the list of matters that will be taken up in a given court term. See also **court calendar**.

double jeopardy A common law and constitutional prohibition against a second trial for the same offense.

drift A state of limbo that makes deviant acts possible.

Drug Enforcement Administration (DEA) Drug Enforcement Administration was created by President Nixon in 1973 to establish a single unified command to combat an all-out global war on drugs.

ducking stool A see-saw device onto which an offender was tied, lowered into a river, and then turned upside down.

due process A right guaranteed by the Fifth, Sixth, and Fourteenth Amendments of the U.S. Constitution and generally understood, in legal contexts, to mean the due course of legal proceedings according to the rules and forms established for the protection of individual rights. In criminal proceedings, due process of law is generally understood to include the following basic elements: a law creating and defining the offense, an impartial tribunal having jurisdictional authority over the case, accusation in proper form, notice and opportunity to defend, trial according to established procedure, and discharge from all restraints or obligations unless convicted.

due process model A criminal justice perspective that emphasizes individual rights at all stages of justice system processing.

Duncan* v. *Barnes 1979 negligence case in which officers violently entered the wrong home and held occupants in humiliating circumstances while they searched for drugs.

duress A legal defense in which the defendant claims he or she was compelled to take part in a crime by others.

Edwards* v. *Balisok A 1997 Supreme Court case that held that prisoners cannot sue for monetary damages for loss of good time until they sue in state court and get their disciplinary conviction set aside.

Eighth Amendment Guarantees the right against excessive bail. Provides protection from cruel and unusual punishment including housing conditions and medical care.

Electronic Communications Privacy Act (ECPA) A law passed by Congress in 1986 establishing the due process requirements that law enforcement officers must meet in order to legally intercept wire communications.

electronic evidence Information and data of investigative value that are stored in or transmitted by an electronic device.

electronic monitoring Devices attached to a probationer or parolee that can provide documentation of the offender's location.

Elmira Reformatory Zebulon Brockway as warden of the Elmira Reformatory tried to humanize prison life and make a prisoner more fit for society. Merged ideas of reformation, early release, and supervision by nonpolice agents into the earliest form of parole in the United States.

emergency search A search conducted by the police without a warrant, which is justified on the basis of some immediate and overriding need, such as public safety, the likely escape of a dangerous suspect, or the removal or destruction of evidence.

emergent theory Theories of crime that focus on gender, social construct, and evolving views of what causes criminal behavior. Feminist, constitutive, and postmodern criminology are examples of the emergent perspective.

entrapment An improper or illegal inducement to crime by agents of law enforcement. Also, a defense that may be raised when such inducements have occurred.

equity A sentencing principle, based on concerns with social equality, that holds that similar crimes should be punished with the same degree of severity, regardless of the social or personal characteristics of the offenders.

Escoe* v. *Zerbst A 1935 Supreme Court case in which the court held that probation "comes as an act of grace to one convicted of crime," and that revocation of probation with hearing or notice to the probationer is acceptable practice.

Estelle* v. *Gamble 1976 Supreme Court case that established inmates' rights to medical treatment while incarcerated.

evidence-based policing (EBP) The use of the best available research on the outcomes of police work to implement guidelines and evaluate agencies, units, and officers.

excessive force The application of an amount and/or frequency of force greater than that required to compel compliance from a willing or unwilling subject.

exclusionary eule The understanding based on U.S. Supreme Court precedent that incriminating information must be seized according to constitutional specifications of due process or it will not be allowed as evidence in a criminal trial.

exculpatory evidence Any information having a tendency to clear a person of guilt or blame.

exigent circumstance Situations in which police are allowed to search a structure without a warrant. This situation includes those when someone is in imminent danger or when there is the possibility of evidence being destroyed. Prompt action is necessary by law enforcement.

Ex parte Crouse A court decision that clarified the power that states had in committing children to institutions.

expert witnesses Witnesses who have special knowledge and skills recognized by the court. They are allowed to express opinions and draw conclusions within their area of expertise. Types of expert witnesses include doctors, psychologists, ballistic specialists, etc.

eyewitness A witness who testifies to having actually seen or experienced some element related to the crime process that either confirms or negates the culpability of the accused.

factual guilt Guilt that deals with the issue of whether the defendant is actually responsible for the crime.

Farmer* v. *Brennan A 1994 Supreme Court case that clarified the concept of deliberate indifference by holding that it required both actual knowledge and disregard of risk of harm.

Federal Victim and Witness Protection Act of 1983 Provided a greater role for victims and witnesses of federal offenses and improved protection.

felony A criminal offense punishable by death or by incarceration in a prison facility for at least one year.

feminist criminology Examines how women are treated differently from men in a society dominated by male power structures. Feminists employ the concept of gender, which argues that society has different expectations of females and males. Feminist criminology includes liberal feminism, radical feminism, and socialist feminism.

Fifth Amendment Provides for protections against double jeopardy and against a defendant being compelled in any criminal case to be a witness against himself, or for a defendant being deprived of life, liberty, or property, without due process of law.

filing The initiation of a criminal case by formal submission to the court of a charging document, alleging that a named person has committed a specified criminal offense.

fine The penalty imposed on a convicted person by a court, requiring that he or she pay a specified sum of money to the court.

First Amendment Congress shall make no law respecting an establishment of religion, or prohibiting the free exercise thereof; or abridging the freedom of speech, or of the press; or the right of the people peaceably to assemble, and to petition the Government for a redress of grievances.

first appearance An appearance before a magistrate during which the legality of the defendant's arrest is initially assessed and the defendant is informed of the charges on which he or she is being held. At this stage in the criminal justice process, bail may be set or pretrial release arranged. Also called *initial appearance*.

fixed sentencing A model of criminal punishment in which an offender is given a fixed term of imprisonment that may be reduced by good time or gain time. Under the model, for example, all offenders convicted of the same degree of burglary would be sentenced to the same length of time behind bars. See also **determinate sentencing**.

fleeting-targets exception An exception to the exclusionary rule that permits law enforcement officers to search a motor vehicle based on probable cause and without a warrant. The fleeting-targets exception is predicated on the fact that vehicles can quickly leave the jurisdiction of a law enforcement agency.

focal concerns A theory developed by Walter B. Miller in which the emphasis on specific values contributes to the involvement in delinquency by members of the lower class. The six focal concerns identified by Miller include: trouble, toughness, smartness, excitement, fate, and autonomy.

forcible rape The carnal knowledge of a female forcibly and against her will. For statistical reporting purposes, the FBI defines forcible rape as "unlawful sexual intercourse with a female, by force and against her will, or without legal or factual consent." Statutory rape differs from forcible rape in that it generally involves nonforcible sexual intercourse with a minor. See also **carnal knowledge** and **rape**.

forfeiture The authorized seizure of money, negotiable instruments, securities, or other things of value. Under federal antidrug laws, judicial representatives are authorized to seize all cash, negotiable instruments, securities, or other things of value furnished or intended to be furnished by any person in exchange for a controlled substance, as well as all proceeds traceable to such an exchange. Also called *asset forfeiture*.

Fourth Amendment Provides right for people to be secure in their persons, houses, papers, and effects against unreasonable searches and seizures.

free will Individuals choose to engage in crime after considering various courses of action and then selecting the one he or she believes is the most desirable.

fruit of the poisoned tree doctrine Doctrine based on the case *Silverthorne Lumber Co.* v. *U.S.* (1920), which posits that if the source of evidence is illegal then any evidence that results from the illegal search cannot be used since it is tainted.

Gagnon* v. *Scarpelli A 1973 Supreme Court decision that established that probationers were entitled to two hearings: preliminary hearing and a more comprehensive hearing, prior to making the final revocation decision.

gain time The amount of time deducted from time to be served in prison on a given sentence as a consequence of participation in special projects or programs.

general deterrence A goal of criminal sentencing that seeks to prevent others from committing crimes similar to the one for which a particular offender is being sentenced by making an example of the person sentenced.

general strain Agnew's theory that strain exists at the individual level, primarily in unavoidable, undesirable and stressful situations

Gilliam* v. *Fabo 1982 unnecessary roughness case in which officers at a police station beat a detainee.

good time The amount of time deducted from time to be served in prison on a given sentence as a consequence of good behavior.

good-faith exception An exception to the exclusionary rule. Law enforcement officers who conduct a search or who seize evidence on the basis of good faith (that is, when they believe they are operating according to the dictates of the law), and who later discover that a mistake was made (perhaps in the format of the application for a search warrant) may still provide evidence that can be used in court.

grand jury A group of jurors who have been selected according to law and have been sworn to hear the evidence and to determine whether there is sufficient evidence to bring the accused person to trial to investigate criminal activity generally, or to investigate the conduct of a public agency or official.

grass eaters Police officers who accept bribes or goods for not issuing tickets, making arrests, etc. These officers do not initiate the corrupt activity, but do not refuse it when offered.

Greenholtz* v. *Nebraska A 1979 Supreme Court decision that established that parole boards do not have to specify the evidence used in deciding to deny parole.

grievance procedure A formalized arrangement, usually involving a neutral hearing board, whereby institutionalized individuals have the opportunity to register complaints about the conditions of their confinement.

Griffin* v. *Wisconsin A 1987 Supreme Court case that ruled that probation officers may conduct searches of a probationer's residence without the need for either a search warrant or probable cause.

Grummett* v. *Rushen 1984 Supreme Court case that determined that female correctional officers could be allowed to supervise male inmates, with minimal accommodations, without violating the inmates' right to privacy.

Guajardo* v. *Estelle A 1977 Supreme Court case that mandated that the prison must provide stamps.

guilty act See ***actus reus***.

guilty but mentally ill (GBMI) A verdict, equivalent to a finding of "guilty," that establishes that the defendant, although mentally ill, was in sufficient possession of his or her faculties to be morally blameworthy for his or her acts.

habitual offender A person sentenced under the provisions of a statute declaring that people convicted of a given offense and shown to have previously been convicted of another specified offense shall receive a more severe penalty than that for the current offense alone.

Haley* v. *Ohio 1948 Supreme Court case that prohibited the use of coerced confessions by juveniles.

halfway house Temporary living situations provide a way for newly released offender to "ease in" to living in the outside world. When in the halfway house, the offender is still under the control of the justice system.

Hamilton* v. *Schiriro 1996 Supreme Court case that allowed Native American inmates the right to sweat lodges.

hands-off doctrine A policy of nonintervention with regard to prison management that U.S. courts tended to follow until the late 1960s. For the past 40 years, the doctrine has languished as judicial intervention in prison administration dramatically increased, although there is now some evidence that a new hands-off era is approaching.

harmless error rule A rule that states that there may be no grounds for appeal, even when evidence is improperly introduced at trial.

hate crime A criminal offense committed against a person, property, or society that is motivated, in whole or in part, by the offender's bias against a race, religion, disability, sexual orientation, or ethnicity/national origin.

Hawes-Cooper Act An act that required prison-made goods conform to the regulations of states through which they were shipped.

Haygood* v. *City of Detroit 1980 exercising poor judgment case in which officers beat and verbally abused a detainee, and used racist slurs during the incident.

hearsay Something that is not based on the personal knowledge of a witness. Witnesses who testify about something they have heard, for example, are offering hearsay by repeating information about a matter of which they have no direct knowledge.

hearsay rule The long-standing precedent that hearsay cannot be used in American courtrooms. Rather than accepting testimony based on hearsay, the court will ask that the person who was the original source of the hearsay information be brought in to be questioned and cross-examined. Exceptions to the hearsay rule may occur when the person with direct knowledge is dead or is otherwise unable to testify.

hedonism The major explanation for human behavior during the eighteenth century; the concept that people would automatically attempt to maximize pleasure and minimize pain.

hedonistic calculus The notion that individuals calculate whether the benefits of committing the crime outweigh the possible penalties.

Helling* v. *McKinney A 1993 Supreme Court case that indicated prison officials are responsible for correcting environmental conditions of prison life that pose a threat to inmate health.

hierarchy rule A pre-NIBRS Uniform Crime Reporting Program scoring practice in which only the most serious offense was counted in a multiple-offense incident.

highway patrol See **state highway patrol**.

Hill* v. *Blackwell A Supreme Court case that established that the prison regulations prohibiting the wearing of beards, even those grown for religious purposes, were held acceptable because of security considerations.

Holt* v. *Sarver 1970 Supreme Court case that created the concept of reasonable sensitivity, the first standard to measure "cruel and unusual punishment."

home confinement House arrest. Individuals ordered confined to their homes are sometimes monitored electronically to ensure they do not leave during the hours of confinement. Absence from the home during working hours is often permitted.

homicide The act of causing the death of another person without legal justification or excuse. See **criminal homicide**.

Houchins* v. *KQED, Inc. A 1978 Supreme Court case that established that news personnel cannot be denied correspondence with prisoners, but they have no constitutional right to interview prisoners or to inspect correctional opportunities available to others.

house arrest Individuals ordered confined to their homes are sometimes monitored electronically to ensure they do not leave during the hours of confinement. Absence from the home during working hours is often permitted.

***Hudud* crime** A serious violation of Islamic law that is regarded as an offense against God. *Hudud* crimes include such behavior as theft, adultery, sodomy, alcohol consumption, and robbery.

Hudson* v. *Palmer 1984 Supreme Court case that held that searches of inmates in a prison did not constitute unreasonable behavior.

hue and cry During medieval times, the method used to alert townspeople of the occurrence of a crime. Anyone within hearing distance was required to give pursuit to apprehend the offender. If the offender was not able to be apprehended, the townspeople were fined by the King.

hundred In England during medieval times the hundred represented the grouping of ten tithings (ten families to each tithing) for purposes of maintaining order in a community.

hung jury A jury that, after long deliberation, is so irreconcilably divided in opinion that it is unable to reach any verdict. This is a mistrial and the prosecutor may choose to try the case again.

illegal search and seizure An act in violation of the Fourth Amendment of the U.S. Constitution, which reads, "The right of the people to be secure in their persons, houses, papers, and effects, against unreasonable searches and seizures, shall not be violated, and no Warrants shall issue, but upon probable cause, supported by Oath or affirmation, and particularly describing the place to be searched, and the persons or things to be seized."

illegally seized evidence Evidence seized without regard to the principles of due process as described by the Bill of Rights. Most illegally seized evidence is the result of police searches conducted without a proper warrant or of improperly conducted interrogations.

Illinois* v. *Montanez The U.S. Supreme Court's refusal to hear this case upholding a lower court's decision that a concerned adult needs to be present during interrogation or the confession is inadmissible.

importation model Inmates bring with them to prison the specific values, roles, and behaviors from the outside world.

In re Caulk A 1984 Supreme Court case that held that prisoners can be forced to take medications in an emergency situation against their will.

In re Gault 1967 Supreme Court case that confirmed a juvenile's right to due process during confinement.

In re Harrell A 1970 Supreme Court case that allowed inmates to meet with counsel for a reasonable length of time.

In re Winship 1970 Supreme Court case that required that a juvenile adjudication be based not on a preponderance of evidence, but on the stricter standard of proof, beyond a reasonable doubt. This is the same standard used in adult criminal cases.

incapacitance The use of imprisonment or other means to reduce the likelihood that an offender will commit future offenses.

incapacitation The use of imprisonment or other means to reduce the likelihood that an offender will commit future offenses.

incarceration An expensive sentencing option that removes dangerous persons from the general public so they are no longer able to continue their criminal activities and the community is better protected.

inchoate offense An offense not yet completed. Also, an offense that consists of an action or conduct that is a step toward the intended commission of another offense.

incident-based reporting Compared with summary reporting, a less restrictive and more expansive method of collecting crime data in which all of the analytical elements associated with an offense or arrest are compiled by a central collection agency on an incident-by-incident basis.

indentured servants Transported felons, from England to the colonies, who were auctioned to the highest bidder to work off their literal debt to the new master who had purchased their labor. Upon completion of the term of obligation (often seven years), the felon became a free citizen.

indeterminate sanctions The use of less, or nontraditional sentences in lieu of imprisonment; sometimes called "alternative sentencing" strategies.

indeterminate sentencing A model of criminal punishment that encourages rehabilitation through the use of general and relatively unspecific sentences (such as a term of imprisonment of from one to ten years).

index crime A now defunct but once inclusive measure of the UCR Program's violent and property crime categories, or what are called Part I offenses. The Crime Index, long featured in the FBI's publication *Crime in the United States*, was discontinued in 2004. The index had been intended as a tool for geographic (state-to-state) and historical (year-to-year) comparisons via the use of crime rates (the number of crimes per unit of population). However, criticism that the index was misleading arose after researchers found that the largest of the index's crime categories, larceny-theft, carried undue weight and led to an underappreciation of changes in the rates of more violent and serious crimes. See **Crime Index**.

indictment A formal, written accusation submitted to the court by a grand jury, alleging that a specified person has committed a specified offense, usually a felony.

individual rights The rights guaranteed to all members of American society by the U.S. Constitution (especially those found in the first ten amendments to the Constitution, known as the Bill of Rights). These rights are particularly important to criminal defendants facing formal processing by the criminal justice system.

industrial era Prisoners served as cheap labor while learning a trade. States were able to generate income from labor, and there was great potential for exploitation of the workers.

information A formal written accusation submitted to the court by a prosecutor, alleging that a specified person has committed a specific offense.

infraction A minor violation of state statute or local ordinance punishable by a fine or other penalty or by a specified, usually limited, term of incarceration.

initial appearance An appearance before a magistrate during which the legality of the defendant's arrest is initially assessed and the defendant is informed of the charges on which he or she is being held. At this stage in the criminal justice process, bail may be set or pretrial release arranged. See also **first appearance**.

innovation A case of adaptation in which the emphasis on the approved goals of society is maintained while legitimate means are replaced by other, nonapproved means.

insanity defense A legal defense based on claims of mental illness or mental incapacity.

institutional strain Anomie produced by the weakening of social institutions such as family, schools, religion, and law.

intake The first step in decision making regarding a juvenile whose behavior or alleged behavior is in violation of the law or could otherwise cause a juvenile court to assume jurisdiction.

intelligence-led policing The collection and analysis of information to produce an intelligence end product designed to inform police decision making at both the tactical and strategic levels. Angus Smith, ed., *Intelligence-Led Policing* (Richmond, VA: International Association of Law Enforcement Intelligence Analysts, 1997), p. 1.

intensive probation supervision (IPS) Form of probation supervision involving frequent face-to-face contact between the probationer and the probation officer.

interlocutory appeal Filed when a judge's decision so impacts the case in progress that to wait to the end of the trial would significantly violate or damage the case.

intermediate sanctions The use of split sentencing, shock probation or parole, shock incarceration, community service, intensive supervision, or home confinement in lieu of other, more traditional, sanctions, such as imprisonment and fines. Also called *alternative sanctions*.

internal affairs The branch of a police organization tasked with investigating charges of wrongdoing involving members of the department.

interrogation The information-gathering activity of police officers that involves the direct questioning of suspects.

involvement Hirschi's element of the bond of social control that measures the degree of activity available for conventional or unconventional behavior.

Irish System Penal Servitude Act passed by Parliament in 1853 allowed the release of well-behaved felons. Sir Walter Crofton adopted ideas from Norfolk Island and the "ticket of leave" concept into the Irish prison system.

Islamic Law A system of laws, operative in some Arab countries, based on the Muslim religion and especially the holy book of Islam, the Koran.

jail A confinement facility administered by an agency of local government, typically a law enforcement agency, intended for adults but sometimes also containing juveniles, which holds people detained pending adjudication or committed after adjudication, usually those sentenced to a year or less.

Johnson* v. *Avery 1969 Supreme Court case that affirmed that inmates must have full access to the legal system, and may also have legal assistance, including consultation with other inmates.

Johnson* v. *Phelan 1995 Supreme Court case that confirmed that opposite sex correctional officers could conduct searches.

Jones* v. *North Carolina Prisoner's Labor Union 1977 Supreme Court case that confirmed a ban on union activities within a prison work environment.

judge Ultimate authority in the courtroom. Safeguards both rights of accused and interests of the public. Determines guilt or innocence of defendant where trial is not before a jury.

jurisdiction The territory, subject matter, or people over which a court or other justice agency may exercise lawful authority, as determined by statute or constitution. See also venue.

jurisprudence The philosophy of law. Also, the science and study of the law.

juror A member of a trial or grand jury who has been selected for jury duty and is required to serve as an arbiter of the facts in a court of law. Jurors are expected to render verdicts of "guilty" or "not guilty" as to the charges brought against the accused, although they may sometimes fail to do so (as in the case of a hung jury).

jury Determines guilt or innocence of a defendant based on the facts presented at a trial. Article II of the U.S. Constitution requires that "[t]he trial of all crimes . . . shall be by jury."

jury selection The process whereby, according to law and precedent, members of a trial jury are chosen.

just desserts A model of criminal sentencing that holds that criminal offenders deserve the punishment they receive at the hands of the law and that punishments should be appropriate to the type and severity of the crime committed.

just desserts era (1995–present) New "get-tough" and zero-tolerance initiatives increased mandatory sentences for violent crimes. Shift from deterrence to punishment with incarceration being a natural consequence for committing crimes. Also included a reduced use of parole.

justice The principle of fairness; the ideal of moral equity.

justice model A contemporary model of imprisonment based on the principle of just desserts.

justice of the peace Edward III of England, in 1861, created the title of justice of the peace. Originally, in 1327, an act identified "good and lawful" individuals to be appointed to "guard the peace."

justification A legal defense in which the defendant admits to committing the act in question but claims it was necessary in order to avoid some greater evil.

juvenile A person subject to juvenile court proceedings because a statutorily defined event or condition caused by or affecting that person was alleged to have occurred while his or her age was below the statutorily specified age limit of original jurisdiction of a juvenile court.

juvenile court A court that has, as all or part of its authority, original jurisdiction over matters concerning people statutorily defined as juveniles.

juvenile disposition The decision of a juvenile court, concluding a dispositional hearing, that an adjudicated juvenile be committed to a juvenile correctional facility; be placed in a juvenile residence, shelter, or care or treatment program; be required to meet certain standards of conduct; or be released.

juvenile justice system Government agencies that function to investigate, supervise, adjudicate, care for, or confine youthful offenders and other children subject to the jurisdiction of the juvenile court.

juvenile petition A document filed in juvenile court alleging that a juvenile is a delinquent, a status offender, or a dependent and asking that the court assume jurisdiction over the juvenile or that an alleged delinquent be transferred to a criminal court for prosecution as an adult.

Kansas City Experiment The first large-scale scientific study of law enforcement practices. Sponsored by the Police Foundation, it focused on the practice of preventive patrol.

Kelly* v. *Robinson A 1986 Supreme Court decision that held that an individual cannot avoid having to make restitution by filing bankruptcy.

Kent* v. *U.S. 1967 Supreme Court case that established the following rights for juveniles being transferred to adult court: right to a transfer hearing; right to be present at a waiver hearing; right to have attorney review reports; judge must state the reasons for transfer.

Knapp Commission A committee that investigated police corruption in New York City in the early 1970s.

labeling theory A social process perspective that sees continued crime as a consequence of the limited opportunities for acceptable behavior that follow from the negative responses of society to those defined as offenders.

landmark case A precedent-setting court decision that produces substantial changes in both the understanding of the requirements of due process and in the practical day-to-day operations of the justice system.

larceny-theft (UCR/NIBRS) The unlawful taking or attempted taking, carrying, leading, or riding away of property, from the possession or constructive possession of another. Motor vehicles are excluded. Larceny is the most common of the eight major offenses, although probably only a small percentage of all larcenies are actually reported to the police because of the small dollar amounts involved.

latent evidence Evidence of relevance to a criminal investigation that is not readily seen by the unaided eye.

law A rule of conduct, generally found enacted in the form of a statute, that proscribes or mandates certain forms of behavior. Statutory law is often the result of moral enterprise by interest groups that, through the exercise of political power, are successful in seeing their valued perspectives enacted into law.

law enforcement The generic name for the activities of the agencies responsible for maintaining public order and enforcing the law, particularly the activities of preventing, detecting, and investigating crime and apprehending criminals.

Law Enforcement Code of Ethics Originally created in 1909 by August Vollmer, chief of police, Berkely, California, as a pledge against participating in corrupt acts or accepting gratuities.

lay witness An eyewitness, character witness, or other person who is not considered an expert.

lease system A system in which prisoners are taken outside of prison to work under the supervision of armed guards.

left realism The basic notion represents a deviation from the Marxist view that all crime is a product of the capitalist system.

legal guilt Guilt that is established sufficient to convince the judge or jury that the defendant is guilty as charged.

legalistic style A style of policing marked by a strict concern with enforcing the precise letter of the law. Legalistic departments may take a hands-off approach to disruptive or problematic behavior that does not violate the criminal law.

less-lethal weapons A weapon that is designed to disable, capture, or immobilize—but not kill—a suspect. Occasional deaths do, however, result from the use of such weapons.

Lewis* v. *Casey A case that overturned *Bounds* v. *Smith*, and claimed that prisoners are not guaranteed to file any and every type of legal claim, but requires that they be provided with the tools to attack their sentences and conditions of confinement.

lex talionis Taken from Hammurabi's Code, approximately 210 B.C.E., that delineated both crimes and punishments. The law of retaliation, based on the concept of an "eye for an eye, a tooth for a tooth."

liberal feminism This perspective in criminology focused on gender discrimination and women's liberation.

life course perspective Developmental theory concept that individuals and their influencing factors change over time, usually in patterned ways

magistrate A judge for a low-level court that has very limited jurisdiction. Magistrate often is not required to have a law degree and handles minor criminal and civil matters.

major crimes See **Part I offenses**.

***mala en se* crimes** Acts that are regarded, by tradition and convention, as wrong in themselves.

***mala prohibita* crimes** Acts that are considered wrong only because there is a law against them.

Malley* v. *Briggs 1986 failure to follow protocol case in which an officer knowingly obtained an improperly supported warrant.

Mallery* v. *Lewis A 1983 Supreme Court case that ruled that magazines that depict deviant sexual behavior can be banned in prisons.

mandatory parole Sometimes called conditional release, legislation that mandates supervised release under specific conditions such as the completion of a percentage of the prison sentence.

mandatory release The release of an inmate from prison that is determined by statute or sentencing guidelines and is not decided by a parole board or other authority. (Jeremy Travis and Sarah Lawrence, *Beyond the Prison Gates: The State of Parole in America* [Washington, DC: Urban Institute Press, 2002], p. 3.)

mandatory sentencing A structured sentencing scheme that allows no leeway in the nature of the sentence required and under which clearly enumerated punishments are mandated for specific offenses or for habitual offenders convicted of a series of crimes.

mandatory waiver A waiver that provides for transfer of juvenile cases to adult criminal court that meet certain age, offense, or other criteria.

mark system The first early release program, the mark system led to recognition of the indeterminate sentence as a useful tool in the reformation of offenders.

Marxist criminology See **radical criminology**.

Marxist feminism This group of feminists see the capitalist system as exploiting subordinate groups for capital production.

mass prison era (1825–1876) Congregated but silent system, communal meals and day labor, no speaking or eye contact allowed, vocational training provided, and corporal punishment and hard labor allowed. Also called the *Auburn system*.

master status Conveys the notion that there are central traits to people's identities binding us to their other characteristics.

McClelland* v. *Facteau 1979 violations of rights case in which the suspect in a traffic stop was not advised of his rights, was questioned aggressively, then beaten.

McKeiver* v. *Pennsylvania 1971 Supreme Court case that denied juveniles the right to a jury trial.

McNamara* v. *Moody Case that upheld the right of prisoners to write vulgar letters to girlfriends since such action did not affect the security of the prison.

McNaughten rule A rule for determining insanity, which asks whether the defendant knew what he or she was doing or whether the defendant knew that what he or she was doing was wrong.

meat eaters Police officers who initiate corrupt activity such as soliciting bribes, taking a share of drugs they confiscate for sale and their own profit, etc.

Mempa* v. *Rhay A 1967 Supreme Court case in which the court held that in probation revocation decisions, both notice and a hearing were required.

mens rea The state of mind that accompanies a criminal act. Also, a guilty mind.

middle-class measuring rod A set of standards that are difficult for the lower-class child to attain that include sharing, delaying gratification, and respecting others' property.

Minnesota* v. *Murphy A 1984 Supreme Court decision that held that a probationer's incriminating statements made to a probation officer may be used as evidence if the probationer did not specifically claim a right against self-incrimination.

***Miranda* rights** The set of rights that a person accused or suspected of having committed a specific offense has during interrogation and of which he or she must be informed prior to questioning, as stated by the U.S. Supreme Court in deciding *Miranda* v. *Arizona* (1966) and related cases.

***Miranda* warnings** The advisement of rights due criminal suspects by the police before questioning begins. *Miranda* warnings were first set forth by the U.S. Supreme Court in the 1966 case of *Miranda* v. *Arizona*.

misdemeanor An offense punishable by incarceration, usually in a local confinement facility, for a period whose upper limit is prescribed by statute in a given jurisdiction, typically one year or less.

mitigating circumstances Circumstances relating to the commission of a crime that may be considered to reduce the blameworthiness of the defendant. See also **aggravating circumstances**.

mixed sentence A sentence that requires that a convicted offender serve weekends (or other specified periods of time) in a confinement facility (usually a jail) while undergoing probationary supervision in the community.

Mobilization for Youth Project A subculture project in New York City designed to increase educational and job opportunities for youths in deprived communities.

modes of adaptation Merton's five ways of adapting to strain caused by restricted access to the socially-approved goals and means.

Monroe* v. *Pape 1961 violations of rights case in which officers conducted a warrantless search at gunpoint, and verbally and physically abused the suspects.

Morrissey* v. *Brewer The 1972 Supreme Court case that held that revocation procedure for parolees require written notice, evidence of violation, and an impartial detached body at hearing. The parolee will have a chance to appear, the right to cross-examine witness, and receive written statement of the outcome of revocation.

motivated offender Cohen and Felson's theory says this must be present first in a predatory criminal event.

motor vehicle theft (UCR/NIBRS) The theft or attempted theft of a motor vehicle. Motor vehicle is defined as a self-propelled road vehicle that runs on land surface and not on rails. The stealing of trains, planes, boats, construction equipment, and most farm machinery is classified as larceny under the UCR/NIBRS Program, not as motor vehicle theft.

murder The unlawful killing of a human being. Murder is a generic term that in common usage may include first- and second-degree murder, manslaughter, involuntary manslaughter, and other similar offenses.

National Center for Victims of Crime (NCVC) This organization maintains multiple national computer databases of victim-related legislation and other resources.

National Organization for Victim Assistance (NOVA) Assists victims of crime and disasters and tries to educate policy makers about victims rights.

National Crime Victimization Survey (NCVS) An annual survey of selected American households conducted by the Bureau of Justice Statistics to determine the extent of criminal victimization—especially unreported victimization—in the United States.

National Incident-Based Reporting System (NIBRS) An incident-based reporting system that collects data on every single crime occurrence. NIBRS data will soon supersede the kinds of summary data that has traditionally been provided by the FBI's Uniform Crime Reporting Program.

National Probation Act An act that allowed federal judges to appoint federal probation officers.

necessity A legal defense based on the claim that the committing the crime was more beneficial than adhering to the law. There is no intent to violate the law.

neglected child A child who is not receiving the proper level of physical or psychological care from his or her parents or guardians or who has been placed up for adoption in violation of the law.

neoclassical criminology A contemporary version of classical criminology that emphasizes deterrence and retribution and that holds that human beings are essentially free to make choices in favor of crime and deviance or conformity to the law.

neutralization theory A theory developed by Gresham Sykes and David Matza that involves a series of rationalizations used by individuals to overcome conventional values. Includes five techniques: denial of responsibility, denial of injury, denial of victim, condemnation of condemners, and appeal to higher loyalties.

Newman* v. *Alabama A 1972 Supreme Court case that found that prison medical services were inadequate.

NLETS An acronym referring to the International Justice and Public Safety Information Sharing Network.

nolo contendere A plea of "no contest." A no-contest plea is used when the defendant does not wish to contest conviction. Because the plea does not admit guilt, however, it cannot provide the basis for later civil suits that might follow a criminal conviction.

Norfolk Island Located off of Australia, Norfolk Island was a penal colony. Convicts earned privileges through good behavior in a staged system with indeterminate sentences.

nullification The jury returns an acquittal that is not consistent with the evidence. This is a rarely used option indicating the jury's disbelief in the law.

occupational crime Any act punishable by law that is committed through opportunity created in the course of an occupation that is legal.

O'Lone* v. *Estate of Shabazz 1987 Supreme Court case that identified some legitimate reasons for restriction of religious practices, particularly as they impact security issues.

offense A violation of the criminal law. Also, in some jurisdictions, a minor crime, such as jaywalking, that is sometimes described as ticketable. See also **summary offense**.

open-field search The courts have determined that an open-field search is not the same as the search of curtilage and is not protected by the Fourth Amendment (*Oliver* v. *U.S.*, 1984).

opening statement The initial statement of the prosecution or the defense, made in a court of law to a judge, or to a judge and jury, describing the facts that he or she intends to present during trial to prove the case.

operational capacity The number of inmates a prison can effectively accommodate based on management considerations.

opportunity theory A perspective that sees delinquency as the result of limited legitimate opportunities for success available to most lower-class youths.

organized crime The unlawful activities of the members of a highly organized, disciplined association engaged in supplying illegal goods and services, including but not limited to gambling, prostitution, loan sharking, narcotics, labor racketeering, and other unlawful activities.

original jurisdiction The lawful authority of a court to hear or to act on a case from its beginning and to pass judgment on the law and the facts. The authority may be over a specific geographic area or over particular types of cases.

parens patriae A common law principle that allows the state to assume a parental role and to take custody of a child when he or she becomes delinquent, is abandoned, or is in need of care that the natural parents are unable or unwilling to provide.

parole A convict is granted conditional release from prison before the completion of the sentence. The parolee must comply with certain conditions of behavior.

parole (probation) violation An act or a failure to act by a parolee (or probationer) that does not conform to the conditions of his or her parole (or probation).

parole board A state paroling authority. Most states have parole boards that decide when an incarcerated offender is ready for conditional release. Some boards also function as revocation hearing panels. Also called *parole commission*.

parole conditions Parole conditions are the general and specific limits imposed upon an offender who is released on parole.

parole revocation The administrative action of a paroling authority removing a person from parole status in response to a violation of lawfully required conditions of parole, including the prohibition against committing a new offense, and usually resulting in a return to prison.

Part I offenses A UCR/NIBRS offense group used to report murder, rape, robbery, aggravated assault, burglary, larceny-theft, motor vehicle theft, and arson, as defined under the FBI's UCR/NIBRS Program. Also called *major crimes*.

Part II offenses A UCR/NIBRS offense group used to report arrests for less serious offenses. Agencies are limited to reporting only arrest information for Part II offenses, with the exception of simple assault.

patria potestas Literally, power of father in Latin.

Peace Officer Standards and Training (POST) Program The official program of a state or legislative jurisdiction that sets standards for the training of law enforcement officers. All states set such standards, although not all use the term POST.

peacemaking criminology A perspective that holds that crime-control agencies and the citizens they serve should work together to alleviate social problems and human suffering and thus reduce crime.

Pell* v. *Procunier 1974 case in which Supreme Court determined that inmates keep all First Amendment rights that don't interfere with acceptable objectives of incarceration.

penal code The written, organized, and compiled form of the criminal laws of a jurisdiction.

penal law See **criminal law**.

penitentiary A prison. See also **Pennsylvania System**.

penitentiary era (1790–1825) Separate and silent system, sought penance in total solitude, and used handicrafts to help maintain sanity. Also called *Pennsylvania System.*

Pennsylvania Board of Probation and Parole* v. *Scott A 1998 Supreme Court case in which the court declined to extend exclusionary rule to apply to searches by parole officers, even where such searches yield evidence of parole violations.

Pennsylvania Department of Corrections* v. *Yeskey A Supreme court case that established that the Americans with Disabilities Act applies to prisons and prison inmates.

Pennsylvania System A form of imprisonment developed by the Pennsylvania Quakers around 1790 as an alternative to corporal punishments. This style of imprisonment made use of solitary confinement and encouraged rehabilitation. See also **penitentiary era**.

peremptory challenge The right to challenge a potential juror without disclosing the reason for the challenge. Prosecutors and defense attorneys routinely use peremptory challenges to eliminate from juries individuals who, although they express no obvious bias, are thought to be capable of swaying the jury in an undesirable direction.

perjury The intentional making of a false statement as part of the testimony by a sworn witness in a judicial proceeding on a matter relevant to the case at hand.

personal and household larceny The unlawful taking or attempted taking, carrying, leading, or riding away of property, from the possession or constructive possession of another. Motor vehicles are excluded. Larceny is the most common of the eight major offenses, although probably only a small percentage of all larcenies are actually reported to the police because of the small dollar amounts involved.

phrenology The chief practitioners of this believed that the characteristics of the brain are mirrored in bumps in the skull.

piece-price system A system in which goods were produced for private businesses under prison supervisions.

pillory Wooden structure that closed over a person's head and hands and forced the offender to remain standing.

plain view A legal term describing the ready visibility of objects that might be seized as evidence during a search by police in the absence of a search warrant specifying the seizure of those objects. To lawfully seize evidence in plain view, officers must have a legal right to be in the viewing area and must have cause to believe that the evidence is somehow associated with criminal activity.

plea In criminal proceedings, the defendant's formal answer in court to the charge contained in a complaint, information, or indictment that he or she is guilty of the offense charged, is not guilty of the offense charged, or does not contest the charge.

plea bargaining The process of negotiating an agreement among the defendant, the prosecutor, and the court as to an appropriate plea and associated sentence in a given case. Plea bargaining circumvents the trial process and dramatically reduces the time required for the resolution of a criminal case.

plea bargain A negotiated agreement among the defendant, the prosecutor, and the court as to an appropriate plea and associated sentence in a given case. A plea bargain circumvents the trial process and dramatically reduces the time required for the resolution of a criminal case.

police brutality Includes a range of behavior that police officers can engage in when dealing with the public from using abusive language to excessive use of force including the use of mace, a baton, or deadly weapon unnecessarily.

police corruption The abuse of police authority for personal or organizational gain. (Carl B. Klockars et al., *The Measurement of Police Integrity*, National Institute of Justice Research in Brief [Washington, DC: NIJ, 2000], p. 1.)

police discretion The opportunity of law enforcement officers to exercise choice in their daily activities.

police ethics The special responsibility to adhere to moral duty and obligation that is inherent in police work.

police professionalism The increasing formalization of police work and the accompanying rise in public acceptance of the police.

police use of force The use of physical restraint by a police officer when dealing with a member of the public. National Institute of Justice, *Use of Force by Police: Overview of National and Local Data* (Washington, DC: NIJ, 1999).

police working personality All aspects of the traditional values and patterns of behavior evidenced by police officers who have been effectively socialized into the police subculture. Characteristics of the police personality often extend to the personal lives of law enforcement personnel.

police–community relations (PCR) An area of police activity that recognizes the need for the community and the police to work together effectively. PCR is based on the notion that the police derive their legitimacy from the community they serve. Many police agencies began to explore PCR in the 1960s and 1970s.

Ponte* v. *Real A 1985 Supreme Court ruling that held that prison officials must provide an explanation to inmates who are denied the opportunity to have a desired witness at their hearing.

Positive School An approach to criminal justice theory that stresses the application of scientific techniques to the study of crime and criminals. Includes a philosophy with several varieties, the first being a product of eighteenth-century Enlightenment philosophy, with its emphasis on the importance of reason and experience.

postmodern criminology A branch of criminology that developed after World War II and that builds on the tenets of postmodern social thought.

power of judicial review The power of the court to review actions and decisions made by lower courts and other government agencies.

precedent A legal principle that ensures that previous judicial decisions are authoritatively considered and incorporated into future cases.

predisposition hearing This report contains background information to help the judge make good decisions based on the youth's history and needs.

preliminary hearing A proceeding before a judicial officer in which three matters must be decided: (1) whether a crime was committed, (2) whether the crime occurred within the territorial jurisdiction of the court, and (3) whether there are reasonable grounds to believe that the defendant committed the crime.

presentence investigation (PSI) The examination of a convicted offender's background prior to sentencing. Presentence examinations are generally conducted by probation or parole officers and are submitted to sentencing authorities.

presumptive sentencing A model of criminal punishment that meets the following conditions: (1) The appropriate sentence for an offender convicted of a specific charge is presumed to fall within a range of sentences authorized by sentencing guidelines that are adopted by a legislatively created sentencing body, usually a sentencing commission. (2) Sentencing judges are expected to sentence within the range or to provide written justification for departure. (3) There is a mechanism for review, usually appellate, of any departure from the guidelines.

presumptive waiver A waiver that shifts the burden of proof to the juvenile to show that the juvenile should not be transferred to adult court.

pretrial release The release of an accused person from custody, for all or part of the time before or during prosecution, on his or her promise to appear in court when required.

PRIDE Act Designed to reauthorize and improve the program of block grants to states, this Act temporarily assists families in need and improves access to child care.

Prior* v. *Woods 1981 negligence case in which police officers mistook the resident of a home as a burglar and killed him.

prison A state or federal confinement facility that has custodial authority over adults sentenced to confinement.

prison argot The slang characteristic of prison subcultures and prison life.

prison capacity The size of the correctional population an institution can effectively hold. There are three types of prison capacity: rated, operational, and design. Paige M. Harrison and Allen J. Beck, *Prisoners in 2005* (Washington, DC: Bureau of Justice Statistics, 2006), p. 7.

Prison Litigation Reform Act of 1996 (PLRA) An act that (1) requires inmates to exhaust their prison's grievance procedure before filing a lawsuit; (2) requires judges to screen all inmate complaints against federal government and to immediately dismiss those deemed frivolous or without merit, (3) prohibits prisoners from filing a lawsuit for mental or emotional injury unless they can also show there has been physical injury, and (4) requires inmates to pay court filing fees.

prison subculture The values and behavioral patterns characteristic of prison inmates. Prison subculture has been found to be surprisingly consistent across the country.

prisoner reentry The managed return to the community of individuals released from prison. Also called *reentry*.

prisonization The process whereby newly institutionalized offenders come to accept prison lifestyles and criminal values. Although many inmates begin their prison experience with only a few values that support criminal behavior, the socialization experience they undergo while incarcerated leads to a much greater acceptance of such values.

private prisons Prison facilities operated for local and state governments by private enterprise for profit.

private protective services Independent or proprietary commercial organizations that provide protective services to employers on a contractual basis.

privatization The movement toward the wider use of private prisons.

proactive policing An approach to policing that involves the police initiating crime control activities through patrol, citizen stops, arrests, etc., rather than waiting to respond to calls for assistance.

probable cause A set of facts and circumstances that would induce a reasonably intelligent and prudent person to believe that a specified person has committed a specified crime. Also, reasonable grounds to make or believe an accusation. Probable cause refers to the necessary level of belief that would allow for police seizures (arrests) of individuals and full searches of dwellings, vehicles, and possessions.

probable cause hearing Held only for warrantless arrests, police demonstrate the reasons for the arrest at the probable cause hearing. Presence of the detainee is not required. Charges may be dismissed at this point, or the case may move forward to the next step.

probation A sentence of imprisonment that is suspended. Also, the conditional freedom granted by a judicial officer to a convicted offender, as long as the person meets certain conditions of behavior.

probation revocation A court order taking away a convicted offender's probationary status and usually withdrawing the conditional freedom associated with that status in response to a violation of the conditions of probation.

probation termination The ending of the probation status of a given person by routine expiration of the probationary period, by special early termination by the court, or by revocation of probation.

probation violation An act or a failure to act by a probationer that does not conform to the conditions of his or her probation.

probation workload The total set of activities required to carry out the probation agency functions of intake screening of juvenile cases, referral of cases to other service agencies, investigation of juveniles and adults for the purpose of preparing predisposition or presentence reports, supervision or treatment of juveniles and adults granted probation, assistance in the enforcement of court orders concerning family problems, such as abandonment and nonsupport cases, and other such functions assigned by statute or court order.

probative value The degree to which a particular item of evidence is useful in, and relevant to, providing something important in a trial.

problem-oriented policing (POP) Begun in the 1970s in an attempt to improve police effectiveness, it was understood that "discretion to design solutions is extremely valuable" for police officers. An early founder of the POP approach is Herman Goldstein.

problem police officer A law enforcement officer who exhibits problem behavior, as indicated by high rates of citizen complaints and use-of-force incidents and by other evidence. (Samuel Walker, Geoffrey P. Albert, and Dennis J. Kenney, *Responding to the Problem Police Officer: A National Study of Early Warning Systems* [Washington, DC: National Institute of Justice, 2000].)

problem-solving policing A type of policing that assumes that crimes can be controlled by uncovering and effectively addressing the underlying social problems that cause crime. Problem-solving policing makes use of community resources, such as counseling centers, welfare programs, and job training facilities. It also attempts to involve citizens in crime prevention through education, negotiation, and conflict management. Also called *problem-oriented policing*.

procedural law The part of the law that specifies the methods to be used in enforcing substantive law. See also **criminal procedure**.

Procunier* v. *Martinez 1974 Supreme Court case that confirmed the right of prison officials to read, but, not censor, inmate mail.

property bond Tangible goods are signed over to the ownership of the state, as collateral for appearance.

property crime A UCR/NIBRS summary offense category that includes burglary, larceny-theft, motor vehicle theft, and arson.

proportionality A sentencing principle that holds that the severity of sanctions should bear a direct relationship to the seriousness of the crime committed.

prosecutor Represents the government or the interests of the community in a criminal trial. Also known as district attorney, state's attorney, county attorney, commonwealth attorney, or prosecuting attorney.

prosecutorial discretion The decision-making power of prosecutors, based on the wide range of choices available to them, in the handling of criminal defendants, the scheduling of cases for trial, the acceptance of negotiated pleas, and so on. The most important form of prosecutorial discretion lies in the power to charge, or not to charge, a person with an offense.

psychoanalysis A theory of human behavior, based on the writings of Sigmund Freud, that sees personality as a complex composite of interacting mental entities.

psychological manipulation Manipulative actions by police interviewers that are designed to pressure suspects to divulge information and that are based on subtle forms of intimidation and control.

Psychological School A perspective on criminological thought that views offensive and deviant behavior as the product of dysfunctional personality. Psychological thinkers identify the conscious, and especially the subconscious, contents of the human psyche as major determinants of behavior.

psychopath A person with a personality disorder, especially one manifested in aggressively antisocial behavior, which is often said to be the result of a poorly developed superego. Also called *sociopath*.

psychopathology The study of pathological mental conditions—that is, mental illness.

psychosis A form of mental illness in which sufferers are said to be out of touch with reality.

public-account system A system in which industries are owned entirely by prisons and the prisons handle the manufacture of goods from beginning to end. The finished goods are sold on the free market.

public works Structures (such as highways, parks, and schools) built at government expense for public use.

punitive era (1938–1945) Prison was to be used for punishment while education, treatment, and work were luxuries. Maximum-security prisons were built in isolated places. Under this system there was an increase in riots and escape attempts.

racial profiling "Any police-initiated action that relies on the race, ethnicity, or national origin rather than (1) the behavior of an individual, or (2) information that leads the police to a particular individual who has been identified as being, or having been, engaged in criminal activity." (Deborah Ramirez, Jack McDevitt, and Amy Farrell, *A Resource Guide on Racial Profiling Data Collection Systems: Promising Practices and Lessons Learned* [Washington, DC: U.S. Department of Justice, 2000], p. 3.)

radical criminology A conflict perspective that sees crime as engendered by the unequal distribution of wealth, power, and other resources, which adherents believe is especially characteristic of capitalist societies. Also called *critical criminology*; *Marxist criminology*.

radical feminism Its primary focus is on the way in which power is constructed and dominated by males in society.

rape Unlawful sexual intercourse, achieved through force and without consent. Broadly speaking, the term rape has been applied to a wide variety of sexual attacks and may include same-sex rape and the rape of a male by a female. Some jurisdictions refer to same-sex rape as sexual battery. See also **forcible rape, sexual battery**.

rated capacity The number of inmates a prison can handle according to the judgment of experts.

rational choice theory A perspective on crime causation that holds that criminality is the result of conscious choice. Rational choice theory predicts that individuals will choose to commit crime when the benefits of doing so outweigh the costs of disobeying the law. Suggests a connection between opportunities for offending, the environmental conditions at the time, and the readiness of the offender to engage in the offense.

reaction formation The process whereby a person openly rejects that which he or she wants or aspires to but cannot obtain or achieve.

real evidence Evidence that consists of physical material or traces of physical activity.

reasonable force A degree of force that is appropriate in a given situation and is not excessive. Also, the minimum degree of force necessary to protect oneself, one's property, a third party, or the property of another in the face of a substantial threat.

reasonable juror Juror who would consider all of the evidence presented fairly and obey the court's instructions requiring proof beyond a reasonable doubt.

reasonable suspicion The level of suspicion that would justify an officer in making further inquiry or in conducting further investigation. Reasonable suspicion may permit stopping a person for questioning or for a simple pat-down search. Also, a belief, based on a consideration of the facts at hand and on reasonable inferences drawn from those facts, that would induce an ordinarily prudent and cautious person under the same circumstances to conclude that criminal activity is taking place or that criminal activity has recently occurred. Reasonable suspicion is a general and reasonable belief that a crime is in progress or has occurred, whereas probable cause is a reasonable belief that a particular person has committed a specific crime. See also **probable cause**.

rebellion This mode of adaptation focuses on the substitution of new goals and means for the original ones.

recidivism The repetition of criminal behavior. In statistical practice, a recidivism rate may be any of a number of possible counts or instances of arrest, conviction, correctional commitment, or correctional status change related to repetitions of these events within a given period of time.

recorder See **court reporter**.

reentry See **prisoner reentry**.

reformatory era (1876–1890) Used indeterminate sentence, provided education and vocational training, early release for good behavior, community parole, and rest cure (solitary confinement) was allowed as punishment. Example is Elmira Reformatory.

reform school An institution for juveniles that emphasizes traditional values and hard work.

regional jail A jail that is built and run using the combined resources of a variety of local jurisdictions.

rehabilitation The attempt to reform a criminal offender. Also, the state in which a reformed offender is said to be.

reinforcement Any event that follows the occurrence of behavior and that alters and increases the frequency of the behavior.

reintegrative shaming The process of humiliating or condemning the offender publically in order to prepare them to reenter the community with better awareness and sensitivity toward the need for conforming behavior

release on recognizance (ROR) Defendant is set free based only on a signed promise to return for further legal proceedings.

remote location monitoring A supervision strategy that uses electronic technology to track offenders sentenced to house arrest or those who have been ordered to limit their movements while completing a sentence involving probation or parole.

restitution A court requirement that an alleged or convicted offender pay money or provide services to the victim of the crime or provide services to the community.

restoration A goal of criminal sentencing that attempts to make the victim "whole again."

restorative justice (RJ) A sentencing model that builds on restitution and community participation in an attempt to make the victim "whole again."

resultant decision See **adjudication**.

retreatism This mode of adaptation involves a rejection of both the goals and means.

retreatist subculture Their primary focus is on drugs, and their gang-related activities are designed to bring them the money for their own drug use.

retribution The act of taking revenge on a criminal perpetrator.

retrospective interpretation Provides us with an idea of how identities can be reconstructed to fit a new label.

revocation The administrative act of determining that the parolee or probationer has failed to comply with behavioral expectations during release. Revocation results in the rescinding of a suspended sentence for a probationer, or the return to incarceration of a parolee.

revocation hearing A hearing held before a legally constituted hearing body (such as a parole board) to determine whether a parolee or probationer has violated the conditions and requirements of his or her parole or probation.

ritualism A mode of adaptation where the goals themselves are rejected and the focus is shifted to the means.

robbery The unlawful taking or attempted taking of property that is in the immediate possession of another by force or violence and/or by putting the victim in fear. Armed robbery differs from unarmed or strong-arm robbery in that it involves a weapon. Contrary to popular conceptions, highway robbery does not necessarily occur on a street—and rarely in a vehicle. The term highway robbery applies to any form of robbery that occurs outdoors in a public place.

role malfeasance In law enforcement, this can be represented by the destruction of evidence, biased testimony, or the protection of "crooked cops."

routine activities theory A neoclassical perspective that suggests that lifestyles contribute significantly to both the amount and the type of crime found in any society.

Ruiz* v. *Estelle A 1982 Supreme Court ruling that found the Department of Corrections lacking in its medical treatment programs.

rule of law The maxim that an orderly society must be governed by established principles and known codes that are applied uniformly and fairly to all of its members.

rules of evidence Court rules that govern the admissibility of evidence at criminal hearings and trials.

Sager* v. *City of Woodlawn Park 1982 failure to properly screen, train, or supervise staff case in which an officer shot a suspect using an inappropriate cuffing technique.

Sandin* v. *Connor 1995 Supreme Court case provided further clarification to due process required in disciplinary action.

Schall* v. *Martin A 1984 Supreme Court case that upheld the right of state to put juveniles in preventive detention, but imposed procedural requirements

scientific jury selection The use of correlational techniques from the social sciences to gauge the likelihood that potential jurors will vote for conviction or for acquittal.

search incident to arrest A warrantless search of an arrested individual conducted to ensure the safety of the arresting officer. Because individuals placed under arrest may be in possession of weapons, courts have recognized the need for arresting officers to protect themselves by conducting an immediate search of arrestees without obtaining a warrant.

search warrant A document issued by a judicial officer that directs a law enforcement officer to conduct a search at a specific location for specified property or person relating to a crime, to seize the property or person if found, and to account for the results of the search to the issuing judicial officer.

secondary deviance This concept suggests that, in addition to audience reaction, there is the possibility an individual will react to the label.

Section 1983 of the Civil Rights Act Prohibits anyone from depriving another of their civil rights.

security threat group (STG) A inmate group, gang, or organization whose members act together to pose a threat to the safety of correctional staff or the public, or who prey upon other inmates, or who threaten the secure and orderly operation of a correctional institution.

self-defense The protection of oneself or of one's property from unlawful injury or from the immediate risk of unlawful injury. Also, the justification that the person who committed an act that would otherwise constitute an offense reasonably believed that the act was necessary to protect self or property from immediate danger.

sentencing The imposition of a criminal sanction by a judicial authority.

sentencing alternatives Judges have an array of treatment and detention options for youths depending on recommendations in the disposition report and the youths' apparent needs.

sequestered jury A jury that is isolated from the public during the course of a trial and throughout the deliberation process.

serial murder The killing of several people in three or more separate events.

service style A style of policing marked by a concern with helping rather than strict enforcement. Service-oriented police agencies are more likely to use community resources, such as drug treatment programs, to supplement traditional law enforcement activities than are other types of agencies.

sexual battery Intentional and wrongful physical contact with a person, without his or her consent, that entails a sexual component or purpose.

sheriff The elected chief officer of a county law enforcement agency. The sheriff is usually responsible for law enforcement in unincorporated areas and for the operation of the county jail.

shire reeve Chief law enforcement officer of a shire, the equivalent of a county in the United States. We derived the term *sheriff* from *shire reeve*.

shock incarceration A sentencing option that makes use of "boot camp"-type prisons to impress on convicted offenders the realities of prison life.

shock probation The practice of sentencing offenders to prison, allowing them to apply for probationary release, and enacting such release in surprise fashion. Offenders who receive shock probation may not be aware that they will be released on probation and may expect to spend a much longer time behind bars.

signature bond Used only in minor offenses. No assessment of danger is made. The accused simply signs a promise to return to court.

Sixth Amendment Guarantees the right to a speedy trial, the right to confront witnesses, and the right to an impartial jury.

Smith* v. *Coughlin A 1984 Supreme Court case that established that prisoners have rights, much the same as people who are not incarcerated, provided that the legitimate needs of the prison for security, custody, and safety are not compromised.

social debt A sentencing principle that holds that an offender's criminal history should objectively be taken into account in sentencing decisions.

social development theory An integrated view of human development that points to the process of interaction among and between individuals and society as the root cause of criminal behavior.

social disorganization A condition said to exist when a group is faced with social change, uneven development of culture, maladaptiveness, disharmony, conflict, and lack of consensus.

social ecology A criminological approach that focuses on the misbehavior of lower-class youths and sees delinquency primarily as the result of social disorganization.

social justice An ideal that embraces all aspects of civilized life and that is linked to fundamental notions of fairness and to cultural beliefs about right and wrong.

social learning theory A psychological perspective that says that people learn how to behave by modeling themselves after others whom they have the opportunity to observe.

social reality Six propositions from theorist Richard Quinney, whose theory incorporated concepts from differential association, social learning, and labeling.

socialist feminism Uniting radical and Marxist principles, this group identifies the oppression of women as a symptom of the patriarchal capitalist system.

sociopath A person with a personality disorder, especially one manifested in aggressively antisocial behavior, which is often said to be the result of a poorly developed superego. Also called *psychopath*.

Solem* v. *Helm 1983 Supreme Court case that established the test of proportionality, for measuring the fairness of a sentence against the severity of the crime.

specific deterrence A goal of criminal sentencing that seeks to prevent a particular offender from engaging in repeated criminality.

Speedy Trial Act A 1974 federal law requiring that proceedings against a defendant in a federal criminal case begin within a specified period of time, such as 70 working days after indictment. Some states also have speedy trial requirements.

split sentence A sentence explicitly requiring the convicted offender to serve a period of confinement in a local, state, or federal facility, followed by a period of probation.

stare decisis A legal principle that requires that, in subsequent cases on similar issues of law and fact, courts be bound by their own earlier decisions and by those of higher courts having jurisdiction over them. The term literally means "standing by decided matters."

state court administrator A coordinator who assists with case-flow management, operating funds budgeting, and court docket administration.

state court system A state judicial structure. Most states have at least three court levels: trial courts, appellate courts, and a state supreme court.

state highway patrol A state law enforcement agency whose principal functions are preventing, detecting, and investigating motor vehicle offenses and apprehending traffic offenders.

state police A state law enforcement agency whose principal functions usually include maintaining statewide police communications, aiding local police in criminal investigations, training police, and guarding state property. The state police may include the highway patrol.

state-use system A system in which prisons manufacture goods only for use by the prison or other government agencies.

status frustration Lower-class children lose ground in the search for status and suffer from this.

status offender A child who commits an act that is contrary to the law by virtue of the offender's status as a child. Purchasing cigarettes, buying alcohol, and being truant are examples of such behavior.

status offense An act or conduct that is declared by statute to be an offense, but only when committed by or engaged in by a juvenile, and that can be adjudicated only by a juvenile court.

statutory decree Mandatory parole, that automatically goes into effect after the offender serves a certain amount of their sentence minus the time for good behavior and other special considerations.

statutory law Written or codified law; the "law on the books," as enacted by a government body or agency having the power to make laws.

Stengel* v. *Belcher 1975 failure to take required or expected actions case in which an off-duty officer failed to identify himself when he intervened in a bar fight, and killed two men.

stocks Wooden structures in which a person is placed in a sitting position with his or her hands locked in front of them and the head remaining free.

stop and frisk The detaining of a person by a law enforcement officer for the purpose of investigation, accompanied by a superficial examination by the officer of the person's body surface or clothing to discover weapons, contraband, or other objects relating to criminal activity.

strain theory These theories require that people be motivated to commit criminal and delinquent acts.

strategic policing A type of policing that retains the traditional police goal of professional crime fighting but enlarges the enforcement target to include nontraditional kinds of criminals, such as serial offenders, gangs and criminal associations, drug-distribution networks, and sophisticated white-collar and computer criminals. Strategic policing generally makes use of innovative enforcement techniques, including intelligence operations, undercover stings, electronic surveillance, and sophisticated forensic methods.

strict liability Liability without fault or intention. Strict liability offenses do not require *mens rea*.

structured sentencing A model of criminal punishment that includes determinate and commission-created presumptive sentencing schemes, as well as voluntary/advisory sentencing guidelines.

subculture of violence Those in this subculture learn a willingness to resort to violence and share a favorable attitude toward the use of violence. A cultural setting in which violence is a traditional and often accepted method of dispute resolution.

subpoena ad testificandum An order (writ) of the court requiring and individual to come before the court and give testimony.

subpoena duces tecum An order (writ) of the court requiring an individual to bring with him or her documents, papers, or other materials for the courts to consider. Also called a *subponea* for *production of evidence*.

subterranean values Respectable values that are present in the larger culture.

suicide by cop Occurs when a citizen intentionally acts in such an aggressive and threatening manner to give the police officer no other option than to take the life of the citizen.

suitable target Something worth stealing or taking, or that has the appearance of worth.

summary offense A violation of the criminal law. Also, in some jurisdictions, a minor crime, such as jaywalking, that is sometimes described as ticketable. See also **offense**.

supervision Official scrutiny in the form of guidance, treatment, supervision, or regulation of behaviors by a state authority, of the convict during the time of his or her conditional release.

suspicionless search A search conducted by law enforcement personnel without a warrant and without suspicion. Suspicionless searches are permissible only if based on an overriding concern for public safety.

symbolic interactionism Developed from a belief that human behavior is the product of purely social symbols communicated between individuals.

Taylor* v. *Sterrett A 1976 Supreme Court case that stated that letters can be opened and inspected for contraband, but not read, in the presence of the inmate.

***Tazir* crime** A minor violation of Islamic law that is regarded as an offense against society, not God.

team policing The reorganization of conventional patrol strategies into "an integrated and versatile police team assigned to a fixed district."

techniques of neutralization These techniques allow individuals to neutralize and temporarily suspend their commitment to societal values, thus providing the freedom to commit delinquent acts. See also **neutralization theory**.

teen court An alternative approach to juvenile justice in which alleged offenders are judged and sentenced by a jury of their peers.

testimony Oral evidence offered by a sworn witness on the witness stand during a criminal trial.

three-strikes rule Statutes that require mandatory sentences for offenders convicted of a third felony.

tithing From the Old English tithe, paying one tenth, it came to represent ten families grouped together for peace-keeping purposes.

tort A wrongful act, damage, or injury not involving a breach of contract. Also, a private or civil wrong or injury.

total institution An enclosed facility separated from society both socially and physically, where the inhabitants share all aspects of their lives daily.

transactional immunity A broad form of immunity that prevents the witness from being prosecuted from any of the testimony the person gives or other source of independently collected evidence related to the crime.

transfer procedures Most states have procedures that direct the process of moving the youth's case to another legal jurisdiction, such as children's court or adult court.

transportation In England in the seventeenth century, criminals were pardoned and shipped to the colonies in America. Contractors in America initially paid government fees to have the felons shipped, which evolved into legal custody.

treason A U.S. citizen's actions to help a foreign government overthrow, make war against, or seriously injure the United States. Also, the attempt to overthrow the government of the society of which one is a member, the only crime specifically mentioned in the U.S. Constitution. (Daniel Oran, *Oran's Dictionary of the Law* [St. Paul, MN: West, 1983], p. 306.)

treatment era (1945–1967) Based on the medical model. Classification and treatment led to rehabilitation. Therapy, training and education were provided. Treatments included extensive sensory deprivation and neurosurgeries.

trial In criminal proceedings, the examination in court of the issues of fact and relevant law in a case for the purpose of convicting or acquitting the defendant.

trial *de novo* Literally, "new trial." The term is applied to cases that are retried on appeal, as opposed to those that are simply reviewed on the record.

Tribble* v. *Gardner 1988 Supreme Court case that established certain guidelines for routine strip searches.

truth in sentencing A close correspondence between the sentence imposed on an offender and the time actually served in prison. (Lawrence A. Greenfeld, "Prison Sentences and Time Served for Violence," Bureau of Justice Statistics Selected Findings, No. 4 [April 1995].)

Turner* v. *Safley 1987 Supreme court case that supported a ban of inmates' writing to each other while incarcerated.

U.S. Constitution Produced by the Constitutional Convention and ratified in 1789, the U.S. Constitution is the oldest written constitution continuously in effect.

undisciplined child A child who is beyond parental control, as evidenced by his or her refusal to obey legitimate authorities, such as school officials and teachers.

Uniform Crime Report (UCR) A statistical reporting program run by the FBI's Criminal Justice Information Services (CJIS) division. The UCR Program publishes Crime in the United States, which provides an annual summation of the incidence and rate of reported crimes throughout the United States.

unsecured bond A bond that is based upon a court-determined dollar amount of bail.

use of force continuum Standard use of force continuum ranges from the mere physical presence of the officer up to and through the use of deadly force by the police officer.

U.S.* v. *Knights A 2001 Supreme Court case in which the court stated that the warrantless search, "supported by reasonable suspicion and authorized by a probation condition, satisfied the Fourth Amendment."

verdict The decision of the jury in a jury trial or of a judicial officer in a nonjury trial.

victim-assistance program An organized program that offers services to victims of crime in the areas of crisis intervention and follow-up counseling and that helps victims secure their rights under the law.

victim-impact statement The in-court use of victim- or survivor-supplied information by sentencing authorities seeking to make an informed sentencing decision.

Victims of Crime Act of 1984 (VOCA) Established a federal compensation fund for victims, including medical expenses, loss of wages, and funeral expenses.

vigilantes Individuals who without legal authorization conduct a trial of an accused. More typical in the Old West.

Violence Against Women Act of 1994 Part of the Violent Crime Control and Law Enforcement Act, funded services to victims of domestic violence and sexual abuse.

violent crime A UCR/NIBRS summary offense category that includes murder, rape, robbery, and aggravated assault.

Vitek* v. *Jones A 1980 Supreme Court ruling that extended the requirement of due process to inmates about to be transferred from prisons to mental hospitals.

voir dire Literal translation is "to see and speak the truth." Process through which prospective jurors are questioned to determine if they are unbiased and can be impartial during the trial. If jurors are found to be unacceptable during the *voir dire*, they can be excused from serving on the jury.

voluntary/advisory guidelines Guidelines that recommend sentencing parameters, but the law does not require that the judge follow them.

waiver hearings Some states require a hearing before any juvenile is transferred to adult court.

Walnut Street Jail A prison established by the Quakers to provide religion and humanity to those imprisoned by allowing them to do penance.

warehousing era (1980–1995) Return to incarceration because increased recidivism and ongoing criminality by offenders in the community-based programs led to a loss of faith in treatment and rehabilitation. Mandatory minimum sentences, truth-in-sentencing legislation and goal of protecting society rather than treating the offender became the main focus.

warrant In criminal proceedings, a writ issued by a judicial officer directing a law enforcement officer to perform a specified act and affording the officer protection from damages if he or she performs it.

warrantless search Search of a structure is permitted under certain circumstances with a warrant: when the suspect may escape, when there is imminent danger, or when the possibility exists that evidence may be destroyed. *U.S.* v. *Reed* (1991).

watch and ward System in Englnad in the 1400s and 1500s in which individuals would patrol at night and call out the time as he patrolled. Intent was to scare off individuals who were engaged in illegal activity by announcing the presence of the watchman.

watchman style A style of policing marked by a concern for order maintenance. Watchman policing is characteristic of lower-class communities where police intervene informally into the lives of residents to keep the peace.

Webster* v. *City of Houston 1994 failure to take required or expected actions case in which an officer killed an unarmed teen, then covered up the killing.

wergild In ancient Germanic law, amount of compensation paid by a person committing an offense to the injured party, or in case of death, to his family.

white-collar crime Crime committed, usually by a person of high social status, in the course of an occupation.

Wickersham Commission A national commission created by Herbert Hoover in 1929. Commission studied all aspects of law enforcement, including issue of corruption.

Wilson* v. *Seiter 1991 Supreme Court case that set the most recent standard to measure cruel and unusual punishment—the test of deliberate indifference.

Wolff* v. *McDonnell 1974 Supreme Court case that differentiated between legal rights at trial and the limited rights of an inmate who is incarcerated and receiving discipline.

workhouses Residences that were intended to foster good work habits in the poor and homeless.

work release Offenders continue to reside within the confines of the institution, but go into the community each day to a job. Intent is to provide offender with work experience, cash flow, and an opportunity to "practice" being in the outside world.

writ of *certiorari* A writ issued from an appellate court for the purpose of obtaining from a lower court the record of its proceedings in a particular case. In some states, this writ is the mechanism for discretionary review. A request for review is made by petitioning for a writ of *certiorari*, and the granting of review is indicated by the issuance of the writ.

writ of *habeas corpus* A writ that directs the person detaining a prisoner to bring him or her before a judicial officer to determine the lawfulness of the imprisonment.

Younger* v. *Gilmore 1971 Supreme Court case that required prisons to provide sufficient legal libraries to allow inmates to conduct research.

Young* v. *Harper A Supreme Court decision that ruled that "an inmate who has been released under a program to relieve prison crowding cannot be re-incarcerated without getting a chance to show at a hearing that the conditions of the program have been met and is entitled to remain free.